MARX AGAINST THE MARXISTS

MARX AGAINST THE MARXISTS

The Christian Humanism of Karl Marx

José Porfirio Miranda

Translated from the Spanish by John Drury

ORBIS BOOKS
Maryknoll, New York 10545

The Catholic Foreign Mission Society of America (Maryknoll) recruits and trains people for overseas missionary service. Through Orbis Books Maryknoll aims to foster the international dialogue that is essential to mission. The books published, however, reflect the opinions of their authors and are not meant to represent the official position of the society.

Library of Congress Cataloging in Publication Data

Miranda, José Porfirio.
  Marx against the Marxists.

  Translation of El cristianismo de Marx.
  Bibliography: p.
  Includes index.
  1. Communism and Christianity. 2. Marx, Karl,
1818-1883. I. Title.
HX536.M5413 1980   335.4'01   80-14415
ISBN 0-88344-322-8

Originally published as El cristianismo de Marx, Mexico, D. F., copyright © 1978 by José Porfirio Miranda. The author has revised portions of the work for the English translation.

English translation copyright © 1980 by Orbis Books, Maryknoll, NY 10545

Contents

Abbreviations   vii

Preface to the English Translation   xi

  1. The Real Motive of the Revolution   1

  2. A History with a Subject   29

  3. A Free Subject   52

  4. Determination in Marx's Thought   69

  5. Marx the Humanist   106

  6. The Moral Content of Marx's Economic Analysis   136

  7. The Moral Conscience of Marx   165

  8. The Gospel Roots of Marx's Thought   197

  9. Marx's Thought as a Conscious Continuation of Early Christianity   224

  10. The God of Historical Eschatology   264

  11. Appendix on Marx's Epistemology   285

Epilogue   310

Index   311

Abbreviations

With the exception of the German-language Marx-Engels Werke, all the
titles listed below are English-language editions of the works of Marx
and Engels.

AD F. Engels. *Anti-Dühring*. Herr Eugen Dühring's
Revolution in Science. New York: International
Publishers, 1939 (hardbound edition).

CAP 1,2 K. Marx. *Capital*. A Critique of Political Economy.
New York: International Publishers, 1967 (paperback edition).

CCPE K. Marx. *A Contribution to the Critique of Political
Economy*. New York: International Publishers,
1970 (paperback edition).

CSF K. Marx. *The Class Struggles In France*. 1895 Introduction by F. Engels. New York: International
Publishers, 1964 (hardbound edition).

CWC F. Engels. *The Condition of the Working Class in
England*. New York: Macmillan, 1958 (hardbound edition).

DN F. Engels. *Dialectics of Nature*. New York: International Publishers, 1940 (hardbound edition).

EOM *The Essentials of Marx*. Contains The Communist
Manifesto; Value, Price and Profit; Wage-Labour
and Capital. New York: Vanguard Press, 1926
(hardbound edition).

EPM K. Marx. *Economic and Philosophic Manuscripts of
1844*. New York: International Publishers, 1964
(paperback edition).

GI Marx and Engels. *The German Ideology*. Part I,
Selections from Parts II and III, Theses on Feuerbach, and the 1857 Introduction to A Critique of
Political Economy. New York: International Publishers, 1970 (paperback edition).

GRU K. Marx. *Grundrisse*. Foundations of the Critique of
Political Economy. New York: Vintage Books,
1973 (paperback edition).*

HF	Marx and Engels. *The Holy Family. Or Critique of Critical Criticism.* Moscow: Progress Publishers, 1975 (hardbound edition).
LF	F. Engels. *Ludwig Feuerbach and the End of Classical German Philosophy.* Peking: Foreign Languages Press, 1976 (paperback edition).
MESC	Marx and Engels. *Selected Correspondence: 1846–1895.* New York: International Publishers, 1942 (hardbound edition).
MESW 1,2,3	Marx and Engels. *Selected Works.* 3 vols. New York: International Publishers (paperback edition).
MEW	*Marx-Engels Werke.* East Berlin: Dietz Verlag. A complete English-language edition based on the *MEW* is being published by Lawrence and Wishart of London, and International Publishers of New York.
MEW/EB	Supplementary volumes of the MEW (Erganzungsband).
NYDT	*New York Daily Tribune.* Two recent collections in this area are highly praised by David McLellan (in his *Karl Marx: His Life and Thought,* New York: Harper & Row, Publishers, 1973): Selections from these NYDT articles in H. Christman, ed. *The American Journalism of Marx and Engels.* New York, 1966; complete edition in Ferguson and O'Neil, eds. *The Collected Writings in the New York Daily Tribune.* New York, 1973.
OF	F. Engels. *The Origins of the Family, Private Property and the State.* New York: International Publishers, 1942 (hardbound edition).
OR	Marx and Engels. *On Religion.* New York: Schocken Books, 1964 (hardbound edition).
POP	K. Marx. *The Poverty of Philosophy.* New York: International Publishers, 1975 (paperback edition).
RFH	F. Engels. *The Role of Force in History: A Study of Bismarck's Policy of Blood and Iron.* New York: International Publishers, 1968 (hardbound edition).
RME	Marx and Engels. *The Russian Menace to Europe: A Collection of Articles, Speeches, Letters and News Dispatches.* Glencoe, Ill: The Free Press, 1952 (hardbound edition).

SCME	Marx and Engels *Selected Correspondence: 1844– 1895*. 3rd rev. ed. Moscow: Progress Publishers, 1975 (hardbound edition).
SUS	F. Engels. *Socialism: Utopian and Scientific*. Peking: Foreign Languages Press, 1975 (paperback edition).
SW	F. Engels. *Selected Writings*. Baltimore: Penguin Books, 1967 (paperback edition).
TEQ	Marx and Engels. *The Eastern Question: Letters and Articles Written Between 1853 and 1856 and Dealing with Events of the Crimean War*. New York: Burt Franklin & Company, 1968 (hardbound reprint).
TGR	F. Engels. *The German Revolutions*. Contains *The Peasant War in Germany* and *Germany: Revolution and Counter-Revolution*. Chicago: University of Chicago Press, 1967 (hardbound edition).
TSV 1, 2, 3	K. Marx. *Theories of Surplus Value*. Also known as Book IV of *Capital*. Moscow: Progress Publishers, 1963–71.
VEW	K. Marx. *Early Writings*. New York: Vintage Books, 1975 (paperback edition).
VFI	K. Marx. *The First International and After: Political Writings III*. New York: Vintage Books, 1974 (paperback edition); part of the Pelican Marx Library published in England by Penguin Books.
VRV	K. Marx. *The Revolutions of 1848: Political Writings I*. New York: Vintage Books, 1974 (paperback edition); part of the Pelican Marx Library published in England by Penguin Books.
VSE	K. Marx. *Surveys From Exile: Political Writings II*. New York: Vintage Books, 1974 (paperback edition); part of the Pelican Marx Library published in England by Penguin Books.
WLCVPP	K. Marx. *Wage-Labour and Capital* and *Value, Price and Profit*. New York: International Publishers, 1976 (combined paperback edition).

Translator's Note: All page references to the *Grundrisse* are to the recently published English-language edition (GRU) except where citations come from early drafts or others contained only in the larger German-language edition. The latter are cited as the "German *Grundrisse*" (*Grundrisse der Kritik der politischen Oekonomie*, Frankfurt: Europäische Verlagsanstalt).

Chapter citations of *Capital* in this volume are those of the English edition of *Capital* (CAP), which differ from the chapter enumeration of the German-language edition.

Preface to
the English Translation

The Christianity of an author does not consist exclusively in his or her affirmation of the existence of God. If the whole doctrine of an author is aimed at provoking a very specific kind of revolution in the world, then the specific motive of this revolution is an incomparable indication as to whether the author's thinking is Christian or not. And this is particularly true if less noble motives are expressly rejected and are shown to be intrinsically incompatible with the detailed analyses and the overall thought of the author (Chapter 1).

Similarly, if Marx's fundamental and thoroughgoing criticism of capitalism centers around the fact that capitalism does not respect human beings as persons, as real subjects and agents, then that analysis turns out to be eminently Christian (Chapter 2). And that is far more substantial and important than explicit professions of faith.

A deterministic conception of the human being and of history cannot be reconciled with Christianity. But if Marx expressly rejects such a conception (Chapter 3), and if he views the primacy of the economic factor in a way that is radically different from the view usually offered by materialism, then we are faced with a philosophical corpus that is far more Christian than is ordinarily presumed. Chapter 4 of this book is the key to a correct interpretation of Marx on this point, which is now being debated all over the world.

I hardly need point out that authentic Christianity means solid, unequivocal humanism. Chapter 5 in this book compiles proofs of the explicit, normative humanism of Marx, which has been denied in recent times by certain forms of snobbery within the Marxist camp and by the caricatures of Marx published by the reactionary forces in order to bring the communist revolution into disrepute. Chapters 5, 6, and 7 show that a profoundly demanding morality is not simply present in some fashion in the thinking of Marx and Engels, but that it actually constitutes the guiding thread of their own economic analyses and the norm of their own personal and political decisions. For Marx, economic science itself is not feasible without a strictly moral conscience.

Chapter 8 shows that the idea which gave rise to Marx's scientific analysis, and which serves as the structure for *Capital*, is the denunciation of the god money—a denunciation which is voiced for the first time in history by Jesus Christ. Marx's economic message is the scientific, demonstrative elaboration of a teaching that is absolutely central to the gospel message. And the so-called "Christian" world has not dared to accept that teaching. Indeed it is not inclined to hear that message, much less comprehend it.

Chapter 9 brings together explicit remarks of Marx and Engels which show that they were aware that their communism is a prolongation and completion of the idea of early Christianity. In Chapter 10 I present and discuss various remarks of the mature Marx dealing with eschatology and the existence of God. Insofar as the latter subject is concerned, I find his thinking and his remarks a bit contradictory and illogical, as I hope the reader will see.

After the original Mexican edition of this book appeared, certain authentic texts came to my attention that are not in the MEW. This forced me to revise some of what I had said in Chapter 10 and in the first two pages of Chapter 9, and those revisions appear here for the first time.

Chapter 11 serves as an Appendix, bringing together some theses of Marx dealing with epistemology. Those theses will not only have a traumatic effect on positivists who call themselves "Marxists," but will also make valuable contributions to the complex of problems surrounding the theory of science.

It is not just the satanic image of Marx concocted by conservatives that is demonstrably false. Equally false is the image of Marx presented by certain revolutionaries who call themselves "Marxists." And curiously enough these two images agree on many points. Today, fortunately we possess a critical edition of the works of Marx and Engels that is almost complete. So we can discuss the issues with a solid basis in the sources—a situation that did not exist twenty years ago.

The present volume is based on the forty-three volumes of the *Marx-Engels Werke* (MEW) and the thick German edition of the *Grundrisse*. For the English-language edition, we have made use of the many translations of Marx's writings that are now available. A detailed overview of these sources is provided in the list of Abbreviations (pp. vii–ix).

In writing this book, I have been very conscious of the many important things published about Marx and his thought, and also of some of the things of lesser importance. The literature has certainly grown enormously in recent years, so that now it is beyond the capacity of any one investigator to keep up with it, much less master it. To mention these works expressly and debate with them directly would have made this book three times as long as it is now. So for pragmatic reasons I will focus on the works of Marx and Engels themselves, only exceptionally referring explicitly to this abundant literature on Marx.

MARX AGAINST THE MARXISTS

1
The Real Motive
of the Revolution

Apart from the history of philosophy, nowhere do we find more varied and differing interpretations of the term "materialism" than in the ranks of Marxists. It would not serve our purpose here to list and group these interpretations, documenting each with quotations from more or less well-known Marxist authors or Marxist parties around the world. Even a mere description of the *status quaestionis* would constitute a book as large as the present one. But it would not help us to construct a unifying criterion or to eliminate the existing confusion.

A more direct and solid way to tackle the question is to show in gradual steps what Marx himself did *not* mean by materialism. If this seemingly negative method helps us to trim away some of the more frequent interpretations of the term "materialism," then our effort will be fruitful. Of course, the passages introduced in the course of this work will also put us on the track of what Marx himself understood by materialism. From a methodological standpoint, however, there is no use in ascertaining the latter if we do not use it to counteract unfounded or untenable interpretations.

I

Now one of the most frequently encountered interpretations is the one that suggests that the socialist revolution will be motivated by hunger. It assumes that the decisive moving force in history is self-preservation, the acquisition of indispensable material goods, utilitarianism. Hobbes maintained that some centuries ago, and many Marxists still hold to the same opinion today. As a theory of revolution, this view also assumes that capitalism will subject the exploited to ever increasing pauperization until the moving force just mentioned finally triggers the revolution.

1

Prescinding from the metaphysical backdrop of this first interpretation, I shall try to show in this chapter that Marx unequivocally rejected this conception of the moving force for the revolution. Marx's materialism is not of that ilk.

Let me begin by mentioning Alfred Schmidt,[1] one of the most relevant Marxist theoreticians of our day. He can hardly disguise his dislike for a passage in Engels' writing that is a fine summary of the latter's thought: "By materialism the philistine understands gluttony, drunkenness, lust of the eye, carnal desire and ostentatious living, avarice, cupidity, covetousness, and stock-exchange swindling—in short, all the sordid vices in which he himself secretly indulges" (MEW 21:282; LF:27). There is good reason for Schmidt to feel uncomfortable with these words in *Ludwig Feuerbach and the End of Classical German Philosophy*. The fact is that many present-day Marxists, including their theoreticians, profess the same philistine conception of materialism that Engels regarded as typical of the bourgeoisie. From Engels' quote it seems fair to conclude that the founders of Marxism would never have maintained that such a materialism be the moving force behind the socialist revolution.

We would betray an ignorance of Marx's writing if we felt that we could appeal to Marx against Engels on this matter. Here is what Marx said about Napoleon III in an article dated 2 July 1858 (NYDT):

> Bonaparte, who won his power only by flattering the basest passions of human beings, can maintain it only by purchasing new accomplices day after day. Thus he has not only restored slavery but also bought the plantation-owners by renewing the slave trade. Everything that degrades the conscience of the nation consolidates the power of Napoleon (MEW 12:511).

We see, therefore, that Marx would not appeal to the success of the revolution to justify stirring up base passions or the degradation of people's consciences. Indeed those who equate liberation with the complete absence of morality must feel it is totally antiquated to talk about "the basest passions of human beings." But it is Marx himself who uses these words and not in a throwaway remark on some secondary topic. Criticism of Napoleon III runs like a thread through much of Marx's adult writing until that rascal lost his crown during the Franco-Prussian War. Marx's penetrating insight and clear-sightedness are even more evident in the remark cited above than in *The Eighteenth Brumaire of Louis Bonaparte* written six years earlier. If Marx felt obliged to condemn the revolution that led to Louis Bonaparte's reign because it led to opportunism and all sorts of sordid behavior, then it is hardly likely that he would ground the socialist revolution on the same sort of utilitarianism. Thus I do not see how certain Marxists can interpret materialism in that vein today, or appeal to a man who said, "Everything that degrades the conscience of the nation consolidates the power of Napoleon."

The following year Marx returned to this theme in the more general context of the philosophy of history. In an article dated 10 February 1859 (NYDT) he talks about the threats and attempted blows that the Carbonari, a secret revolutionary society, were directing against Louis Napoleon:

> The mysterious intervention of such a force—invisible, of course, but familiar to him after the pistol of Pianori and the bomb of Orsini—was peculiarly suited to upset the mind of a man who sees no other causality in history except the ordinary political one of self-seeking (MEW 13:173).

The pursuit of personal gain is the core of the materialism which we are considering here. According to Marx, Napoleon III was completely mistaken in thinking that it is the only important moving-force in history. Like the thief, Napoleon III thought that everyone was like himself. Since he was never motivated by anything but self-seeking and personal advantage he assumed that all human beings were like that and interpreted the events of history accordingly. Marx could scarcely have imagined that his own followers would end up imputing the same philosophy of history to himself.

Now I am aware of the retort that the brand of materialism under discussion will give. It maintains that those who think they are guided by motives other than self-profit are victims of an idealist and subjectivist delusion, that they simply are not conscious of their real motives. The point here, however, is not to debate whether this particular brand of materialism is true in itself or not. It is to see whether Marx himself professed it. Here is what Marx says to Freiligrath in a letter dated 23 February 1860:

> We both realize that each of us in his own way, setting aside all private interests and moved by the purest motives, has for years waved the banner of the most wretched and labor-ridden class over the heads of the philistines. So it seems to me we would be committing the sin of pettiness against history if we now broke with one another for trifles that are nothing more than misunderstandings (MEW 30:461 f.).

In a letter to Siegfried Meyer dated 30 April 1867, Marx says: "If one chose to be an ox, one could of course turn one's back on the agonies of humanity and look after one's own skin" (MEW 31:542; MESC:219).

Both these letters postdate *A Contribution to the Critique of Political Economy* and its Introduction in which, it is commonly said, Marx espouses materialism. But the person who wrote the articles and letters cited above obviously did not think that the quest for self-profit was the only motive and cause operative in history, not even in the last analysis. Hence Marx's materialism must be of a different sort, to say the very least.

Marx uses the term "gross materialism" *(Grob-Materialismus)* to describe the quest for personal profit and advantage. This is evident in his letter to Engels dated 19 December 1860 (MEW 30:131), which should be compared with his letter dated 6 December of the same year (MEW 30:123f.). The term itself should be enough to warn us that Marx's understanding of materialism does not coincide with the view of the Marxists under discussion here. And the reader should note that I am citing texts that come from Marx's mature years and that are accepted as such even by the most vehement proponents of a distinction between the "young" Marx and the "mature" Marx. In his *Theories of Surplus Value* Marx's historical review finally comes to Hodgskin, the author of *Labour Defended,* for whom Marx professed great admiration. After citing a few passages from this author, Marx sums up the matter:

> These are simply further elaborations of Galiani's thesis: ". . . the real wealth . . . is man." The whole objective world, the "world of commodities," vanishes here as a mere aspect, as the merely passing activity, constantly performed anew, of socially producing men. Compare this "idealism" with the crude, material fetishism into which the Ricardian theory develops in the writings "of this incredible cobbler," McCulloch, where not only the difference between man and animal disappears but even the difference between a living organism and an inanimate object. And then let them say that as against the lofty idealism of the bourgeois political economy, the proletarian opposition has been preaching a crude materialism directed exclusively towards the satisfaction of coarse appetites (MEW 26/3:263).

From this passage we should not infer that Marx professes idealism, since he puts the word in quotes—though perhaps it is a question of terminology. What is clear is that his materialism is not "directed exclusively towards . . . coarse appetites." Any such crude materialism is a calumny against socialism, yet that is precisely the sort of crude materialism that some Marxists now impute to Marx. According to Marx, this sort of crude materialism is typical of the bourgeois economy and contrasts sharply with the socialist revolution. Marx emphasizes the difference between the two tendencies precisely because the one cannot be reduced to the other, even in the last analysis. In his *Instructions for Delegates to the Geneva Congress* (of the First International), Marx wrote this about the role of trade unions:

> They must look carefully after the interests of the worst paid trades, such as the agricultural labourers, rendered powerless by exceptional circumstances. They must convince the world at large that their efforts, far from being narrow and selfish, aim at the emancipation of the downtrodden millions (MEW 16:197 f.; VFI:92).

Of course, those who today equate materialism with self-seeking will find a way around Marx's words. They will say that the best way to achieve one's own interests is to be concerned about the welfare of others, and so forth. Unfortunately that is Jeremy Bentham, not Karl Marx, talking. When Marx sets up a contrast between two things, he really means that one cannot be equated with the other. The Marxists we are considering here are, of course, perfectly free to advocate any sort of utilitarianism or preestablished harmony they wish. However, they do not have a right to attribute such views to Marx. There is a school of thought that holds that in the last analysis self-seeking is the ultimate moving force behind human action, either consciously or unconsciously. Indeed, that is the central dogma of utilitarianism as propagated by Jeremy Bentham. Here is what Marx has to say about Bentham in Book I of *Capital*: "Had I the courage of my friend Heinrich Heine I should call Mr. Jeremy a genius of bourgeois stupidity" (MEW 23:637, ftn. 63; CAP 1:609–10, ftn. 2). In the same section Marx questions the principle of utility on the basis of the principle of nature:

> To know what is useful for a dog, one must study dog-nature. This nature itself is not to be deduced from the principle of utility. Applying this to man, he that would judge all human acts, movements, relations, etc., by the principle of utility, must first deal with human nature in general and then with human nature as modified in each historical epoch. Bentham makes short work of it. With the dryest naiveté he takes the modern shopkeeper, especially the English shopkeeper, as the normal man (MEW 23:637, ftn. 63; CAP 1:609, ftn. 2).

In short, Marx makes the same accusation against Bentham that he had made against Louis Napoleon. Like the thief, he thinks that everyone thinks like himself. The bourgeois Englishman in search of his own profit thinks that he is the perfect exemplar of human nature. Marx never dreamed that some of his own followers would accept this bourgeois definition of what it means to be a human being. Still less did he dream that they would attribute it to him as one of the basic principles on which Marxism stands or falls.

Now we can apply the point more explicitly to the matter of the socialist revolution whose motivating force concerns us here. On 4 February 1878 Marx wrote a letter to Wilhelm Liebknecht regarding the Russo-Turkish War. As usual Marx takes sides on the basis of what will best serve the proletarian revolution, and in this case he sides with the Turks. But notice his reasoning:

> We definitely take sides with the Turks—for two reasons. Firstly, we have studied the Turkish peasantry—i.e., the mass of the Turkish people—and we clearly find them to be *the most capable and moral representatives of the peasantry in Europe.* Second, *a Russian defeat would greatly accelerate the social revolution in Russia,* for which there are elements in massive quantities, *and hence accelerate insurrection throughout Europe* (MEW 34:317).

The element of geopolitical strategy is clearly a factor in Marx's stand, but it is deliberately given second place. First place goes to the capability and morality of those with whom Marx sides. Thus the moral factor, far from being subsumed under or reduced to a political strategy, is the most important factor of all. Why? Obviously because the revolution and the subsequent realization of socialism can only be accomplished by human beings who are capable and moral. I shall return to this point again. Right now I simply want to ask the reader if people are accurately interpreting the thought of Marx when they say that the primordial motive of the proletarian revolution is the satisfaction of material needs. In an article dated 12 September 1847 for the *Deutsche-Brüsseler Zeitung* Marx wrote: "To those proletarians who do not wish to be treated like garbage, courage, self-awareness, pride, and a sense of independence are more important than bread" (MEW 4:200).

Whatever reservations might be pleaded by those who like to divide Marx's life up into distinct periods, he never went back on the kind of sentiments expressed in the above analysis.

II

Now let us go back over the same topic in somewhat more systematic terms, for what is at stake here is Marx's whole economic analysis. Those who maintain that the revolution will be motivated by hunger must assume the hypothesis that capitalism will lead to the ever increasing pauperization of the workers. Since the facts do not bear out this prediction, these materialists necessarily split into two groups. The orthodox faction continues to hope against hope, to wait for the pauperization of the proletariat that is nowhere in sight, and hence to keep postponing the revolution. The revisionist faction, on the other hand, recognizes that the proletariat is not becoming increasingly impoverished; it maintains that the message of the revolution no longer has any addressee.[2] Meanwhile the capitalists and their ideologues mock both groups, and Marxism in the bargain, since both agree on the importance of the prophecy about pauperization. Indeed, the latter is the most important element undermining the prestige of Marxism on the level of theory.

On the practical level this interpretation of materialism has prevented us from making the revolution. According to the materialist hypothesis, its motivating force must be people's rebellion against a decreasing degree of consumption on their part. The revolutionary message is so construed that only this motive, and no other, will move the minds and hearts of the proletariat. Thus, devoid of any real basis, this message remains ineffectual and lost in the air. By this definition of materialism, moreover, to envision any other motive force would be to fall into the snares of idealism and spiritualism.

However, Marx's own view cannot be reconciled with this prediction of growing pauperization. His statements on this matter are clear, frequently reiterated, and completely central to his theory of value. So true is this that we cannot understand his theory of value unless we grasp this point. How can we explain the fact that it is missed by people who have dedicated their whole lives to studying Marx? The only explanation is that they approach Marx with the *a priori* assumption that he must be interpreted in line with their understanding of materialism, even though it may be incorrect.

That many Marxists unwittingly help the capitalist campaign against Marxism by their confusion on this point is not the worst result. Worse still is the negative result that Marx's economic message is simply not proclaimed, that his incomparable contribution to the consciousness raising of humanity is not transmitted to its addressee. Rosdolsky and Sombart,[3] for example, saw clearly that the theory of pauperization was incompatible with Marx's theory of value. Unfortunately they did not proceed to ask themselves the question that becomes critical at that point: what exactly is the economic message of Marx? In other words, what is the real motive of the revolution?

Here let me anticipate the answer I would offer to this question by pointing to the root of the matter. With an increase in productivity, that is to say, with an increase in the number of physical goods produced per normal work hour, the value of each article produced decreases; for the value of a commodity depends on the amount of labor time that is socially necessary for its production. Since a work hour is now embodied in a thousand articles of the same sort rather than in a hundred, then the value of one such article is now one thousandth of a normal man hour rather than one hundredth. When there is increased productivity in every branch of activity, then the value of all the individual goods produced is diminished.

In the commodity system of production, labor power is a commodity too. Like other commodities its value is measured by the amount of labor required to reproduce itself as labor power. Obviously this amount of labor is concretized in a certain amount of consumer goods, e.g., food, clothing, housing, and entertainment. In other words, the value of labor power is crystallized in the quantity of consumer goods required for the subsistence of the laborer. So when the value of consumer goods diminishes, then the value of the commodity known as labor power also diminishes *even though the physical quantity of goods consumed by the worker may remain exactly the same as before.* Moreover, this is also true even when the quantity of goods consumed by the proletariat increases, *if productivity increases faster.* In that case, too, the value of labor power decreases.

Let us assume that at the end of a certain period workers are consuming twice as much as they did before. If productivity has increased four times during the same period, then the value of labor power has been cut in half. Now let us consider the situation in agriculture and husbandry in round numbers. In 1750 the productivity of workers in this field was so small that the labor of one family was only enough to feed two families (itself and one other). Today in the United States the agricultural labor of one family is enough to feed twenty-seven families (itself and twenty-six others). So even though the consumption of the proletariat, their standard of living, may have quadrupled between 1750 and today, the value of their labor power would have diminished almost seven times.

Let us assume for a moment that the number of hours in the working day remains constant. If the value of labor power diminishes, then there is an increase in the amount of value produced by the laborer and appropriated by the capitalist. Now let us say that a century ago four of the eight hours of the working day were required to produce the consumer goods needed by the workers. The value produced in the other four work hours is what remained in the hands of the owner of the business. Let us call the work of the first four hours necessary labor, and that of the last four hours surplus labor. As we noted above, the value of consumer goods and hence of labor power decreases with every increase in productivity. The number of hours of necessary labor keeps decreasing while the number of hours of surplus labor keeps increasing. Thus exploitation keeps increasing even though the worker's standard of living may remain constant, for now he is consuming the same physical quantity of goods even though the latter have now decreased in value. This holds true even if the pressure of labor unions may have succeeded in increasing the consumption of the worker fourfold over the last hundred years. If productivity has increased forty times, then the exploitation of the worker is greater even though there may be no pauperization of the proletariat.

To repeat, this analysis is explicit and central in Marx's work. The theory of necessary pauperization at an increasing rate cannot be applied to workers in the capitalist system. At best it might be applicable to the unemployed. But that is a horse of a different color since the revolution is supposed to be grounded specifically on the workers.

A brief survey of the documentary evidence on this point might properly begin with Engels, for the phrase and a half in the *Communist Manifesto*, that has opened the door to the theory of pauperization may well have come from Engels' pen. At least we find something resembling it in his earlier work, *The Condition of the Working Class in England*, published in German three years before the *Communist Manifesto*. In 1886 he wrote the following in an introduction to the forthcoming English edition of his early work.

> It will be hardly necessary to point out that the general theoretical standpoint of this book—philosophical, economical, political— does not exactly coincide with my standpoint today. Modern international Socialism, since fully developed as a science, chiefly and almost exclusively through the efforts of Marx, did not as yet exist in 1844 (MEW 21:254 f.; CWC:363–64).

In other words, the statements in that book which might be interpreted as a prediction of pauperization could only have occurred to the founders of Marxism before Marx discovered his theory of value and undertook his scientific analysis of capitalism. And the same must be said of the phrase and a half in the *Communist Manifesto* that was written in 1847.

For another printing in 1892 of the English edition of his book on the condition of the working class, Engels makes this clear statement:

> Thus the development of production on the basis of the capitalistic system has of itself sufficed—at least in the leading industries, for in the more unimportant branches this is far from being the case— to do away with all those minor grievances which aggravated the workman's fate during its earlier stages (MEW 22:267; CWC:362).

So it is not only the interpretation of the facts that has changed. The economic facts themselves have eliminated the grievances of the worker, so a prophecy about pauperization is now untenable.

A year earlier, in 1891, the German Social Democrats asked Engels to give them a critique of the draft agenda that they would be discussing in Erfurt during the week of 14 to 21 October. (The draft agenda itself can be found in MEW 22:596–98.) Engels reacted to the following phrase in the draft (4): "The number and poverty of the proletarians grows increasingly greater." In his reply Engels underlined the word "poverty" and made this comment:

> This is not true, in the absolute terms expressed here. The organization of the workers and their ever growing opposition may well block the *increase in poverty*. What will increase *for sure* is the *insecurity of their existence*. That is what I would put (MEW 22:231).

In 1881, when Marx was still alive, *The Labour Standard* published a series of articles by Engels that constitutes a veritable treatise on economic and labor questions. The last paragraph of the central article entitled "The Wages System" begins as follows:

> Thus the Trade Unions do not attack the wages system. But it is not the highness or lowness of wages which constitutes the economical degradation of the working class, this degradation is comprised in the fact that, instead of receiving for its labour the full produce of this labour, the working class has to be satisfied with a portion of its own produce called wages (MEW 19:253; SW:103).

His conclusion is, "And therefore there is no real redemption for the working class until it becomes owner of all the means of work" (ibid.). Clearly, then, the motive for rebelling against the capitalist system is not the highness or lowness of wages, it is the very existence of the wage system itself. In an article on "Trade Unions" in the same series we find Engels saying:

> There are plenty of symptoms that the working class of the country is awakening to the consciousness that it has for some time been moving in the wrong groove, that the present movement for higher wages and shorter hours exclusively, keep it in a vicious circle out of which there is no issue; that it is not the lowness of wages which forms the fundamental evil, but the wages system itself (MEW 19:260; SW:109).

The above quotations touch upon a matter that is crucial for Marx's socialism. If it is a matter of improving the level of consumption in materialistic terms, then there really is no reason to abolish capitalism. Readers may find it hard to believe that I must emphasize this point at this late date in the twentieth century, but the fact is that the materialist mentality has thrown everything out of focus. If socialist propaganda continues to try to foster this sort of materialism, then it will only succeed in driving the workers into the arms of capitalism. For that is precisely the philosophy that capitalism must inculcate to consolidate its own position.

Those who stump for the passage in the *Communist Manifesto* on pauperization (MEW 4:473) apparently do not wish to pay serious attention to the joint preface written by Marx and Engels for the 1872 German edition. By that time the *Manifesto* was already a classic document and its text could not be altered. However, Marx and Engels note that "here and there some detail might be improved" in the general principles, which is where we find the sentence on pauperization. And they also note that their program in the *Manifesto* has become antiquated in some details "in view of the gigantic strides of modern industry since 1848, and of the accompanying improved and extended organization of the working class" (MEW 18:95 f.; VRV:66). In his preface to the 1888 English edition, Engels cited this section from their joint preface of 1872.

Now let us consider Marx's own analyses that are incompatible with the theory of pauperization. The first thing to be noted here is that they are central aspects of his whole system. In Book I of *Capital* we find this section, which could hardly be more explicit.

The value of labour-power is determined by the value of a given quantity of necessaries. It is the value and not the mass of these necessaries that varies with the productiveness of labour. It is possible that this mass, owing to an increase of labour productiveness, increase simultaneously and in the same proportion for the worker and for the capitalist, without any change in the proportion between price of labour-force and the price of surplus-value. If the value of labour-power be 3 shillings, and the necessary labour-time amount to 6 hours, if the surplus-value likewise be 3 shillings and the surplus-labour 6 hours, then if the productiveness of labour were doubled without altering the ratio of necessary labour to surplus-labour, there would be no change of magnitude in surplus-value and price of labour-power. The only result would be that each of them would represent twice as many use-values as before, these use-values being twice as cheap as before. Although labour-power would be unchanged in price, it would be above its value. If, however, the price of labour-power had fallen, not to 1s. 6d., the lowest possible point consistent with its new value, but to 2s. 10d. or 2s. 6d., *still this lower price would represent an in-*

creased mass of necessaries. In this way it is possible with an increasing productiveness of labour, *for the price of labour-power to keep on falling, and yet this fall to be accompanied by a constant growth in the mass of the labourer's means of subsistence*. But even in such case, the fall in the value of labour-power would cause a corresponding rise of surplus-value and thus the abyss between the labourer's position and that of the capitalist would keep widening (MEW 23:545 f.; cf. CAP 1:523; my italics).

If Marx were alive today, and if he wanted to analyze what has happened in the industrialized nations and what is happening right now, he would not say anything different from what he said above. He foresaw that the productivity of capitalism could increase indefinitely and that therefore the quantity of goods consumed by the workers would also continue to grow. In other words, the workers' standard of living would continue to improve without this signifying any diminution in the degree of exploitation. It is the latter that Marx is talking about above when he refers to the relationship between surplus value and the price of labor power. Marx also sees the irrefutable theoretical possibility that the worker's standard of living and the degree of exploitation might grow simultaneously. Hence he also realized that an improvement in the consumption of workers could go hand in hand with an intensification in the contrast between their standard of living and that of the capitalist. So it is completely absurd for anyone to think that the man who foresaw developments so clearly would maintain that the social revolution would be motivated by hunger or by an ever increasing squeeze insofar as material necessities is concerned. In the same Book I of *Capital* we find this lengthy passage.

Since the capital produces yearly a surplus-value, of which one part is yearly added to the original capital; since this increment itself grows yearly along with the augmentation of the capital already functioning; since lastly, under special stimulus to enrichment, such as the opening of new markets, or of new spheres for the outlay of capital in consequence of newly developed social wants, etc., the scale of accumulation may be suddenly extended, merely by a change in the division of the surplus-value or surplus-product into capital and revenue, the requirements of accumulating capital may exceed the increase of labour-power or of the number of labourers, the demand for labourers may exceed the supply, and, therefore, *wages may rise*. This *must, indeed, ultimately be the case* if the conditions supposed above continue. For since in each year more labourers are employed than in its predecessor, *sooner or later a point must be reached*, at which the requirements of accumulation begin to surpass the customary supply of labour, and, therefore, *a rise of wages takes place* (MEW 23:641; CAP 1:613; my italics).

Keeping this lengthy passage in mind, we must now add six shorter passages from the same Chapter 23 of Book I to make clear the thrust and scope of Marx's thesis on the question we are considering here:

Under the conditions of accumulation supposed thus far, which conditions are those most favourable to the labourers, their relation of dependence upon capital takes on a form endurable, or, as Eden says: "easy and liberal" (MEW 23:645; CAP 1:617).

Instead of becoming more intensive with the growth of capital, this relation of dependence only becomes more extensive, i.e., the sphere of capital's exploitation and rule merely extends with its own dimensions and the number of its subjects (MEW 23:645a; CAP 1:617–18).

A larger part of their own surplus-product, always increasing and continually transformed into additional capital, comes back to them in the shape of means of payment, so that they can extend the circle of their enjoyments; can make some additions to their consumption-fund of clothes, furniture, etc., and can lay by small reserve-funds of money. But just as little as better clothing, food, and treatment, and a larger peculium, do away with the exploitation of the slave, so little do they set aside that of the wage-worker (MEW 23:646; CAP 1:618).

In the controversies on this subject the chief fact has generally been overlooked, viz., the differentia specifica of capitalistic production (MEW 23:646 f.; cf. CAP 1:618).

The conditions of its sale, *whether more or less favourable to the labourer,* include therefore the necessity of its constant re-selling, and the constantly extended reproduction of all wealth in the shape of capital (MEW 23:647; CAP 1:618–19; my italics).

Altogether, irrespective of the case of a rise of wages with a falling price of labour, etc., such an increase only means at best a quantitative diminution of the unpaid labour that the worker has to supply. This diminution can never reach the point at which it would threaten the system itself (MEW 23:647; CAP 1:619).

The seven sections of Chapter 25 quoted above clearly show that Marx foresaw that capitalism would *necessarily* tend to raise the workers' standard of living. It is not just that he foresaw the theoretical possibility of an improvement or increase in the consumption of the workers without any diminution in their exploitation by the capitalist. He foresaw that this would in fact happen of necessity. But just as a better pittance does not stop a slave from being a slave, so a better wage does not stop the wage laborer from being a wage slave. *The real motive of the revolution is this irritating situation itself*, not the growing squeeze of material necessities. Marx's own formulations are so clear that the materialist thesis about the motive of the revolution must be regarded as an original creation devoid of any relationship with Marx and completely undemonstrable.

Once the capacity of workers to form a coalition had been verified, it was only natural to assume that they would not allow their standard of living to decline, that they would snatch a part of the growing wealth for themselves. Here is what Marx says in *Theories of Surplus Value:*

> For example, the workers themselves, although they cannot prevent reductions in the *value* of their wages, will not permit them to be reduced to the absolute minimum; on the contrary, they achieve a certain quantitative participation in the general growth of wealth (MEW 26/3:306; cf. TSV 3:312; my italics).

In the first long quote from Book I of *Capital* above, Marx made it clear that the exchange value of wages can diminish even though their real purchasing power may increase. Marx makes the same point in his 1865 lectures on "Value, Price and Profit." In them he notes:

> By virtue of the increased productivity of labor, the same amount of the average daily necessaries might sink from three to two shillings, or only four hours out of the working day, instead of six, be wanted to reproduce an equivalent for the value of the daily necessaries. The working man would now be able to buy with two shillings as many necessaries as he did before with three shillings. Indeed, the *value of labor* would have sunk, but that diminished value would command the same amount of commodities as before. Then profits would rise from three to four shillings, and the rate of profit from 100 to 200 percent. Although the laborer's absolute standard of life would have remained the same, his *relative* wages, and therewith his *relative social position*, as compared with that of the capitalist, would have been lowered (MEW 16:142; EOM:158; my italics).

The general economic explanation for this is stated by Marx a bit earlier in the same work: "The values of commodities are directly as the times of labor employed in their production, and are inversely as the productive powers of the labor employed" (WMEW 16:127; EOM:141).

That is why the workers cannot prevent either the value of their own labor from diminishing or the surplus value stolen from them from increasing. However, not only can they prevent their own standard of living from sinking, they can even make it rise—though the degree of exploitation and the social abyss between capitalist and workers increases at the same time. Such is the economic machinery of capitalism. Its ironclad logic cannot be modified. No one can change that logic without destroying the system altogether.

In *Theories of Surplus Value* Marx says: "The worker, therefore, justifiably regards the development of the productive power of his own labor as hostile to himself" (MEW 26/2:576; TSV 2:573). It is a terrible thesis, and its explanation is to be found in still another terrible thesis in Book III of *Capital:*

> Given the necessary means of production, i.e., a sufficient accumulation of capital, the creation of surplus-value is only limited by the labouring population if the rate of surplus-value, i.e., the intensity of exploitation is given; and no other limit but the intensity of exploitation if the labouring population is given (MEW 25:253; CAP 3:243).

Moreover, as early as 1849, when Marx had just finished studying the matter in Ricardo's work, he had already arrived at the key distinction between real wages and relative wages; he saw the possibility of real wages rising and relative wages falling simultaneously. Here is what he said in *Wage-Labour and Capital:*

> The real wage expresses the price of labor in relation to the price of other commodities; the relative wage, on the contrary, expresses the proportionate share which living labor gets of the new values created by it as compared to that which is appropriated by stored-up labor or capital (MEW 6:413; EOM:100).

> Real wages may remain the same, or they may even rise, and yet the relative wages may none the less have fallen. Let us assume, for example, that the price of all the means of subsistence has fallen by two-thirds, while a day's wages have only fallen one-third, as for instance, from three shillings to two. Although the laborer has a larger amount of commodities at his disposal for two shillings than

he had before for three, yet his wages are nevertheless diminished in proportion to the capitalist's gain. The capitalist's profit—the manufacturer's, for instance—has been augmented by a shilling, since for the smaller sum of exchange-values which he pays to the laborer, the laborer has to produce a larger sum of exchange-values than he did before. The share of capital is raised in proportion to the share of labor. The division of social wealth between capital and labor has become more disproportionate. The capitalist commands a larger amount of labor with the same amount of capital. The power of the capitalist class over the laboring class is increased; the social position of the laborer has deteriorated, and is depressed another degree below that of the capitalist (MEW 6:414; EOM:101).

Not only do these passages rule out the view that the moving force behind the revolution is to be the growing pursuit of material necessities, but these passages also hint at a very different set of motives. In *Wage-Labour and Capital* we find this refutation of capitalist apologetics:

The meaning of the statement that the laborer has an interest in the rapid increase of capital is merely this; the faster the laborer increases his master's dominion, the richer will be the crumbs that he will get from his table; and the greater the number of laborers that can be employed and called into existence, the greater will be the number of slaves dependent upon capital (MEW 6:416; EOM:103).

When capital is increasing fast, wages may rise, but the profit of capital will rise much faster. *The material position of the laborer has improved, but it is at the expense of his social position.* The social gulf which separates him from the capitalist has widened (MEW 6:416; EOM:103–4; my italics).

Finally, the meaning of the most favorable condition of wage-labor—that is, the quickest possible increase of productive capital—is merely this: The faster the working classes enlarge and extend the hostile power that dominates over them, the better will be the conditions under which they will be allowed to labor for the further increase of bourgeois wealth and for the wider extension of the power of capital, and thus contentedly to forge for themselves the golden chains by which the bourgeoisie drags them in its train (MEW 6:416; EOM:104).

This clearly is a motive for revolution, but it has nothing to do with materialism. Indeed it would be impossible to carry out the revolution for Marx's reasons if the workers were materialists. We have already seen how indignant Marx was over the maneuvers of Louis Napoleon to "buy" the various segments of the French population on the grounds of material interests. In another section of his article dated 18 March 1858 (NYDT), Marx comments on his attempts to buy off the working class:

> It seems that the mass imprisonments, the deportations, and the general-security measures designed to root out the republican element have been as sterile as the *cités ouvrières,* the recently founded workshops, and *all other attempts to buy off the conscience of the French working class* (MEW 12:413; my italics).

According to Marx, then, the motives for making the revolution are perceived by the moral conscience of human beings more than by the human stomach. Note the point that Marx makes in *Wage-Labour and Capital:* an improved standard of living tends to make the working class feel satisfied to forge the golden chains that bind it. The other texts cited above make the same point in different words. We do well to ponder the nature and quality of the indignation that they are trying to provoke. It is the same sort of indignation that Marx is trying to provoke in Book III of *Capital* when he talks about private ownership of land:

> One part of society thus extracts tribute from another for the permission to inhabit the earth, as landed property in general assigns the landlord the privilege of exploiting the terrestrial body, the bowels of the earth, the air, and thereby the maintenance and development of life (MEW 25:782; CAP 3:773–74).

> To the buyer, as previously indicated, the rent appears merely as interest on the capital with which he has purchased the land and consequently his title to the rent. In the same way, the slave-holder considers a Negro, whom he has purchased, as his property, not because the institution of slavery as such entitles him to that Negro, but because he has acquired him like any other commodity, through sale and purchase. But the title itself is simply transferred, and not created by the sale. The title must exist before it can be sold, and a series of sales can no more create this title through continued repetition than a single sale can (MEW 25:784; CAP 3:776).

From the standpoint of a higher economic form of society, private ownership of the globe by single individuals will appear quite as absurd as private ownership of one man by another. Even a whole society, a nation, or even all simultaneously existing societies taken together, are not the owners of the globe. They are only its possessors, its usufructuaries, and, like *boni patres familias,* they must hand it down to succeeding generations in an improved condition (MEW 25:784; CAP 3:776).

The same reason in that case would also serve to justify slavery, since the returns from the labour of the slave whom the slave-holder has bought, merely represent the interest on the capital invested in this purchase. To derive a justification for the existence of ground-rent from its sale and purchase means in general to justify its existence by its existence (MEW 25:637; CAP 3:624).

These words show that Marx is not the positivist that some of his followers are. According to them, communism is not justified because it is more humane, or just, or moral than capitalism. It is justified simply because it is, or will be, a fact. Marx says, however, that a thing is not justified by its mere existence. If the positivist Marxists retort that nothing requires justification, then we can only direct their attention to the passages we have cited above. In them it is apparent that capitalism is not as justified as communism, that private property is not as justified as the absence of private property. We can get at least that much out of Marx's text. What else is Marx saying when he refers to communism as a higher economic form of society and when he calls private property and slavery "absurd"? When he talks about a title being transferred and yet not created, Marx is obviously requiring some justification. If anything is obvious in these passages it is the deliberate presence of value judgments, i.e., the negation of positivism.

In fact, however, these passages present more than a simple comparison between capitalism and communism. The relative evaluation is not one of mere degrees. For in them Marx says that capitalism is unjust and that communism is the realization of justice. That is a real, solid motive for revolution. If Marx's banner has attracted millions of human beings, it has certainly not been because it lacked value judgments and moral estimates. Quite the contrary is true. It has attracted people because it appeals to their elemental sense of justice.

Marx does not accept the argument that runs: "For the simple reason that it is a fact." Today some of his followers accuse people of being idealists if they do not reduce their arguments to that simplistic one. Marx's reply to them is: slavery, too, is a fact. This reply assumes that one has already passed a *moral judgment* on slavery and that the judgment is unquestionably correct. The issue is so clearly settled that one need only compare capitalism to slavery in order to reject it. The argument based on mere fact is an argument based on brute force. It is the denial of rationality, though paradoxically positivism sees itself as the very model of scientific reasoning. Those who rely solely on that argument have given up the idea of being right or reasonable. Marx, on the other hand, *wrote to prove that the communist movement is right and reasonable.* Otherwise he would not have written:

> The capitalist has always appropriated to himself the commodity "labour" *before* he pays for it. The fact however that he only buys it in order to make a profit out of the resale of its product is no *reason* for his making this profit. It is a motive (MEW 26/1:290; TSV 1:314).

The correct translation of the German word *Grund* is "justifying reason." If Marx emphasizes the word in the text above, he does so deliberately to make a distinction between moral reasons and brute facts. Here are two more passages worth considering:

> By saying, therefore, that profit is justified *by the fact* that the capitalist "saves" his capital out of profit and that he fulfils the function of accumulating, one merely says that the capitalist mode of production is justified because it exists—this, however, applies equally to the modes of production which preceded it and those which will succeed it (MEW 26/3:413; TSV 3:421).

> In relation to the moneyed capitalist, the industrialist is the one who works, but the one who works as a capitalist, that is, as *an exploiter of other people's labour.* But in relation to the workers it is *strange* to plead that the exploitation of their labour costs the capitalist labour and that, therefore, they have to pay him for this exploitation; it is the plea of the slave-driver addressed to the slave (MEW 26/3:497; cf. TSV 3:507).

Here again Marx need only draw a parallel between slavery and capitalism to reject the arguments used to justify the latter. This assumes that the conscience of humanity had already formed its moral judgment of slavery and Marx adopts that judgment as his own. Consider this ironic passage in his article dated 2 July 1853 (NYDT):

> If parliament prohibits an industrialist from forcing his workers to labor for twelve, sixteen, or even more hours, then the *Times* says: "England is no longer a place where a free man can live." It is like

the gentleman from South Carolina who was hauled before a London court and found guilty for publicly whipping a Negro he had brought from Overseas. The gentleman exploded, saying: "Don't tell me that a country where one is prohibited from whipping one's own Negro is a free country!" (MEW 9:193).

Here is a passage from another article dated 14 July 1853 (NYDT):

> In a social order grounded on class-antagonism, we must be willing to fight if we want to prevent slavery not only with words but with deeds. If we are to correctly appreciate the value of strikes and coalitions, we must not let ourselves be deceived by the apparent insignificance of their economic results. We must, first and foremost, take due account of their moral and political effects (MEW 9:70 f.).

III

I don't want to go on with this anthology of texts interminably. Enough has been adduced to show that Marx's view cannot be reconciled with those who ground the revolution on a materialist motive. In the remainder of this chapter I should like to consider the whole issue of the declining rate of profit, and then move on to Marx's explicit and explosive testimony on the systematic importance of the theme we have been exploring in this chapter.

Some Marxist theoreticians think that the declining rate of profit in capitalism is bound to produce the growing pauperization of the workers. Facts and events have proved otherwise, but here we are not concerned with debating the issue in and for itself. Insofar as exegesis of Marx's texts is concerned, his statements predicting a *real* rise in the consumption level of the proletarian class would argue against any belief in growing pauperization. Aside from the passages already considered, there is this statement in an article which Marx wrote for the *Almanacco Repubblicano* in 1874: ". . . the very noteworthy fact that English industry can sell its commodities at a lower price than that of any other country, whereas wages in England are higher than in any other country of Europe" (MEW 18:303). In *Theories of Surplus Value* Marx made the same point, expressing it in terms of a general law pure and simple:

> The more productive one country is relative to another in the world market, the higher will be its wages as compared with the other. In England, not only nominal wages but [also] real wages are higher than on the continent. The worker eats more meat, he satisfies more needs (MEW 26/2:8; TSV 2:16–17).

These and other similar statements make one thing quite clear: whatever result Marx may have drawn from the law of a declining rate of profit, its effect would not be to pauperize the workers. As we shall see, however, Marx did draw a very important conclusion from the law of the declining rate of profit. It is worth pointing out that Marx is very wary and cautious in talking about that law. He hedges his remarks with if's, and's, and but's when he talks about this law that had become an obligatory topic in economic tracts, due to the influence of the classic authors. Consider this passage in *Theories of Surplus Value:*

> It is an incontrovertible fact that, as capitalist production develops, the portion of capital invested in machinery and raw materials grows, and the portion laid out in wages declines. This is the only question with which both Ramsay and Cherbuliez are concerned. For us, however, the main thing is: does this fact explain the decline in the rate of profit? (A decline, incidentally, which is far smaller than it is said to be.) Here it is not simply a question of the quantitative ratio, but of the value ratio (MEW 26/3:356 f.; TSV 3:364–65).

In Book III of *Capital,* where he dedicates Part III to this topic, we find him saying:

> There must be some counteracting influences at work which cross and annul the effect of the general law, and which give it merely the characteristic of a tendency, for which reason we have referred to the fall of the general rate of profit as a tendency to fall (MEW 25:242; CAP 3:232).

> The rise in the rate of surplus-value . . . does not abolish the general law. But it causes that law to act rather as a tendency, i.e., as a law whose absolute action is checked, retarded, and weakened, by counteracting circumstances (MEW 25:244; CAP 3:234).

> Thus, the law acts only as a tendency. And it is only under certain circumstances and only after long periods that its effects become pronounced (MEW 25:249; CAP 3:239).

Sometimes he says that the law is suppressed. At other times he says that it is not formally suppressed, but that its complete realization cannot take place. Even when it is reduced to the role of a mere tendency, still it only operates in certain circumstances. In short, it is not a law whose results can be foreseen with certainty because it is conditioned by many variables. When we do not find some opposing tendency appearing on the horizon to balance it, we may find another tendency that nullifies it. And this give-and-take can go on indefinitely, unless a decisive factor of another type intervenes: e.g., the socialist revolution that Marx wants to initiate.

After treating "Counteracting Influences" in Chapter 14 of Book III of *Capital,* Marx goes on to consider the internal contradictions of this law in Chapter 15. The most noteworthy point for us here is to see what Marx focuses on in this connection. He focuses on the fact that in capitalism there are two mutually contradictory tendencies at work. It is important for us to see the nature of these two tendencies. It is equally important for us to realize that Marx does not foresee any one-track development or outcome but rather a perduring state of contradiction between the two tendencies:

> The contradiction, to put it in a very general way, consists in that the capitalist mode of production involves a tendency towards absolute development of the productive forces, regardless of the value and surplus-value it contains, and regardless of the social conditions under which capitalist production takes place; while, on the other hand, its aim is to preserve the value of the existing capital and promote its self-expansion to the highest limit (i.e., to promote an ever more rapid growth of this value) (MEW 25:259; CAP 3:249).

These are the two tendencies: (1) a tendency to develop productivity and (2) a tendency to develop and increase profit. As ultimate goals and norms for action, the two are obviously contradictory. But that does not mean that the first tendency is definitely going to overcome the second and eventually destroy it—unless some extraneous factor of a different sort intervenes and wipes out the whole system, replacing it with socialism. Marx nowhere maintains that the capitalist machinery itself must necessarily keep reducing the rate of profit more and more; and no one can demonstrate that by basing his argument on Marx's premises. What underlies Marx's thinking can be found in this passage on the following page of Book III:

> The *real barrier* of capitalist production is *capital itself.* It is that capital and its self-expansion appear as the starting and the closing point, the motive and the purpose of production; that production is only production for *capital* and not vice versa, the means of production are not mere means for a constant expansion of the living process of the *society* of producers. The limits within which the preservation and self-expansion of the value of capital resting on the expropriation and pauperization of the great mass of producers

can alone move—these limits come continually into conflict with the methods of production employed by capital, for its purposes which drive towards unlimited extension of production, towards production as an end in itself, towards unconditional development of the social productivity of labour. The means—unconditional development of the productive forces of society—comes continually into conflict with the limited purpose, the self-expansion of the existing capital. The capitalist mode of production is, for this reason, a historical means of developing the material forces of production and creating an appropriate world-market and is, at the same time, a continual conflict between this its historical task and its own corresponding relations of social production (MEW 25:260; CAP 3:250).

Here Marx is denouncing the fact that capitalism has turned the end into the means and the means into the end. In this perversion whose moral character is clear, Marx sees the real limitation of capitalism and the motive behind the socialist revolution. For this subsisting contradiction, this institutional knot, will not be unravelled on its own.

The commentators have not stopped to consider the fact that in *Theories of Surplus Value* Marx drew up a careful and deliberate balance sheet on the whole problem of the declining rate of profit:

Apart from the terror which the law of the declining rate of profit inspires in the economists, its most important corollary is the presupposition of a constantly increasing concentration of capitals, that is, a constantly increasing decapitalization of the smaller capitalists. This, on the whole, is the result of all laws of capitalist production. And if we strip this fact of the contradictory character which, on the basis of capitalist production, is typical of it, what does this fact, this trend towards centralization, indicate? Only that production loses its private character and becomes a social process, not formally—in the sense that all production subject to exchange is social because of the absolute dependence of the producers on one another and the necessity for presenting their labour as abstract social labour (by means of money)—but in actual fact (MEW 26/3:440 f.; TSV 3:447).

In this deliberate evaluation we are told that the only important result of the famous law of the declining rate of profit is the growing concentration of capital resources and the consequent socialization of production. What Marx predicted in this connection, then, is not the pauperization of the proletariat but the rise of mammoth trusts; and that is precisely what happened. The relationship is an obvious one. If we get a small

measure of profit from every million dollars of capital, then the only way
to compensate for this is to increase the number of millions involved. In
short, we must increase the mass of capital. This breaks the small
capitalists, who are then absorbed into the mammoth enterprises. Book
I of *Capital* tells us why this concentration is important:

> Centralisation of the means of production and socialisation of
> labour at last reach a point where they become incompatible with
> their capitalist integument. This integument is burst asunder. The
> knell of capitalist private property sounds. The expropriators are
> expropriated (MEW 23:791; CAP 1:763).

In other words, the socialist revolution must intervene to provide a
way out of the situation. But nowhere does Marx say that it will be
motivated by hunger or by the growing squeeze of necessity. Indeed
Book III of *Capital* informed us that the extraction of surplus value has
no limits in and of itself:

> Given the necessary means of production, i.e., a sufficient ac-
> cumulation of capital, the creation of surplus-value is only limited
> by the labouring population if the rate of surplus-value, i.e., the
> intensity of exploitation is given; and no other limit but the inten-
> sity of exploitation if the labouring population is given (MEW
> 25:253; CAP 3:243).

IV

We can pick up the main theme of this chapter once again by examining the truly dramatic testimony of Marx regarding the important place
that the motive for the revolution has in his system. In this case we are
dealing with one of the most classic works of the mature Marx (1875): his
Critique of the Gotha Programme and the letter that accompanied it. In a
sense it is a summary of *Capital* designed to prevent people from
confusing his socialism with other brands of socialism. The central
passage is composed of three paragraphs:

> Since Lassalle's death the scientific insight has made headway in
> our party that wages are not what they *appear* to be, namely the
> value or price of labour, but only a disguised form of the *value or
> price of labour power.* Thereby the whole of the former bourgeois
> conception of wages was thrown overboard once and for all, as
> well as all criticism of it, and it became clear that the wage labourer
> is only allowed to work for his own livelihood, i.e., *to live,* if he
> works a certain amount of time without pay for the capitalist (and

thus also for the latter's fellow consumers of surplus value); that the whole capitalist system of production turns on the prolongation of this free labour through the extension of the working day and through the development of productivity, the increasing intensification of labour power, etc.; and that the system of wage labour is consequently a system of slavery, increasing in severity commensurately with the development of the social productive forces of labour, irrespective of whether the worker is then better or worse paid. And now, after this insight has gained more and more ground in our party, there comes this return to the dogmas of Lassalle, even though people must be aware that Lassalle *knew nothing* of the true nature of wages and that he followed the bourgeois economists in mistaking the appearance of the matter for its essence.

It is as if, among slaves who have finally got behind the secret of slavery and broken out in rebellion, one slave, still the prisoner of obsolete ideas, were to write in the programme of the rebellion: Slavery must be abolished because the provisioning of slaves in the slave system cannot exceed a certain low maximum!

The mere fact that the representatives of our party were capable of making such a monstrous attack on an insight which has gained wide acceptance among the mass of the party is surely sufficient proof of the criminal levity and complete lack of conscience with which they set to work on the formulation of the compromise program (MEW 19:25 f.; VFI:352).

Here we would do well to see the connection between this statement and the passages cited earlier in this chapter. A key phrase is this one: "The system of wage labour is consequently a system of slavery, increasing in severity commensurately with the development of the social productive forces of labour, *irrespective of whether the worker is then better or worse paid.*" As we have seen before, the comparison with slavery is a sufficient argument for Marx. We are dealing here with the motive for the revolution, and Marx expresses indignation over the argument based on the provisioning of the workers. Indeed, in the sentence preceding the section cited above Marx calls such an argument a "really outrageous step back."

Even more significant for our purposes here is the fact that Marx sees in the formulation of the program a lack of moral conscience. *Gewissen* means "moral conscience." No speaker of German would equate it with the term *Bewusstsein*, which means "psychological consciousness," "awarenesss," "cognizance." In his accompanying letter to Bracke (5 May 1875) Marx says: "Apart from that it is my duty not to approve, even by diplomatic silence, a programme which in my opinion is thoroughly reprehensible and demoralizing for the party" (MEW 19:13; VFI:340). Since Marx ends his *Critique of the Gotha Programme* with the shattering phrase, *"Dixi et salvavi animam meam"* ("I have spoken and saved my soul"), we must take him seriously and literally when he writes in his letter about "duty" and a program that is "demoralizing for the party." It is not demoralizing in the sense of discouraging. Indeed Lassalle's dogma, the iron law of wages, would hardly discourage revolutionary spirits. Instead it would enflame them to fight to the death against capitalism as would the laments of the slave with obsolete ideas about their low provisioning under slavery.

Marx's point is that it would enflame them with motives that severely debase the moral sense of the workers. It "demoralizes" them in the most literal sense of that word. Marx has a moral duty to speak out against a program that would ground the revolution on materialistic motives. To repeat once more: the conception of materialism I have been attacking in this chapter is a wholly original creation of some Marxists. It has nothing to do with Marx and it is false to attribute it to him. He fought against it with his whole economic system, fully realizing that he had a moral duty to combat it.

Only an upright man of real conscience would end a commentary with the words *"Dixi et salvavi animam meam"* (MEW 19:32; VFI:359). It is something one says only once or twice in a whole lifetime. Of course it implies that he believes in the soul—something incomprehensible to those who believe that the only moving force is a materialistic one. The people to whom Marx addressed this critique in 1875 kept it from being published during his lifetime and for many years afterward. It was only through strenuous and even violent efforts on the part of Engels that the *Critique of the Gotha Programme* and the accompanying letter to Bracke were finally published in 1891. Even then some of the most incisive phrases were excised. The full text was not published until a few short years ago. Thus it is a dramatic document. One might say that Marx sensed what was going to happen. Marx himself, however, cannot be blamed for what materialists have done with his whole message. He said what he had to say, and thereby saved his soul. *Frevelhaft*, translated as "criminal" above, really means "sacrilegious." That is what Marx thinks of those who claim that the proletariat will fight for materialistic motives, when his whole economic message was designed to enable them to fight for motives that elevate the moral level of all humanity. Such materialists are guilty of "criminal levity and complete lack of conscience."

The technical terms Marx underlines in the first sentence of the text cited above are not abstruse ones. The value of a commodity is measured by the amount of labor necessary to (re)produce it. Now what is reproduced by the provisions or necessaries that are the equivalent of wages is not labor but labor power. Labor is the use made of the commodity known as labor power. Moreover, the use value of a commodity is not bought or sold or paid; it is simply enjoyed as usufruct. In the sales process we do not pay the use value of a thing but rather the exchange value. The use that is made of a commodity after its purchase is an entirely different matter; it is not governed by the law of the exchange of equivalents. Here is what Marx says in Book I of *Capital:*

> The law of exchange requires equality only between the exchange-values of the commodities given in exchange for one another. From the very outset it [Miranda: the law of exchange] pre-supposes even a difference between their use-values and it has nothing whatever to do with their consumption, which only begins after the deal is closed and executed (MEW 23:611; CAP 1:585).

Now it so happens that the curious commodity known as labor power is of a peculiar sort: its use value is the performance of labor and hence the creation of value. But this does not affect the transaction in which the employer purchases this commodity known as labor power. Instead it is the consumption which the purchaser makes of what he purchased. Therein lies the whole secret of the economic system known as capitalism.

Having clarified these technical terms, the discovery of which by Marx is absolutely decisive, we can now sum up the revolutionary message in the following terms. It is not precisely a matter of eating better. Capitalism consists in the fact that the proletariat are not permitted to labor to maintain themselves—to live, in other words—unless they agree to labor for nothing a certain number of hours during the day in order to enrich the capitalist. Since the capitalists are the owners of the means of labor, they are the ones who give or refuse permission to labor. To produce their own basic provisions, the proletarians need the permission of the capitalists. In other words, they need the permission of the capitalists to live. They won't get this permission unless they agree to work a certain length of time exclusively for the benefit of the capitalists. It does not matter here whether the means of production were acquired properly or improperly (though in fact they were acquired improperly). What is certain is that I am not permitted to produce the necessaries I need to live unless I agree to work gratis for the enrichment of the wealthy. Now this is in fact slavery, and the fact that I am well fed does not change the situation one bit. Our masters keep us in slavery, forcing us to labor for their benefit. We cannot withdraw from all this and go out and produce our sustenance on our own because all the means of production belong to the capitalists. That is being a slave, and juridical formalities to the contrary are sheer hogwash.

This is the "poverty" which we are told in Book I of *Capital* (MEW 23:675 and 790; CAP 1:645 and 762) continually grows with the further development of the capitalist mode of production. For every sale of labor power necessarily entails that the proletarians must come back to sell their labor power time and again. With each appropriation of surplus value there is a growth in capital and hence in its absolute dominion over the means of production. The materialists really had to indulge in amazing obfuscation to interpret this "poverty" as "pauperization." For Marx himself tells us: "It follows, therefore, that in proportion as capital accumulates, the lot of the labourer, be his payment high or low, must grow worse" (MEW 23:675; CAP 1:645). The materialistic interpreters of Marx forget that he used the word "poverty" in the title of one of his books: *The Poverty of Philosophy*. He was obviously not trying to say that philosophers were dying of hunger.

Now it is time to explore the situation of the laborer under capitalism more deeply, to probe further into the message of Marx. To do that, however, we need more categories than those associated with the theme of this chapter.

Notes

1. A. Schmidt, *Der Begriff der Natur in der Lehre von Marx*, Frankfurt: Europäische Verlag, 1974, p. 34, and ftn. 72; Eng. trans., *The Concept of Nature in Marx*, Atlantic Highlands, N.J.: Humanities Press, 1972.

2. H. Marcuse, *Un ensayo sobre la liberación*, Mexico City: Mortiz, 1969; English edition, *Essay on Liberation*, Boston: Beacon Press, 1969. J. Habermas, *Theorie und Praxis*, Frankfurt: Suhrkamp, 1974, p. 229; Eng. trans., *Theory and Practice*, Boston: Beacon Press, 1974.

3. R. Rosdolsky, *Zur Entstehungsgeschichte des Marxschen "Kapital,"* Frankfurt Europäische Verlagsanstalt, 1974, pp. 330–66. Sombart is cited in ibid., p. 334. Some of Sombart's works available in English are *Jews and Modern Capitalism*, New York: Macmillan, 1962 (paperback edition); *Krieg und Kapitalismus: War & Capitalism*, New York: Arno Press, 1975; *Luxury and Capitalism*, Ann Arbor, Mich.: University of Michigan Press, 1967; *The Quintessence of Capitalism*, New York: Howard Fertig, 1967; *Socialism and the Social Movement*, Clifton, N.J.: Kelley, reprint of 1909 edition.

2
A History
with a Subject

The workers that the revisionists declare to be incapable of making the revolution are the materialistic workers who only make a move when they are suffering from hunger or when they want to upgrade their consumption. Unfortunately there are two things wrong with that point of view. First of all, Marx did not compose his message with those addressees in mind. Secondly, it is simply false to say that the western proletariat is materialistic in that sense. Having falsified Marx's message, Marxism addresses a materialistic message to addressees who do not exist and who therefore do not respond.

I

But the neo-orthodoxy of Stalin and Althusser is much worse. To deny that the proletariat is the active subject or agent of the revolution, it denies that there is any subject at all. If the capitalists could manage to have a group of their theoreticians infiltrate the ranks of the oppressed, that is precisely the thesis that such a group would have to propound. How can the workers unite around a philosophy which prohibits them from using such words as "justice" and "injustice" on the grounds that these moralistic and spiritualistic categories go hand in hand with the bourgeoisie? In the last fifteen years or so, more nonsense has been spouted by this version of materialism than we have heard for a long time.

If there is no subject to engage in revolutionary activity, then materialism consists in contemplation and we are stuck with a philosophy that proposes to interpret the world rather than to change it. We are thrown back to the materialism of the eighteenth century as if Marx had never existed. And the crowning touch is that those who deny the existence of an active revolutionary subject claim to find support for their view in Marx's rejection of the humanism of Feuerbach. Yet Marx's criticism of Feuerbach, and of all previous materialists, is clearly stated in the first of his *Theses on Feuerbach*.

> The chief defect of all hitherto existing materialism (that of Feuer-
> bach included) is that the thing, reality, sensuousness is conceived
> only in the form of the *object or of contemplation,* but not as
> *sensuous human activity, practice,* not subjectively (MEW 3:5;
> GI:121).

Because of this failure to recognize the active subject, Feuerbach failed to grasp "the significance of 'revolutionary,' of 'practical-critical,' activity" (ibid.).

Nothing could be more astounding. In order to launch a thesis directly opposed to the thinking of Marx, these Marxists appeal to one of Marx's works in which he directly attacks the very thesis they wish to promulgate.

There is more to be added here. First of all, it is not true that bourgeois philosophy regards humanity as an active subject of history; and second, it is not true that Marx believed that bourgeois philosophy regarded humanity as an active subject of history. Both the fact itself and Marx's view of the matter have been completely twisted. Here is what Copleston has to say about Voltaire, one of the main figures of the French Enlightenment.

> He was not a democrat in the sense of wishing to promote popular
> rule. True, he advocated toleration, which he thought to be neces-
> sary for scientific and economic progress; and he disliked tyranni-
> cal despotism. But he mocked at Rousseau's ideas about equality,
> and his ideal was that of a benevolent monarchy, enlightened by
> the influence of the *philosophes.* He mistrusted dreamers and
> idealists; and his correspondence shows that in his opinion the
> rabble, as he pleasingly called the people, would always remain a
> rabble.[1]

I cite this passage because it describes the most characteristic thrust of the Enlightenment: to treat the people as an object rather than as a subject. This thrust is all the more intense insofar as the Enlightenment figure in question inclined toward materialism. Ranciere cites a highly pertinent passage from Bentham's *Panopticon:*

> If we could find some means to control everything that might
> happen to a group of human beings, a means to arrange everything
> around them so that we might produce the impression we wanted
> to produce, a means to be sure of all their actions, relationships,

and living circumstances so that nothing would escape or con-
travene the desired effect, then there is no doubt that such a means
would be a very useful and forceful one which rulers could apply to
different matters of the utmost importance.[2]

Here the underlying thesis is that of Helvetius: education can do everything; it makes us what we are.[3]

Marx was completely objective in grasping the core of this bourgeois
line of thought. In the third of his *Theses on Feuerbach* he summed it up
and then attacked it:

> The materialist doctrine concerning the changing of circumstances
> and upbringing forgets that circumstances are changed by men and
> that it is essential to educate the educator himself (MEW 3:5 f.;
> GI:121).

In his classic study of *The Idea of Progress*, J. B. Bury showed that a
belief in the omnipotence of education as a way of molding and determining the human beings of a given generation was a common denominator
in Enlightenment thinking, particularly among such materialists as Helvetius.[4] Education, that is, the impact of economic, social, cultural, and
political factors, would prevail over the biological factors inherited from
one's forebears. In any case the proponents of the Enlightenment felt
they could form a small group that would systematically alter circumstances and mold people accordingly. So in his third thesis on
Feuerbach Marx goes on to say: "This doctrine must, therefore, divide
society into two parts one of which is superior to society" (MEW 3:6;
GI:121).

The doctrine in question, then, is clearly related to the class struggle in
Marx's mind. It is an instrument used by the bourgeoisie in that struggle.
Denying that the people are an active subject is not Marx's view at all
(see his first thesis on Feuerbach); it is the thesis of the bourgeois class,
which he opposes with all his might. In the history of ideas we shall
hardly find as great a distortion as the one Althusser attempts on this
point. And this distortion constitutes the absolute core of his philosophy
and of his whole interpretation of Marx.

The purpose of this book, of course, is to study the thought of Marx,
not to debate the issue as to whether history is a process without an
active subject. But the reader might do well to consider briefly the net
result of the following paragraph from a logically consistent Althusse-
rian:

> Those who participate in the process without the information
> required to appreciate its dynamics precisely can imagine that a
> variety of options and alternatives exists and that their execution

will depend on their own free, personal behavior. If a limited view of the whole complex of determinations nurtures the illusion that there is a plurality of options, exhaustive knowledge of these determinations erases that illusion. There is not one situation in history where the course of events, which might have gone one way or another, has depended on the chance intervention of a free subjectivity. Among other reasons, because the activity of historical agents is never a free, undetermined activity.

Aside from the fact that this is warmed-over Laplace, theses such as this attempt to convince us that we are puppets at the mercy of a pervasive cosmic machine. Whether we will it or not, that machine produces all the acts and decisions which we, in our ignorance, think to be dependent on ourselves; for it even produces in us the illusion of being free. If such doctrines had their ways we would stop believing that various options were open to us; we would submit to the current of determinism which holds sway over plants, animals and things. In fact human beings are not born free; they make themselves free through their activity. Thus if we submitted to the determinist point of view, we would stop fashioning ourselves as free beings and sink back into the determinism that pervades the rest of the cosmos. That point of view seeks to recruit automatons and engagingly preaches nonresponsibility. Such a thesis objectively tries to *become* true, but it *is* not true. Yet its plan is not impossible *a priori*. Humanity emerged from the determinism of matter; it can sink back into that determinism if it decides to stop being human, as this point of view would have it do. The only thing which I cannot understand is how anyone could ever associate this thesis with the name of Karl Marx.

The materialism which I discussed in Chapter 1 could be called motivational materialism. The materialism under discussion here might be called materialism as the be-all and the end-all. In this context Althusser's thought is not just another Parisian fashion; it is symptomatic of a whole group of thinkers. For them, materialism comes *first*. Only then comes the communist revolution, if it is feasible. If the latter is not feasible, so much the worse for it because the real aim and goal is materialism for its own sake. They seek to take hold of the proletarian revolution in order to use it as a way of spreading materialism. They have no real regard for the thought of Marx himself. Instead they seek to use Marxism in order to inculcate materialism in the people.

Contrary to some other materialists in this camp, however, Althusser is open and frank about this matter. In his response to Lewis he points out that the category of subject "is meaningless for dialectical materialism. The latter rejects that category purely and simply, even as it rejects such problems as the existence of God."[5] Though Althusser offers the latter problem merely as an example, there is actually a close connection between the two issues. Indeed the two are linked by all the exigencies of logic, as Hegel demonstrated once and for all. If subjects exist, then God exists. In "Ideology and the Ideological Apparatus of the State," Althusser brings out this inescapable logical tie-up:

> Religious ideology is addressed to individuals to transform them into subjects. It appeals to Peter, the individual, to turn him into a subject who is free to obey or disobey . . . the commands of God. . . . This multitude of religious subjects can exist only on the absolute condition that there is *another* unique, absolute *Subject:* i.e., God.[6]

That is the reason why Althusser expressly denies the existence of subjects. Marx does not enter the picture at all. Moreover, the logic here is undeniable. A conglomeration of beings who are merely objects could not give rise to the slightest innerness or subjectivity. Only an absolute moral summons from God gives rise to subjectivity in the finite world.

Here we have a fine major premise for a great syllogism. What Althusser forgets quite often is that he is presenting his own theory as an interpretation of Marx. Hence his minor premise should consider whether Marx himself did or did not recognize the existence of subjects. That is what we seek to do in this volume. I should like to know, for example, what Althusserians are going to do with passages such as the following from the mature work of Marx. In his 1857 "Introduction" to the CCPE Marx says:

> In the succession of the economic categories, as in any other historical, social science, it must not be forgotten that their subject—here, modern bourgeois society—is always what is given, in the head as well as in reality, and that these categories therefore express the forms of being, the characteristics of existence, and often only individual sides of this specific society, this subject, and that therefore this society by no means begins only at the point where one can speak of it *as such;* this holds *for science as well* (MEW 13:637; GRU:106).

Marx tells us quite plainly that no matter what economic categories we may be using, we must always remember that they are *forms of being of the subject* that is society. The danger is that the historical and social sciences will hypostasize their categories, as if the latter were entities existing in themselves. Strickly speaking, however, we should talk not about "production" but about the producing subject, not about "culture" but about real subjects who cultivate themselves. The various categories are merely ways in which the subject exists; and the subject is society, or the human being, or humanity, as the case may be. The only reality we designate by the category "production" is the producing human being, the producing subject, the producing society.

Marx will not reiterate this point on every page of his subsequent work. He will not explicitly allude to this subject of economics. But he wants the reader to realize, once and for all, that he is talking about forms of being of this subject; that this subject exists, both in external reality and in the mind of the scientist who is talking about it. So what author does Althusser have in mind when he tells us that history and economics do not have a subject? Could Marx have been any more explicit in spelling out his methodology, his program, and his line of attack?

Althusser is reading Marx in the same official edition (MEW) that I am using here, and he cites the same pages as I do. On page 109 of the Spanish edition of *Lire le capital*, Althusser cites some sections from the same page of the MEW (13:637) and the same paragraph that I gave just above.[7] How could anyone who has read that passage maintain that history and economics have no subject according to Karl Marx? Or is it simply a matter of broadcasting "interpretations" of Marx on the assumption that no one will take the trouble to read what Marx has to say? Here is another section from the 1857 "Introduction":

> Some determinations belong to all epochs, others only to a few. [Some] determinations will be shared by the most modern epoch and the most ancient. No production will be thinkable without them; however, even though the most developed languages have laws and characteristics in common with the least developed, nevertheless, it is just those things which are not general and common that determine their development. The determinations valid for production as such must be precisely discerned. In their unity—which arises since *the subject, humanity, and the object, nature,* are the same for all—their essential difference must not be forgotten (MEW 13:617; cf. GRU:85; my italics).

Here we are told that some characteristics or traits are common to all social formations or economic systems. Without them there could be no production at all. But we must be clear as to what these common traits are, so that we do not forget the differences between various formations and systems. And the most obvious of these common characteristics is the fact that in all social formations the subject is humanity and the object is nature. Could we find a clearer denial of Althusser's thesis?

Before proceeding to cite other passages that are equally convincing, I want to point up the importance of the 1857 "Introduction," which is now found in the *Grundrisse*. In actual fact Marx originally planned it as an "Introduction" to his *Contribution to the Critique of Political Economy* (1859). He changed his mind about using it in that volume because he wanted his readers to "advance from the particular to the general" (CCPE:19). He felt that the "Introduction" anticipated results that yet remained to be substantiated. But originally it was an introduction to that volume; and Marx frequently referred to the CCPE in *Capital*, regarding it as the first part of the latter work (e.g., MEW 25:792 refers to MEW 13:133 f., MEW 26/1:275 to MEW 13:107; MEW 26/1:298 to MEW 13:101 f. and 80 f.; MEW 26/1:41 to MEW 13:44 f.; MEW 26/1:21 to MEW 13:49–59; MEW 26/1:144 to MEW 13:107, MEW 26/3:110 to MEW 13:118–120; MEW 26/3:127 to MEW 13:21 and 34; MEW 26/3:131 to MEW 13:50 f., MEW 26/3:290 to MEW 13:21–24, 34 f.; and 130 f., MEW 26/3:512 to MEW 13:41 and 68 f.). Thus the "Introduction" to the CCPE should be regarded as an introduction to *Capital*. Furthermore, as we have seen, Marx establishes a close tie-up between the existence of a subject and the scientific nature of any economic treatise.

For Althusser, who is a good positivist, science as such recognizes no subjects. For Marx, sound science presupposes the existence of a subject. It is an inescapable datum because such a subject does exist in reality and because the mind of the scientist cannot prescind from it. In the *Grundrisse* Marx uses the category of "subject" to distinguish between different social formations:

> In the slave relation, he belongs to the individual, particular owner, and is his labouring machine. As a totality of force-expenditure, as labour capacity, he is *a thing [Sache]* belonging to another, and hence *does not relate as subject* to his particular expenditure of force, nor to the act of living labour. In the serf relation he appears as a moment of property in land itself, is an appendage of the soil, exactly like draught-cattle. In the slave relation the worker is nothing but a living labour-machine, which therefore has a value for others, or rather is a value. The totality of the free worker's labour capacity appears to him as his property, as one of his moments, over which he, *as subject,* exercises domination, and which he maintains by expending it (GRU:464–65; my italics).

This passage is particularly valuable because it shows us that Marx is using the term "subject" deliberately in its authentic sense. By contrast, things and animals do not have interiority: i.e., subjectivity. Marx is not using the term "subject" unconsciously, as just another word in the language that people use without knowing exactly what it means. Other passages from the *Grundrisse* should confirm that point:

The only thing distinct from *objectified* labour is *non-objectified* labour, labour which is still objectifying itself, *labour* as subjectivity. Or, *objectified* labour, i.e., labour which is *present in space,* can also be opposed, as *past labour,* to labour which is *present in time*. If it is to be present in time, alive, then it can be present only as the *living subject,* in which it exists as capacity, as possibility: hence as *worker* (GRU: 72).

The only contrast to *objectified* labor is *non-objectified* labour; to *objectified* labour, *subjective* labour. Or, in contrast to labour that is past in time but present in space, living labour that is present in time. As labour that is present in time, not objective, hence as yet not objectified, labour can only be present as potency, possibility, capability; as the *labour-power* of the living subject (German *Grundrisse:* 942).

These two passages spell out the difference between objects and subjects. Objects include the means and instruments of production, capital, and commodities; they are past labor, objectified labor, labor already converted into space and matter. By contrast, the subject is the laborer as living labor power. Marx insists on affirming the existence of this subject, contrasting this subject with everything that is not subject though it has been produced by subjects. On another page of the same work (GRU:296) he talks about the "subjective existence of labour itself. Labour not as an object, but as activity; not as itself *value,* but as the *living source* of value." He then proposes the following thesis: using anacoluthon with a vengeance:

Thus, it is not at all contradictory—or, rather, the in-every-way mutually contradictory statements that labour is absolute poverty as object on one side, and is, on the other side, the general possibility of wealth *as subject* and as activity—are reciprocally determined and follow from the essence of labour, such as it is presupposed by capital as its contradiction and as its contradictory being, and such as it, in turn, presupposes capital (GRU: 296; my italics).

In this passage and in the preceding ones Marx explicitly brings out the nature of the worker as a subject. And this is true, not only in the mental consideration of philosophers, but also in reality. As he points out elsewhere: "In general, relations can be established as existing only by being *thought,* as distinct from the subjects which are in these relations with each other" (GRU:143). Thus Marx stresses the subject nature, not only of humanity or of labor considered collectively but also of the individual workers. Consider this on the production process:

The conditions and objectifications of the process are themselves equally moments of it, and its only *subjects* are the *individuals*, but *individuals* in mutual relationships, which they equally reproduce and produce anew (GRU:712; my italics).

The *Contribution to the Critique of Political Economy* (1859) is just as insistent on the personal character of the subjects of economics:

Lastly, it is a characteristic feature of labour which posits exchange-value that it causes the social relations of *individuals* to appear in the perverted form of a social relation between *things*. The labour of *different persons* is equated and treated as universal labour only by bringing one use-value into relation with another one in the guise of exchange-value. Although it is thus correct to say that exchange-value is *a relation between persons,* it is however necessary to add that it is a relation hidden by a *material* veil (MEW 13:21; CCPE: 34; my italics).

II

It should be clear that Marx is not afraid to spell out his point of view. To those who deny that history has any subject he would reply that they are looking at the surface appearances, at the outer wrappings. Of course the commodity mode of production, the capitalist system, makes the relationships between persons look perverted: for in that system they show up as relations between things. That is precisely why Marx engaged in his economic analysis: to help people see economic relations as they really are, as relations between subjects. He never dreamed that later followers of his would go back and focus on appearances once again. Still less did he dream that they would turn this focus into a dogma and then propagate it as his great discovery and his central message. Marx's herculean task was to dereify economics and help the subjects to emerge. Now we find some of his followers claiming that Marx's central message is that there are no subjects at all. I cannot imagine a greater falsification of a thinker's position.

In *Theories of Surplus Value* we find the following passage, which is even more forceful than the ones transcribed above:

Man himself is the basis of his material production, as of any other production that he carries on. All circumstances, therefore, which affect man, the *subject* of production, more or less modify all his functions and activities, and therefore too his functions and activities as the creator of material wealth, of commodities. In this respect it can in fact be shown that *all* human relations and functions, however and in whatever form they may appear, influence material production and have a more or less decisive influence on it (MEW 26/1:260; TSV 1:288).

This passage is also devastating for another type of materialism which we will consider in a later chapter, for it presents production as determined by human beings rather than vice versa. I shall come back to this passage again in that context. Right now the point is that Marx explicitly rejects the view that the economic process does not have a subject. Various historical factors affect production because they affect humanity. Since man is the *subject* (Marx's own italics) of production, everything that alters human beings also alters their productive activity (i.e., production). Materialism has suffered the same fate as late scholasticism did. Its proponents have come to believe that every substantive or term is matched by a corresponding entity outside the mind that exists on its own. In fact, the only reality of these forms of being is the living, acting subject. When we use the term "production," we are really talking about the producing subject, the human being who produces. Hence in Book I of *Capital* Marx says:

> Darwin has interested us in the history of Nature's Technology, i.e., in the formation of the organs of plants and animals, which organs serve as instruments of production for sustaining life. Does not the history of the productive organs of man, of organs that are the material basis of all social organisation, deserve equal attention? And would not such a history be easier to compile, since, as Vico says, human history differs from natural history in this, that *we have made the former,* but not the latter? (MEW 23: 392, ftn. 89; CAP 1:372, ftn. 3; my italics).

Here I am limiting myself strictly to the testimony that appears in Marx's strictly economic works. Even within these limits we have not yet seen the main pieces of Marx's testimony. I call them "main" because of this: the fact that the human being is the subject of economics and history is one of the main criteria that Marx uses to pass judgment on capitalism and condemn it. In *Theories of Surplus Value* he says:

> The very great difference is whether the available means of production confront the workers as capital and can therefore be employed by them only in so far as it is necessary for the increased production of surplus-value and surplus-produce for their employers, in other words whether the means of production employ the workers, or whether the workers, *as subjects,* employ the

means of production—in the accusative case—in order to produce
wealth for themselves (MEW 26/2:583; TSV 2:580; my italics).

On the capitalist conception of the issue Marx has this to say:

> In this conception, the workers themselves appear as that which
> they are in capitalist production—mere means of production, not
> an end in themselves and not the aim of production (MEW 26/
> 2:549; TSV 2:548).

The criterion for attacking capitalism is the fact that the workers are
subjects and cannot be treated as objects. In capitalism the means of
production and capital join to *use human beings* for the production
of surplus value. In communism human beings, as subjects—a point
stressed by Marx—use the instruments of production for their own
human ends. Instead of denying man as subject—a denial invented with
a strange cynicism by Althusser in this case—Marx takes the affirmation
of the subject as his explicit norm.

> This passage reminds one of Carey. But with him it is not the
> labourer who uses capital, but capital which uses the labourer
> (MEW 26/3:251; TSV 3:254).

> His [Ricardo's] expression "capital, or the means of employing
> labour" is, in fact, the only one in which he grasps the real nature
> of capital (MEW 26/3:111; TSV 3:115).

> The objective conditions of labour—created, moreover, by labour
> itself—raw materials and working instruments, are not *means
> employed by labour as its means,* but, on the contrary, they are *the
> means of employing labour.* They are not employed by labour;
> they employ labour. For them labour is a means by which they are
> accumulated as capital, not a means to provide products, wealth
> for the worker (MEW 26/3:111; TSV 3:115).

> It is that capital and its self-expansion appear as the starting and the
> closing point, the motive and the purpose of production; that
> production is only production for *capital* and not vice versa, the
> means of production are not mere means for a constant expansion
> of the living process of the *society* of producers (MEW 25:260;
> CAP 3:250).

Like the other passages cited above, this passage from Book III of
Capital (composed after 1867) condemns the very essence of capitalism.

For in capitalism we find that capital is the end whereas persons are only means. Clearly there is a moral judgment being passed here, but that does not concern us directly right now. The point worth noting is that one cannot talk about ends in themselves or about the perversion of the proper relationship between ends and means unless one assumes that some subject exists, for the end in question is the subject. We can understand why the shibboleth of Althusser and his followers is "a process without subject(s) or end(s)." Marx, however, explicitly assumes the existence of subjects: ". . . in other words whether the means of production employ the workers, or whether the workers, as subjects, employ the means of production—in the accusative case—in order to produce wealth for themselves" (MEW 26/2:583; TSV 580). In *Theories of Surplus Value* we also find the following two paragraphs:

> Even from the standpoint of this purely formal relation—the *general* form of capitalist production, which is common both to its less developed stage and to its more developed stage—the *means of production,* the material conditions of labour—material of labour, instruments of labour (and means of subsistence)—do not appear as subsumed to the labourer, but the labourer appears as subsumed to them. He does not make use of them, but they make use of him. And it is this that makes them capital. Capital *employs* labour. They are not means for him to produce products, whether in the form of direct means of subsistence, or of means of exchange, commodities. But he is a means for them—partly to maintain their value, partly to create surplus-value, that is, to increase it, absorb surplus-labour.
>
> Already in its simple form this relation is an inversion—personification of the thing and materialisation of the person; for what distinguishes this form from all previous forms is that the capitalist does not rule over the labourer through any personal qualities he may have but only in so far as he is "capital"; his domination is only that of materialised labour over living labour, of the labourer's product over the labourer himself (MEW 26/1:366; TSV 1:390).

III

The dominion of labor as object over labor as subject: that is the definition of capitalism. As we shall see in later chapters, Marx's whole analysis, from his study of value in Book I of *Capital* to his study of that monster—interest-bearing capital—in Book III, is a denunciation of this reversal. Marx condemns the personification of things and the reification of persons, unmasking the fact that in capitalism the object dominates the subject. If one gets rid of the notion of subject, then Marx's whole work goes up in smoke. If a focus on subjects is immature, then the whole work of Marx is immature. We are left with nothing but the work of so-called Marxists who have come after Marx. We are not surprised to find Althusser being forced (in the 1975 Amiens thesis) to keep pushing back the "mature" Marx to a later and later date. Now he tells us that we find the mature Marx around 1871! If that is the case, then *Capital* itself is an immature work. Pretty soon we will be told that the mature Marx is to be found later than Marx's own lifetime (1818–1883).

After the section just cited above from *Theories of Surplus Value,* Marx goes on to say that even the organization of labor, which in itself does not consist of things, confronts the laborer as a thing. It has the same alien and reified character as tools themselves:

> In fact, the unity [of labour] in cooperation, the combination [of labour] through the division of labour, the use for productive purposes in machine industry of the forces of nature and science alongside the products of labour—all this confronts the individual labourers themselves as something *extraneous* and *objective,* as a mere form of existence of the means of labour that are independent of them and control them, just as the means of labour themselves [confront them] in their simple visible form as materials, instruments, etc., as functions of *capital* and consequently of the *capitalist* (MEW 26/1:1:367; TSV 11390–91).

In capitalism this whole complex of things, including their intangible organization, constitutes the object that uses the subject. The capitalist dominates insofar as he himself is capital. The laborers are mere means for the ends of this complex known as capital. Does that strike some Marxists as an antiquated way of analyzing the basic problem of capitalism? Well that is the explicit and emphatic analysis of Marx himself in all his economic works without exception.

Marx does not just recognize subjects in the plural—which is the most important thing. He also recognizes them as a collective subject:

> Freedom in this field can only consist in *socialised man, the associated producers,* rationally regulating their interchange with Nature, bringing it under their common control, instead of being ruled by it as by the blind forces of Nature; and achieving this with the least expenditure of energy and under conditions most favorable to, and worthy of, their human nature (MEW 25:828; CAP 3:820; my italics).

In Chapter 5 of this book I shall return to human nature as a moral criterion, showing how much in line with traditional humanism Marx was in this respect. Right now I want to cite other places where Marx talks about a collective subject. Again in Book III of *Capital* we find this passage:

> We have already mentioned savings yielded in the production process through cooperative use of means of production by the *aggregate,* or *socially combined, labour* (MEW 25:90 f.; CAP 3:80; my italics).

Both in Book I of *Capital* and in the *Grundrisse* this collective subject plays an important role:

> The collective labourer now possesses, in an equal degree of excellence, all the qualities required for production, and expends them in the most economical manner, by exclusively employing all his organs, consisting of particular labourers, or groups of labourers, in performing their special functions (MEW 23:369; CAP 1:349).

> The collective labourer, formed by the combination of a number of detail labourers, is the machinery specially characteristic of the manufacturing period (MEW 23:369; CAP 1:348).

> Since the collective labourer has functions, both simple and complex, both high and low, his members, the individual labour-powers, require different degrees of training, and must therefore have different values (MEW 23:370; CAP 1:349).

> Even where the only task is to *find* and to *discover,* this soon requires exertion, labour—as in hunting, fishing, herding—and production (i.e., development) of certain capacities on the part of the subject (GRU:492).

> The conquest of the forces of nature by the *social intellect* is the precondition of the productive power of the means of labour as developed into the automatic process. . . (GRU:709; my italics).

> The development of fixed capital indicates to what degree *general social knowledge* has become a direct force of production, and to what degree, hence, the conditions of the process of social life itself have come under the control of the *general intellect* and been transformed in accordance with it (GRU:706; my italics).

Let me add two more passages, one from Book II of *Capital* and one from *Theories of Surplus Value:*

If we conceive society as being not capitalistic but communistic, there will be no money-capital at all in the first place, nor the disguises cloaking the transactions arising on account of it. The question then comes down to the need of society to calculate beforehand how much labour, means of production, and means of subsistence it can invest, without detriment, in such lines of business as for instance the building of railways which do not furnish any means of production or subsistence, nor produce any useful effect for a long time, a year or more, while they extract labour, means of production and means of subsistence from the total annual production. In capitalist society, however, where *social reason* always asserts itself only post festum, great disturbances may and must constantly occur (MEW 24:316 f.; CAP 2:315; my italics).

Thus *interest* in itself expresses precisely the existence of the conditions of labour as *capital* in their social contradiction and in their transformation into personal forces which confront labour and dominate labour. It sums up the *alienated* character of the conditions of labour in relation to the activity of the subject (MEW 26/3:485; TSV 3:494).

By way of summary I might point out that "subject" or "subjects" is mentioned more frequently in the *Grundrisse* (1857–58) than in the 1857 "Introduction" to the CCPE. They are mentioned just as frequently, if not more frequently, in Book III of *Capital* (after 1867) as they are in Book I of *Capital* (published in 1867). Taken all together, Marx's allusions to the subject or subjects of history are an integral part of his economic works. They are explicit, insistent, and completely central both to his methodology and to the content of his analysis. Indeed we would have to assume the existence of subjects in every page of his work, even though he does not allude to them on every page. Thus Althusser's thesis is nothing more than hogwash. Totalitarian governments and the capitalist communications media know that bold statements, however cynical they may be, have the effect of catching people off balance. The people assume that no one would dare to tell monumental lies if they could be disproved in a minute. Thus a feeling of collective paralysis prevents people from comparing statements like those of Althusser with those of Marx himself. Yet one need only open the German-language *Grundrisse* (p. 8) to find this passage:

Rather, it is always a certain social body, *a social subject,* which is active in a greater or sparser totality of branches of production (GRU:86; my italics).

Althusser repeatedly cites a phrase from Marx's *Marginal Notes on A. Wagner* (1879–80). He mutilates the passage, and I must tell the reader that his use of the citation is fraudulent.[8] Althusser cites the passage as follows: "My method does not start from the human being but from the economically given social period. . . ." Marx himself writes: "[Wagner] has not even noticed that my *analytical* method, which does not start with *the* human being but with the economically given social period, has nothing in common with the method of German professors which consists in joining concepts" (MEW 19:371).

Marx italicizes both the adjective "analytical" and the article. The method of Wagner and his fellow professors is to weave together universal concepts such as "*the* human being." Proceeding deductively rather than analytically, they derive all sorts of concepts and conclusions. Marx's works, which Wagner failed to understand, begin by analyzing concrete realities, i.e., concrete human beings who are imbedded in the economic mode of production that is proper to the sociohistorical period in which they live. These concrete human beings really exist, while "the human being" or "man" is a pure abstraction. Indeed Marx's polemics against this abstraction is the main theme of the twenty preceding pages in this particular work. No commentator can isolate the phrase in question without considering why Marx underlines the definite article, and the matter is crystal clear:

> "The" human being? If we are talking about the category "human being," the latter has "no" needs whatsoever. If we are talking about a human being confronting nature as an individual, then we must view him as a non-gregarious animal. If we are talking about a human being already living in some form of society—and Mr. Wagner assumes this for "the" human being in question possesses at least language, if not a university education—then our point of departure must be to spell out the specific character of this social human being, i.e., the specific character of the society in which he lives; for in that case production, the process of making a living, already possesses some specific character.
>
> For a professional school-master, however, the relations of human beings with nature are assumed from the start to be, not *practical* (established by action) but theoretical (MEW 19:362).

We now see clearly why Marx underlines the article in the phrase which Althusser mutilates. This universal known as "*the* human being" is not a real human being. It has no needs of any sort and hence it does not need to work or to produce. But the human being as the subject of the production process is real; and to understand that human being one must start by analyzing the social formation or economic system in which he finds himself. Marx's method begins with precisely that sort of analysis. Althusser takes a fatal leap and concludes that Marx is an anti-humanist. Just the opposite is true. Marx is so much the humanist that he is interested only in real-life human beings, not in abstractions.

Since Wagner criticizes Marx's theory of value, let us see what answer Marx gives him:

> If Mr. Wagner says that this is "no general theory of value," he is quite right in his sense of the term. For by a general theory of value he means pedantic scrutiny of the word "value." This would even allow him to remain in the traditional, German professor's confusion of "use value" with "value," since both terms contain the word "value" (MEW 19:358).

Marx could just as well go on to say: My *analytical* method does not start off from value in the abstract. Althusser would then use that assertion to show that Marx denied value altogether; and from there he would proceed to fashion a new version of Marxism-Leninism that would undoubtedly have great success among Latin American materialists. In all likelihood he would tell us that only the bourgeoisie, because of its overdetermined idealism, asserts that the commodities made by it have value; that nothing is so important to the capitalist ideology that has infected even great Marxists like John Lewis as the notion that human labor produces value; that Marx only flirted with this idea now and then in his "immature" period, for authentic Marxism-Leninism supposes a lifetime struggle to get beyond such typically humanist notions as exchange value; and that from 1883 on, Marx hardly ever mentioned the word "value." By this tack he would presumably prove that the authentic Marx is to be found only in his maturity (1883 and afterwards)! The ideological apparatus of the capitalist state, you see, is undermining the proletariat by citing such Marxian texts as the 1875 *Critique of the Gotha Programme* (VFI:339–359). In fact, the theoretical class struggle is so severe that authentic Marxism-Leninism must be fought out even in the midst of Marxists and the proletariat!

IV

Althusser sometimes likes to cite another truncated phrase: "Society is not composed of individuals." His technique here is about as "scientific" as his citation of the *Marginal Notes on A. Wagner.* But one sample is enough to show the quality of the merchandise. There might be some value in discussing another mutilated text if Stalinists showed any serious desire to know the thought of Karl Marx. Such is not the case. They make the same boast as Althusser: they seek to use philosophy for political ends (see footnote 6). Indeed we can even go back further, to Lenin, for example. In his *Materialism and Empirio-criticism* he shows not the slightest concern about objectivity. He attributes to Mach, Avenarius, and Haeckel theses that are directly contrary to the views of those people. It is not that Lenin tries to draw conclusions that flow logically from their premises. Instead he reads into their words views that are exactly the opposite of what they say.[9]

This approach, which was not invented by Lenin, evoked much indignation from Marx and Engels in an earlier day, as we shall see. Althusser, however, goes even further and uses Stalin's approach. As should be evident already from our discussion of the quotation from the *Marginal Notes on A. Wagner*, the basic idea is to cite phrases, allegedly from Marx, that are not his at all. For example, in *On Dialectical and Historical Materialism* (Part III, "Second Fundamental Trait") Stalin cites a sentence from *The German Ideology* as if it were the thought of Marx. In fact, in this passage Marx is summarizing the thinking of Hobbes.[10] And Johannes Lanz points out an even more glaring falsification in Stalin's work entitled *Anarchism or Socialism*.[11]

Now my readers should realize that some people think this is the proper revolutionary approach; that love of truth is an ideological principle espoused by bourgeois idealism. Such a view is quite consonant with the "absolute materialism," the "materialism as the be-all and the end-all," that is the topic of this chapter.[12] In the minds of these people it makes no sense to ask whether something is true or not, for the distinction between true and false is meaningless to them. Here, of course, my purpose is to show whether they have a right to call themselves followers of Marx—though they may well be justified in calling themselves followers of Lenin or Stalin. Here is Marx's opinion of such self-interested views:

> But when a man seeks to *accommodate* science to a viewpoint which is derived not from science itself (however erroneous it may be) but from *outside, from alien, external interests*, then I call him *"base."*
>
> It is not a base action when Ricardo puts the proletariat on the same level as machinery or beasts of burden or commodities, because (from his point of view) their being purely machinery or beasts of burden is conducive to "production" or because they really are mere commodities in bourgeois production. This is stoic, objective, scientific. In so far as it does not involve *sinning* against his science, Ricardo is always a philanthropist, just as he was in *practice* too.
>
> The parson Malthus, on the other hand . . . *seeks,* as far as he can, to sacrifice the demands of production to the particular inter-

ests of existing ruling classes or sections of classes. And to this end he *falsifies* his scientific conclusions. This is his *scientific* baseness, his sin against science (MEW 26/2:112 f.; TSV 2: 119–120).

Gemein, here translated as "base," also means ordinary, common, indecent, and vulgar. Whatever the meaning be, this passage expresses Marx's indignant and systematic disapproval of introjecting extra-scientific ends into scientific investigation. It is his attack on the political use of scientific investigations. It does not matter to Marx at all that Ricardo's science might have antiproletarian consequences. That is not his criterion, though it is the criterion of present-day pseudo-Marxists when they look at science and ideology. They want to use science for political purposes, and they see that as the highest form of Marxism. Yet that is precisely what Marx rejects in the above passage! Marx and their brand of materialism are poles apart:

> Ricardo's ruthlessness was not only *scientifically honest* but also a *scientific necessity* from his point of view (MEW 26/2:111; TSV 2:118).

According to the materialism we are considering in this chapter, it is idealistic to talk about scientific honesty or about a scientific obligation. When they talk about Marx, therefore, they must be talking about Groucho or one of the other Marx brothers; for the founder of scientific socialism expressly called for such honesty.

In an article dated 10 October 1859 (NYDT), Marx has this comment on the *Times* report of official bulletins about the war in China:

> It is worth noting that the *Times,* though moved by the waves of passion, managed to eliminate from its review of the original reports all those sections which speak favorably of the Chinese already indicted. To confuse things may well be the work of passion; but to mutilate them seems much more like the work of cold reason (MEW 13:517).

In the CCPE Marx feels that the economist Friedrich List cannot grasp things because of his practical bent:

> Friedrich List has never been able to grasp the difference between labour as a producer of something useful, a use-value, and labour as a producer of exchange-value, a specific social form (since his mind being occupied with practical matters was not concerned with understanding) (MEW 13:24, ftn.; CCPE:37, ftn. 1).

Engels writes in the same sense in a letter dated 11 August 1884 and addressed to Lafargue:

When we now talk about a "man of science," of economic science, then one must not have any ideal. One works up scientific results. If, beyond that, one wants to be a party man, then one struggles to implement these results in practice. But one who holds an ideal cannot be a man of science, because he has a preconceived opinion (MEW 36:198).

In a letter to Charlotte Engels dated 10 December 1884, Engels talks about his relationship with his nephew, Emile: "What we share in common is the fact that we both are concerned with scientific questions, without any regard for direct, practical usefulness" (MEW 36:247 f.).

In a letter to Marx dated 4 July 1877, he tells him the same thing that he is writing to the editorial board of the new review *Zukunft,* which had been founded by the Social Democratic Party of Marx and Engels:

However respectable they may be in the realm of political agitation, the resolutions of a congress are worth nothing in science; they do not suffice to establish the scientific character of a review, since that cannot be established by *fiat* (MEW 34:56).

Clearly Engels agrees with Marx on this point. There is nothing surprising about that, for that is the criterion of anyone dedicated to serious, objective investigation, be it in the last century or our present one. At least it is true of anyone who has seen the current quibbles about science and ideology for what they really are, i.e., political agitation. While the latter may be quite respectable insofar as they seek to promote the revolutionary aims of communism, they are worth nothing as science. If some materialists think that Marx changed his mind regarding scientific standards, it is because they have not read him. In his 1894 Preface to Book III of *Capital* Engels has this to say about the correct way to use and cite the works of other authors:

No doubt Dr. Stiebling has the best intentions, but when a man wants to deal with scientific questions he should above all learn to read the works he wishes to use just as the author had written them, and above all without reading anything into them that they do not contain (MEW 25:29; CAP 3:21).

We know that Marx thought and acted and judged things in the same way. For example, there is the interminable polemics that surrounded his citation of Gladstone in the 1864 *Inaugural Address of the Interna-*

tional Working Men's Association (MEW 16:5; VFI:75). He was challenged on this point by an anonymous attacker, who turned out to be Lujo Brentano. In *Der Volksstaat* of 10 June 1872 Marx published his first article proving the legitimacy of his citation (MEW 18:89–92). A second article covering the same issue, and defending the same criterion of scientific and scholarly accuracy, appeared on 7 August 1872 (MEW 18:108–115). After Marx's death his daughter, Eleanor, carried on the defense of her father's scientific precision in the newspaper *To-Day*, writing about the matter in February (MEW 22:162 f.) and March (MEW 22:166–170) of 1884. On the publication of the fourth German-language edition of Book I of *Capital* in 1890, Engels devoted his Preface to the same affair (MEW 23:41–46; CAP 1:26–31). He also wrote an article for the *Neue Zeit,* which appeared early in 1891 (MEW 22:587 f., ftn. 163). As if that were not enough, in 1891 Engels published a whole book proving the scientific accuracy of the famous Gladstone quote (MEW 22:93–185).

The materialism we are considering in this chapter maintains that the very concept of truth itself is ideological. In Book I of *Capital,* which this brand of materialism regards as its maximum expression, Marx expresses himself very differently:

> Ricardo originally was also of this opinion, but afterwards expressly disclaimed it, with the scientific impartiality and *love of truth* characteristic of him (MEW 23:461, ftn. 213; CAP 1:438, ftn. 1; my italics).

Obviously in praising Ricardo, Marx is implying that the same qualities should be displayed by all those who devote themselves to scientific investigation. In Book III of *Capital* he inculcates the same standard:

> The well-meaning desire to discover in the bourgeois world the best of all possible worlds replaces in vulgar economy *all need for love of truth* and inclination for scientific investigation (MEW 25:852; CAP 3:844, ftn. 53; my italics).

In a letter dated 10 April 1889 and addressed to Kautsky, Engels describes the conversion of Conrad Schmidt to socialism: "Schmidt came to us on his own without anyone prompting him, in fact despite many indirect warnings from me, and *simply because he could not resist the truth"* (MEW 37:187; my italics).

These passages should also suggest something to those who think that the quest for self-gain is the only decisive moving force in history (see Chapter 1). Let me now cite three short phrases from Book I of *Capital:*

Tucker was a parson and a Tory, but, for the rest, an honourable man and a competent political economist (MEW 23:788, ftn. 248; CAP 1:760, ftn. 2).

Mandeville, an honest, clear-headed man . . . (MEW 23:643; CAP 1:615).

Is it a scientific advance to make cowardly concessions to public opinion? (MEW 23:313, ftn. 183; CAP 1:296, ftn. 2).

Finally, on 8 November 1867 Engels, in his review of *Capital* that appeared in the *Elberferder Zeitung*, has this to say about Marx and his work:

With his unusual assertions Marx now appeals, not to the masses, but to men of science. . . . Lassalle was a practical agitator, and to confront him, in practical agitation, the daily press, and meetings suffice. Here, by contrast, we have a systematic, scientific theory. Here there is nothing for the daily press to decide. Here only science can have the last word (MEW 16:215).

Notes

1. See F. Copleston, *A History of Philosophy*, vol. 6, Part I, New York: Doubleday & Company, Image Books, 1964, p. 37.
2. This passage from Bentham is cited by Jacques Rancière, *La leçon d'Althusser*, Paris: Gallimard, 1974, p. 21.
3. See Claude A. Helvetius, *On Man*, Eng. trans., London, 1777, 2: 392 and 395.
4. J.B. Bury, *The Idea of Progress: An Inquiry into Its Origin and Growth*, originally published in 1915; 1932 reprint published in paperback by Dover Press.
5. *Para una crítica de la práctica teórica*, Spanish trans., Buenos Aires: Siglo XXI, 1974, p. 77.
6. *La filosofía como arma de la revolución*, 7th ed., Spanish trans., Mexico City: Siglo XXI, 1974, p. 135.
7. *Para leer el capital*, Spanish trans., Mexico City: Siglo XXI, 1976, p. 109; French original entitled *Lire le capital;* Eng. trans., *Reading Capital*, Humanities Press, 1977 (paperback edition).
8. For example, he uses it as an epigraph in *Marxism and Humanism*.
9. See the very vituperative but irrefutable study of A. Pannekoek, *Lenin filósofo*, Buenos Aires: Siglo XXI, 1973. For those who have directly studied Marx, even though they may disagree with him, Lenin's commentary on him is crude and misrepresentative to a degree scarcely imaginable.

10. See Stalin's *On Dialectical and Historical Materialism* in the critical edition published by I. Fetscher, Berlin: Ed. Diestenberg, 1956; also see J. Stalin, *Dialectical and Historical Materialism,* New York: International Publishers, 1940 (paperback edition).

11. In the review *Ost-Europa* 3:197 ftn.

12. For Althusser the very concept of truth is ideological. See the Spanish edition of his *Curso de filosofía para científicos,* Ed. Diez, 1975, pp. 57, 86,116; and passim in his other works. Also see Oscar del Barco in the review *Dialéctica,* no. 3 (1977), Universidad de Puebla.

3
A Free Subject

Economic determinism is the next version of materialism that we shall consider. In one and the same paragraph of the *Inaugural Address of the International Working Men's Association* (1864), Marx affirms the reality of the collective subject and rejects economic determinism. Here is what he says:

> This struggle about the legal restriction of the hours of labour raged and more fiercely since, apart from frightened avarice, it told indeed upon the great contest between the blind rule of the supply and demand laws which form the political economy of the middle class, and social production controlled by social foresight, which forms the political economy of the working class. Hence the Ten Hours Bill was not only a great practical success; it was the victory of a principle; it was the first time that in broad daylight the political economy of the middle class succumbed to the political economy of the working class (MEW 16:11; VFI:79).

The *Soziale Ein- und Vorsicht* (translated as ''social foresight'' above) is the same collective intellect that Marx was telling us about before. It is the collective subject of economics and history. As we have already seen, no materialism that denies the existence of subject or subjects can plausibly appeal to Karl Marx. The above paragraph is another corroboration of that fact. But it also challenges the version of materialism that proposes economic determinism.

According to the latter view, the laws governing economic reality impose determinism on the actions of human beings. We imagine that we are choosing freely between different possibilities. This is mere fantasy and ignorance, for in fact all our actions are determined inexorably by the economic structure of society. The above paragraph by Marx is a crushing denial of any such view. According to him, it is the bourgeoisie that appeals to the determinism of economic laws; by contrast, the economic theory of the revolutionary class is grounded on a rejection of any such determinism.

When the working class managed to get a law passed that limited the working day to ten hours, they undoubtedly won a great practical victory. Even more important, however, they proved the falsity of the deterministic theory espoused by the theoreticians of the middle class. According to the latter, the length of the working day, the amount of the worker's salary, their standard of living, and everything else in this area did not depend one bit on the good or bad will of human beings; they were all determined by the iron laws of economic reality. According to Marx, the victory of the workers on the Ten Hours Bill was a victory for the principle that it is human beings who determine economics rather than vice versa.

It should be noted here that some Marxists maintain that determinism exists only while the commodity mode of production exists, or perhaps only during the capitalist stage when commodity production reaches its most refined and systematic point. According to these Marxists, determinism will come to an end when we arrive at communism. Now I myself do not see how any materialist can claim that determinism ceases to exist at some point, but that in itself is a different question which does not concern us directly here. What we want to know is whether even this chronologically limited materialism can appeal to Marx for support. It cannot. The above passage from Marx indicates that the reduction in the hours of the working day was obtained during the capitalist period, during the very period when determinism is in full swing according to certain Marxists. Right in the middle of this period, according to Marx, we find the victory of an important principle. That concrete victory did not have to do with the destruction of capitalism. It simply vindicates the principle that human beings can control the world of economics rather than being determined by the latter. Once again we find that some so-called followers of Marx are propounding a thesis that runs directly counter to his own view. Indeed they are propounding a thesis which Marx attributes to the bourgeoisie and which he attacks.

Before proceeding to present and analyze the thinking of Marx, I wish to assure my readers that I am not attacking adversaries who do not exist. Lenin, for example, explicitly maintains the thesis of determinism: "The idea of determinism maintains the obligatory nature of human actions and rejects the absurd fictitiousness of free will."[1] And I have already cited the warmed-over Laplace of a contemporary in the preceding chapter. This is not some chance exaggeration. The fact is that any good materialist is logically obliged to deny human freedom. I, on the other hand, maintain that determinism cannot be reconciled with the thinking of Marx, and that he himself explicitly rejected it and attacked it with all his might.

I

This is a basic issue. Aside from the texts that will be cited below, the paragraph from the 1864 *Inaugural Address* shows that Marx's thought cannot be reconciled with that of Lenin. It is not my fault. The same irreconcilability can be documented with respect to other themes or ideas that are equally basic. Of course we can offer an excuse for Lenin because he was not familiar with more than a third of Marx's writings, for the simple reason that much of those writings had not yet been published. This important fact is disguised by many Marxists. Still there is good reason to doubt that familiarity with the complete writings of Marx would have stopped Lenin from offering misleading or false interpretations. For Lenin had the habit of reading his own thinking into works that said exactly the opposite of what he maintained. It is doubtful that even the complete works of Marx and Engels would have made him change his own mind.

In the first draft of *The Civil War in France,* written in April 1871 while the Commune was in the midst of its struggles, Marx again attributes to capitalists the belief in economic determinism that some later Marxists would attribute to himself:

> A great lot of workshops and manufactories have been closed in Paris, their owners having run away. This is the old method of the industrial capitalists, who consider themselves entitled "by the spontaneous action of the laws of political economy" not only to make a profit out of labour, as the condition of labour, but to stop it altogether and throw the workmen on the pavement—to produce an artificial crisis whenever a victorious revolution threatens the "order" of their "system" (MEW 17:528; VFI:236).

In the first draft of his letter to Vera Zasulich (February–March 1881), Marx wrote the following:

> One must proceed with great caution in reading the histories of primitive communities written by bourgeois authors. They are not afraid to go so far as falsification. Take Sir Henry Maine, for example, who was a diligent collaborator of the British government in its violent destruction of the communities of India. He hypocritically assures us that all the noble efforts of the government to preserve these communities failed in the face of the spontaneous violence of economic laws! (MEW 19:386).

In Chapter 24 of Book I of *Capital* Marx explains how the capitalist divides up the mass of surplus value which he extracts from the labor of his workers. Some goes into consumption, and some is set aside as accumulated capital. At one point Marx puts it this way:

> One portion is consumed by the capitalist as revenue, the other is employed as capital, is accumulated.
> Given the mass of surplus-value, then, the larger the one of these parts, the smaller is the other. Caeteris paribus, the ratio of these parts determines the magnitude of the accumulation. But it is by the owner of the surplus-value, by the capitalist alone, that the division is made. *It is his deliberate act* (MEW 23:617 f.; cf. CAP 1:591; my italics).

In Chapter 25 of the same Book I Marx is talking about demographic growth within capitalism. In passing he takes a shot at Malthus's law, which is supposed to be an iron, incontrovertible one:

> The labouring population therefore produces, along with the accumulation of capital produced by it, the means by which itself is made relatively superfluous is turned into a relative surplus-population; and it does this to an always increasing extent. This is a law of population peculiar to the capitalist mode of production; and in fact every special historical mode of production has its own special laws of population, historically valid within its limits alone. *An abstract law of population exists for plants and animals only, and only in so far as man has not interfered with them* (MEW 23:660; CAP 1:631–32; my italics).

It is clear that Marx is contrasting nature with history, as he did earlier in his footnote on Darwin and Vico (see page 38 in this volume). It is we human beings who make history for ourselves. Incontrovertible laws exist only for nature, for plants and animals; and even here they exist only insofar as human beings do not intervene to alter them and thus turn them into history. The assertion that Marx was a determinist is a joke, and not a very funny one at that. In Chapter 15 of Book I of *Capital* Marx writes this in praise of Britain's labor legislation:

> It is evident that the English legislature, which certainly no one will venture to reproach with being overdosed with genius, has been led by experience to the conclusion that a simple compulsory law is sufficient to enact away *all the so-called impediments, opposed by the nature of the process,* to the restriction and regulation of the working-day. Hence, on the introduction of the Factory Act into a given industry, a period varying from six to eighteen months is fixed within which it is incumbent on the manufacturers to remove all technical impediments to the working of the Act. Mirabeau's

"Impossible! ne me dites jamais ce bête de mot!" is particularly applicable to modern technology (MEW 23:501; CAP 1:477; my italics).

Engels had made the same point in his *Outlines of a Critique of Political Economy:* "And what is impossible to science?" (MEW 1:521; EPM:222). That was written back in 1844.

The italicized phrase above is *"alle sog. Naturhindernisse der Produktion"* in German. Marx is referring to the alleged impediments imposed by the nature of the production process. He is mocking those who maintain that determinism is imposed on us by the mode of production, and he is saying that it is the capitalists who maintain this point of view.

Both Engels' phrase and Marx's basic passage in Book I of *Capital* against deterministic laws of population allude to a theme that we can better tackle in our next chapter, i.e., the effectiveness of human science in dominating and overcoming the supposedly iron laws of nature. Marx, we know, completely rejected Lassalle's "iron law of wages." In the *Critique of the Gotha Programme* he tells us that Lassalle *knew nothing* of the true nature of wages (VFI:352). Marx rejected that iron law, originally Ricardo's, because in large measure it was based on the determinism of Malthus. The latter maintained that human population growth would involve a geometric progression as opposed to the arithmetic progression in the reproduction of plants and animals, and hence the means of subsistence.

Here it should be pointed out that Marx saw a "deliberate distortion" in any interpretation of his doctrine that stressed the importance of the economic factor to the point where it diminished or undermined human freedom and initiative. In a letter to Engels dated 26 November 1869, Marx makes this comment on the recent book written by Carey, an American:

> As for the deliberate distortion that, because in a country with developed production the natural fertility of the soil is an important condition for the production of surplus-value (or, as Ricardo says, affects the rate of profit), therefore the converse must also follow that the richest and most developed production will be found in the most naturally fertile lands, so that it must stand higher, e.g., in Mexico than in New England. I have already answered this in *Capital* [CAP 1:513] (MEW 32:404; MESC:273).

Any such total dependence of the production process on the fertility of nature could indeed be an indication that humans are not free. In the passage in Book I of *Capital,* however, Marx explicitly asserts that the capitalist mode of production "is based on the dominion of man over

Nature'' (MEW 23:536; CAP 1:513). Hence the mode of production and
its degree of development are not in direct proportion to the degree of
fertility of nature. Earlier in *The German Ideology,* Marx and Engels had
said:

> As individuals, it is not as pure egos that they enter into mutual
> dealing; it is as individuals whose production forces and neces-
> sities have reached a specific degree of development. And, to be
> sure, this mutual dealing in turn determines their production and
> necessities. Hence it was precisely the personal and individual
> conduct of the individuals, their reciprocal conduct as individuals,
> which created the existing circumstances and each day creates
> them anew (MEW 3:423).

There could be no clearer denial of determinism. It is the personal
conduct of human beings that determines socioeconomic circumstances, not vice versa. We need not appeal solely to this early work of
1846 either. The testimony of Engels in 1890 is even more important
because it explicitly rejects Dühring's deterministic interpretation of
Marx. In an article for the *Berliner Volksblatt* on 5 October, Engels
rejects:

> the extravagant assertion of the metaphysician Dühring . . . as if
> Marx had maintained that history took place in some wholly au-
> tomatic way, without the intervention of human beings (who,
> however, are the ones who make history), or that economic rela-
> tions play with human beings as if they were so many pawns on a
> chess-board (when those relations are the work of human beings!)
> (MEW 22:83).

In *Theories of Surplus Value* we find a passage as formal as any to be
found in scholastic philosophy:

> In the same way the existence of the human race is the result of an
> earlier process which organic life passed through. Man comes into
> existence only when a certain point is reached. But once man has
> emerged, he becomes the permanent pre-condition of human his-
> tory, likewise its permanent product and result, and he is pre-
> condition *only as his own product and result* (MEW 26/3:482; TSV
> 3:491; my italics).

Human beings are both the product and the producers of history. But
we must note how human beings fulfill the function of being the producers or precondition of history. They fulfill this function, not as products

of history but as products of themselves. If human beings fulfilled this function as products of history, then they could not really be the precondition of history. In that case they would be so many particles in a cycle of mutual causations. Their alleged role as precondition would actually be caused by history itself, and there would be no reason to call them the permanent precondition of history. Marx is telling us that neither in the first nor the last instance is their function as the precondition of history to be reduced to their function as a product of history: "He is precondition *only* as his own [*sein*] product and result." The German word here is *sein,* not *ihr.*

In *The Poverty of Philosophy* (1847) Marx had engaged in polemics with Proudhon on this point:

> P. J. Proudhon the economist understands very well that men make cloth, linen or silk materials in definite relations of production. But what he has not understood is that these definite social relations are just as much produced by men as linen, flax, etc. (MEW 4:130; POP:109).

It is well worth comparing these two last passages from Marx's writings. The point at issue is the same in both, but it is expressed more formally and explicitly in *Theories of Surplus Value* than in *The Poverty of Philosophy*. If humanity's function as the cause of social relations were caused in the last analysis by those social relations, then there would be no reason for Marx to engage in polemics with Proudhon; for that is the position of Proudhon. According to Marx, Proudhon did not come to realize that human beings, in their role as causes of social relations, are not caused by the latter though they may be caused in everything else. The above passage from *Theories of Surplus Value* makes the same point. While humanity is also a product of history, it is not in that capacity that humanity produces history. Comparison of the two passages shows that Marx did grow more precise in the later one, but his defence of human liberty is as strong and forceful in 1847 as it is in his later *Theories of Surplus Value.*

Since we have delved a bit into Marx's earlier life, let us also note an article in the *Rheinische Zeitung* dated 12 May 1842. It is an article Marx chose to republish in 1851:

> Liberty is so much the essence of humans that even its enemies realize it when they attack its existence. They wish to expropriate as a precious jewel for themselves what they reject as an adornment of human nature. . . . If the speaker were consistent, he would have to reject, not the free press, but the press. According to him it would be okay only when it was not a product of liberty; that is to say, when it was not a *human* product (MEW 1:51).

The thesis that "liberty is the essence of humans" is such an imposing one that we could never assume it had been taken back unless an author explicitly retracts it. The passages cited above and many others clearly prove that Marx always identified what it means to be free with what it means to be a human being.

II

Before we proceed with our compilation of passages from Marx concerning liberty, we must note that the term "liberty" or "freedom" is used in two distinct senses. It is used in a psychological (or metaphysical, if you will) sense and also in a political sense. In the first usage liberty is the faculty or capacity of choosing or not choosing, or choosing this or that. This is the capability that plants and animals lack. Because it characterizes humans, Marx identifies it with the human essence. Another way of defining it is to see it as internal control over one's own actions. Confronted with some (real or possible) object, the human will can choose it or not, can decide for or against it. Rather than being determined in this act, the will makes its own determination. By contrast, it is the appetite of animals that decides whether they will pursue or flee from some object, they do not have dominion over their own acts. In the political sense liberty lies in the fact that a human being is not prevented by social institutions and authorities from fleshing out this self-determination in external acts and thus assuming personal responsibility for choosing and pursuing his or her goals in life.

In the 1842 passage just cited, Marx defends political liberty with respect to the press, appealing to the psychological or metaphysical liberty that is identical with what it means to be a human being. In *On the Jewish Question* (1843) we read:

> *Political* emancipation is certainly a big step forward. It may not be the last form of general human emancipation, but it is the last form of human emancipation *within* the prevailing scheme of things. Needless to say, we are here speaking of real, practical emancipation (MEW 1:356; VEW:221).

From the overall context we know that Marx regards socioeconomic emancipation as a more authentic achievement and fuller realization than political freedom. Yet he also feels that political freedom (which is typical of modern countries) is really a great step forward. It is real, practical liberation. It is not just the merely imaginary liberation envisioned by mystifying idealistic philosophies.

In 1859, thus in his mature years, Marx wrote an article for *Das Volk* (20 August 1859). In it he commented on the lockout conducted by London construction companies against bricklayers who belonged to a

"society" organized to defend their rights. Marx says this in support of
the bricklayers:

> They felt that to detach themselves from the "society" and to give
> up all organization would be to turn themselves formally into
> slaves of the capitalists and to spurn *the little modicum of indepen-
> dence* left to the modern proletariat (MEW 13:487; my italics).

In a strictly economic analysis Marx formulates against Adam Smith
the following thesis in the *Grundrisse*. It boldly upholds human freedom:

> It seems quite far from Smith's mind that the individual, "in his
> normal state of health, strength, activity, skill, facility," also needs
> a normal portion of work, and of the suspension of tranquillity.
> Certainly, labour obtains its measure from the outside, through the
> aim to be attained and the obstacles to be overcome in attaining it.
> But Smith has no inkling whatever that this overcoming of obsta-
> cles is in itself a *liberating activity*—and that, further, the external
> aims become stripped of the semblance of merely external natural
> urgencies, and become posited as aims which the individual him-
> self posits—hence as self-realization, objectification of the sub-
> ject, hence *real freedom,* whose action is, precisely, labour
> (GRU:611; my italics).

Those who deny liberty maintain that this is mere appearance. As
Marx sees it, it is the absence of liberty that is merely appearance. Here
we are not interested in deciding which view is correct. The point here is
that a writer who reduces economic determinisms to "the semblance of
merely external natural urgencies" can hardly be invoked as the
spokesman of a school of thought which maintains that freedom of the
will is a figment of the imagination and that everything is determined by
economic factors. The above paragraph again indicates that Marx as-
cribes determinism to bourgeois theoreticians, and that he himself regards humanity as free no matter what the prevailing mode of production
may be. The freedom espoused in the above passage is what I have
called psychological or metaphysical freedom: labor itself is an exercise
of freedom, and indeed of real freedom. Here is another passage from
the *Grundrisse:*

> Hence not a single category of the bourgeois economy, not even
> the most basic, e.g., the determination of value, becomes real
> through free competition alone: i.e., through the real process of
> capital, which appears as the interaction of capitals and of all other
> relations of production and intercourse determined by capital.

Hence, on the other side, the insipidity of the view that free competition is the ultimate development of human freedom; and that the negation of free competition = negation of individual freedom and of social production founded on individual freedom (GRU:651–52).

In *On the Jewish Question* Marx asserted that political emancipation is not the ultimate form of emancipation, though it certainly is real emancipation. Here he moves to the economic sphere. He clearly acknowledges that there is real freedom in capitalism, but he insists that it is not the fullest development of freedom. He rejects the liberal bourgeois thesis that the denial of free competition is a denial of individual freedom. Thus in the second passage from the *Grundrisse* cited above Marx is dealing with political freedom; in the first he is dealing with psychological or metaphysical freedom. This is corroborated by an article dated 12 October 1861 (NYDT) in which he comments on the American Civil War:

> The peoples of Europe know that the Southern slave-owners began this war with a statement that the permanence of slave-owner dominion could no longer be reconciled with the permanence of the Union. Hence the peoples of Europe know that a fight for the permanence of the Union is a fight against the dominion of slave-owners; and that in this fight we have *the highest form of popular self-government ever attained* waging war against the most vile and shameful form of human enslavement ever recorded in the annals of history (MEW 15:327; my italics).

Even then Marx was of the opinion that the American democracy (of the Northern states) was the highest form of political freedom as yet attained in history. This does not mean it is the ultimate form, or that communism will not attain an immensely superior freedom; but it is real freedom. In short, we have now seen that Marx affirms the existence of both psychological liberty and political liberty.

To fill in the gaps, I must note briefly that in its retreat determinism makes four twists and turns. First, it says that freedom is a fiction and a subjective fantasy. Then it says that the only real freedom is external, political freedom. Then it says that the only real freedom is economic freedom. Finally it asserts that in any case neither political nor economic freedom will be attained until we have communism.

I have already noted that it is inconsistent for materialism to hold that there can be freedom for even a moment. Here, however, the point is that Marx rejects each and every one of these four assertions. He maintains that it is the absence of freedom that is mere semblance; that purely political emancipation is real freedom, though not the ultimate; that capitalist freedom is real, though it is not the supreme degree of freedom either; and that human labor itself already implies freedom, so that freedom exists not only before communism but from the moment that labor exists.

III

Before adding three more crushing passages from Marx, I think we would do well to consider the testimony of Engels. Whether we are free or not is obviously a vital topic, and one that occurs much in conversation. Engels, therefore, would be a fine witness to the thinking of Marx. In his 1892 Introduction to the English edition of *Socialism: Utopian and Scientific* Engels clearly affirms the existence of freedom and the libertarian character of modern democracy:

> Let us, however, not forget that if English law continues to express the economic relations of capitalistic society in that barbarous feudal language which corresponds to English pronunciation— you write London and pronounce it Constantinople, said a Frenchman—that same English law is the only one which has preserved through ages, and transmitted to America and the Colonies, the best part of that old Germanic *personal freedom,* local self-government, and independence from all interference but that of the law courts which on the Continent has been lost during the period of absolute monarchy, and has nowhere been as yet fully recovered (MEW 19:537; SUS:31; my italics).

In this passage we find two of the things we have already seen in Marx's writings: the freedom of the human being *in se* is maintained, and Anglo-Saxon democracy, even while still under capitalism, is valued as the highest form of political liberty as yet attained. Earlier, in his pamphlet on *The Role of Force in History* (1888), Engels had made this assertion:

> English law has a history in which a good deal of old German freedom survived beyond the Middle Ages; which does not know the Police State, for it was nipped in the bud in the two revolutions of the seventeenth century; and which culminated in two centuries of uninterrupted development of civil liberty (MEW 21:458; RFH:102–103).

We are not interested in examining or debating this historical thesis of Engels. The important point for us here is that Engels unequivocally affirms freedom. On 28 May 1892 Engels responded to the German worker August Siegel who had consulted him about his plan to work in the Scottish mines. Without mentioning the word "freedom" directly, Engels' reply is very much along the lines of his above statement:

> It would be most useful for you to get an exact picture of the labor situation here so that later, from your own personal experience, you can help the Germans to realize how much better they can do under the capitalist economy, provided that they defend themselves (MEW 38:352).

In a letter addressed to Kautsky on 5 March 1892, Engels makes this interesting comment in connection with the repression unleashed by the government in Berlin: "Liberalism is the root of socialism. Hence if one wishes to proceed *radically,* one must destroy liberalism; then socialism will wither of its own accord" (MEW 38:288).

In a letter addressed to the Viennese Isidore Ehrenfreund, Engels asserts:

> The stronger capital is, so much the stronger will the wage-earning class be; and hence so much closer will we be to the end of capitalist domination. Hence for us Germans, among whom I include the Viennese, I want to see a nice healthy growth of the capitalist economy, certainly not any swamping stagnation" (MEW 22:50).

In an article dated 12 April 1853 (NYDT), Engels had something much more profound to say about freedom:

> Russia is decidedly a conquering nation. She has been so for a whole century until the great movement of 1789 created an enemy to be feared by her, an enemy of powerful effectiveness. We refer to the European revolution, the explosive force of democratic ideas and *the impulse of freedom that is innate in humanity* (MEW 9:17; my italics).

After the explicit statements above concerning the existence of freedom, it does not really matter whether the final phrase of the last translation might perhaps better be translated "the impulse freedom." The important thing is that Engels links freedom with human nature just as Marx does. His interpretation of the French Revolution is also important, since it links up with his comment to Kautsky on liberalism as the root of socialism. In *The Role of Force in History* Engels has this to say when he is recounting the reactions of Germans in the Rhineland to the growing power of France in 1859:

Old memories of the French, who really had brought freedom, were re-kindled in the minds of the peasantry and of the petty bourgeoisie (MEW 21:416; RFH:42).

In *Anti-Dühring* Engels formulates this thesis of the utmost importance on the philosophical level:

> Freedom . . . is therefore necessarily a product of historical development. The first men who separated themselves from the animal kingdom were in all essentials as unfree as the animals themselves, but each step forward in civilization was a step towards freedom (WMEW 20:106; AD:125–26).

In Chapter 9 of this volume I will reexamine this thesis and try to integrate it into its real and proper context. We have already noted that humanity is not born free but rather makes itself free. It is not that freedom will exist only in communism. That is not true at all, for quite the contrary is the case. Every civilization embodying real progress has brought with it a greater degree of freedom for humanity.

Just before the passage cited above Engels broaches the topic that Marx considered in connection with Adam Smith in the *Grundrisse*: humanity's overcoming of the obstacles posed by physical and economic laws as an exercise of freedom as a subject. Here is how Engels puts it:

> Freedom does not consist in the dream of independence of natural laws, but in the knowledge of these laws, and in the possibility this gives of systematically making them work towards definite ends (MEW 20:106; AD:125).

Now some people who deny freedom cut off Engels' remark just before the "and" in the second line above. Then, appealing to Engels, they say that freedom consists solely in knowing and accepting natural necessity, in admitting that there is no real freedom at all. One could hardly imagine a more arbitrary interpretation or a worse example of bad faith. When I freely choose to bounce on a trampoline, I am taking advantage of the law of gravity for my purposes of exercise or recreation. When we take advantage of the laws of aerodynamics to travel from New York to Florence in a matter of hours, we are not obeying natural laws; instead we are getting those laws to obey us. As Engels says on the same page, "Freedom of the will therefore means nothing but the capacity to make decisions with real knowledge of the subject" (MEW 20:106; AD:125). Put another way: "Freedom therefore consists in the control over ourselves and over external nature which is founded on knowledge of natural necessity; it is therefore necessarily a product of historical development" (ibid.).

What is clear at any rate is that even in *Anti-Dühring* Engels insistently affirms the existence of freedom in human willing. That the degree of freedom depends on the degree of knowledge is a thesis that is quite true; and it can be found in such thinkers as Plato, Aristotle, Thomas Aquinas, and Hegel.

In an article on "A Working Men's Party" in *The Labour Standard* (23 July 1881), Engels concludes with this remark:

> The work-people of England have *but to will it,* and they are the masters to carry every reform, social and political, which their salvation requires. Then why not make that effort? (MEW 19:279; SW:112, my italics).

In Engels' 1892 Preface to the second German edition of his *Condition of the Working Class in England,* he remarks:

> The superstitious belief in the "great liberal party," which has dominated the English workers for almost forty years, has come apart. They have witnessed convincing examples that they, the workers, are the decisive force in England, *if only they will it,* and know what they want (MEW 22:330; my italics).

It would be difficult to formulate a more explicit affirmation of the existence of human freedom. Thus determinists cannot appeal to Engels any more than they can appeal to Marx.

IV

Let us get back to Marx. In Chapter 2 of this volume I stressed the methodological importance of his 1857 Introduction to the CCPE for all his economic work. This Introduction ends with a three–page section that is merely an outline of topics to be developed. Commentators have belittled this section, forgetting that it is of the utmost importance precisely because of its programmatic character. It is divided up into eight points which are numbered as such. Here I want to cite number 7, with all its italics and parentheses.

> *This conception appears as necessary development.* But legitimation of chance. How. (Of freedom also, among other things.) (Influence of means of communication. World history has not always existed; history as world history a result.) (GRU: 109).

One could not say more explicitly that Marx's famous "determination" must be understood in some way that is not deterministic. In fact the German verb *bestimmen*, which unfortunately is customarily translated as "to determine," means many different things that have nothing to do with determinism. This major mistake in translation is due in large measure to translations into languages derived from Latin, where the basic word is some form of *determinare*. The crucial passage in question is to be found in Marx's Preface to *A Contribution to the Critique of Political Economy*. Marx says: "It is not the consciousness of men that determines their existence, but their social existence that determines their consciousness" (MEW 13:9; CCPE:21). In the 1857 Introduction cited above, however, Marx notes that neither human freedom nor contingency is excluded; and that was intended as an "Introduction" to the CCPE. How, then, can commentators neglect or disregard such a clear and explicit remark in talking about "determinism" in Marx?

In an article for the NYDT entitled "The General Mood in Berlin" (28 April 1860), Marx sums up the latest developments in the capital of Prussia for his American readers. The paragraph in question here has to do with the fact that Friedrich Wilhelm IV, a ferocious oppressor of civil liberties, has just gone crazy and been forced to abdicate:

> People congratulated each other in low tones, saying that the worst was passed and that the specter of ten years of repression had stopped suffocating their spirits. This absurd motif was played in every key, with the inevitable counter-theme that the change had not been caused by any insistent rescue-efforts on the part of the subjugated Prussians but by the sick condition in the head of the Prussian king. In other words, it was a work of nature, not the work of human beings (MEW 15:39).

Here we have the real thinking of Marx about freedom. It is not just that Marx distinguishes clearly between what is the work of natural laws and what is the result of free human decision making and effort. This he does of course, so clearly that one cannot be a faithful interpreter of Marx if one claims that in the last analysis one is reducible to the other; if that were the case, Marx would not have gone to so much trouble to emphasize the difference between them. Nor is it just that Marx actually recognizes the existence of human freedom in some way. What stands out clearly is Marx's high valuation of such freedom and its resultant deeds. What is really worthwhile in Marx's eyes is what human beings achieve through their own free decision-making, effort, and struggle. He has little regard for changes which in the last analysis are the end result of natural laws.

Deterministic Marxism, then, is due to sheer ignorance of the written works of Marx. In the article just cited, Marx drives the point home two pages later.

In short, insofar as the great international drama now unfolding on the European stage is concerned, it would seem that our friends in Berlin are concerned only as spectators. They sit in the balcony and applaud or boo, but they have nothing to do with the action (MEW 15:1).

Finally, I want to introduce into evidence the *Circular Letter* of Marx and Engels to Bebel, Liebknecht, Bracke, and all the other leaders of the German Social Democrats (17–18 September 1879). In a letter to Sorge on 19 September, Marx wrote that in the *Circular Letter* ''our standpoint is set forth without reserve'' (MEW 34:413; SCME:308). And in the *Circular Letter* itself, Marx and Engels conclude: ''As far as we are concerned, nothing stands in the way of its communication to the members of the Zurich commission'' (VFI:375).

Reading the following passages, one should recall that they were written only three and a half years before Marx's death. In the third and final section of the *Circular Letter,* Marx and Engels assail the Manifesto of three Socialists in Zurich: Hochberg, Bernstein, and Schramm. These three wrote a manifesto to criticize the attacks of the left wing of their party on those who had founded the movement: Lassalle, Strousberg, etc. First Marx and Engels summarize some of the opinions expressed in the Manifesto:

Another offence against form was evident in the ''exaggerated attacks on the 'founders','' who, of course were ''only children of the age''; ''it would have been better to abstain from the abuse of Strousberg and such people.''

After summarizing the views expressed in the Manifesto, Marx and Engels launch their own counter-attack:

Unfortunately all people are ''only children of the age,'' and *if this is an adequate excuse* nobody may be attacked any more and all polemics and all struggle on our part must come to an end; we simply put up with all the kicks from our opponents because we, in our wisdom, know of course that they are ''only children of the age'' *and cannot act any other way.* Instead of repaying their kicks with interest we should rather feel pity for the poor souls (MEW 19:163; VFI:372; my italics).

There is enormous force in this ironic passage. In terms of philosophic content it dovetails with Marx's attack on Proudhon for forgetting that human beings produce their social relations just as they produce material goods *(The Poverty of Philosophy),* and with his assertion in *Theories of Surplus Value* that human beings are the presupposition of history insofar as they are their own products, rather than merely the products of history. Every individual is a child of his or her time, but our free actions are not caused by our historical era or time. In other words, we are not children of our time in every respect. If we were, then we could not "act any other way." Our conduct would be fixed in a deterministic way, and that would obviously constitute "an adequate excuse" for all our follies.

What the above passage brings out more explicitly than the passages in *The Poverty of Philosophy* and *Theories of Surplus Value* is the moral aspect of responsibility. One might almost say that here Marx and Engels adopted the very vocabulary of a classic treatise on freedom. In other words, if a human being, given all the prerequisites for action, can only act in one way, then that human being is not free; if, on the other hand, given the same prerequisites, a human being can act or not act, act in one way or another, then that human being is free. To be sure, even his most dissimilar actions bear the qualitative stamp of his time. Today's criminal deed is not identical with the criminal deed of the Renaissance; today's hero is not identical with the hero of the Middle Ages. But a human being can choose between heroism and crime.

Notes

1. Lenin, *Sochinenia,* 4th ed., I:142.

4

Determination in Marx's Thought*

Chapters 3 and 4 in this volume form a unit, but the plethora of material warrants a division into two chapters. This also accords with my procedure in this work, which is to proceed step by step, making sure that one point is established before moving on to the next. From the final pages of the previous chapter it should be evident that Marx's famous "determination" does not imply any denial of human freedom. That point should not be forgotten by the reader as we move along in the present chapter.

I

To express the notion of "determinism" the German language uses the Latinism *eterminismus* and its cognates (e.g., *deterministisch*), or some equivalent circumlocution. Neither the verb *bestimmen,* the noun *Bestimmung,* nor the past participle *bestimmt* signifies or connotes the idea of determinism in themselves. Thus it is wholly invalid to cite passages where Marx and Engels use *bestimmen* and its cognates in order to interpret their thought in deterministic terms.

There is much danger in the procedure of using the verb "to determine" and its cognates to translate *bestimmen* and its cognates, though we have little other recourse. However, it is worth noting that *Bestimmung* can often be translated as the substantive "characteristic" and *bestimmen* as "to appoint" or "to designate." Curiously enough, even the Spanish verb *determinar* and its cognates do not necessarily imply the notion of determinism. If I say that this book is printed on a *deter-*

Translator's note: "Determination" is here used in contrast to "determinism." It refers to Marx's use of *Bestimmung* and its cognates in contrast to the German term *Determinismus* and its cognates. Miranda's treatment clearly brings out the import of this contrast.

minado tipo de papel, no thought of determinism enters the reader's mind. The phrase simply means that a *specific* kind of paper was used, not just any old paper.

On a more philosophical level, the use of the word "determination" connotes that every entity is composed of a set of characteristics or notes or traits that define or describe it. These constitutive features are called "determinations," by contrast with generic concepts that are indeterminate. The latter do not provide any feature or set of features to designate unequivocally a concrete, individual entity. The generic concept, animal, for example, is indeterminate. We need the further determination "rational" to relate it to the species *Homo.* And we need a whole series of further determinations to relate this concept to a given "determinate" individual. There is no determinism of any sort in our use of this terminology, and this is even more true in German.

We cannot possibly understand the juridical reality of a society if we prescind from that society's mode of production. Thus the economic reality "determines" (i.e., "specifies"; Ger. *bestimmt*) the juridical reality in a given society, in the sense that it really gives it a specific nature. For example, we cannot establish slave ownership if the mode of production is a wage-earning system. In short, our concept of the juridical sphere of a society will remain "indeterminate" if we do not take its mode of production into account.

Use of the verb "to condition" is much less problematical. A cause is one thing, a condition is obviously something else. The use of "if" and a conditional clause brings out the import of "conditioning" in this sense. If there isn't any mode of production, then there can't be legislation, art, religion, science, politics, or anything else. Among human beings the material "conditions" everything, since not even human beings could exist if the material factor were not present. There simply would be no humanity at all. This type of "conditioning" has been presumed and affirmed from Aristotle to Hegel. And in authentic biblical thought immortality includes the resurrection of bodies. The German verb for "to condition" is *bedingen.*

It should be pointed out here that, in the view of Marx and Engels, it is not enough to appeal in some vague way to the material factor, the economic factor, or economic circumstances; yet that is precisely what some Marxists do. Economic factors include the mode of distribution, the mode of exchange, and many other things, including the mode of advertising and publicity. Marx himself, however, always rejected explanations based on distribution or exchange. There is a kind of mythology which believes that it has settled all problems when it utters the word "economic."

The characteristic approach of Marx himself is to investigate the mode of production as the decisive factor. This embraces two facets: (1) the production forces; (2) the social relations of production, such as the system of ownership or the class struggle. Suppose, for example, we are investigating the rise of capitalism and the downfall of feudalism. It is not enough to appeal to the growth of commerce. I make this point because the version of materialism that we are considering here, unlike the versions in previous chapters, is very vague and imprecise. It is a sort of "materialistic mysticism" whose theses are often hard to lay hold of.

The curious thing is, and this leads us into the subject matter of this chapter, that the earliest use of the terms "Marxism" and "Marxist" is associated with precisely this particular version of materialism. And both Marx and Engels explicitly rejected it.

The defenders of capitalism have found much ammunition to use against the revolutionary movement in Marx's assertion: "As for me, one thing I do know is that I am not a Marxist." This should not upset us or prevent us from facing the facts. Authentic communism has nothing to hide. We can no longer run scared when the bourgeoisie launches campaigns to discredit us. Moreover, the kind of materialism that Marx was repudiating in his famous assertion has done more to discredit the revolution than any capitalist campaign.

The phrase from Marx is historical. He used it in a conversation with his son-in-law, Paul Lafargue, when the latter told him the views of the French communists who were calling themselves Marxists. We know it from a letter of the Russian G. A. Lopatin, addressed to M. N. Oschanina and sent from London on 20 September 1883 (MEW 21:489). We also know it from a letter of Engels to Bernstein dated 3 November 1882 (MEW 35:388), while Marx was still alive. In addition there is a letter of Engels to Conrad Schmidt dated 5 August 1890 (MEW 37:436; MESC:472), and another letter of Engels to Lafargue himself dated 27 August 1890 (MEW 37:450). Finally, there is an article of Engels published in *Der Sozialdemokrat* on 13 November 1890 (MEW 22:69). So we have five documents. Though they all come to us by way of Engels, Lafargue could have published some disclaimer. He never did, even after Engels' death. And if Engels was inventing something in his letter to Bernstein, Engels knew that he was risking a disclaimer by Marx himself, who was still alive.

When the phrase was uttered, Marx was referring to French Marxism (MEW 35:388; VFI:68, ftn. 61). But as Engels' other three documents indicate, German Marxism of a slightly later date was of the same type as that which Marx was referring to in his remark. The standpoint of this Marxism is "the dependence of philosophy, etc., on the material conditions of existence" (MEW 37:436; MESC:472). According to Engels in his 1890 article, this Marxism "is characterized firstly by a greatly mistaken understanding of the conception it claims to defend, and secondly by gross ignorance of the historical facts which are decisive in each case" (MEW 22:69).

These are the very traits of the Marxism under consideration in this chapter. And just as it was historically the first version of Marxism, so it continues to be the Marxism *par excellence* in many theoretical and practical circles. Notice that there is an inner logic to this point of view. It cannot help but remain in "gross ignorance of the historical facts which are decisive in each case," because no fact can be decisive if the mode of production is the determining thing. How can facts be decisive in any case if the mode of production is the determining thing in all cases?

Now it is possible that some careless phrases of Marx or Engels may serve as a pretext for this brand of Marxism, but in this case Marx and Engels offered an explicit retraction or its equivalent; for they disavowed specific doctrinal movement that claimed to be based on their views. In his famous letter to Bloch dated 21 September 1890, Engels concludes:

> *Marx and I are ourselves partly to blame for the fact that younger writers sometimes lay more stress on the economic side than is due to it.* We had to emphasise this main principle in opposition to our adversaries, who denied it, and we had not always the time, the place or the opportunity to allow the other elements involved in the interaction to come into their rights. *But when it was a case of presenting a section of history, that is, of a practical application, the thing was different and there no error was possible.* Unfortunately, however, it happens only too often that people think they have fully understood a theory and can apply it without more ado from the moment they have mastered its main principles, and those even not always correctly. And I cannot exempt many of the more recent "Marxists" from this reproach, for the most wonderful rubbish has been produced from this quarter too (MEW 37:465; MESC:477; my italics).

Aside from the retraction, or what comes down to that, this passage offers us the key to the matter: if we want to understand the thrust and import of Marx's and Engels' theoretical statements, we must see how they themselves apply them in analyzing and evaluating concrete historical facts. However, this involves the awesome task of studying the writings of Marx and Engels, and the Marxists in question do not have the heart for it. They claim that the theoretical formulas suffice. In the passage above Engels makes it very clear that it is the meaning and import of the main theoretical principles that are at stake here. They are of no use if people do not know what they mean, and the only way to find that out is to see how they are applied to historical facts and events. This is where the huge mass of articles and letters written by Marx and Engels fits into the overall system. In them Marx and Engels offer flesh-and-blood analyses of important historical events and try to capture their import. I fully realize that anyone might well be frightened off by a collection of forty-four volumes, one in which a volume of six hundred pages is a small one. But there is really no other way to dispel the arbitrariness, confusion, and dogmatism that now prevail.

In the second section of this chapter, therefore, I shall try to give readers a concrete picture of the way in which Marx and Engels study and analyze historical events. I shall concentrate on some of their writings that are less well known. This second section will be the largest one in this chapter. In the third section we will see Marx and Engels repeatedly stating that historical events are unpredictable. In the fourth section we will consider their views of important figures in history (the problem of great men and geniuses). The fifth section offers an anthology of their statements about the irreducible historical efficacy of science. Finally, in the sixth section, we shall consider the theoretical texts that present Marx's authentic thesis about the mode of production as the *base*. It is the key to Marx's conception of history.

II

When two consecutive massacres were committed in Sicily by the troops of Francis II, the Bourbon King of Naples, Marx published an article in the NYDT entitled "Sicily and the Sicilians" (17 May 1860). In it he traces the suffering, oppression, and enslavement of the Sicilians by one ruler after another in the course of history: Polyphemus and Ceres, Dionysius, the Roman Empire, the Arabs, the Aragonese, the Hapsburgs, and the Bourbons. He talks about the "horrible cruelties" of the Romans, the treachery of the Bourbons, the "shameful" excuses of the British, the "bloodthirsty idiot of Naples," and the "cry of indignation" that should sound out through Europe over "the fiscal, political and administrative pressure weighing down on all classes of the people." And that is all (MEW 15:43–45). There is not a word about production forces or the class struggle.

For the whole Crimean War (MEW 9,10, and 11 ; see TEQ), Marx and Engels offer the same kind of explanations that you and I would offer if we had been in possession of the same military and historical information. Neither the war in general nor particular battles, neither the partial triumphs nor the defeats, are explained in terms of the mode of production. All the explanations are similar to the one below for the defeat of the Russians at the decisive battle of Inkerman:

Later, when the Russians showed up in greater numbers, the British found themselves surrounded by the larger Russian force even as the troops of Napoleon had found themselves surrounded by the Mamelukes at the foot of the pyramids. The staunchness of the troops, who possess that full measure of self-confidence which only men of a highly civilized nation can possess, and British superiority in arms and marksmanship did the rest (Engels, NYDT, 14 December 1854; MEW 10:567).

Engels goes on to say: "The Russians are the worst marksmen of all the troops we know, and they proved it in this instance. Otherwise they should have been able to crush every one of the British soldiers on the scene." On 4 January of the following year Marx offers the same explanation in the *Neue Oder Zeitung;* and he even borrows Engels' allusion to the battle of Napoleon's troops around the pyramids (MEW 10:592).

A good "Marxist" would add that the production forces of England and France were superior to those of Russia, which explains their superiority in war. Marx and Engels do not insert that, nor does it seem to have interested them as an explanatory factor. As they see it, a satisfactory explanation is to be found in "that full measure of self-confidence which only men of a highly civilized nation can possess." Or as Marx puts it in his article:

> The Russians, rather inimical to originality in general, copied Napoleon's plan of operation. But once the strategic phase had been completed and the tactical maneuvers had to begin, the mask of Western civilization was stripped away and the Tartar was revealed (MEW 10:592).

The ultimate explanation for the outcome of the battle, according to Marx and Engels, is the difference between western civilization and barbarianism. If someone else had tried to bring in the economic factor as well, they would have replied that such an approach revealed gross ignorance of the facts that are in each case decisive.

On 25 July 1859 (NYDT) Marx wrote about the intervention of Louis Napoleon in Italy, which resulted in a bloody war in Lombardy between the French and Italians on one side and the Austrians on the other. Marx offers this explanation for the war:

> There is hardly need to present additional proofs that this man [Louis Napoleon] is as egotistic as he is unscrupulous; and that, having shed the blood of fifty thousand human beings *to satisfy his own personal ambitions,* he is ready to deny and disavow all of the alleged principles in the name of which he led them to slaughter (MEW 13:421; my italics).

This explanation in terms of personal ambition is about as remote as one could be from any that a "Marxist" would have to offer. That is why Marx said that he himself was not a Marxist. When Mazzini's new manifesto reached him, he wrote the following on 17 June 1859 (NYDT) about Mazzini:

> He has just performed an admirable act of moral valor and patriotic loyalty, raising his solitary voice against a Babel of obfuscation, blind fanaticism and egotistical falsehood even though it might jeopardize his own popularity (MEW 13:365).

Marx then proceeds to transcribe the entire manifesto, and that is the whole of his report. A good "Marxist" would feel obliged to play down the admirable nature of Mazzini's act, explaining his moral valor in terms of the compelling laws of the class struggle and the mode of production in the underdeveloped European countries of that era. That is why Engels maintained that this brand of Marxism did not understand the concept it claimed to be defending.

Toward the end of the 1880s Karl Kautsky, a Marxist, wrote a history of the French Revolution and sent the manuscript to Engels for his critique. On 20 February 1889 Engels made this major observation:

> I would say much less about the mode of production. In each instance there is a huge gap between it and the *factual events* about which you are writing. Thus the mode of production is immediately presented as a *pure abstraction* which obscures things even more rather than clarifying them (MEW 37:155).

The events in question here are those of the French Revolution, one of the most important events in all of human history. Yet Engels says to leave the mode of production alone because that only causes confusion and explains nothing. If only the Marxists of our present day would really read Marx and Engels! On the prehistoric period of human history, Engels makes an even stronger statement in a letter to Conrad Schmidt dated 27 October 1890:

> . . . the low economic development of the prehistoric period is supplemented and also partially conditioned and *even caused* by the false conceptions of nature. And even though economic necessity was the main driving force of the progressive knowledge of nature and becomes ever more so, *it would surely be pedantic to try and find economic causes* for all this primitive nonsense (MEW 37:492; MESC:482; my italics).

On 21 September 1857 (NYDT) Marx published a quantitative study, "The Income of the British in India." After a careful reporting of the balance sheet, he ends his article with these astonishing words:

> If one adds to this the whole series of interminable conquests and ongoing acts of aggression in which the possession of India has involved the British, then one might well ask oneself if this dominion, viewed overall, is not liable to cost just as much in expenditures as the British might hope to take in as revenue (MEW 12:284).

Hence *objectively* economic reasons do not explain the British conquest of India, and Marx feels it is quite legitimate to make such a statement. Clearly he can reconcile it with his own conception of history. And remember that this is the year (1857) in which he wrote his Introduction to the CCPE. The usual brand of Marxism must have badly misunderstood something in Marx's theory of history.

On the occasion of the Spanish revolution in 1854, Marx plunged into the study of Spanish history in the first half of the nineteenth century. He wrote what amounts to a whole treatise on revolutionary Spain, though the NYDT published only a few chapters. Perhaps the most valuable section, which was published at the time, is his analysis of the Cortes of Cadiz and the 1812 Constitution. This article was published on 24 November 1854. Here I cite Marx's formulation of the problem and then the final paragraph in which Marx offers his conclusion:

> How are we to explain the striking phenomenon of this 1812 Constitution, which the crowned heads of Europe were later to stigmatize at their meeting in Verona as the most subversive product of Jacobinism? . . . And how are we to explain, on the other hand, its sudden disappearance without leaving a trace . . . ? If the origin of this Constitution is an enigma, its disappearance is no less an enigma. . . .
>
> After careful study of the 1812 Constitution, then, we come to the *conclusion* that it, far from being a slavish imitation of the 1791 French Constitution, must be regarded as a *pristine, original creation of the life of the Spanish spirit*. It restored ancient national institutions, introduced reforms which had been openly demanded by the most famous writers and statesmen of the eighteenth century, and it made inevitable concessions to the prejudices of the people (MEW 10:464 and 473; my italics).

Marx's article ends with this last paragraph. At the start of his next article (10 December 1854) Marx explains the progressive makeup of the

Cádiz assembly as being due to "various favorable circumstances" (MEW 10:473). He enumerates these circumstances, and none of them is of an economic nature. It is not just that he does not talk about the mode of production. He does not even talk about economics in vague, imprecise terms. The principal circumstance is the fact that the most reactionary provinces were not permitted to hold elections for deputies or representatives, and that the overseas provinces did not do so in time. By way of replacement, representatives were chosen in Cádiz itself; and the people chosen were revolutionaries who had come to Cádiz for that very reason. Even more important here, however, is Marx's conclusion after "careful analysis." Marx himself tells us that it is his conclusion: the historical cause of the 1812 Constitution was the spiritual or intellectual life of Spain.

According to Marxism, no causal explanation can stop there because in the last analysis the intellectual life and everything else must be reduced to the mode of production. Yet these are the historical studies of Marx to which Engels refers in his letter to Bloch, telling him that one must look to them to see the practical application of his general, theoretical principles. And remember that Engels insists that the authentic Marx cannot be reconciled with Marxism. Obviously the irreconcilability lies in the fact that, according to Marx, the historical causes *cannot be reduced* to one. In his analysis of the 1812 Cádiz Constitution, for example, Marx concludes that it is a product of the intellectual life—the life of the spirit—of the Spanish people.

In subsequent articles Marx explains the disappearance of this Constitution, because of military defeats (which he enumerates), the heavy-handed interference of the Russian ambassador in Madrid, and the success of the reactionaries in getting the people to identify the Cádiz representatives as Francophiles who favored the intervention of Napoleon and who were therefore unpatriotic. There is nothing about the mode of production.

In one of the first articles Marx advances a reason that is very much a fortuitous and anecdotal one: "The Spanish revolution was shipwrecked at the very start by its desire to be decent and legitimate" (MEW 10:450; NYDT, 20 October 1854). This basically dovetails with what he says in his 1871 letter to Kugelmann: "It [history] would on the other hand be of a very mystical nature, if 'accidents' played no part . . . which include the 'accident' of the character of those who at first stand at the head of the movement" (MESC:310–11). In his article dated 27 October 1854 Marx writes: "Hence the members of the Cortes did not fail because they were revolutionaries, as French and English writers assert; they failed because their leaders were reactionary and failed to make use of the high moment for revolutionary action'' (MEW 10:458).

The entire Volume 14 of the MEW is especially noteworthy. It contains articles by Engels on highly interesting military affairs, and articles by Marx on outstanding military leaders in history. These were written between 1857 and 1860 for the *New American Cyclopedia*. They do not mention economic causes for the events they relate, and that is not due to forgetfulness. They do not say that one particular general was opposed to another because they belonged to different social classes. When they do deal with such antagonisms, they offer other reasons. When Marx recounts the enduring tension between Napoleon I and Bernadotte, for example, he explains it by saying that one was a genius and the other a mediocrity:

> [Bernadotte] was too much the Gascon not to appreciate . . . the gap between a genius like Napoleon and a man of talent like himself. Hence their mutual antipathy (MEW 14:154).

Now any talk about "geniuses" would prompt Marxists to label it sweetly as idealism, not to mention much less any attempt to explain facts and events in terms of different human endowments. But let us see how Marx explains the antagonism between two nations in his article dated 14 February 1857 (NYDT):

> This political antagonism between the Afghans and the Persians, *based on differences in origin,* intermingled with historical memories, and kept alive by border disputes and territorial claims, is simultaneously sanctioned by a religious antagonism. The Afghans are Muslims of the Sunni sect, i.e., of the orthodox Mohammedan faith, whereas Persia is the citadel of the heretical Shiites (MEW 12:118; my italics).

According to Marx the economic factor—territorial claims—is not the cause of their antagonism; it is one of the factors that keep the antagonism alive. The basis or root cause is their difference in origin, which is interlaced with historical memories that can readily fan feelings of rancor and revenge. Marxism has gone off the track somewhere in its interpretation of Marx's thought when it assumes that all the underlying causes are to be viewed as economic. And this article about Persia was also published in the same year that Marx wrote his Introduction to the CCPE.

From the same year we have one of the many articles that Marx devoted to the life of the British Parliament (NYDT, 7 April 1857). Consider this brief but penetrating analysis of the Peelites:

In contrast to the Whigs, the Tories, and the Manchester school, the Peelite fraction* did not represent a class or parts of any class. It was purely a parliamentary clique, which could count on friends outside the walls of both chambers but was never capable of raising an army (MEW 12:180).

Thus the historical existence of the influential Peelite group is not explained in terms of socioeconomic causes related to the class struggle. So we can conclude at the very least that reducing everything to production relationships was not something which Marx, as historian, regarded as very important.

Now let us consider an article of Engels dated 22 June 1860 (NYDT). The importance of the historical event in question is brought out in the article itself, and in any case we know the decisive role which Garibaldi played in the struggle for Italian independence. To what does Engels attribute the successes of this great leader and strategist? Here is what he says:

> After receiving contradictory pieces of information, we finally got some trustworthy reports on the details of Garibaldi's astonishing march from Marsala to Palermo. It is truly one of the most portentous military feats of the century, and it would be inexplicable if it were not for the nimbus that goes before the victorious revolutionary general. Garibaldi's success proves that the troops of the kingdom of Naples are still fearful of this man, who has held aloft the banner of Italian revolution in battle against French, Neapolitan, and Austrian troops; and that the people of Sicily have not lost faith in this man or in the national cause (MEW 15:60).

As we have seen, in the Crimean War the cause of victory was the higher degree of civilization on one side. In the Sicily campaign it was Garibaldi's charisma. And what about the mode of production? Not a word, thank you.

It is to such concrete analyses as these that Engels was alluding when he wrote that "Marxism" prevents people from discovering and analyzing "the decisive facts in each case." And Engels was right. As a cause, the mode of production is always present and operative. It obviously does not explain why a war is won in one case and lost in another, since it is present as a factor in both instances. Once we acknowledge its presence, we must still seek out the decisive factors and events in each given case if we really want to explain anything. To simply point to the forces and relations of production is akin to saying that the victory of

---

* *Translator's Note:* I have retained the word "fraction" (Ger. *Fraktion*) after reading Fernbach's comment on Marx's use of the word in VSE:11.

Austerlitz was due to the presence of breathable oxygen in the atmosphere. Such an explanation leaves us right where we started, since there was oxygen both at Austerlitz and at Waterloo.

Now let us see how Marx describes the defeat of the Confederate army in the campaign in Maryland (NYDT: 12 October 1863). This defeat, according to Marx, "has decided the outcome of the American Civil War" (MEW 15:551). The campaign was a surprise initiative on the part of the Confederate side, and indeed in circumstances very favorable to them. Here is what Marx writes:

> And yet the breakthrough into Maryland took place under the most favorable possible circumstances: an ignominious series of unexpected defeats for the North; the Union army demoralized; Stonewall Jackson, the hero of the day; Lincoln and his government, the butt of children's jokes; the Democratic Party further strengthened in the North and taking for granted the presidency of Jefferson Davis; France and England lying in wait to openly proclaim the legitimacy of the slave states that they now recognize within! *"E pur si muove."* Despite everything, reason triumphs in world history.
>
> Even more important than the campaign in Maryland is Lincoln's Proclamation. . . . In the history of the United States and humanity, Lincoln will occupy the place right next to Washington! (MEW 15:552 f.).

Marx's admiration for Lincoln is undeniable. In the section omitted in the second paragraph Marx offers a penetrating analysis of the modest style of this great man, who performs the most transcendent feats without a fuss and issues "eternally memorable decrees" as one might dispatch the ordinary correspondence of the day. But the significant thing in the section cited above is that Marx attributes greater weight to the activity of Lincoln than to the military victory of the Union army in the Maryland campaign, even though he says that the latter campaign has decided the outcome of the Civil War! And all these events are under the guidance of reason which, despite setbacks, always triumphs in history! I have never read a less materialistic exposition of history than this one. The real Marx cannot be reconciled with Marxism, and in his letter to Bloch Engels tells us clearly why that is so.

Now let us move on to the Spring of 1871. People have just learned of a world tragedy in the most authentic sense of the word, i.e., the fall of the Paris Commune. Marx and Engels had given it all their support, much more than they had to. Ludwig Kugelmann, a typical Marxist, wrote the following to Marx from Hannover on 15 April: "The defeat will strip the workers of their leaders for a long time. It seems to me that for some time to come the proletariat will have more need of enlightenment than of armed struggle. To attribute the failure to this or that contingency—isn't that the same as falling into the same mistakes for which the petty bourgeois were reproached so roundly in the *18th Brumaire?''* (MEW 33:746, ftn. 243). Marx gave this reply on April 17:

> World history would indeed be very easy to make, if the struggle were taken up only on condition of infallibly favourable chances. It would on the other hand *be of a very mystical nature if "accidents" played no part.* These accidents themselves fall naturally into the general course of development and are compensated for, again, by other accidents. But acceleration and delay are very dependent on such "accidents," which include *the "accident" of the character of those who at first stand at the head of the movement.*
>
> The decisive, unfavourable accident this time is *by no means to be found in the general conditions of French society,* but in the presence of the Prussians in France and their position right before Paris (MEW 33:209; MESC:310–11; my italics).

In very Marxist terms Kugelmann would reject any historical explanation for the fall of the Commune that did not come down to necessary causes of a socioeconomic nature. Marx replies that this conception of history is a mythical one. The fall of the Paris Commune, an historical reality of the utmost importance for the realization of communism in France, is explained by Marx in terms of such contingent and irreducible factors as the character of the people involved and the unfortunate accident of the presence of Prussian troops in France.

Communism will certainly become a reality, both in France and the rest of the world. But chance, the individual temperament of certain people, and their free decisions have held back the arrival of communism for more than a century. Indeed it may be a matter of two hundred or three hundred or even more years. In a letter dated 14 July 1893, which is actually a brief lecture on his and Marx's basic view, Engels writes the following to Franz Mehring (who wrote the major biography of Marx):

> In fact, if Richard Coeur-de-Lion and Philip Augustus had introduced free trade instead of getting mixed up in the crusades, we should have been spared five hundred years of misery and stupidity (MEW 39:37 f.; MESC:512).

So there is a point worth making here. The free decision of a pair of extraordinary individuals can accelerate or retard human history for five hundred years or more. And readers should note that these letters addressed to militant Marxists are better than any books in showing what Marx and Engels regarded as compatible with the theoretical principles they had formulated on the dialectics of history and its causes. If the tenor of the general principles seems to rule out such concrete possibilities, the reason is that they have been misconstrued. For their real import is to be inferred unmistakably from the concrete applications that Marx and Engels make of them in their evaluation of historical events.

III

In creating their science of history Marx and Engels did not think that it made historical events predictable with any certainty. If they had thought that, they would not have repeatedly stressed the absolute unpredictability of those events. The concept of a science of history does not include the notion that historical events are predictable. Insofar as Marx and Engels are concerned, the only predictable event is the final outcome: communism. Time and again in their writings, Marx and Engels refer to events as unpredictable. In this section I want to offer various samples of their attitude on this matter.

In a letter to Bebel dated 19 February 1892, Engels mentions the two currents or tendencies evident among the German bourgeoisie. One is pacifist while the other seeks open confrontation with the surviving vestiges of feudalism. Engels goes on to say: "Which of these two currents predominates at the moment is determined by accidents— personal, local, etc." (MEW 38:281). Later he says: "As I said above, how long this conflict goes on depends on personal contingencies" (MEW 38:282).

In a letter to Marx dated 2 March 1852, Engels talks about the possibility or probability of a general economic crisis. Then he adds: "However, all this is guess-work" (MEW 28:35).

Here we have two statements separated by a lapse of forty years. In both, the prediction is purely conjectural. His concept of historical science does not include the notion of predictive certainty.

In 1891 Bebel wrote to Engels saying that, according to his calculations, the collapse of German capitalism would occur around 1898. On 26 October Engels replied: "I would be very cautious about predicting any such thing" (MEW 38:189).

On 7 February 1865 Engels wrote the following to Marx:

> To be sure, it will not occur to Bismarck to question for long the right of the chamber to a budget. Otherwise he would not obtain

either money or credit, both of which he needs badly. However, history can always founder anew on one sort of trifle or another (MEW 31:62).

On 6 June 1884 Engels wrote to Bebel:

If the revolution in Russia is not to be put off for a few years, there will have to be either some unpredictable complications or a couple of nihilist thunderbolts. In neither of these cases is any prediction possible (MEW 31:62).

In a letter to Marx dated 11 June 1863, Engels offers this pessimistic comment on the Polish uprising of that year:

The quality of the insurgents is no longer what it was in March and April, the best fellows have been used up. These Polacks are quite incalculable, however, and the business may still turn out well all the same, although the prospects are less (MEW 30:353; MESC:149–150).

In a letter to Marx dated 10 April 1866, Engels comments on the fact that Napoleon III is looking for a quarrel with Bismarck:

If they do in fact come to blows, for the first time in history the outcome will depend on the attitude of Berlin. If the Berliners attack at the right moment, the matter can be settled in fine fashion—but who can rely on *them?* (MEW 31:207).

Writing to Marx on 15 November 1862 about Wilhelm I and his skirmishes with Prussian liberals, Engels has this to say: "Provided the old ass does not take fright again. He is certainly in top form, but in the case of these Prussians one cannot rely on anything, not even on their foolishness" (MEW 30:299).

In still another letter to Marx dated 22 January 1852, Engels has this to say about the expansionist designs of Louis Napoleon: "Piedmont, Switzerland, and Belgium will not be handed over by England or by the Holy Alliance. The affair is so beautifully bungled that in the end pure chance must decide" (MEW 28:11).

Writing to Laura Lafargue (Marx's daughter) on 17 August 1891 in mixed German and French, Engels says at one point: "France is the unexpected" (MEW 38:145). On 12 October 1885 he had written to Paul Lafargue: "France is the country of the unexpected, and I would be cautious about expressing a definitive opinion" (MEW 36:369). Writing to the same party on 7 February 1888, Engels says: "The French are unpredictable and capable of all sorts of unexpected things. So I simply wait" (MEW 34:57).

During another Russo-Turkish war, which involved the English and the French as usual, Engels offered this comment on the Russian campaign to Marx on 24 July 1877: "Despite all the follies of the Turks, this year's campaign has failed for all practical purposes—provided that the unpredictable does not assert itself here!" (MEW 34:57).

Thus in the eyes of Engels the Prussians, the Russians, the Poles, the Turks, the French, the English, and the entire Holy Alliance are unpredictable. How can one make a scientific prognosis in such circumstances? When Engels does offer some prediction, he always adds some provisory clause. Writing from England to Bebel on 30 August 1883, he says: "And a general labor movement will not come into existence here—save for the unexpected—unless the workers feel that England's world monopoly has collapsed" (MEW 36:58). For the sake of preciseness I should add that Engels regarded the French as the most unpredictable people on earth.

This stress on unpredictability is not to be found solely in Engels' personal letters. In the newspaper *Le Socialiste* he reiterates his view of France on 17 October 1885: "France is the country of the unexpected" (MEW 21:226). In 1887 he wrote an Introduction to a pamphlet written by Sigismund Borkheim, in which he foresaw a world war taking place at some point in the future. But he stressed the *"absolute impossibility of predicting* how it will turn out and who will emerge as the victor. Only one result is absolutely certain: a general exhaustion and the establishment of the conditions for the *final* victory of the working class" (MEW 21:351; my italics). This final section of the Introduction was published by *Der Sozial-Demokrat* on 15 January 1888.

Marxism might at least expect that on military and war matters, on which he was a recognized expert, Engels would have offered predictions based on certainty. Alas, that is not the case. In the third chapter of his pamphlet on *The Foreign Policy of Russian Czarism* (1890), Engels refers to "the absolute unpredictability of the odds, the total uncertainty as to who would finally emerge as the victor from this gigantic conflict" (MEW 22:45; RME:52). In his article for *Der Sozial-Demokrat* dated 8 March 1890, he mentions "the fear of all parties in the face of the absolutely unpredictable possibilities of the world war, which now is the only one possible" (MEW 22:9). In his 1891 Introduction to *The Civil War in France*, Engels again talks about "a war about which nothing is certain except the absolute uncertainty of its outcome" (MEW 17:616), a war which does not break out "because even the strongest of the big military powers are stricken with fear over the absolute unpredictability of the final outcome" (MEW 17:616). In an article for *Le Socialiste* dated

6 November 1886, Engels had written: "A localization of the war is therefore impossible. The war will become a general one. Given the credibility of the knaves who govern Europe, it is impossible to predict how the two sides will align themselves" (MEW 21:315).

The most interesting feature of this whole matter is that it was Marx who explained to Engels why even the most scientific military data do not allow one to make any certain predictions. But the reason he gives for that is equally valid for the science of history as a whole. In a letter to Engels dated 8 January 1868 Marx says:

> You have already proven your reputation twice: once as a tactical prophet (at the time of the battle of Sebastopol), and the second time as a strategist (during the Austro-Prussian conflict). *But the stupidity of which human beings are capable* is something which cannot be foreseen even by *the minds of the most prudent* (MEW 32:14; my italics).

A historical or social science can say: if you want A, you must do B. Or it can say if B happens, then A will take place. The causal or conditional relations between B and A are the object of rigorous analysis. But no science can tell us if B, the conditioning factor, will take place. Therefore it cannot tell us if the resulting event, A, will take place or not. As Marx puts it, the realization or nonrealization of the conditioning factor, B, depends on the stupidity of which human beings are capable; and even the minds of the wisest and most prudent people cannot foresee that. Thus science can discern the strategic or tactical connection between B and A in exact terms. Indeed its nature as a science lies in such discernment. But the fulfillment or nonfulfillment of the condition depends on personal factors, and so we cannot foresee which of the alternative possibilities will in fact be verified.

Indeed the final sentence of Engels cited above goes right to the heart of military matters and the application of science to them: "Given the credibility of the knaves who govern . . . it is impossible to predict how the two sides will align themselves." One can estimate and even measure fairly accurately the stock of accumulated arms and available reserves. But the alignment of these various supplies and reserves is something that depends on the personal decisions of those at the head of given governments or movements at a particular point in time. They may be outright knaves capable of the most absurd alliances, the most monstrous treacheries, and the most craven cowardice. Here, for example, is what Engels had to say about Louis Napoleon on 21 February 1852 in the weekly *Notes to the People:* "a relatively unknown adventurer in whose hands chance has placed the executive authority of a great republic" (MEW 8:221).

However, the above sentence of Marx is not his only statement about the irreducible indeterminacy of events. Referring to Louis Napoleon by his nickname, he wrote this to Engels on 9 December 1851:

> Will he try a coup again, if the election proves to be adverse? Will the majority vote? The Orleans have already left for France. It is difficult, if not impossible, to make a prediction in a drama whose hero is Crapulinski (MEW 27:383 f.).

Many people are familiar with Marx's comments as to whether such democratic countries as England, the United States, and Holland must necessarily go through an armed revolution to arrive at socialism. Marx consistently states that such a revolution is possible, though not necessary. It all will depend on circumstances, and of course on the decisions of those who head various factions and movements at a given moment. In a letter to Henry Mayers Hyndman dated 8 December 1880, Marx writes that his party "does not regard an English revolution as absolutely necessary but, in accordance with historical precedents, as definitely possible" (MEW 34:482). In his *Speech on the Hague Congress* (8 September 1872), which he delivered in Amsterdam after the Hague Congress of the International was over, Marx said this:

> We know that heed must be paid to the institutions, customs and traditions of the various countries, and we do not deny that there are countries, such as America and England, and if I was familiar with its institutions, I might include Holland, where the workers may attain their goal by peaceful means (MEW 18:160; VFI:324).

IV

We saw above that in 1863 Marx attributed greater importance to Lincoln's proclamation than to the decisive victory of the Union army in the Maryland campaign. Here let us consider the words Marx published on 20 May 1865 in the *Bee-Hive* newspaper, after the death of Lincoln:

> Lincoln was one of those rare human beings who manage to be great without ceasing to be good. Indeed so great was the modesty of this great and good man that the world discovered he was a hero only after he had fallen as a martyr (MEW 16:98 f.).

Now there are illogical and inconsistent materialists, but the above words certainly could not be spoken by a consistent materialist. One cannot admire people at all if one believes that everything which happens is the necessary result of economic causes. To merit admiration, an action or a life must be the product of real human freedom. If a human being is compelled to do what he or she does, then such words as "genius" and "hero" must be dropped from our vocabulary.

On the lips of Marx and Engels these words retain their full meaning and force precisely because they did not think that all historical causes are ultimately economic and material. After decades of misrepresentation, it is time for us to take seriously the fact that Marx denied he was a Marxist. In an article dated 19 November 1861 for *Die Presse,* Marx had this to say about Turgot:

> Turgot was the leader of the new economic school of the eighteenth century, the school of the physiocrats. He was one of the intellectual heroes who overthrew the old regime (MEW 15:375).

Marx was very far from thinking that social circumstances manipulate individuals in a deterministic way, thereby stripping them of all responsibility and merit for their decisions and actions. As we saw above, he admired Mazzini for coming out at a certain point in time and challenging all the forces of obfuscation and egotism. Now we see him praising the heroic attitude of Turgot and others and saying that its historical effectiveness was such as to overthrow the absolutist regime.

Doctrines that propose to rule out the possibility of admiring human beings who deserve admiration do little service for humanity. They would condemn all to mediocrity without reservation. And while mediocrity is not a crime, the cultivation of mediocrity is. I cannot help but wonder if nihilistic envy does not lie behind these doctrines that support entropy. Theirs is the thesis of Mephistopheles: "For all things that arise, deserve to suffer their demise" (*Faust* 1340).

In *Theories of Surplus Value* Marx has this to say about Quesnay's *Tableau Économique:* "This was of extreme genius conception, incontestably of the greatest genius for which political economy had up to then been responsible" (MEW 26/1:319; cf. TSV 1:344). He uses such terms as "brilliant" and "genious" and so forth to describe the work of Adam Smith (MEW 26/1:59; cf. TSV 1:85) and that of William Petty (MEW 26/1:334; cf. TSV 1:358). In his 1859 CCPE he alludes to Friedrich Engels' "essay of genius on the critique of economic categories" (MEW 13:10; cf. CCPE:22). As we have already seen, he referred to Napoleon I as a genius in his article on Bernadotte for the *New American Cyclopedia.* And in Book I of *Capital* he talks about "the brilliancy of Aristotle's genius" (MEW 23:74; CAP 1:60).

As for Engels, he regarded Garibaldi both as a military genius and a hero (MEW 15:64 and 155). In *The Role of Force in History* he adds these words that need no commentary:

And in Garibaldi, Italy possessed a hero like those of Antiquity, a man who could, and did, perform miracles. He put an end to the whole kingdom of Naples with his thousand volunteers, actually united Italy and tore holes in the artificial web of Bonapartist policy (MEW 21:415; RFH:41).

Without mentioning the many times he refers to Marx as a genius, we note how often he praised other people. In March 1852 he refers to the socialist Robert Blum as a hero and martyr (MEW 8:74). In his "preliminary notice" of 1874 he refers to Owen, Saint-Simon, and Fourier as men of genius (MEW 18:516). In an article dated 8 October 1885 for *Der Sozial-Demokrat,* he points up the "peculiarities" of genius of Weitling (MEW 21:214). In his 1891 Preface to *The Origin of the Family, Private Property and the State* he points up the contributions of genius of Bachofen and Morgan (MEW 21:482; cf. OF:Preface). In his 1882 pamphlet, *On the Primitive History of the Germans,* he refers to Zeuss and Grimm as "scholars of genius" (MEW 19:463). In one of his early writings he depicts David Friedrich Strauss as a genius (MEW EB III:429). In 1883 and 1888 respectively he applies the adjective "heroic" to Marx's eldest daughter, Jenny Marx Longuet, and to Vera Zasulich (MEW 19:332; MEW 21:354). And a remark of his in *The Foreign Policy of Russian Czarism* is particularly noteworthy:

> This was the situation in Germany at the time of Peter the Great. This truly great man—great in quite a different way than Frederick II, the obedient friend of Peter's successor, Catherine II—was the first who fully understood the situation of Europe, so marvelously favorable for Russia (MEW 22:19; RME:30–31).

This remark speaks volumes. The founders of scientific socialism fully realized that there were objective criteria for determining when the epithet "a great man" did and did not correspond to reality. This is a far cry from any brand of Marxism for which no such thing as great men exist at all.

Engels also saw the possibility of a small group of heroic human beings having a real impact on history. In a letter to Vera Zasulich dated 23 April 1885, he writes about the possibilities of revolution in Russia:

> This is one of the exceptional cases where it is possible for a handful of people to *make* a revolution, i.e., with one small push to cause a whole system which (to use a metaphor of Plekhanov's) is in more than labile equilibrium, to come crashing down, and thus by one action, in itself insignificant, to release uncontrollable explosive forces. Well now, if ever Blanquism—the phantasy of

overturning an entire society through the action of a small conspiracy—had a certain justification for its existence, that is certainly in Petersburg. . . .

Supposing these people imagine they can seize power, what does it matter? Provided they make the hole which will shatter the dyke, the flood itself will soon rob them of their illusions. But if by chance these illusions resulted in giving them a superior force of will, why complain of that? People who boasted that they had *made* a revolution have always seen the next day that they had no idea what they were doing, that the revolution *made* did not in the least resemble the one they would have liked to make. That is what Hegel calls the irony of history, an irony which few historic personalities escape (MEW 36:304 and 307; MESC:437–38).

Here Engels recognizes the possibility of ideas producing an overwhelming force that cannot be adequately explained in terms of socioeconomic circumstances. In exceptional cases a handful of heroic people can play a decisive role, and no one would deny that such cases are exceptional. And insofar as his remark on the irony of history is concerned, this factor is so nonmaterialistic that he alludes to Hegel. It dovetails with the Hegelian thesis that Marx proposed with regard to the Maryland campaign in the American Civil War: despite everything, reason triumphs in history.

We shall return to this in Chapter 10, when we consider a point that has already come up in this chapter. As we have seen, the unpredictability of history did not undermine the conviction of Marx and Engels that the outcome of history would be the triumph of communism. Here, however, I simply want to point out that both Marx and Engels appeal to a higher principle which guides history, and which human agents and protagonists are incapable of controlling.

Insofar as the historical impact of groups and exceptional individuals situated in the right place at the right time is concerned, Engels makes an important point in an article for *Der Volksstaat* dated 6 October 1874. In it he alludes to Louis XV of France, Isabella of Spain (a contemporary of Engels), and the Bakunist Alliance that had set itself up as a rival to the International. Here Engels is challenging the views of Peter Lavrov:

Our friend Peter is of the opinion that private affairs are as sacred as private correspondence, and that they should not be published in political debates. If we grant absolute validity to this principle, then all historiography is ruled out. The relations of Louis XV with Du Barry or la Pompadour were private affairs, but *without them the prehistory of the French Revolution is unintelligible*. Or, to come down closer to the present: If an innocent Isabella somewhere marries a man who, according to informed sources (the adviser, Ulrich, for example), cannot tolerate women and loves men only; if she, in her abandonment, takes men wherever she can find them; then that is a purely private affair. But if this innocent Isabella is also the queen of Spain and one of her bucks is a young official named Serrano; if this Serrano, as a reward for his feats in bed, is promoted to field marshal and chief minister; if he is subsequently displaced and deposed by another; if he then joins with other unfortunate companions and drives his unfaithful little darling out of the country; if through a series of adventures he finally ends up as dictator of Spain and is so prominent that Bismarck moves heaven and earth to get the great powers to recognize him; then the private history of Isabella and Serrano is an official part of the history of Spain. In that case someone who proposed to write the modern history of Spain, who knew about all this and deliberately failed to inform the reader of this little affair, *would in fact be falsifying history.* And if one attempts to describe the history of a faction like the [Bakuninist] Alliance, which includes not only deluded people but also a high collection of deceivers, adventurers, villains, police informers, swindlers and cowards, should one falsify the history by remaining silent about the singularly base acts of these people on the grounds that they are "private matters"? (MEW 18:538 f.; my italics).

This long citation needs no lengthy comment. It is an outright rejection of any so-called Marxist interpretation that ultimately seeks to reduce all historical causes to the forces and relations of production. This brand of Marxism would probably answer that socioeconomic conditions are responsible for making it possible for these moral failings to exist and hence to play a decisive role. Fair enough. But to make something possible is not the same as to cause it to actually exist. The former comes down to a conditioning factor or precondition. Scientific investigation, however, must also point up the actual cause of the matter under study. Causes and conditions are two very different things.

As we saw earlier, Marx maintains that human beings are the basis of history, not insofar as they are the product of history, but insofar as they are the result and product of their own decisions. After ascertaining that certain socioeconomic conditions have made the events under study possible, the responsible historian must still examine and analyze the most important thing: the characteristics and vicissitudes and personal decisions that caused the events to move from merely being possible to becoming the only ones that actually took place amid a host of possibilities. To suppress these causes is, in the eyes of Engels, to falsify history.

In an article for *Vorwärts* dated 16 November 1892, Engels discussed England's industrial monopoly over the world. Turning his attention to the United States, he writes:

> The protectionist tariff established in America since the Civil War bears witness to the intention of Americans to shake off the yoke of this monopoly. Thanks to the prodigious natural resources and the intellectual and moral qualities of the American race, this goal has already been achieved by now (MEW 22:334).

Leaving aside the word "race," which is a lapse on Engels' part, the idea is clear enough. Without a rich store of natural resources the Americans could not have broken England's world monopoly. But that alone would not do it either. Intellectual and moral qualities were needed to turn the possibility into a reality. The point is the same one which Engels made in another context, and which we cited in Chapter 3. Once the material possibilities are given, human beings must then "will" to turn them into a reality (MEW 19:279; 22:330). There is clearly a gap between the presence of certain social and economic possibilities and the realization of these possibilities through effective decision.

V

In the 1861 article cited above (p. 87), Marx referred to Turgot as "one of the intellectual heroes who overthrew the old regime." Thus he clearly attributes effectiveness to certain human beings in their role as intellectuals. He also attributes efficacy to the sciences, which are of course embodied in human beings. Exploring past history and the fall of feudalism in the *Grundrisse,* Marx has this to say about the dissolution of the feudal communities:

> The *development of science alone*—i.e., the most solid form of wealth, both its product and its producer—was sufficient to dissolve these communities (GRU:540).

> The feudal system, for its part, foundered on urban industry, trade, modern agriculture (even as a result of individual inventions like gunpowder and the printing press) (GRU:540).

It is worth noting that gunpowder was an invention imported from China, as Engels points out in *The Peasant War in Germany.* So it can in no way be explained as the result of the development of production in the West.

In the above passages Marx says that scientific ideas are effective enough to produce a complete change in the history of a people or a civilization, to topple the existing structure. And this is clearly one of Marx's mature works. It is certainly true that the degree of development in the natural sciences goes hand in hand with the degree of wealth in a nation or society. But there have been wealthy countries that did not develop any science. Wealth, then, is a condition rather than a cause of science. More precisely, it is a circumstance that favors the growth of science.

The point can be put another way which is quite similar. If there is to be some scientific solution, this logically requires that first there be some problem to be solved. If there is no problem, there can hardly be a solution. But the mere existence of the problem is not enough to guarantee that there will be a solution as well. Talent must come along to figure out the solution. Otherwise all the problems posed by humanity would automatically be solved. Note how carefully Marx chooses his words in this paragraph from Book I of *Capital:*

> The sporadic use of machinery in the 17th century was of the greatest importance, because it supplied the great mathematicians of that time with a practical basis and stimulant to the creation of the science of mechanics (MEW 23:369; CAP 1:348).

The function of the mathematicians was the *creation,* the real causation, of the science known as mechanics. Industrial production and its machinery offered the practical circumstance or point of application. Thus it served as a stimulus, but it was not the cause of the science of mechanics. It served simply as a "practical basis" (Ger. *Anhaltspunkt*). At this same point in the text Marx offers a footnote which says a great deal:

> The subordinate role which he [Adam Smith] assigns to machinery gave occasion in the early days of modern mechanical industry to the polemic of Lauderdale, and, at a later period, to that of Ure. A. Smith also confounds differentiation of the instrument of labour, in which the detail labourers themselves took an active part, with the invention of machinery; in this latter, it is not the workmen in manufactories, but learned men, handicraftsmen, and even peasants (Brindley), who play a part (MEW 23:369, ftn. 44; CAP 1:348, ftn. 4).

If the industrial workers had taken an active part in the creation of new machines, that would be an indication that scientific invention was caused by industry itself. Historically speaking, however, we know that they were not the originators of these inventions. The latter were invented by learned men, handicraftsmen, and even farmers. Here dogmatic Marxism would interpose an objection, of course. It would insist that material production was exercising causality here, whether it be through the workers or through the scientists. This is a typical a priori hypothesis thrown out blindly. The causality proposed by it is similar to the divine *concursus* proposed by theologians of the school of Bañez. God is always at work in the background, though we may not know how his *concursus* works or have any verifiable proof of its causal intervention.

Adam Smith, too, sought to reduce the cause of inventions to the division of labor in manufacturing. Marx here rejects that view, stressing that learned men, not the producers, invented the various advances in science. Not only does the "Marxist" thesis fail to dovetail with Marx's own interpretation; it actually runs directly counter to his.

On 28 January 1863, while he was at work on *Capital,* Marx wrote a letter to Engels in which he summed up the results of his study of the origin of modern machinery. Here I wish to cite the main section. For the information of my readers, Cardanus (1501–76) was a famous Italian man of science and a doctor; Jacques de Vaucanson (1709–82) constructed many automatic machines that made him famous and perfected many machines used in the French silk industry. Here is what Marx says:

> The re-reading of my technical-historical extracts has led me to the opinion that, apart from the discoveries of gunpowder, the compass and printing—those necessary pre-requisites of bourgeois development—the two material bases on which the preparations for machine industry were organised within manufacture during the period from the sixteenth to the middle of the eighteenth century (the period in which manufacture was developing from handicraft into actual large-scale industry) were the *clock* and the *mill* (at first the corn mill, that is, a water-mill). Both were inherited from the ancients. (The water-mill was introduced into Rome from Asia Minor at the time of Julius Caesar.) The clock is the first automatic machine applied to practical purposes; the whole theory of the *production of regular motion* was developed through it. Its nature is such that it is based on a combination of half-artistic handicraft and direct theory. Cardanus, for instance, wrote about (and gave practical formulae for) the construction of clocks. German authors of the sixteenth century called clockmaking "learned handicraft" (i.e., not of the guilds) and it would be possible to show from the development of the clock how entirely different the relation between theoretical learning and practice was on the basis of the handicraft from what it is, for instance, in large-scale industry. There is also no doubt that in the eighteenth century the idea of

applying automatic devices (moved by springs) to production was first suggested by the clock. It can be proved historically that Vaucanson's experiments on these lines had a tremendous influence on the imagination of the English inventors (MEW 30:321; MESC:142–43).

Antiquity had both the clock and the mill, yet it did not develop machine industry. Marx adopts the phrase used by German authors of the sixteenth century to describe clockmaking: "learned handicraft (i.e., not of the guilds)." Thus it was not production, not even the handicraft production of the guilds, that was the cause of western science. The invention of automatic machines is rooted in the theory of mechanics concerned with uniform motion—an abstract branch of theory if there ever was one. Even the practical basis is not to be sought for in the handicraft production of the guilds; it is to be found in half-artistic handicraft. Thus the whole theory of uniform motion is based on a combination of half-artistic handicraft and *direct* theory. And to Marx it is evident that the relationship between theory and practice in that stage of development was completely different from the one that now prevails in modern industry.

Science is an historical factor that cannot be reduced to material production. That is why Marx explains the differing degree of development in industry as opposed to agriculture by the differing degree of development in their corresponding sciences *rather than vice versa.* This is a key point that many commentators have missed or disregarded. In Book III of *Capital* (Chapter 45) Marx explains why the productivity of agriculture has not kept pace with that of the processing industries: "Such a fact could be explained—aside from all other circumstances, including in part decisive economic ones—by the earlier and more rapid development of the mechanical sciences, and in particular their application compared with the later and in part quite recent development of chemistry, geology and physiology, and again, in particular, their application to agriculture" (MEW 25:768; CAP 3:760). In his letter to Engels dated 2 August 1862, Marx makes much the same point:

> . . . this proves that agriculture has not yet reached the same stage of development as industry. (Which is very easy to explain, for, apart from everything else, the presupposition of industry is the older science of mechanics, the presupposition of agriculture the entirely new sciences of chemistry, geology and physiology) (MEW 30:266; MESC:132).

This is really explaining, not beating around the bush. For the same basic reasons, Marx offers this prediction in *Theories of Surplus Value:*

But when industry reaches a certain level the disproportion must diminish; in other words, productivity in agriculture must increase relatively more rapidly than in industry. This requires: (1) The replacement of the easy-going farmer by the businessman, the farming capitalist; transformation of the husbandman into a pure wage-labourer; large-scale agriculture, i.e., with concentrated capitals. (2) In particular, however: Mechanics, the really scientific basis of large-scale industry, had reached a certain degree of perfection during the eighteenth century. The development of chemistry, geology and physiology, the sciences that *directly* form the specific basis of agriculture rather than of industry, does not take place till the nineteenth century and especially the later decades (MEW 26/2:103 f.; TSV 2:110).

According to Marx, then, the true foundation of modern production is science properly so called. There is no question of then grounding again this foundation on the mode of production or the forces of production. That could go on *ad infinitum,* as Marx indicates when he censures Adam Smith for reducing the value of labor to the value of foodstuffs, and then the value of foodstuffs to that of labor. Marx deliberately makes a distinction between productive handicraft and learned handicraft in order to point up *direct* theory as a foundation for the modern industrial mode of production. If "in the last analysis" scientific theory could be reduced once again to the mode of production, then the proffered explanation for the different degrees of development in industry and agriculture would explain nothing.

In the *Grundrisse* Marx talks about "the *objective unity* of the *machinery,* of fixed capital, which, as *animated monster,* objectifies the scientific idea" (GRU:470):

The development of fixed capital indicates to what degree general social knowledge has become a *direct force of production* . . . (GRU:706).

At this point a pedant might say that scientific thinking is work too, so that everything is reducible to work. This is merely playing with words. The point at issue is whether everything can be reduced to the mode of *material production* as the cause. Science is labor, but it is spiritual or intellectual labor. Here is how Marx describes it in three brief phrases in Book III of *Capital:*

. . . new developments of the universal labour of the human spirit (MEW 25:114; CAP 3:104).

. . . progress in the field of intellectual production, notably natural science and its practical application (MEW 25:91; CAP 3:81).

. . . the development of intellectual labour, especially in the natural sciences . . . (MEW 25:92; CAP 3:82).

These passages make it clear that the natural sciences have historical impact and effectiveness. They cannot be causally reduced to the mode of production or to economic factors in general. For the sake of completeness, however, I should like to introduce another argument from Marx's *Theories of Surplus Value,* and then conclude this section with some testimony from Engels.

At one point in *Theories of Surplus Value* Marx is discussing the definition that political economy gives of productive work. He notes:

The product of mental labour—science— always stands far below its value, because the labour-time needed to reproduce it has no relation at all to the labour-time required for its original production. For example, a schoolboy can learn the binomial theorem in an hour (MEW 26/1:329; TSV 1:353).

This disproportion shows that material production is not the cause of science, just as it is not the cause of any of the other creations of the human spirit. Again in *Theories of Surplus Value* we read:

If the music is good and if the listener understands music, the consumption of music is more sublime than the consumption of champagne, although the production of the latter is a "productive labour" and the production of the former is not (MEW 26/1:271; TSV 1:298).

Marx probes even deeper in his polemics against Rossi. The latter maintains that the intellectual labor of the magistrate is at least indirectly productive because national production could not function without the administration of justice. Again we have the eternal confusion between a condition and a cause. One could just as well argue that the oxygen in the atmosphere is productive for the very same reason. However, the way in which Marx replies to Rossi is very enlightening:

It is precisely this labour which participates indirectly in production (and it forms only a part of unproductive labour) that we call unproductive labour. Otherwise we would have to say that since the magistrate is absolutely unable to live without the peasant, therefore the peasant is an indirect producer of justice! And so on. Utter nonsense! (MEW 26/1:266; TSV 1:293–94).

On the basis of this criterion it is quite clear that the labor of material production is not a producer of science even indirectly. And as we have seen above (p. 95) the natural sciences, by contrast with jurisprudence and art, are directly productive in the material sense. For in these sciences (e.g., mechanics, chemistry, geology and physiology) "general social knowledge has become a *direct force of production*" (GRU:706).

The attribution of productive efficacy to the sciences is deeply rooted in the outlook and system of Marx. Indeed it is such an integral part of his system that Marx repeatedly feels obliged to point out that this fact does not in any way entitle the capitalists to expropriate for themselves the surplus product that is produced by scientific innovation. Marx carries out this obligation to the hilt, discussing the issue in Book I of *Capital* (MEW 23:119, 407, 408, 411 f., and 535), Book III of *Capital* (MEW 25:91, 92, 113, 114), and *Theories of Surplus Value* (MEW 26/1:64f. 253; MEW 26/3:183).

Marx distinguishes between an increase in productivity and an increase in value. These two things are indeed distinct, as we saw in Chapter 1 of this volume. Consider the machines and the raw materials or semifinished materials used. The labor embodied in a commodity consists of the labor contained in the machinery and the raw or semifinished materials used. However: "The amount of labour contained in these two elements before the new commodity is produced is obviously not increased merely because they become production elements of a new commodity" (MEW 26/3:20; TSV 3:26). Insofar as the value of the machinery is used up, it is *transferred* proportionally to the product in equal parts; it does not *increase*. Unlike human labor power, machinery does not produce a greater value than it itself possesses. It simply *transfers* its own value to the commodities that are fashioned by it; and there is no increase of value in this transference. Moreover, the merit and worth of inventions is that of the scientists who make them. It is part of the spiritual or intellectual labor of the whole society, of human history and civilization. By what right should this redound to the capitalists specifically?

However, this point is not the one that directly interests us here. What interests us here is the fact that Marx felt obliged to make the point. This means that the productive efficacy of the sciences is an indisputable datum in Marx's whole system. It was clear from the start that business leaders would appeal to this efficacy to justify the pillage and expoliation that is part and parcel of the capitalist system.

On the efficacy of the sciences, and their irreducibility to some other cause, we must also refer to Engels' youthful work entitled *Outlines of a Critique of Political Economy* (1844). We are justified in bringing it up here because in 1859 Marx spoke highly of it in the Preface to his CCPE (MEW 13:10; CCPE:22). In Book I of *Capital* he cites it at least four times (MEW 23:89, 166, ftn. 5, 178, ftn. 33, and 663, ftn. 81). He also mentions Engels' arguments in a letter dated 9 August 1862 (MEW 30:275; MESC: 137–38) and a letter dated 8 January 1868 (MEW 32:12; MESC:232). So although Engels may have had some misgivings about his work later, Marx never ceased to regard his findings as valid. Here is what Engels said in 1844:

> . . . and, besides capital, a third factor which the economist does not think about—I mean the spiritual element of invention, of thought, alongside the physical element of sheer labor. What has the economist to do with the spirit of invention? Have not all inventions come flying to him without any effort on his part? Has *one* of them cost him anything? Why then should he bother about them in the calculation of production costs? Land, capital and labor are for him the conditions of wealth, and he requires no more. Science is no concern of his. What does it matter to him that he has received its gifts through Berthollet, Davy, Liebig, Watt, Cartwright, etc.—gifts which have benefited him and his production immeasurably? He does not know how to calculate such things; the advances of science go beyond his figures. But in a rational order which has gone beyond the division of interests as it is found with the economist, the spiritual element certainly belongs among the elements of production and will find its place, too, in economics among the costs of production. And here it is certainly gratifying to know that the promotion of science also brings its material reward; to know that a single achievement of science like James Watt's steam engine has brought in more for the world in the first fifty years of its existence than the world has spent on the promotion of science since the beginning of time (MEW 1:508 f.; EPM: 208).

The clear import of these words is that the contribution of science to material production cannot be reduced or equated to what the extrascientific realm (the realm of production) contributes to science in a causative way. Thus science is creative in the strict sense, even from the economic point of view. In this work Engels uses that fact to refute Malthus. Marx felt that his refutation remained valid, both against Malthus and against Ricardo's law about increasing land rent. But the reader should note that if science is dependent on the production process then Malthus is right rather than Engels and the latter's argument is totally invalid:

> . . . there still remains a third element which, of course, never means anything to the economist—science—whose progress is as unceasing and at least as rapid as that of population. What progress does the agriculture of this century owe to chemistry alone— indeed, to two men alone, Sir Humphrey Davy and Justus Liebig! But science increases at least as much as population. The latter increases in proportion to the size of the previous generation, science advances in proportion to the knowledge bequeathed to it by the previous generation, and thus under the most ordinary conditions also in geometrical progression. And what is impossible to science? (MEW 1:52; EPM:222).

The final statement would be absurd if the efficacy of science ultimately depended on determinations imposed by the material nature of the mode of production. For then the possibilities of science would not be unlimited as Engels here presumes, and his argument against Malthus would fall apart.

In one sense this would be the proper place to deal with the historical efficacy of scientific socialism. However, we must postpone treatment of that question until we have examined the specific way in which that efficacy is exercised. For unlike that of the natural sciences, it does not consist in a direct impact on productivity or an increase in production. So we shall hold off consideration of the issue until the end of Chapter 5.

VI

Now that we have established the fact that not all historical causes are reducible to the economic factor in the last analysis, we must face up to Marx's central thesis and ask ourselves what he means when he insists on the decisive importance of the mode of production. For it can be said without exaggeration that this thesis, along with Marx's analysis of the value of labor power, constitutes Marx's major contribution to economics, the historical sciences, the social sciences, and philosophy.

Why does Marx refer to the mode of production as the basis? This is how he formulates the matter in *Theories of Surplus Value:*

> The usurer in all pre-capitalist modes of production has a revolutionary impact only in the political sense, in that he destroys and wrecks the forms of property *whose constant reproduction in the*

same form constitutes the stable basis of the political structure
(MEW 26/3:520; TSV 3:531; my italics).

That is almost a deliberate definition. The mode of production, which
includes production forces and relations of production, is the basis
because it is the way in which a society reproduces itself in exactly the
same form that it already has. Here production relations are the forms of
ownership. They constitute the basis because when the group in question materially produces its nourishment and other means of subsistence, it also reproduces the same forms of property and ownership that
it already has. The first step in trying to understand Marx's thought is to
understand this equation: *the mode of production is the mode of reproduction.*

The fact that a social system reproduces itself as it was, produces itself
again in exactly the same form, is really decisive. To talk about a specific
society is to include the notion of its stability, its ongoing perdurance for
a certain period of time. No momentary sort of functioning (of what?)
makes a specific society what it is. It is a specific society only
if it reproduces itself—which is to say, only if it endures in the
same form. That is why the mode of production is the basis:
if a society does not reproduce itself, then the term "society"
itself is meaningless. We would be left with a completely ephem-
eral and fleeting phenomenon. Indeed it would not exist at all,
for its existence would cease as soon as we ended our talk about
it.

Let us suppose some other factor intervening from the outside in a
society or arising in some other way. If that factor does not alter the way
in which a society reproduces itself, then in fact it does not alter anything. The society still reproduces itself as it was prior to the intervention of that outside factor, and things remain exactly as they were
before. If people do not explain this thought of Marx, how can they
explain his thought at all?

Of course a society is made up of the individuals who compose it. But
these individuals would cease to exist if they did not reproduce themselves, if their interchange of substances with nature ceased. The mode
of production of the means of subsistence is the mode of reproduction of
the individuals themselves. And in reproducing themselves through the
process of production, the individuals reproduce the same social relationships in which they found themselves before. Thus the result of this
process (i.e., the social relationships that are reproduced) is more important than the articles and material goods produced by the process. With
regard to capitalist society specifically, Marx has this to say in the
Grundrisse:

Finally, the result of the process of production and realization is, above all, the reproduction and new production of the relation of capital and labour itself, of capitalist and worker. This social relation, production relation, appears in fact *as an even more important result of the process than its material results* (GRU:458; my italics).

The production of capitalists and wage labourers is thus a chief product of capital's realization process. Ordinary economics, which looks only at the things produced, forgets this completely (GRU:512).

The reproduction of the individuals is not the reproduction of individuals in general, but of capitalists and wage laborers as such; hence it is the reproduction of the social relations of capitalist production. The same holds true for other forms of society. Thus feudal production reproduces its social relations, that is, lords and serfs; and production based on slavery reproduces masters and slaves as such.

The thesis is even broader in scope. If we clearly distinguish between production properly so called and such things as hunting and food gathering without instruments, then we must maintain that every mode of production is social. The individual who is not in society does not produce. Robinson Crusoe was a producer because he had learned to produce in society and hence was still in society (see GRU:83–84). An individual living outside any form of society would simply live by food gathering. He would not be a human being because it is our relationship with others that makes us humans. He would be a nongregarious animal.

Now the point is that there is no such thing as production in general. Production is always a certain mode of production. Real human beings are beings living in the context of a specific mode of production and its corresponding social relations. There can be no science of man that is not a social science, and the most basic datum for every human science is the mode of production. That is why Marx says that his thesis is at bottom tautological:

But the fact that pre-bourgeois history, and each of its phases, also has its own *economy* and an *economic foundation* for its movement, is at bottom only the tautology that human life has since time immemorial rested on production, and, in one way or another, on *social* production, whose relations we call, precisely, economic relations (GRU:489).

The base, then, is economic. *But Marx himself never made the absurd claim that all the factors or causes which alter that base are economic.* Whatever the various factors or influences might be, they alter nothing if they do not alter the mode of production; for it is through the latter that society reproduces itself just as it was before the outside factors intervened. If a change is to truly change anything, then it must crystallize in the mode of production. But the idea that all the causes of such change must be economic, at least in the last analysis, is something that Marxism pulled out of its own hat; and it cannot be reconciled with the thought of Marx himself.

On two previous occasions in this book I pointed up the programmatic and methodological importance of the 1857 Introduction to the CCPE for Marx's whole economic effort. Well, in that work Marx expressly makes the point that I have just presented:

> The questions raised above all reduce themselves in the last instance to the incidence of general-historical relations into production . . . (MEW 13:629; cf. GRU: 97).

Here the historical circumstances or factors are called general precisely in order to distinguish them from economic factors, to contrast them with factors relating to the mode of production. The important thing is how causes of a varied nature affect the mode of production of a given society, how they alter it. The decisive thing is their impact on the mode of production. But this does not mean that the causes must be of an economic nature or that they must necessarily have originated in the mode of production. The mode of production and reproduction is "the determining element . . . *in the last instance*" (Engels, MEW 37:463; cf. MESC:475) because all other causes must have some impact on it if they are to have any real effect at all, but not because the ultimate origin of these other causes is necessarily economic. Marxism should have given more thought to the fact that "in the last instance" was not applied to Marx's thesis for the first time by Engels in 1890. Marx himself used the phrase "in the last instance" thirty-three years earlier, in the passage of his 1857 Introduction which I cited above.

Now it is clear why Engels insisted that we must investigate and find out what facts are decisive in each case. They may have to do with politics, individual temperament, education, personal heroism, lack of character, and so forth. Of course the only way to find out how decisive they are is to see how they affect the base, the mode of production, in the long or short run. The base does not "determine" what social factor will be the determining one in a given case; it does not decide that by some sort of authoritative decree. It is simply that the characteristic (i.e., "determination") of being decisive cannot be understood without taking account of the base and the impact of the decisive factor on it.

In Book III of *Capital* Marx is explaining how surplus value was extorted from the direct producers in medieval society. He says at one point: "Under such conditions the surplus-labour for the nominal owner of the land can only be extorted from them *by other than economic pressure . . ."* (MEW 25:799; CAP 3:791; my italics). And in a footnote on the same page Marx adds: "After conquering the land, the immediate aim of the conqueror was to seize the human beings as well" (MEW 27:799; cf. CAP 3:791).

In the crucial section on "The So-called Primitive Accumulation" (Part VIII in Book I of *Capital*), we find the following sentence that is often read and quoted by Marxists:

> *In actual history it is notorious that* conquest, enslavement, robbery, murder, *briefly force, play the great part* (MEW 23:742; CAP 1:714; my italics).

In tracing the history of the rise of capitalism in that section, Marx comes to the point where laborers have been transformed into wage laborers and the whole mechanism of capitalism reproduces itself automatically. He then notes that direct violence is no longer necessary. But note how he puts it: "Direct force, outside economic conditions, is of course still used, but only exceptionally" (MEW 23:765; CAP 1:737). So we see that according to Marx all the force, conquest, robbery and murder noted earlier are extraeconomic factors. Could there be a clearer statement that not all historical factors are economic? Indeed he says that it is well known that such noneconomic factors "play the great role."

In the same section (Part VIII) of Book I, Marx describes the enclosure of communal lands within private estates that marked the start of the agricultural revolution: "We leave on one side here the purely economic causes of the agricultural revolution. We deal only with the forcible means employed" (MEW 23:751; CAP 1:723). Thus it is plain that the violence and force which Marx describes in such great detail is not reducible to any economic factor.

In his major study of April 1868, *On the nationalization of the land,* Marx makes a similar point:

> In the course of history conquerors, using laws which they themselves promulgate, seek to give a certain social confirmation to the property-right which *derives originally from violence* (MEW 18:59; my italics).

All these statements are clear and explicit. There is no sense in making a distinction between economic and extraeconomic factors, as Marx does, if everything comes down to economics in the last instance. Where Marx says that something "derives originally from violence," then there is nothing to be done and Marxists must disagree. In their eyes it must ultimately derive from some economic factor. Where Marx talks about "extraeconomic violence," they must talk about intraeconomic violence. And if we are talking about the thought of Karl Marx, then I am deeply sorry but it is they who have some explaining to do.

Insofar as Marx's thought is concerned, the preponderant role of the mode of production is something which not only can be reconciled with the historical analyses we have examined in this chapter but in fact *does not need to be reconciled.* All these factors—spiritual, personal, cultural, and so forth—can have an impact on the mode of production. So Marx himself can make statements like the following:

> Thus all the progress of civilization [constitutes a productive force] (GRU:308).

> The community itself appears as the first great force of production . . . (GRU:495).

> From the standpoint of the direct production process it can be regarded as the production of *fixed capital,* this fixed capital being man himself (GRU:711–12).

> The revolutionary class itself [is a productive force] (MEW 4:181).

> Force is the midwife of every old society pregnant with a new one. It is itself an economic power (MEW 23:779; CAP 1:751).

The reason for all this is given in a passage from *Theories of Surplus Value* that we have already noted:

> Man himself is the basis of his material production, as of any other production that he carries on. All circumstances, therefore, which affect man, the *subject* of production, more or less modify all his functions and activities, and therefore too his functions and activities as the creator of material wealth, of commodities. In this respect it can in fact be shown that *all* human relations and functions, however and in whatever form they may appear, influence material production and have a more or less decisive influence on it (MEW 26/1:260; TSV 1:288).

The revolutionary import of Marx's thesis, which we have examined in this chapter, lies in its antireformism. All efforts and philanthropic reforms are able to be absorbed by the system until and unless they change the mode of production. And to change the latter is to change the socioeconomic system itself and replace it with another. Perhaps the greatest scientific and revolutionary merit of Marx lies in the fact that he *demonstrated* that point. It is certainly one of the greatest contributions that any human being has made to humanity.

However, this message could not possibly be revolutionary if extra-economic factors, the ones directly within our grasp, could not alter the mode of production or direct the revolution against the prevailing mode of production. To maintain that those factors cannot alter the mode of production is to preach a message that is as antirevolutionary as any message could be. It is to succumb to fatalism. We would then have to sit and wait, hoping that the mode of production will change on its own—or not change at all. In either case it would not depend on us at all.

5
Marx the Humanist

Readers unfamiliar with the sociopolitical literature of the last fifteen years or so would find it hard to believe that anyone has ever denied the humanism of Marx. Their incredulity is well founded, and their ignorance of such negations is no real loss.

On the one hand there have been conservative campaigns motivated by hatred for the Communist revolution and explicitly designed to discredit it. People in this camp feel dangerously attacked when they are told that communism is the one and only logical realization of the humanism that the West claims to profess; and so they deny the humanism of Marx. However, they do not examine Marx's writings nor do they take the trouble to grasp the real content of his economic analyses. Right from the start they pin the label of "antihumanist" on any and every movement that assails the bastions of self-interest they have erected for themselves.

On the other side, a more subtle calumny against Marx comes from the ranks of revolutionaries themselves. Motivated by hatred of everything that is not Marx's, they end up attacking everything that is Marx's. If real materialism is to be consistently logical, it must reject any and all humanism. Our advantage today lies in the fact that many materialists are finally getting around to admitting this negation of Marx which inevitably follows from their premises.

I

Fortunately we do not have to engage in prolonged polemics with either of these two views. The humanism of Marx is so clear and central to his system that one need only offer a brief anthology of his mature writings. The documents speak for themselves.

At the urging of Marx himself, Engels wrote a review of the recently published Book I of *Capital* for the *Demokratisches Wochenblatt* (21 and 28 March 1868). In the final paragraph of the second installment we find this summary of Marx's thought by Engels:

106

Just as sharply as Marx stresses the evils of capitalist production, so also does he clearly prove that this social system has been necessary so as to develop the productive forces of society to a level which will make it possible for *all* members of society to develop equally in a manner *worthy of human beings*. All earlier forms of society have been too poor to do this (MEW 16:241 f.; SW:184; my italics).

According to Engels, then, the governing criterion of *Capital* is completely humanist: not every kind of development can be considered "worthy of human beings" (*menschenwürdig*). Engels goes on to say that the workers will have to take over the means of production that are now monopolized by a privileged few. For capitalism does not allow this personal development that is worthy of human beings to be possible for *all* the members of society. As we shall see, Engels' interpretation of *Capital* is completely faithful to Marx's own thought.

In his 1891 Introduction to the third German edition of *The Civil War in France,* Engels recounts a historical incident associated with the fall of the Paris Commune. This is how he puts it:

The Prussian troops surrounding the northern half of Paris had orders not to allow any fugitives to pass; but the officers often shut their eyes when the soldiers paid more obedience to *the dictates of humanity* than to their general's orders; particular honor is due to the Saxon army corps for *its humane conduct* in letting through many workers who had obviously been fighting for the Commune (MEW 22:195; also see MEW 17:621 f.; SW:306; my italics).

So it is not just that in fact certain kinds of development are worthy of human beings and others are not. Here Engels talks about things that ought to be. There are dictates of humanity. There is a normative, obligatory humanism.

Here I shall not go into the fact that the phrase "more obedience to . . . than to . . ." is a clear allusion to the Acts of the Apostles: "Better for us to obey God than men" (Acts 5:29). The German phrase which Engels uses, *"mehr gehorchen . . . als . . ."* is the phrase Luther used in his translation of the Bible.

More noteworthy, however, is the fact that Marx also used the phrase, "the dictates of humanity," and meant it just as seriously as Engels did. In an article on "English Atrocities in China" (NYDT, 10 April 1857), Marx writes:

The inoffensive citizens of Canton, who submitted peacefully to the occupation, were massacred; their houses were levelled to the

ground and the dictates of humanity were trodden under foot
(MEW 12:164).

When someone recognizes the existence of dictates of humanity, he or
she is professing the only authentic humanism there is, i.e., one that
imposes moral obligations and sets norms for human life and its actions.
Those who say that Marx was not a humanist simply do not know what
they are talking about. This 1857 article shows that Marx did not just
profess humanism in private. He publicly espoused it as a criterion in his
published works.

Let us get back to Engels for a moment. In *Socialism: Utopian and
Scientific* (1880) Engels describes the animalistic jungle of capitalism.
His words make clear that when he is talking about humanity and
humanism, he knows exactly what he is saying:

> Between individual capitalists, as between whole industries and
> whole countries, advantages in natural or artificial conditions of
> production decide life or death. The vanquished are relentlessly
> cast aside. It is the Darwinian struggle for individual existence,
> transferred from nature to society with a fury raised to the nth
> power. The brutish state of nature appears as the peak of human
> development (MEW 19:216; SUS:83).

Here Engels condemns not only capitalism itself but also the doctrines
that serve as apologetics for it. Why? Because these doctrines depict
capitalism as the peak of human development. Engels' formulation
makes it clear that he means "human" specifically in contrast to the life
of brutish animals and other beings inferior to human beings. Here is
the proper place to present Marx's identical opinion on social Darwinism. It is in a letter to Laura and Paul Lafargue dated 15 February
1859:

> The struggle for existence in English society—the war of all against
> all (*bellum omnium contra omnes*)—prompted Darwin to discover
> the struggle for existence as the dominant law in animal and vege-
> table life. By contrast, Darwinism views this as a decisive reason
> why human society is never to be emancipated from its animal
> essence (MEW 32:592).

Like Engels, Marx is of the opinion that the struggle and competition
of all against all is incompatible with the human standpoint which they
regard as normative. The same polemical tone against social Darwinism
(Spencer) can be found in a letter of Engels to Lange dated 29 March
1865: "Nothing discredits modern bourgeois development so much as

the fact that it has not yet succeeded in getting beyond the economic forms of the animal world'' (MEW 31:466; MESC:198).

During the Russo-Turkish conflict, the *New York Daily Tribune* published an article entitled ''What Is Really at Stake in Turkey'' on 12 April 1859. It is one of the articles which Engels wrote at Marx's express bidding, and for which Marx assumed authorship and responsibility. It was not sent by Engels to New York from Manchester, where he was living, but by Marx from London after he had signed his own name to it. In that article we read the following:

> Russia is decidedly a conquering nation. She had been so for a whole century until the great movement of 1789 created an enemy to be feared by her, an enemy of powerful effectiveness. We refer to the European revolution, the explosive force of democratic ideas and the impulse of freedom that is *innate in humanity* (MEW 9:17; my italics).

When the yearning for liberty is considered *innate in humanity,* we are dealing with pure, unadulterated humanism. The use or nonuse of the word ''essence'' does not matter in the least. In his corrections of the Erfurt Program of the Social Democrats (1891), Engels proposes this rewording: ''In their struggle for humanity they [the Social Democrats] find themselves blocked by the antiquated political conditions of Germany'' (MEW 22:597).

So the struggle of socialism and of the proletarian revolution is a struggle for humanity. Engels did point out the danger in such forms of expression, of course, but that danger did not prevent him and Marx from using them with their full force. Talking about Robert Owen in *Socialism: Utopian and Scientific,* Engels has this to say:

> He transformed a population, which originally consisted of the most diverse and for the most part very demoralized elements and which gradually grew to 2,500, into a model colony, in which drunkenness, police, magistrates, lawsuits, poor law relief and any need for charity were unknown. All this simply by placing the people in conditions *more worthy of human beings,* and especially by having the rising generation carefully brought up (MEW 19:198; SUS:58; my italics).

In the previous passage we read about a development more worthy of human beings; here we read about conditions more worthy of human beings. This obviously presumes that there are life-styles worthy of human beings and life-styles unworthy of them. And the underlying criterion is the species nature of humanity in particular.

II

Engels and Marx fully realized that the defenders of capitalism also appealed to such things as "the human being," "humanity," and "society as a whole." The latter used these terms hypocritically to foster peace and harmony, to deny and suppress the class struggle, and to maintain the capitalist exploitation which can only be destroyed through class struggle. These phony advocates of humanity and brotherhood are called "wolves in sheep's clothing" by Engels (MEW 21:255; also see MEW 22:270 and 321). Rarely in history has the phrase of Jesus of Nazareth been applied so pointedly and accurately.

The objection of Marx and Engels to the dangerous misuse of humanist philosophy is not averted by the affirmation that we will be able to convince the exploiters that their humanism is false. The goal is not to convince them but to overthrow them. (As Jesus and the whole Bible tell us, there is such a thing as obstinacy and hardness of heart.) But granting the proviso that authentic humanism must be fleshed out in the class struggle, Marx and Engels have no difficulty in proclaiming themselves humanists. Their views certainly have a better claim to that title than do the hypocritically humanist professions of the bourgeoisie. The latter talk about "humanity" but think only about their own privileged little segment of humanity, which lives by exploiting the rest of humanity. The word "humanity" finds its true meaning only on the lips of communists. In his 1883 Preface to the German edition of the *Communist Manifesto,* Engels makes it clear that the key idea of their humanism comes from Marx:

> That this struggle has now reached a stage in which the exploited and oppressed class (the proletariat) cannot free itself from the exploiting oppressor class (the bourgeoisie) without at the same time freeing *society as a whole* once and for all from exploitation, oppression and class struggle—that fundamental thought belongs uniquely and exclusively to Marx (MEW 21:3; my italics).

Engels repeats this assertion in the 1888 Preface to the English edition of the *Communist Manifesto:*

> The Manifesto being our joint production, I consider myself bound to state that the fundamental proposition, which forms its nucleus, belongs to Marx. That proposition is . . . that the history of these class struggles forms a series of evolutions in which, nowadays, a stage has been reached where the exploited and oppressed

classes—the proletariat—cannot attain its emancipation from the sway of the exploiting and ruling class—the bourgeoisie— without, at the same time, and once and for all, emancipating *society at large* from all exploitation, oppression, class distinctions and class struggles (MEW 21:367; VRV:65; my italics).

As far as the utterances of Marx himself are concerned, we have already noted his stress on the dictates of humanity and his attack on antihuman social Darwinism. Now consider the following passage, which is a profession of humanism through and through. It is from the annual report of the General Council of the International to the September 1868 Brussels Congress. It was composed, delivered, and defended by Marx, and it was published by him on 10 September 1868. It concludes with these words:

> Profoundly convinced of the greatness of its mission, the International Working Men's Association will allow itself neither to be intimidated nor misled. Its destiny, henceforward, coalesces with the historical progress of *the class that bear in their hands the regeneration of mankind* (MEW 16:322 f.; VFI:99; my italics).

Here the incontrovertible humanism of Marx is formulated in the clearest and most forceful terms possible. He does not back away an inch from his boldly class-based position. On the contrary, he makes it clear that the future of humanity depends exclusively on the working class. But his focus is 100 percent humanist: the goal is the regeneration of humanity. A formulation of such depth and pregnancy must have cost many hours of reflection. But in this case it would be better to say that it is the natural fruit of Marx's authentic humanism as it matured over many years. If we did not know which member of the General Council had been entrusted with the task of drawing up this report, the philosophical imprint on the above passage itself would justify us in the inference that it was certainly drawn up by Marx. It is a pity that some Marxist theoreticians lack what it takes to fashion a real creative synthesis. Instead they tumble to one or another extreme and feel they must condemn the opposite point of view.

In his *Letter to the Labour Parliament,* which was published in the *People's Paper* on 18 March 1854, Marx offered another striking proof of his humanism:

> If the Labour Parliament proves true to the idea that called it into life, some future historian will have to record that there existed in the year 1854 two parliaments in England, a parliament at London,

and a parliament at Manchester—parliament of the rich, and a parliament of the poor—but that men sat only in the parliament of the men and not in the parliament of the masters (MEW 10:126).[1]

In Chapter 48 of Book III of *Capital* Marx discusses the difference between human freedom outside of work and human freedom in work itself. He clearly prefers the former because he thinks that real freedom begins only "where labour which is determined by necessity and mundane considerations ceases." But he goes on to write this about human freedom in work:

> Freedom in this field can only consist in socialised men, the associated producers, rationally regulating their interchange with Nature, bringing it under their common control, instead of being ruled by it as by the blind forces of Nature; and achieving this with the least expenditure of energy and *under conditions most favourable to, and worthy of, their human nature* (MEW 25:828; CAP 3:820; my italics).

So right in *Capital* we find Marx telling us that some modes of living and working are more favorable to human nature and some are less so; that some conditions are worthy of human nature and some are not. This is pure, unadulterated humanism; and it mentions human nature explicitly. In Chapter 17 of Book I of *Capital* we read the following:

> The value of a day's labour-power, is, as will be remembered, estimated from its normal average duration, or from the normal duration of life among the labourers, and from corresponding normal transformations of organised bodily matter in motion, *in conformity with the nature of man* (MEW 23:549; CAP 1:527; my italics).

There can be no doubt that in Marx's mind human nature is an objective reality, and a reality of a normative rather than a precisely physical character. In Chapter 15 of Book I Marx formulates the transcendent programmatic thesis that served as a guideline for Engels in his 1868 review of *Capital*. Marx puts it this way:

> Moreover, it is obvious that the fact of the collective working group being composed of individuals of both sexes and all ages, must necessarily, under suitable conditions, become a source of *human* development; although in its spontaneously developed, brutal, capitalistic form, where the labourer exists for the process

of production, and not the process of production for the labourer, the fact is a pestiferous source of corruption and slavery (MEW 23:514; cf. CAP 1:490; my italics).

It should be noted that here Marx puts the word *human* rather than his usual *menschlich*, thus highlighting the qualitative and humanist thrust of his argument. He is talking about real human development, not about the development of humanity. He does not want his readers to misinterpret his important thesis, to assume that he is saying that the organization of labor must necessarily contribute to the economic development of the world. Recalling Engels' 1868 review of *Capital*, we can only conclude that this book is one of the most deliberately and explicitly humanist works ever written. That is why Marx so emphatically endorses the thesis of Galiani—"The real wealth . . . is man"—in both *Theories of Surplus Value* (MEW 26/3:263; TSV 3:267) and the *Grundrisse* (GRU:846). That is also why Marx praises Ricardo so highly at one point in *Theories of Surplus Value*. We should look at this passage closely so as to appreciate its profound place in Marx's analysis:

> It is one of Ricardo's great merits that he examined relative or proportionate wages, and established them as a definite category. Up to this time, wages had always been regarded as something simple *and consequently the worker was considered as animal.* But here he is considered in his social relationships. The position of the classes to one another depends more on relative wages than on the absolute amount of wages (MEW 26/2:420 f.; TSV 2:419; my italics).

This point is of fundamental importance in Marx's system. Failure to take due note of it prompted people to impute a brand of materialism to him that was totally alien to his thinking, as we saw in Chapter 1 of this book. The unfavorable or disproportionate social contrast is indeed a *human* motive for the communist revolution, but the level of consumption by itself is not. Those who take note only of the latter, according to Marx, treat human beings as mere animals. That is why Marx was so incensed by the distortion of his thought in the Gotha Programme. Those who deny the humanism of Marx act as if they had never read *Capital*. God knows what author they are talking about!

Of equivalent or even greater systematic importance is the charge that Marx brings against Adam Smith in Book II of *Capital*, where he accuses him of a lack of humanism. Because Smith was incapable of treating the human being as a human being, says Marx, he could not comprehend the creation of value, which is due exclusively to human labor power:

To what extent Adam Smith has blocked his own way to an understanding of the role of labour-power in the process of self-expansion of value is proven by the following sentence, which in the manner of the physiocrats places the labour of labourers on a level with that of labouring cattle. "Not only his (the farmer's) labouring servants, but his labouring cattle are productive labourers" (Book II, Ch. 5, p. 243). (MEW 24:216, ftn. 24; CAP 2:214, ftn. 24).

We shall return to this point in Chapter 11 of this book, for Marx's whole theory of value, his whole epistemology, and his whole theory of science are at stake here. There is a huge gap between him and Adam Smith for precisely that reason. Indeed Marx repeatedly blasted Adam Smith for this phrase of his, and for his inability to set a proper value on human beings as such. See Chapter 19 of Book II of *Capital* (MEW 24:361 and 373) and *Theories of Surplus Value* (MEW 26/1:235; MEW 26/3:181).

Marx was not posing when he cited Terence's maxim in his letters: *Homo sum, humani nil a me alienum puto* ("I am a human being; I consider nothing human alien to me"). It is the most characteristically humanist maxim in all literature. See, for example, Marx's letter to Freiligrath dated 23 February 1860 (MEW 30:461) and his letter to Engels dated 14 December 1853 (MEW 28:314). One thing seems clear: if Marx had not been a humanist, he certainly would not have used that particular phrase or given it as his motto in parlor games.[2]

Here is another comment of Marx in a letter to Engels dated 9 May 1865:

> Although the bourgeoisie dislike . . . Potter as the chief organizer of strikes, they nevertheless support him against our people because they scent venality in him; whereas they know that our people are real human beings (MEW 31:115).

Marx's humanism is obviously of a moral nature, and it includes incorruptibility. Here, however, I want to stress the testimony of Marx's economic treatises. In Book I of *Capital* he denounces the darwinian jungle known as free competition. His words speak volumes:

> The division of labour within the society brings into contact independent commodity-producers, who acknowledge no other authority but that of competition, of the coercion exerted by the pressure of mutual interests; *just as in the animal kingdom* the war

of all against all more or less preserves the conditions of existence of every species (MEW 23:377; CAP 1:356; my italics).

On the piecework system of work and payment, Marx has this to say in Book I: "a process which *brutalizes* the adult workman, and ruins his wife and children" (MEW 23:501; CAP 1:77; my italics).

At one point Marx talks about the workers who are reduced to performing the most simplified tasks so that production can be mechanized as much as possible and therefore increase in productivity. He describes the boys, mostly between eleven and seventeen, who are given this work:

> A great part of them cannot read, and they are, as a rule, utter savages and very extraordinary creatures. . . . As soon as they get too old for such child's work . . . they are discharged. . . . They become recruits of crime (MEW 23:509; CAP 1:485).

It is not the place, here, to go on to show how division of labor seizes upon, not only the economic, but every other sphere of society, and everywhere lays the foundation of that all engrossing system of *specializing and sorting men, that development in a man of one single faculty at the expense of all other faculties,* which caused A. Ferguson, the master of Adam Smith to exclaim: "We make a nation of Helots, and have no free citizens" (MEW 23:375; CAP 1:354; my italics).

Division of labour in manufacture . . . increases the social productive power of labour, not only for the benefit of the capitalist instead of for that of the labourer, but it does this by crippling the individual labourers (MEW 23:386; CAP 1:364).

Moral degradation . . . intellectual desolation (MEW 23:421; CAP 1:399).

Within the capitalist system . . . all means for the development of production transform themselves into means of domination over, and exploitation of, the producers. *They mutilate the labourer into a fragment of a man, degrade him to the level of an appendage of a machine,* destroy every remnant of charm in his work and turn it into hated toil. They estrange from him the intellectual potentialities of the labour-process in the same proportion as science is incorporated in it as an independent power . . . (MEW 23:674; CAP 1:645; my italics).

These human sacrifices are mostly due to the inordinate avarice of the mine owners (MEW 25:98; CAP 3:88).

The last quote is from Book III of *Capital*. Here are a few more passages from the same Book III:

Over-work, the *transformation of the labourer into a work horse,* is a means of increasing capital, or speeding up the production of surplus-value (MEW 25:96 f.; CAP 3:86; my italics).

Not to mention the absence of all provisions to render the production process *human,* agreeable, or at least bearable (MEW 25:97; CAP 3:86; my italics).

The capitalist mode of production is generally, despite all its niggardliness, altogether too prodigal with its human material (MEW 25:97; CAP 3:86).

Capitalist production . . . more than any other mode of production . . . squanders human lives, or living labour, and not only blood and flesh, but also nerve and brain (MEW 25:99; CAP 3:88).

Book I of *Capital* had spoken in similar terms of "the unrestricted waste of human life" (MEW 23:499; CAP 1:475):

The vampire will not loose its hold on him "so long as there is muscle, a nerve, a drop of blood to be exploited" (Engels) (MEW 23:319 f.; CAP 1:302).

But in its blind unrestrainable passion, its werewolf hunger for surplus-labour, capital *oversteps* not only the *moral,* but even the merely physical *maximum bounds* of the working-day (MEW 23:280; CAP 1:264–65; my italics).

The capitalist . . . in this industry . . . risks nothing by a stoppage of work, but the skin of the worker himself. Here then he sets himself systematically to work to form an industrial reserve force that shall be ready at a moment's notice; during one part of the year he decimates this force by *the most inhuman toil,* during the other part, he lets it starve for want of work (MEW 23:502; CAP 1:478; my italics).

In these citations it is obvious that Marx heaps one negative evaluation of capitalism on another. But note that the criterion used by him is as positive as it can be. It is the humanist criterion that distinguishes between what is human and what is inhuman. If we want to find positive evaluation of the work process in *Capital,* we must look to what Marx says about socialism. Here are some samples:

From the factory system budded, as Robert Owen has shown us in detail, the germ of the education of the future, an education that will, in the case of every child over a given age, combine productive labour with instruction and gymnastics, not only as one of the methods of adding to the efficiency of production, but as the only method of producing *fully developed human beings* (MEW 23: 507 f.; CAP 1:483–84; my italics).

Fanatically bent on making value expand itself, he [the capitalist] ruthlessly forces the human race to produce for production's sake; he thus forces the development of the productive powers of society, and creates those material conditions which alone can form the real basis of *a higher form of society, a society in which the full and free development of every individual forms the ruling principle* (MEW 23:618; CAP 1:592; my italics).

Obviously if socialism is to be regarded as a *higher* form of society, its greater merit cannot lie simply in the fact that it is chronologically *later* than capitalism. There must be some human criterion of evaluation to compare "fully developed human beings" with a situation of "moral degradation" and "intellectual desolation." Few versions of humanism proceed as analytically as that of Marx did in this respect.

III

There is a set of concepts used by Marx and Engels, perhaps elaborated more by Engels in his writings, that is very precise and pregnant. The concepts clearly were introduced into the picture by Marx insofar as historical and economic realities are concerned. In any case both Marx and Engels make a distinction between "human" in the *species* sense and "human" in the *social* sense. The act of producing made human beings human in the species sense (see Section VI of Chapter 4 in this volume). Communism will make human beings human in the social sense. In the Introduction to his *Dialectics of Nature* (1876) Engels writes:

Only conscious organization of social production, in which production and distribution are carried on in a planned way, can lift mankind above the rest of the animal world as regards the social aspect, in the same way that production in general has done this for men in their aspect as species (MEW 20:324; DN:19).

That is why Engels describes communism in the following terms in his *Anti-Dühring*:

> The struggle for individual existence comes to an end. And at this point, in a certain sense, man finally cuts himself off from the animal world, leaves the conditions of animal existence behind him and enters conditions which are really human (MEW 20:264; AD:309).

That is why Marx is correct and precise when he says the following about the social formation of capitalism in his 1859 CCPE:

> The prehistory of human *society* accordingly closes with this social formation (MEW 13:9; CCPE:22; my italics).

In the species sense, the human realm began as soon as there was production and association. In the social sense, the human realm will begin when capitalism comes to its end. So today we are still in the prehistory of human *society,* but not in the prehistory of the human realm altogether (i.e., as a species reality). To say this is not at all to relativize the normative force of human nature; instead it is to take it more seriously than anyone ever has.

As we have already seen in this chapter, Marx and Engels appealed to the dictates of humanity as a solid and universally valid criterion to pass judgment on the conduct of the British in China and on the soldiers of Saxony after the fall of the Paris Commune. They also used this criterion to assert that some circumstances are more worthy of human beings than others. They also maintained that the yearning for freedom is innate in humanity. Thus their criterion of what is human in the social sense enabled them to pass judgment on societies as a whole, as social formations, and to assert that so far no societies have been truly human. In their view only the future communist society will be truly human in the social sense.

For this reason people make a radical mistake when they interpret the following statement of Engels in a relativistic sense:

> A really human morality which transcends class antagonisms and their legacies in thought becomes possible only at a stage of society which has not only overcome class contradictions but has even forgotten them in practical life (MEW 20:88; AD:105).

If he were a relativist, Engels could not have written in the absolute terms we find throughout his writings. In his book on *The Origins of the Family, Private Property and the State,* Engels makes it clear that monogamy itself, for example, clearly represents progress. Insofar as moral progress is concerned, here are some strange statements from a would-be relativist:

> Only now were the conditions realized in which through monogamy . . . the greatest moral advance we owe to it could be achieved: modern individual sex-love, which had hitherto been unknown to the entire world (MEW 21:71; OF:61).

> And as sexual love is by its nature exclusive . . . the marriage based on sexual love is *by its nature* individual marriage (MEW 21:82; OF:72).

In an ethnological article on the marriage customs of primitive tribes entitled "A Recently Discovered Case of Group Matrimony" and published in *Die Neue Zeit* in 1893, Engels has this caution for the reader:

> It should also be noted . . . that group marriage is not at all like the brothel-fantasy our petty bourgeoisie might imagine it. It is not as if these peoples carry out in public the same erotic life that our bourgeois people practice in secret (MEW 22:351).

There is no solid ground for the relativistic interpretation of Engels' thought that some people propose. The "nature" which he regards as the ground of individual marriage is clearly human nature. And he goes on to argue that the human nature of sexual love calls for monogamy, among other things.

Aside from the books, articles, and letters of Marx already cited in this chapter, I also want to mention the humanitarian campaign that Marx and his daughter Jenny waged against the cruel treatment of the Irish Fenians by British jailers. In the Spring of 1870 Jenny published a series of articles in *La Marseillaise.* Her father helped her write and edit these articles, and in fact the third article in the series was written completely by Marx. He also published another article on his own in the Brussels *L'Internationale.* It was in two parts, which were published on 27 February and 6 March of that year (MEW 16:401–6). He also got the General Council of the International to pass several resolutions and to include a section on the "Question of the General Council's Resolutions on the Irish Amnesty" in a circular to the Federal Council of the International in French Switzerland (MEW 16:401–6; see VFI:117–19 and 163–64). The point I want to bring out here, however, is the quality of Marx's humanism. That can best be seen in a letter to Engels dated 5 March 1870, in which he asks for Engels' support:

> With these two periodicals *L'Internationale* and *La Mar-seillaise*—we will now unmask the British on the continent. If some day you find something that will fit one of these periodicals, you should get involved in *our good work* (MEW 32:455; my italics).

On the same day he summarized the whole process in a letter to Paul and Laura Lafargue. He went on to say: "Of course you realize that I am not guided solely by feelings of humanity. There are other reasons, too" (MEW 32:656). He then proceeds to talk about England's vulnerability in Ireland. The fact remains, however, that feelings of humanity prompted him to this "good work" and that he urged Engels to join him in it.

In a letter to Johann Philipp Becker dated 6 February 1862, Marx had used the word "human" in the same sense:

> The ancients say—it was Aeschines, I believe—that one should try to procure worldly goods so as to be able to help one's friends in need. What profound human wisdom there is in that remark! (MEW 30:620).

Here again Marx resorts to the Latin root word *humanus* (whence comes the word "humanism") rather than to his usual German word *menschlich*. Here is also the place to cite his remark in a letter to Kugelmann dated 17 March 1868: "Amid the machinery of the world friendship is the only personally important thing" (MEW 32:540). I will not quote from his letter to his wife dated 21 June 1856 (MEW 29:532–36) because it is often cited. But in it Marx makes clear that he is not dedicating himself to humanity in the abstract: neither to the human being of Feuerbach nor to the collection of atoms that constitutes humanity for Moleschott and all logically consistent materialism.

The circular of the General Council of the Fenians (i.e., Irish guerrilla fighters), which Marx himself drew up and pushed through the General Council, contained the following paragraph and then went on to plead for a reduction of the death sentence imposed on five Fenian prisoners accused of the murder of a policeman:

> Even if the judgment of the Manchester jury and the statements of the witnesses . . . had not been tarnished by the British government, the latter would now have to choose between the bloody

practice of old Europe and the *generous humanity* of the young republic across the Atlantic (MEW 16:219; see VFI:159, ftn. 4; my italics).

In an article for the NYDT dated 4 August 1858, Marx writes about the sorry state of the mentally ill in England. Here is the concluding paragraph:

> Generally speaking, there are few horse paddocks in England that would not look like ladies' boudoirs compared to the wards for the mentally ill in the workhouses, few in which the treatment of the quadrupeds could not be called tender and loving by comparison with the treatment given to the mentally ill (MEW 12:538).

On 25 December 1861, *Die Presse* published an article in which Marx assailed the 1856 international declaration of maritime rights. In substance the declaration exempted commercial shipping from bombardment and capture in wartime. The important thing here is the criterion upon which Marx based his criticism of the declaration:

> In fact the declaration of 1856 conceals *great inhumanity* under its philanthropic wording. It transforms what was a country's war into a government's war. *It grants property an immunity which it denies to the person*. It frees commerce from the horrors of war, so that the merchant and trading classes are rendered indifferent to the horrors of war. . . . An innovation which would permit English commerce to carry on commerce with the enemy in neutral ships while soldiers and sailors are fighting for the honor of the nation (MEW 15:428; my italics).

Marx's criterion could not be more explicit or more humanist. He cannot tolerate a regulation that protects commerce (i.e., things) but does not protect persons. Thus a great lack of humanity underlies the philanthropic wording of the declaration. Here we have the same criterion that prompted his comparison of the treatment of stable horses and that of human beings in mental asylums. It never occurs to Marx that attentiveness to human beings must be evaluated in terms of the criterion of productivity. Such an approach would offer grounds for defending the maritime declaration and the lack of concern for the mentally ill, as well as for rejecting his attacks in *Capital* against the capitalist mode of production. Human beings are values in themselves, whatever their productive capabilities may be. On 1 August 1854 (NYDT), Marx published an article entitled "The English Bourgeoisie." The following paragraph from that article is pertinent here:

When it [the Ten Hours Law] took effect, the reports of the district inspectors reveal the shameful cunning, the niggardly and wily meanness through which it was evaded. To every subsequent attempt of parliament to obtain *more humane conditions* for the workers, the representatives of the bourgeoisie have replied with cries of "communism." Mr. Cobden has done this with great frequency. For years now the owners have been trying to extend the working day in the factories *beyond what is humanly tolerable* and, by unscrupulously implementing the piece-work system and setting some workers against others, to lower the pay of the skilled worker to the level of the unskilled worker. This approach finally drove the Amalgamated Engineers to rebel, and the brutal expressions that became current among the masters proved how little could be expected of them *in the way of any noble or human sentiment* (MEW 10:647; my italics).

The new materialism which calls itself "Marxist," and which makes fun of noble sentiments, must be informed that its nihilism goes against the explicit theses Marx fought for with all his might. The above citation lays down the coordinates of the conscious humanism in the framework of which we must evaluate the moral judgments that crop up countless times in Marx's writings. Time and again we come across such words as shameful, cunning, meanness, unscrupulous, and so forth. The fact that all these moral categories sound antiquated to certain dilettantes of philosophy and life never kept Marx from using them, or identifying himself fully with them, or giving his life for what they signify.

Before we focus on the humanist base of Marx's economic system, we would do well to note that Marx's humanism does not signify naturalism—a frequent misinterpretation of his thought. The antinaturalism of Marx will concern us more fully in the latter half of Chapter 9. However, we can anticipate the topic here by quoting his remarks on the primitive communities of India which appeared in the NYDT on 25 June 1853:

We must not forget that this *undignified,* stagnatory, and vegetative life, that this passive sort of existence evoked on the other part, in contradistinction, wild, aimless, unbounded forces of destruction, and rendered murder itself a religious rite in Hindustan. We must not forget that these little communities were contaminated by distinctions of caste and by slavery, that they subjugated man to external circumstances instead of elevating man to be the sovereign of circumstances, that they transformed a self-developing social state into never-changing natural destiny, and thus brought about a *brutalizing* worship of nature, exhibiting its degradation in the fact that man, the sovereign of nature, fell down on his knees in adoration of Kanuman, the monkey, and Sabbala, the cow (MEW 9:132; VSE:306; *my italics*).

In the eyes of Marx these primitive communities closely bound to nature simply vegetate. That is undignified, unworthy of human beings, because it means that nature has dominion over them instead of their having dominion over nature. As I said, we shall return to this point in Chapter 9. Here I simply want to bring out the fact that Marx's humanism is diametrically opposed to any return to nature, for there is a tendency in some circles to equate his humanism with that.

The ground and basis of Marx's humanism is unlimited respect for the person as an end in himself or herself. Throughout his economic analysis Marx attributes the utmost systematic importance to the criterion that distinguishes between means and ends, between subject and object, between human beings and things. To point up this fact right from the start, I want to bring up a topic that apparently has nothing to do with that criterion: the rate of profit. Marx examines it in Chapter 2 of Book III of *Capital*:

> The way in which surplus-value is transformed into the form of profit by way of the rate of profit is, however, a further development of the inversion of subject and object that takes place already in the process of production (MEW 25:55; CAP 3:45).

Even Marx's fight against the sovereignty which the rate of profit establishes in economics as a whole is bound up with his fundamental fight against capitalism's reduction of the person of the worker to a mere thing, of the subject to a mere object. In Chapter 25 of Book I of *Capital* ("The General Law of Capitalist Accumulation") Marx had described capitalism as

> a mode of production in which the labourer exists to satisfy the needs of self-expansion of existing values, instead of, on the contrary, material wealth existing to satisfy the needs of development on the part of the labourer. As, in religion, man is governed by the products of his own brain, so in capitalistic production, he is governed by the products of his own hand (MEW 23:649; CAP 1:621).

As we shall see in Chapter 8 of this volume, this thesis is clearly and deliberately taken from the many biblical denunciations of idolaters, who bow down before their own handiwork (e.g., Ps. 135:15; Ps. 115:4; Deut. 31:29; Jer. 32:30; 25:7; 44:8; Bar. 6:50 f.; Wisd. of Sol. 13:10). The noun *Machwerk* is the typical one in German-language translations of the Bible. Thus Marx's contention is that humanity's domination by the work of its own hands holds true even more in economics than in religion.

But even apart from this clear allusion to the Bible, Marx's rejection in humanist terms of the fact that humans now exist for the sake of wealth rather than vice versa is perhaps, technically speaking, the central thesis of *Capital*. His analysis of the commodity form brings out the varying stages that must follow upon one another. Once the production of commodities as such, as opposed to the production of goods for consumption, is introduced into the world, then one is forced to introduce the medium of exchange known as money. From there one is forced to end up with the existence of capital as such, and consequently capitalism. But capital is precisely that form of wealth which does not exist for humans but rather makes them exist for its sake.

Thus we get the crucial, antireformist message of Marx: eliminating the production of commodities is the same thing as establishing communism; so long as commodity production is not eliminated entirely, the dominion of wealth over human beings must necessarily arise again and again, and with it the inversion of the proper relationship between subject and object, ends and means. With one and the same argument Marx refutes both reformism on the one hand and all apologetics for commodity production as the only possible—hence "natural" and unchangeable—form of production on the other hand. Let us see how Marx sums up the matter in his basic chapter on the commodity in Book I (Chapter 1) of *Capital:*

> Political economy has indeed analysed, however incompletely, value and its magnitude, and has discovered what lies beneath these forms. But it has never once asked the question why labour is represented by the value of its products and labour-time by the magnitude of that value. These formulae, which bear it stamped upon them in unmistakable letters that they belong to a state of society in which *the process of production has the mastery over man instead of being controlled by him,* such formulae appear to the bourgeois intellect to be as much a self-evident necessity imposed by Nature as productive labour itself. Hence forms of social production that preceded the bourgeois form are treated by the bourgeoisie in much the same way as the Fathers of the Church treated pre-Christian religions (MEW 23:94 f.; CAP 1:80–81; my italics).

From the above paragraph it is obvious that Marx's basic criterion for judging what is inhuman—the inversion of the relationship between subject and object—is imbedded in *Capital* as early as his analysis of the commodity, which is the cement of the whole work. Thus, when he comes to criticize the rate of profit in Book III, he can relate it back to the foundation he laid down in Book I. The rate of profit is simply "a further development of the inversion of subject and object that takes place already in the process of production" (MEW 23:55; CAP 3:45). Book II of *Capital* and *Theories of Surplus Value* will do the same thing time and again. Even later sections of Book I of *Capital* will link up their points with the basic principle established in Chapter 1. Here, for example, is what Marx says in Chapter 25:

> The law by which a constantly increasing quantity of means of production, thanks to the advance in the productiveness of social labour, may be set in movement by a progressively diminishing expenditure of human power, this law in a capitalist society— *where the labourer does not employ the means of production, but the means of production employ the labourer*—undergoes a complete inversion and is expressed thus: the higher the productiveness of labour, the greater is the pressure of the labourers on the means of employment, the more precarious, therefore, becomes their condition of existence, viz., the sale of their own labour-power for the increasing of another's wealth, or for the self-expansion of capital (MEW 23:674; CAP 1:644–45; my italics).

The basic question here had been formulated by J. H. von Thünen: "How has the labourer been able to pass from being master of capital— as its creator—to being its slave?" Marx cites the question in Book I of *Capital* and then says: "It is Von Thünen's merit to have asked this question. His answer is simply childish" (MEW 23:659, ftn. 77a; CAP 1:621, ftn. 1). The reason is that no correct answer could be given without analyzing the form of the commodity and the whole production process that is affected by it. That is the task which Marx undertakes in Book I of *Capital*. But this is not simply *one* of the messages of *Capital*, nor is the humanist focus simply *one* of the aspects of Marx's work. It is *the* message of Marx and his work.

Even the highly abstract and technical analyses of Book II of *Capital* cannot be carried out if one prescinds from the difference between subject and object, person and thing. Consider these two passages from Chapter 11:

> The real substance of the capital laid out in wages is labour itself, active, value-creating labour-power, living labour, which the capitalist exchanges for dead, materialized labour and embodies in his capital, by which means, and by which alone, the value in his hands turns into self-expanding value (MEW 24:223; CAP 2:221).

In the process of production the instruments of labour, as components of the productive capital, are not opposed to labour-power as fixed capital any more than material of labour and auxiliary substances are identified with it as circulating capital. Labour-power confronts both of them as a personal factor, while those are objective factors—speaking from the point of view of the labour-process (MEW 24:224; CAP:221–22).

People cannot understand anything about Marx's analysis if even for a moment they lose sight of the difference between subject and object, person and thing. Human nature, the nature of human beings, is normative for Marx; and in his view human nature consists in being a subject.

Now let us turn to Book I of *Theories of Surplus Value*. Back in Chapter 2 of this volume we cited two paragraphs of major importance from that work (see p. 40 above). In them Marx railed against "the personification of the thing and the reification of the person" (MEW 26/1:366). He complained that capitalism completely reverses the relationship between human beings and the means of production. The former are used by the latter; instead of human beings using the latter as means, the latter use human beings as their means. As a result, it is not as a person that the capitalist exercises dominion over the worker, "but only insofar as he is 'capital' " (ibid.). The following passage explains the latter point a bit more:

But as personified capital he produces for the sake of production, he wants to accumulate wealth for the sake of accumulation of wealth. In so far as he is a mere functionary of capital, that is, an agent of capitalist production, what matters to him is exchange-value and the increase of exchange-value, not use-value and its increase (MEW 26/1:253 f.; TSV 1:282).

Since the human being is not an end in capitalism, people do not produce to satisfy the needs of society. To do that would be to be swayed by use-values, by the aims of consumption and real wealth. Capitalist society, however, produces to increase exchange-value and turns society as a whole into a means to that end. Book II of *Theories of Surplus Value* reminds us:

It must never be forgotten that in capitalist production what matters is not the immediate use-value but the exchange-value and, in particular, the expansion of surplus-value. This is the driving motive of capitalist production, and it is a pretty conception that—in order to reason away the contradictions of capitalist production—abstracts from its very basis and depicts it as a production aiming at the direct satisfaction of the consumption of the producers (MEW 26/2:495; TSV 2:495).

This last sentence alludes to the analysis made of the base (i.e., of the production process) in Book I of *Capital* and in the CCPE. The production process is governed by exchange value, and for that very reason it must consist in the production of commodities as such. Bourgeois apologetics had been able to dissemble and camouflage this complete inversion of means and ends, which is the very essence of the capitalist mode of production, precisely because no one had come along before Marx to analyze it with implacable rigor. We would be in a fine fix now if we were to cater to the positivist whims of Marxists themselves and to prescind from Marx's analysis, an analysis which for the first time applied the humanist criterion with all its consequences to the most technical and detailed economic facts. Again in Book II of *Theories of Surplus Value* Marx has this to say about Ricardo's formulations:

> In this conception the workers themselves appear as that which they are in capitalist production—mere means of production, not an end in themselves and not the aim of production (MEW 26/2:549; TSV 2:548).

And with regard to overproduction:

> What after all has over-production to do with absolute needs? It is only concerned with demand that is backed up by ability to pay. It is not a question of absolute over-production—over-production as such in relation to the absolute need or the desire to possess commodities. In this sense there is neither partial nor general over-production; and the one is not opposed to the other (MEW 26/2:507; TSV 2:506).

And in fact how can we talk about overproduction when millions of human beings lack the most basic necessities? Doesn't such talk prove that there is a complete inversion of ends and means in capitalist production? How can humanity continue to put up with a system that channels all the resources of the world (including humanity itself) into obtaining a profit rather than into satisfying the needs of human beings?

In Chapter 2 of this book, I also cited several explicitly humanist passages from Book III of *Theories of Surplus Value*. For the basic criterion of humanism is wholly grounded on the fact that the essence of a human being is to be a subject. However, there is more testimony on this matter in Book III. For example, when Marx discusses the two forms adopted by surplus value, bank interest and industrial profit, he notes that in them the character and form of capital are complete "as the subjectification of objects and the objectification of subjects" (MEW 26/3:484; TSV 3:494).

When Marx alludes explicitly to the contradiction that capital is turned into an end while the worker merely becomes a means of production, he says the following:

> In this contradiction political economy simply expressed the essence of capitalist production or, if you will, of wage labor, of labor alienated from itself. Over against this labor stands the wealth which it created as alien wealth, its own productivity as the productivity of its product, its enrichment as impoverishment, its social power as the power of society over it (MEW 26/3:467).

> What is capital regarded not as the result of, but as the prerequisite for, the process [of production]? What makes it capital before it enters the process so that the latter merely develops its immanent character? The social framework in which it exists. The fact that living labour is confronted by past labour, activity is confronted by the product, man is confronted by things, labour is confronted by its own materialized conditions as alien, independent, self-contained subjects, personifications, in short, as *someone else's property* and, in this form, as "employers" and "commanders" of labour itself, which they appropriate instead of being appropriated by it (MEW 26/3:467; TSV 3:475–76).

> The producer is therefore controlled by the product, the subject by the object, labour which is being embodied by labour embodied in an object, etc. In all these conceptions, past labour appears not merely as an objective factor of living labour, subsumed by it, but vice versa; not as an element of the power of living labour, but as a power over this labour. The economists ascribe a false importance to the material factors of labour compared with labour itself in order to have also a *technological* justification for the *specific social form*, i.e., the *capitalist form*, in which the relationship of labour to the conditions of labour is turned upside-down, so that it is not the worker who makes use of the conditions of labour, but the conditions of labour which make use of the worker (MEW 26/3:271; TSV 3:275–76).

Marx never imagined that even some Marxists would deny the character of subject to human beings and join in the justifications of capitalism offered by bourgeois apologists. In Book III of *Theories of Surplus*

Value Marx points up the merit of the economic analysis of Richard Jones, who succeeded Malthus in the chair at Haileybury:

> 1) *The independent, material form of wealth disappears* and wealth is shown to be simply the activity of men. Everything which is not the result of human activity, of labour, is nature and, as such, is not social wealth. The phantom of the world of goods fades away and it is seen to be simply a continually disappearing and continually reproduced objectivization of human labour. All solid material wealth is only transitory materialization of social labour, crystallization of the production process whose measure is time, the measure of a movement itself.
>
> 2) The manifold forms in which the various component parts of wealth are distributed among different sections of society lose their apparent independence. Interest is merely a part of profit, rent is merely surplus-profit. Both are consequently merged in profit, which itself can be reduced to *surplus-value,* that is, to unpaid labour. The value of the commodity itself, however, can only be reduced to labour-time. . . . But from the moment that the bourgeois mode of production and the conditions of production and distribution which correspond to it are recognized as *historical,* the delusion of regarding them as natural laws of production vanishes and the prospect opens up of a new society, [a new] economic social formation, to which capitalism is only the transition (MEW 26/3:421 f.; cf. TSV 3:429).

Let me add one final citation from the same Book III. It is in the same vein of denunciation that we saw in the early part of *Capital:*

> The capitalist directly produces exchange-value in order to increase his profit, and not for the sake of consumption. . . . In every industry each individual capitalist produces in proportion to *his* capital irrespective of the needs of society and especially irrespective of the supply of competing capitalists in the same industry (MEW 26/3:117; TSV 3:120–21).

I will not belabor the point that if one proposes to denounce capitalism as an inversion of the relationship between end and means, one must be absolutely convinced that human beings are "an end in themselves" *Selbstzweck* (MEW 26/2:549; TSV 2:548). Such a conviction cannot be held by capitalists or by materialists who falsely call themselves Marxists. But it is the conviction that underlies all authentic humanism such as that of Marx. What Marx adds to this humanism is a convincing demonstration that in essence and structure capitalism treats human beings as mere means, so that the inversion can be eliminated only by eliminating the capitalist system.

As far as Marx's other economic writings are concerned, I need only add a couple of sample passages from the *Grundrisse:*

> . . . the objective conditions of labour assume an ever more colossal independence, represented by its very extent, opposite living labour, and . . . social wealth confronts labour in more powerful portions as an alien and dominant power. The emphasis comes to be placed not on the state of being *objectified,* but on the state of being *alienated,* dispossessed, sold; on the condition that the monstrous objective power which social labour itself erected opposite itself as one of its moments belongs not to the worker, but to the personified conditions of production, i.e., to capital. To the extent that, from the standpoint of capital and wage labour, the creation of the objective body of activity happens in antithesis to the immediate labour capacity—that this process of objectification in fact appears as a process of dispossession from the standpoint of labour or as appropriation of alien labour from the standpoint of capital—to that extent, this twisting and inversion is a *real* [phenomenon], not a merely *supposed* one existing merely in the imagination of the workers and the capitalists (GRU:831).

> The recognition . . . of the products as its own, and the judgement that its separations from the conditions of its realization is improper—forcibly imposed—is an enormous [advance in] awareness, itself the product of the mode of production resting on capital, and as much the knell to its doom as, with the slave's awareness that he *cannot be the property of another,* with his consciousness of himself as a person, the existence of slavery becomes a merely artificial, vegetative existence, and ceases to be able to prevail as the basis of production (GRU:463).

IV

These passages could not be more explicit. Marx expects that the revolution that will overthrow capitalism will follow from the workers' conscious realization that they are persons, and that it is not right that the means of production do not belong to them.

I shall conclude this chapter by pointing out one obvious connection between it and Chapter 1, and an equally obvious connection between it and Chapter 4. In Marx's eyes, stirring up indignation is not incompatible with rigorous scientific analysis. If the phenomenon analyzed is objectively a cause for indignation, then taking cognizance of that phenomenon will make people indignant. In such a case their indignation is justified because their realization of the situation is objective and scientific. We get subjectivism when the reaction of the subject does not correspond to the reality of the object. Such subjectivism tends to become paranoia and autism when in principle and methodology it isolates the reactions of the subject so that they are not affected at all by the object under study, however scientifically the latter may be scrutinized and described.

In Chapter 1, I cited various examples of the same point brought out in the last passage of the *Grundrisse* cited above: in order to offer motivation for the communist revolution, Marx felt it was enough to point up the parallelism between capitalism and slavery. The impetus to revolution is the indignation provoked by the very reality which is brought to light through Marx's analysis.

The real ending of Book I of *Capital* is the final two pages of Chapter 32 (23 in the German edition), for the following chapter is merely an appendix to it. It begins with these words:

> Along with the constantly diminishing number of the magnates of capital, who usurp and monopolise all advantages of this process of transformation, grows the mass of misery, oppression, slavery, degradation, exploitation; *but with this too grows the indignation of the working-class,* a class always increasing in numbers, and disciplined, united, organised by the very mechanism of the process of capitalist production itself (MEW 23:790; cf. CAP 1:763; my italics).

That is why Engels had this to say in his Preface to the 1890 edition of the *Communist Manifesto:* "For the final triumph of the statements expressed in the *Manifesto* Marx *relied solely and exclusively on the intellectual development of the working class;* the latter must necessarily result from united action and discussion" (MEW 4:584 f.; my italics). In his 1867 *Instructions for Delegates to the Geneva Congress* of the International, Marx himself had written: "The more enlightened part of the working class fully understands that the future of its class, and, therefore, of mankind, *altogether depends upon the education of the rising working generation*" (MEW 4:584 f.; cf. VFI:89; my italics).

I will not divert the reader with a long catalogue of citations in which Marx clearly is trying to arouse indignation in his readers. There are in fact many such passages, akin to the following statements which can be found in Book I of *Capital:*

> . . . the civilised horrors of over-work are grafted on the barbaric
> horrors of slavery, serfdom, etc. (MEW 23:250; CAP 1:236).

> Compulsory working to death is here the recognised form of
> over-work (MEW 23:250; CAP 1:235).

> But the over-work beyond this amount is in many cases, to use the
> words of the English official report, "truly fearful" (MEW 23:273;
> CAP 1:258).

> The cheapening of labour-power, by sheer abuse of the labour of
> women and children, by sheer robbery of every normal condition
> requisite for working and living, and by the sheer brutality of
> over-work and night-work, meets at last with natural obstacles that
> cannot be overstepped (MEW 23:494; CAP 1:470).

The prophetic indignation of Marx is indistinguishable from that of
Jesus Christ (Matt. 23 and John 2:12–22) and the Old Testament
prophets. It plays such an important and recurring role in his work that it
does not need to be documented. It crops up frequently in his articles for
the press:

> It is understandable that the working population should become
> indignant over this excess taxation (*Neue Oder-Zeitung,* 7 March
> 1855; MEW 11:107).

> . . . chief participant in an extremely irritating action (NYDT, 2
> March 1855; MEW 11:103).

> No voice in all of Europe raises a cry of indignation (NYDT, 17
> May 1860; MEW 15:45).

> . . . the most crude and revolting form of military despotism (*The
> Daily News,* 19 January 1871; MEW 17:284).

> By the whipping of women and other fearful brutalities they [the
> Hungarian generals] have covered themselves with ignominy
> (NYDT, 6 June 1859; MEW 13:335).

In all of these cases Marx's indignation is objectively justified and is
an essential part of his message and its thrust. This is probably more true
of *Capital* than of any other of his works.

This links up with the theme of my previous chapter (Section V). The specific and irreplaceable historical efficacy of scientific socialism is the conscious presupposition of Marx's whole effort to arouse the proletariat. Deliberate efforts to enlighten and arouse indignation in people would be ridiculous if history were going to accomplish what it has to accomplish whether they existed or not. Increasing productivity is not the only way in which science serves as an indispensable cause in altering the course of history. Of course scientific socialism must exert some impact on the mode of production specifically; otherwise it would not be effective and society would continue to reproduce itself in its present form. But scientific socialism is the solution to a problem, and a solution is not wholly brought about by the mere existence of the problem (the capitalist mode of production in this case). Scientific socialism, therefore, has another role to play. In an obituary notice entitled "The Burial of Karl Marx," which appeared in *Der Sozialdemokrat* on 22 March 1883, Engels wrote this:

> For Marx was, before anything else, a revolutionary. To cooperate in one way or another in the overthrow of capitalist society and the government institutions created by it; to cooperate in the liberation of the modern proletariat, *whom he was the first to make aware of the conditions underlying their emancipation:* that was truly the vocation of his life. . . . For Marx science was a *moving force* in history, a revolutionary force (MEW 19:336; my italics).

It is not correct, then, that the ideas of scientific socialism arose first in the minds of the workers. According to Engels, in fact, it was Marx who gave them those ideas. Of course, the analysis of capitalist production could not exist if capitalist production itself did not exist; but that is a precondition, not a cause. To those who might suggest that his science was produced by industry, Marx would undoubtedly reply in somewhat the same vein as he replied to Adam Smith with regard to the natural sciences. He would say that the evidence for a causal nexus belies any such hypothesis because his science arose in learned circles, not in laboring circles. In fact Marx had this to say about his economic work in a letter to Kugelmann dated 28 December 1862: "The *scientific* efforts to revolutionize a science can never be really popular. But once the scientific foundation is laid, then popularization is already easy" (MEW 30:640).

Clearly the chronological order is: (1) in the minds of scientific scholars; (2) popularization. It is absurd to suppose that Marx's view was otherwise, that he thought that his scientific socialism began on the level of the people and then entered the mind of a scholar named Karl Marx. When Marx was buried on 17 March 1883, Engels had this to say among other things in his brief graveside eulogy:

> Marx saw his economic theories transformed into the indisputable starting principle of socialism throughout the world (MEW 19:334).

In a letter dated 14 October 1892, Engels wrote to Laura Lafargue about the miners of Carmaux who had been on strike since August:

> Carmaux demonstrates not only the progress of our ideas among the ranks of the workers but also the fact that the bourgeoisie and the government *know* it (MEW 38:493 f.).

In a letter to Marx himself dated 14 October 1868, Engels informs him that the Cologne newspaper reports

> that in Gladbach the cotton *manufacturers* have become convinced that the working day is too long. They are forming an association among themselves to reduce it from 13 to 12 hours (12 October issue). Already you see how your book is exercising practical influence, on the bourgeoisie as well (MEW 32:183).

In a letter to Bebel dated 30 August 1883, Engels talks about a substantial group of Britishers who are organizing a Democratic Federation in London. He goes on to say:

> The only important thing is that now at last they are obliged openly to proclaim our theory as their own, whereas during the period of the International it seemed to them to be imposed on them from outside; and also that recently a lot of young people stemming from the bourgeoisie have appeared on the scene who, to the disgrace of the English workers it must be said, understand things better and take them up more enthusiastically than the workers themselves (MEW 36:57; SCME:343).

In a letter to Florence Kelley Wischnewetsky dated 3 December 1887, Engels had this to say:

> And I have always found that a good book finds its way and has an impact, no matter what the scribblers may say (MEW 36:727).

Notes

1. The original is in English. There is a photocopy of the original in MEW 10, opposite page 128. In this case I think the editors of the MEW made a serious mistake in translating ''men'' by the German word for ''males.'' There may well have been women in the Labour Parliament. Even if there were not, Marx here undoubtedly was using the word ''men'' in the sense of ''human beings,'' as he often did.

2. In one of the back Appendices of his latest book on Marx, David McLellan gives Marx's answers to a Victorian parlor game. For his favorite maxim, Marx cites this maxim of Terence. See D. McLellan, *Karl Marx: His Life and Thought,* New York: Harper & Row, Publishers, 1973.

6

The Moral Content of Marx's Economic Analysis

Those who deny that Marx's message is a moral one and appeal to his writings to prove their point proceed in a curious way. They cut short Marx's statements, usually about half-way through, and then try to offer an interpretation on that basis. In many instances Marx is still in the protasis of his statement; he has not yet gotten to the main clause of his sentence.

Marx's discourse is profound and his statements are often lengthy. He will begin with some sort of conditional or concessive clause—e.g., "although it is true that . . ."—and then write on in this vein, piling clause upon clause and gradually building to a high point. Then there comes a pause and a "however" or "nevertheless," and Marx begins to offer his own thinking as he descends to a close. The interpreters in question interrupt his sentence half-way through and present that to their readers as if that were the whole of Marx's statement. Obviously such an interpretative approach is invalid.

This present chapter could also have been entitled the "apparent immorality" of Marx's analysis. However, we have already seen how profoundly moral Marx's humanism is, and so such a title would be artificial and affected. We would do better to offer a concise exposition of the core of Marx's economic analysis. From within that context it will be much easier to clarify the real import of certain negations uttered by Marx, negations that have been spread around the world and commented on with much fanfare by both Marxist and anti-Marxist authors but that are, in fact, the very opposite of a negation of morality. Simply for the sake of brevity I will refrain from referring explicitly to these commentaries and will try to offer a positive presentation of Marx's own thought.

I

In Book I of *Capital* we read the following passage, which will start us out in the right direction:

> Ricardo never concerns himself about the origin of surplus-value. He treats it as a thing inherent in the capitalist mode of production, which mode, in his eyes, is the natural form of social production. Whenever he discusses the productiveness of labour, he seeks in it, not the cause of surplus-value, but the cause that determines the magnitude of that value. . . . In fact these bourgeois economists instinctively saw, and rightly so, that it is very dangerous to stir too deeply the burning question of the origin of surplus-value (MEW 23:539; CAP 1:515–16).

According to Marx, the real problem is the *existence* of surplus-value, not its greater or lesser quantity. The issue to be explored is why surplus value began to exist and why it continues to exist, not why it tends to be larger or smaller. Its magnitude is one thing, its very existence is quite another thing:

> Suppose now such an eastern bread-cutter requires 12 working-hours a week for the satisfaction of all his wants. Nature's direct gift to him is plenty of leisure time. Before he can apply this leisure time productively for himself, a whole series of historical events is required; before he spends it in surplus-labour for strangers, compulsion is necessary. If capitalist production were introduced, the honest fellow would perhaps have to work six days a week, in order to appropriate to himself the product of one working-day. The bounty of Nature does not explain why he would then have to work 6 days a week, or why he must furnish 5 days of surplus-labour. It explains only why his necessary labour-time would be limited to one day a week. But in no case would his surplus-product arise from some occult quality inherent in human labour (MEW 23:538; CAP 1:515).

Here we would do well to recall what some of these terms mean and how Marx views them. Necessary labour refers to the number of working hours required to produce the maintenance of the worker, or the number of hours he must work in order to produce the goods he needs for his own subsistence. Surplus labor refers to the number of hours that he actually works above and beyond the hours of necessary labor.

Marx also makes a distinction between use value and exchange value. (When he uses the term "value," it should be understood as exchange value.) Use value is the quality of an object whereby its physical properties are capable of satisfying some real or apparent needs of the person who consumes or uses it. Exchange value is the capacity of an object to be interchanged for other objects. These two kinds of value are so far from being identical that air, for example, has enormous use value but no exchange value at all.

Those who deny Marx's theory of value have not gone back in their imagination to the time when there was no commodity because there was nothing to exchange, because human work produced only what was necessary for basic subsistence. Exchange value did not exist; only use value existed. Surplus labor did not exist; only necessary labor existed. If nature was more fertile in one region than in other places, then the people there worked less time; and in any case they only produced what was necessary to live. They produced goods for use, not commodities. There was no wealth because wealth is the portion of the total product that is not consumed.

Surplus labor began to exist when people began to devote a part of their free time to making tools—the most rudimentary being hunting and fishing equipment. The first wealth in human history was made up of these objects fashioned by surplus labor. Surplus labor also included the time employed in looking for and collecting certain objects that attracted people's attention (rare stones, feathers, metals) and that were promptly reduced to a merely ornamental function.

By definition the values produced by surplus labor are surplus value. Obviously only these can be objects of exchange and barter. By definition the product of necessary labor is consumed. Originally exchange value could consist only of surplus value; everything else was use value.

As productivity increased—i.e., the yield in products per work hour—the number of hours of necessary labor kept on diminishing. With good arrows or snares people could catch more game in a hour than they could with their bare hands. Human beings had more free time at their disposal, and they could devote it either to surplus labor or leisure.

For barter, value had to be put on objects in some way. Circumstances being equal, the only possible measure was the number of work hours needed to produce or find the object in question. For example, no one would trade a deer for a rabbit because the hunt for the former entails more hours of human effort. No one would trade a gold bracelet for an onyx bracelet because under ordinary circumstances it takes more hours to find and extract gold than to find and extract onyx. With the growth of productivity human beings could also accumulate foodstuffs and clothing, and so they began to trade these types of objects as well. But the measure of value was the number of work hours, as mentioned above, because there could be no other.

The measure of value was concretized in a particular kind of object, in cows, for example. This particular diamond is worth so many cows. This shipment of maize is worth fewer cows than the diamond is. Later it became more practical to take as the unit for measuring value a certain class of objects that concentrated a great deal of value in a small weight, that was readily transportable, and that could be conserved without undergoing alteration. Thus gold and silver became generally accepted as the measure of value.

However, no class of objects could have fulfilled this function if there had been no common denominator between that class and all other classes of objects. The need for a mediator between heterogeneous types is not solved by a type that is as heterogeneous from them as they are from each other. The only common denominator present in all the exchangeable objects is the labor employed in producing them. Objects are not comparable or commensurable with each other on the basis of their respective physical qualities. The historical fact of interchange shows that human beings attributed value to the various types of objects (including gold and silver) on the basis of the amount of labor required for the production of each.

Let us get back, then, to the origin of value (exchange value). The accumulation of wealth can only come about insofar as the workers produce it in hours of work that are not needed to produce the goods required for the sustenance of the workers. Thus the origin of exchange value is identical with the origin of surplus labor and with the origin of surplus value.

During the Middle Ages the difference between necessary labor and surplus labor was very tangible. The serfs performed necessary labor in their own fields and surplus labor in the fields or castle of their lord. It was obviously extraeconomic forces that forced them to perform surplus labor. Today the direct laborers perform both types of labor in the same place because they do not possess their own means of production as did the medieval serfs (i.e., their own fields). But neither the serfs nor today's laborers would perform surplus labor if there were real freedom. As we saw in Marx's critique of the Gotha Programme, the modern proletariat is not allowed to work for its own subsistence unless it does a certain number of hours of surplus labor for the benefit of those who own the means of production.

The working masses would have every right to refuse to work more than they are required to produce their own means of subsistence. Here someone might object that there is a need to create reserves of goods and to increase the quantity of the means of production. I would answer that with a question of my own: why do these reserves of goods and the increased means of production have to belong to people other than the workers? The working masses could refuse to work unless this surplus remained in their hands as owners. If they are constrained to work, they are constrained by hunger and violence. The new means of production fashioned by the workers will undoubtedly belong to the owners of business, but by virtue of coercion, plunder, and spoliation.

Now this formulation of the issue could have been presented in the thirteenth century. The powerful of that age would have solved the issue by violence, even as today's potentates do. And the means of production accumulated over the last seven centuries have the same origin, i.e., forced surplus labor. The actual ownership of the means of production enjoyed by the business people is what makes them think they have a right to keep the product of today's surplus labor. But all this property is surplus value that has been snatched from the workers by violence. It is contaminated in its very origin, and the fact that the current owners have purchased it changes nothing. As Marx puts it:

> In the same way, the slave-holder considers a Negro, whom he has purchased, as his property, not because the institution of slavery as such entitles him to that Negro, but because he has acquired him like any other commodity, through sale and purchase. But the title itself is simply transferred, and not created by the sale. The title must exist before it can be sold, and a series of sales can no more create this title through continued repetition than a single sale can (MEW 25:784; CAP 3:776).

All the materialized value in the world was produced by surplus labor and hence is surplus value. That holds true for the means of labor that exist today as well. The fact that these means have been purchased by the present business owners does not give them any right because the title to ownership must exist before it can be purchased. Just as one sale or purchase cannot create this title, so neither can a series of such sales endlessly repeated.

What I have expounded in the present chapter is the very core of Marx's economic analysis. Can anyone of sound judgment maintain that this analysis prescinds from morality? Doesn't Marx's analysis demonstrate the injustice and illegitimacy of private ownership of the means of production?

II

Now let us see where mistaken interpretation of Marx comes from. In Book I of *Capital* Marx is explaining that only labor power produces more value than it itself contains. He puts it in these words:

> But the past labour that is embodied in the labour-power, and the living labour that it can call into action; the daily cost of maintaining it, and its daily expenditure in work, are two totally different things. The former determines the exchange-value of the labour-power, the latter is its use-value. The fact that half a day's labour is necessary to keep the labourer alive during 24 hours, does not in any way prevent him from working a whole day. Therefore, the value of labour-power, and the value which that labour-power creates in the labour-process, are two entirely different magnitudes (MEW 23:207 f.; CAP 1:193).

But then Marx proceeds to add a most important analysis that has occasioned the mistaken views about his allegedly amoral standpoint:

> . . . this difference of the two values was what the capitalist had in view, when he was purchasing the labour-power. The useful qualities that labour-power possesses, and by virtue of which it makes yarn or boots, were to him nothing more than a conditio sine qua non; for in order to create value, labour must be expended in a useful manner. The decisive point was the specific use-value which this commodity possesses of being *a source not only of value, but of more value than it has itself.* This is the special service that the capitalist expects from labour-power, and in this transaction he acts in accordance with the "eternal laws" of the exchange of commodities. The seller of labour-power, like the seller of any other commodity, realises its exchange-value, and parts with its use-value. He cannot take the one without giving the other. The use-value of labour-power or in other words, labour, belongs just as little to its seller, as the use-value of oil after it has been sold belongs to the dealer who has sold it. The owner of the money has paid the value of a day's labour-power; his, therefore, is the use of it for a day; a day's labour belongs to him. The circumstance that on the one hand the daily sustenance of labour-power costs only half a day's labour, while on the other hand the very same labour-power can work during a whole day, that consequently the value which the use during one day creates, is double what he pays for that use, this circumstance is, without doubt, a piece of good luck for the buyer, but by no means an injury to the seller (MEW 23:208; cf. CAP 1:193–94).

Those who have seen a hint of amorality in this passage have missed the point completely. What we have here is antireformism, not just expressed as a wish but spelled out in black and white. This brilliant passage asserts that the wage contract does not infringe any of the rights stipulated by the eternal laws of commodity interchange. It thereby shows that if people want to suppress social injustices, they must suppress the production of commodities as such. So long as the commodity mode of production persists, the ongoing plunder of surplus value by the business owners is not only legal but absolutely inevitable.

I said above that Marx's misinterpreters mutilate what he says. Here we find a clear example of this practice. What they do in this case is take the last two sentences, or the passage beginning with "the seller of labour-power . . ." and leave out the preceding clause which sets the proper stage for it: "in this transaction he acts in accordance with the 'eternal laws' of the exchange of commodities." Everything that follows that clause is an explanation of how those laws work. So long as the wage system, or capitalism, is maintained, exploitation does not depend on the good or ill will of the owners; the system itself entails exploitation. The whole passage above, like the whole work in question, is a procommunist allegation proved with reasoning rather than with mere rhetoric.

As early as the *Economic and Philosophic Manuscripts of 1844* Marx had written: "M. Michel Chevalier accuses Ricardo of abstracting from morality. But Ricardo allows political economy to speak its own language. If this language is not that of morality, it is not the fault of Ricardo" (MEW/EB 1:551; VEW:362–63). These three sentences, too, have been flourished left and right. But what they say is that the economic reality called capitalism is immoral.

A. Wagner had interpreted Book I of *Capital* in exactly the opposite way from that of the mistaken proponents of Marx's amorality. Wagner had gone to the other extreme, claiming that the capitalist simply robs and subtracts things from the worker according to Marx. In his reply Marx explains his view in the manner we have indicated above:

> In reality, however, in my exposition the profit of capital is not "only a *subtraction* or 'robbery' committed against the worker." On the contrary, I present the capitalist as a necessary functionary of capitalist production; and I show very amply that he not only "subtracts" or "robs" but also compels *surplus-value to be produced,* that is to say, that he first helps to create what he is going to subtract. Furthermore, I show at length that even when *only equivalents* are exchanged in the interchange of commodities, the capitalist—to the extent that he pays the worker the true value of his labor-power—wins the surplus-value by full right; that is to say, by the lawful right that corresponds to this mode of production. But none of that means that the "profit of capital" is a *"constitutive" element* of value; it simply and solely proves that in the value

not "constituted" by the labor of the capitalist there is a portion which he can "legally" appropriate for himself, that is to say, without infringing the lawful right which accords with the interchange of commodities (MEW 19:359).

Book I of *Capital* was speaking in exactly the same sense when it pointed out that the wage contract does not represent any injustice committed against the seller of labor power. (The German term *Unrecht* used by Marx can mean "injustice" or "illegality.") The two times that Marx employs the word *Recht* ("law" or right") in his *Marginal Notes on A. Wagner's Lehrbuch* (1879–80), he very carefully adds a qualifying phrase, either "the right which accords with this mode of production," or "the right which accords with the interchange of commodities." Just as in *Capital* he pointed out that we are dealing here with the eternal laws of commodity interchange.

That is why it is not "only a robbery." The capitalist is behaving in accordance with the prevailing laws, and those laws do not depend on the whims of the legislators but are a necessary result when the economic system consists in the production of exchange values. If you want to alter something, you must replace the mode of production. When Wagner talked about Marx's theory as seeing capitalism as nothing more than robbery, the implication was that there was a specific act in violation of the prevailing laws. But in this case, replies Marx, the existing laws not only do not prohibit the robbery but actually give it legal shape and status. And of course the "eternal" nature of the laws governing commodity exchange is purely conditional: that is to say, if the mode of production is based on commodities, then those laws must necessarily govern the situation.

Marx's antireformism is implacable, as befits the person who has discovered the key to the whole social problem. To talk about more or less justice in capitalism is to presume that there can be justice without changing the mode of production, that capitalism can be just. In Book III of *Capital* Marx confronts Gilbart. According to the latter, natural justice demands that if someone borrows money to make a profit with it, then he must pay a part of his profits to the lender. Marx offers this comment, which has been misinterpreted as a relativist one:

> To speak here of natural justice, as Gilbart does, . . . is nonsense. The justice of the transactions between agents of production rests on the fact that these arise as natural consequences out of the production relationships. The juristic forms in which these economic transactions appear as wilful acts of the parties concerned, as expressions of their common will and as contracts that may be enforced by law against some individual party, cannot,

being mere forms, determine this content. They merely express it. This content is just whenever it corresponds, is appropriate, to the mode of production. It is unjust whenever it contradicts that mode. Slavery on the basis of capitalist production is unjust; likewise fraud in the quality of commodities (MEW 25:351 f.; CAP 3:339–40).

Note well what Marx is trying to say. To talk about natural justice within the capitalist system is to imply that capitalism is the natural mode of production and can be just, when in fact it is the most refined systematization of exploitation. In particular, to talk about natural justice when the business owner and the banker split the profit is like talking about natural justice when a band of thieves split their take. When it is a question of interest-bearing capital, the participants obey the laws of the capitalist mode of production and the laws of the State give juridical form to this content. The contract is just in that sense, but it has nothing to do with natural justice. Natural justice remains wholly outside the capitalist system of production, and a little further on we shall hear Marx passing judgment on that whole system in the name of natural justice.

If one talks with capitalists living today, one quickly realizes that the danger of declaring the wage system and commodity production to be natural is far from being an imaginary one. It is unthinkable to those people that one could imagine the possibility of another mode of production. Their rustic ingenuousness is astounding. They are like peasants buried in some remote valley amid the hills who cannot believe that anything else might possibly exist besides the things they have seen all their lives. Consider Marx's analysis of this same mentality in Book I of *Capital,* where he is talking about Proudhon:

> Proudhon begins by taking his ideal of justice of "justice éternelle," from the juridical relations that correspond to the production of commodities: thereby, it may be noted, he *proves,* to the consolation of all good citizens, *that the production of commodities is a form of production as everlasting as justice.* Then he turns around and seeks to reform the actual production of commodities, and the actual legal system corresponding thereto, in accordance with this ideal. What opinion should we have of a chemist, who, *instead of studying the actual laws of the molecular changes in the composition and decomposition of matter, and on that foundation solving definite problems,* claimed to regulate the composition and decomposition of matter by means of the "eternal ideas" of "naturalité" and "affinité"? Do we really know any more about "usury," when we say it contradicts "justice éternelle," "équité éternelle," "mutualité éternelle," and other

"verités éternelles" than the fathers of the church did when they said it was incompatible with "grâce éternelle," "foi éternelle," and "la volonté éternelle de Dieu"? (MEW 23:99f., ftn. 38; CAP 1:84–85, ftn. 2; my italics).

The capitalists *cannot* pay the worker the full product of his labor, which is what superficial brands of socialism demand. Essentially such versions of socialism are reformist. Only with the means of production themselves could they pay the workers the complete result of their work. But then the business owners would cease to be capitalists, and the system itself would cease to exist; we would end up in communism. Until we understand and appreciate that point, we have not understood Marx's economic message:

> But strange to say, the great majority of my bourgeois critics upbraid me as though I have wronged the capitalists by assuming, for instance in Book I of *Capital,* that the capitalist pays labour-power at its real value, a thing which he mostly does not do! (MEW 24:504; CAP 5:09).

As we saw in Marx's reply to A. Wagner, even assuming that there never is any fraud and that equivalent values are interchanged, the capitalist would still have full right to keep the surplus value. For the right in question here is bound up with the commodity mode of production. In that mode of production the value of labor power is *in fact* the value of the necessaries required for the sustenance of the worker; and that is what the capitalist actually pays. There is no "only a robbery"; all there is here is the capitalist mode of production.

That is why Marx asks Proudhon: what do we gain by knowing that usury contradicts eternal justice? In what way does our knowledge of usury in those terms represent an advance over what the church fathers already knew? What we must do is study the real laws of production and find a solution on the basis of that study. And the real-life laws tell us that as long as the capitalist mode of production persists, it is impossible for the business owners to stop expropriating the surplus value for themselves and sharing it with their usurious lenders. The spoliation is systematic and structural, not personal. So how can they say that I do the capitalists an injustice?

The antimoralistic interpreters of Marx have been led astray by Marx's jibes about the goddesses justice, equity, liberty, mutuality, and fraternity. But here they have missed the boat. What Marx is saying is that we resolve nothing by appealing to these principles; that instead we must probe to see where exactly the injustice lies and attack it there. Otherwise all our moral rhetoric will be merely reformist. It will only help to shore up capitalism by giving the impression that there can be justice in the capitalist system. This reply to Proudhon and Gilbart in *Capital* was to some extent already implied in Marx's earlier criticism of the rhetorical feminism of George Frederick Daumer. In February 1850 Marx and Engels wrote this in the *Neue Rheinishche Zeitung:*

> It goes without saying that Mr. Daumer does not say one word about the actual social situation of women, but on the contrary deals with woman as such (MEW 7:202).

If we are not to talk about abstractions such as "woman" or "justice," we must analyze the split of society into two classes—the possessors and the dispossessed; and we must recognize and explore the fact that legislation and rights must be structured in such a way as to preserve property ownership by transmitting it from one generation to another. For without this structuring the capitalist mode of production would collapse. If Daumer had wanted to be concrete and to talk about real living women existing today, then he would have had to show, as we saw in Chapter 5, that the production process is not a means to serve subjects, their development as persons, and the most authentic relations between them; that it is rather an end to whose service persons are to be subjected by stifling everything in them that is an obstacle to such service.

Marx's mockery of the goddesses justice, equity, and so forth can be found in his letter to Sorge dated 19 October 1877. There he expresses his repudiation of a socialism that seeks "to replace its materialistic basis (which demands serious objective study from anyone who tries to use it) by modern mythology with its goddesses of Justice, Liberty, Equality, and Fraternity" (MEW 34:303; SCME:290).

Trying to solve things with rhetorical combinations of those lofty principles is to proceed as if Marx had not contributed anything, as if he had not demonstrated the concrete roots of the ongoing plunder committed against the working classes. That does not mean, however, that Marx prescinds from justice or is guided by who knows what else. It simply means that Marx wants real, radical, definitive justice rather than the justice of bombastic rhetoric. Engels put the point very well in his article "A Fair Day's Wage for a Fair Day's Work," which was published in *The Labour Standard* on 7 May 1881:

> But what is a fair day's wage, and what is a fair day's work? How are they determined by the laws under which modern society exists and develops itself? For an answer to this we must not apply to the science of morals or of law and equity, nor to any sentimental

feeling of humanity, justice, or even charity. What is morally fair, what is even fair in law, may be far from being socially fair. Social fairness or unfairness is decided by one science alone—the science which deals with the material facts of production and exchange, the science of political economy (MEW 19:247; SW:98).

Here is the reason why Marx and Engels leave aside the science of morality and take up economic science: they want to be able to make a decision about justice or injustice on the basis of sound knowledge of the underlying cause. That is not prescinding from morality but rather providing the means for justice to be realized. Only economic analysis can tell us what goes to make up justice and injustice. Let us stay with Engels' article for a moment. A page later he writes:

> The transaction, then, may be thus described—the workman gives to the capitalist his full day's working power; that is, so much of it he can give without rendering impossible the continuous repetition of the transaction. In exchange he receives just as much, and no more, of the necessities of life as is required to keep up the repetition of the same bargain every day. The workman gives as much, the capitalist gives as little, as the nature of the bargain will admit. *This is a very peculiar sort of fairness* (MEW 19:248; SW:99; my italics).

In writing the last sentence cited here, Engels was obviously speaking in the name of a sort of justice or fairness that is real justice. Only someone who had a criterion of authentic fairness could write ironically about "a very peculiar sort of fairness." This passage confirms what was said in the previous passage cited: only objective economic analysis enables us to know what goes to make up justice; moral science lacks a sufficient number of elements for making such a judgment and spelling it out unmistakably.

As Marx said in his attack on Proudhon in *Capital,* we will simply continue with perorations against usury and we will have made no progress since the time of the church fathers unless we undertake an economic analysis that gets to the bottom of the matter. Far from being amoral, the position of Marx and Engels is a more demanding morality than any before it. This is confirmed by the following passage from the same article by Engels:

> The capitalist, if he cannot agree with the labourer, can afford to wait, and live upon his capital. The workman cannot. He has but wages to live upon, and must therefore take work when, where,

and at what terms he can get it. The workman has no fair start. He is fearfully handicapped by hunger. Yet, according to the political economy of the capitalist class, that is the very pink of fairness (MEW 19:248; SW:99).

Here again the irony is obviously grounded on some criterion of what real justice is. Since the extortion and blackmail described above is the utmost to which the capitalist system can aspire in the way of justice or fairness, scientific socialism evidently wants a system that goes much further—or rather, a system of authentic justice. And only economic analysis can decide that.

In *Socialism: Utopian and Scientific* (1880), Engels sums up Marx's contribution in these crystal-clear terms:

> The earlier socialism certainly criticized the existing capitalist mode of production and its consequences. But it could not explain this mode of production, and, therefore, could not get the mastery of it. It could only simply reject it as evil. The more violently it denounced the exploitation of the working class, which is insepar- able from capitalism, *the less able was it clearly to show in what this exploitation consists and how it arises.* But for this it was necessary, on the one hand, to present the capitalist mode of production in its historical interconnection and its necessity for a specific historical period, and therefore also the necessity of its doom; and, on the other, to lay bare its essential character, which was still hidden. *This was done by the discovery of surplus-value.* It was shown that the appropriation of unpaid labour is the basic form of the capitalist mode of production and of the exploitation of the worker effected by it; that even if the capitalist buys the labour-power of his worker at the full value it possesses as a commodity on the market, he still extracts more value from it than he paid for; and that in the last analysis this surplus-value forms those sums of value from which there is heaped up the constantly increasing mass of capital in the hands of the possessing classes. The process both of capitalist production and of the production of capital was explained (MEW 19:208 f.; SUS:72–73; my italics).

In other words, pre-Marx brands of socialism were not able to pin-point in what the exploitation consisted. Thus their protests, criticisms, and rejections remained up in the air; they were reduced to invoking the goddess justice. Through his discovery of surplus value Marx was the first to demonstrate that there was exploitation and to pinpoint its exact nature. Far from prescinding from justice or injustice, Marx gave real, precise content to these words.

Now let us see how Marx himself describes the contrast between scientific socialism and the versions of socialism that preceded it. It is a priceless passage, which will utterly astonish all superficial Marxists who gaily mock utopian versions of socialism. We find it in the first draft (1871) of *The Civil War in France:*

> From the moment the working men's class movement became real, the fantastic utopias evanesced, *not because the working class had given up the end aimed at by these utopians, but because they had found the real means to realize them,* and in their place came a real insight into the historic conditions of the movement and a more and more gathering force of the militant organization of the working class. But the last two ends of the movement proclaimed by the utopians *are the last ends proclaimed by the Paris revolution and by the International. Only the means are different,* and the real conditions of the movement are no longer clouded in utopian fables (MEW 17:557; VFI:262; my italics).

If we were to try to formulate the relationship between Marx's socialism and that which went before, we could not be more explicit and precise than Marx was in the above passage. The ideals of justice espoused by earlier brands of socialism remain perfectly intact. Only the means to realize those ideals of justice are now different. And the reason for this, says Marx in all modesty, is that the real historical conditions have now been discovered; or, as Engels puts it, the reason is that Marx discovered surplus value—the real functioning and basic form of the capitalist mode of production.

This would be the place to cite again the passage from the *Critique of the Gotha Programme* that was presented in Chapter 1 of this volume (see pp. 24–25). With the discovery of surplus value it becomes evident that wages are not payment for labor but rather for labor power, since that is what is reproduced with the foodstuffs whose value is equivalent to wages. Hence labor power really is worth what the employer pays. If the use of this peculiar commodity (labor power) produces value, that is lucky for the purchaser, but the latter commits no wrong by paying for the commodity what it is worth. There is nothing to be done, for such are the eternal laws governing the exchange of commodities. If we want to change something, as all the various brands of socialism do, we must replace the present mode of production with another that does not produce commodities. And that is communism. *That is why* Marx and Engels make the following statement in their *Circular Letter* of 1879:

> When the class struggle is rejected as a disagreeable "coarse" phenomenon, nothing remains as the basis of socialism other than

"true love of humanity" and empty phrases about "justice" (MEW 34:406; VFI:373).

If we want to abolish the capitalist mode of production, the class struggle is unavoidable. Aside from a fight aimed at the elimination of capitalism, the only feasible course is to exhort people to love, and talk endlessly and vaguely about justice. Seeking the establishment of justice, Marx's message proposes to be much more realistic and effective than escapist courses disguised as worry and concern.

The commodity mode of production—or, the production of commodities as such—existed long before capitalism. The point brought out by the first five chapters of Book I of *Capital* is that once the production of commodities arises in history, the latter will inevitably lead to capitalism. As Marx puts it in the *Grundrisse:* "It is just as pious as it is stupid to wish that exchange value would not develop into capital, nor labour which produces exchange value into wage labour" (GRU:249).

That is why Marx's analysis does not need to focus on the fraud committed by capitalists in their transactions. The uninterrupted looting of surplus value does not depend on that. Or, as Marx puts it in his reply to A. Wagner:

> I show at length that even when *only equivalents* are exchanged in the interchange of commodities, the capitalist—to the extent that he pays the worker the true value of his labor-power—wins the surplus-value by full right; that is to say, by the lawful right that corresponds to this mode of production (MEW 19:359).

We do well to note here that this supposition—i.e., that only equivalents are exchanged—is a deliberate and systematic one on Marx's part and runs through all the volumes of *Capital* and *Theories of Surplus Value*. It is the assumption "that all commodities, including labour-power, are bought and sold at their full value" (MEW 23:333; CAP 1:314). Indeed Marx reflects explicitly on the fact that he is making this supposition throughout the works cited above (see MEW 23:542; MEW 24:32, 70, 120, 131, 353; MEW 25:60, 61, 118, 123, 159, 163, 186 f., 203; MEW 26/1:106; MEW 26/2:493, 515; MEW 26/3:192).

The supposition, then, is a systematic phenomenon worthy of notice. Daily experience tells us that fraud is committed in many capitalist transactions. The unwary reader might therefore be tempted to criticize this abstract supposition of Marx, to say that he is too far removed from reality in using it throughout his work. This objection, however, loses sight of Marx's basic point which underlies his whole treatment, namely, that the injustice of capitalism does not depend on fraud and deceit due to the moral perversity of persons; the system itself consists in the ongoing expoliation of surplus value. The two adversaries that Marx is aiming at throughout his work are the ardent defendants of capitalism on the one hand and on the other hand the proponents of reformism who think that the social problem can be solved by correcting certain things. These two adversaries were on Marx's mind from the very start of his economic investigation. Here is what Marx writes to Engels in a letter dated 22 July 1859 with regard to the CCPE which had appeared a month before:

> You have forgotten to write me whether you are thinking about making some point with regard to my work. . . . In the event that you write something, it should be kept in mind: (1) that Proudhonism is demolished root and branch, (2) that already in its simplest form, that of the commodity, the *specifically* social and by no means *absolute* character of bourgeois production is analyzed (MEW 29:463).

Let us pick up the thread again by reiterating that an abstract appeal to justice is not enough to point up exactly what constitutes injustice. Though Marx scoffs at such appeals, this does not mean that he is no longer being guided by the ideal of justice. It means exactly the opposite: he wants to spell out concretely and scientifically how we arrive at justice. The official proceedings of the meeting of the General Council of the International held on 6 July 1869 record some words of Marx which elucidate the matter in the same vein that we have seen above:

> Pointing up the social necessity is a stronger argument than appealing to the demands of abstract right. Any and every form of oppression has been justified in terms of abstract right; now is the time to put an end to that agitation. *The question is how this right is to be made real* (MEW 16:558; my italics).

Right does not cease to be the norm for Marx, but the important thing is how right and justice can be turned into reality. The ideals and aims of socialism before Marx are maintained: "only the means are different." In *Value, Price and Profit,* originally an address in English delivered at two sessions of the General Council of the First International (20 and 27 June 1865), Marx brings out the same point in the following passage:

> The cry for an *equality of wages* rests, therefore, upon a mistake, is an inane wish never to be fulfilled. It is an offspring of that false and superficial radicalism that accepts premises and tries to evade conclusions. Upon the basis of the wages system the value of labouring power is settled like that of every other commodity; and as different kinds of labouring power have different values, or

require different quantities of labour for their production, they *must* fetch different prices in the labour market. To clamour for *equal or even equitable retribution* on the basis of the wages system is the same as to clamour for *freedom* on the basis of the slavery system. What you think just or equitable is out of the question. The question is: What is necessary and unavoidable with a given system of production? (MEW 16:131 f.; VPP:39–40 in WLCVPP).

All of Marx's writings explain the issue in the same way. Those who have seen a rejection of the moral criterion of justice in Marx's thesis— i.e., that the capitalist does not wrong anyone by keeping the surplus value—prove that they did not keep on reading *Capital*. Here I am going to cite a long passage from Chapter 24 of Book I in which Marx spells out the balance sheet of the capitalist mode of production and makes it clear that it is the real result. This end result was constantly present in Marx's mind as he presented his reasoning in Book I:

> . . . insofar as each single transaction invariably conforms to the laws of the exchange of commodities, the capitalist buying labour-power, the labourer selling it, and we will assume at its real value; insofar as all this is true, it is evident that the laws of appropriation or of private property, laws that are based on the production and circulation of commodities, become by their own inner and inexorable dialectic changed into their very opposite. The exchange of equivalents, the original operation with which we started, has now become turned round in such a way that there is only an apparent exchange. This is owing to the fact, first, that the capital which is exchanged for labour-power is itself but a portion of the product of others' labour appropriated without an equivalent; and, secondly, that this capital must not only be replaced by its producer, but replaced together with an added surplus. The relation of exchange subsisting between capitalist and labourer becomes a mere semblance appertaining to the process of circulation, a mere form, foreign to the real nature of the transaction, and only mystifying it. The ever repeated purchase and sale of labour-power is now the mere form; what really takes place is this—the capitalist again and again appropriates, without equivalent, a portion of the previously materialised labour of others, and exchanges it for a greater quantity of living labour. At first the rights of property seemed to us to be based on a man's own labour. At least, some such assumption was necessary since only commodity-owners with equal rights confronted each other, and the sole means by which a man could become possessed of the com-

modities of others, was by alienating his own commodities; and these could be replaced by labour alone. Now, however, property turns out to be the right, on the part of the capitalist, to appropriate the unpaid labour of others or its product, and to be the impossibility, on the part of the labourer, of appropriating his own product. The separation of property from labour has become the necessary consequence of a law that apparently originated in their identity (MEW 23:609 f.; CAP 1:583–84).

In a less profound analysis but a more succinct style the *Grundrisse* had said the same thing: the processes of capitalism "are merely the realization of *equality and freedom,* which prove to be inequality and unfreedom" (GRU:249).

In the passage from *Capital* just cited above, Marx expressed his real message. All his earlier remarks, to the effect that there was no robbery involved and that lawful right was respected, were only the superficial guise borrowed from the sphere of circulation and commodity exchange and donned by the capitalist production process. Viewed from the inside, however, that process is really violent expoliation for which no retribution is given. The exchange of equivalents is the disguise that capitalism must necessarily wear. Hence when Book I of *Capital* was finally published, Engels rightly made the following comment on it in his review for the *Elberferder Zeitung* (2 November 1867):

> Fifty sheets of scholarly writing to show us that all the capital of our bankers, merchants, manufacturers and big landholders is nothing else but the accumulated but unpaid labor of the working class! (MEW 16:214).

And this is the book which neo-Marxists claim is devoid of moral judgments! The whole book is one big moral judgment, but proved by reasoning rather than by rhetoric. In the same book review Engels adds this:

> If all the accumulated capital of the possessor class is nothing else but "unpaid labor," it would seem to follow directly from this that this labor is to be paid later—i.e., that all the capital in question is to be transferred to labor (MEW 16:214).

On the same date (2 November 1867) the *Düsseldorfer Zeitung* published another review of Engels:

> And those who have eyes to see, see here quite clearly proposed the necessity of a social revolution. Here there is no question of

workers' associations with state capital, as was the case with the late Lassalle. Here it is clearly a question of the *suppression of capital* (MEW 16:216).

In another review of *Capital,* written for the *Rehinische Zeitung* on 12 October, Engels has this to say about Marx's work:

> After undertaking investigations that were obviously sincere and that were carried out with undeniably specialized preparation, he arrives at the conclusion that the whole capitalist "mode of production" must be abolished (MEW 16:210 f.).

In the review for the *Düsseldorfer Zeitung* cited above, Engels goes on to say: "Marx is and continues to be the same revolutionary that he has always been; and in a scientific piece of writing he certainly would be the last to hide his viewpoints in this vein" (MEW 16:216). On the following page Engels spells the matter out more fully:

> All the basic doctrines of the socialist theory, which are more or less familiar, come down to the fact that in present-day society the worker does not succeed in getting paid for the full value of the product of his labor. This assertion constitutes the guiding thread of the present work also. Only in this case it is spelled out more rigorously, studied with more consistent regard for its consequences, linked more closely with the principles of national economy or contrasted more directly with them, than it has ever been done before (MEW 16:217).

As we recall, Marx's view is that the worker is paid the value of his labor power but not the value of the product of his labor. According to the eternal laws of commodity production, he is not and need not be paid the latter value. Engels summarizes his thought well on this point, and shows where it necessarily leads.

It is not just that there is a moral judgment here, i.e., that the capitalist system involves plunder and exploitation. Marx's work, as Engels points out, leads to a categorical imperative of an undoubtedly moral nature: the capitalist system *must* be eradicated. Marx's whole economic analysis is designed to give grounds for this duty, this obligation. An observation in the *Grundrisse* is relevant here:

> This creation [of value] is identical with the appropriation of alien labour *without exchange,* and for that reason the bourgeois economists are never permitted to understand it clearly (GRU: 553).

The bourgeois never really understand morality. For that reason they have postulated a science devoid of value judgments so that they can understand everything right away. Marx never suspected that some of his own followers would champion the same postulate of voluntary intellectual blindness and psychic mutilation. But the most astounding thing of all is that they attribute to Marx the same tomfoolery for which he himself reproaches the bourgeois.

III

However, there is a second part to Marx's central balance sheet, his overall evaluation of capitalism on the basis of economic analysis. This second part is of the utmost importance, and we do not want to overlook it here. Marx writes:

It is every bit as important, for a correct understanding of surplus-value, to conceive it as a mere congelation of surplus labour-time, as nothing but materialised surplus-labour, as it is, for a proper comprehension of value, to conceive it as a mere congelation of so many hours of labour, as nothing but materialised labour. *The essential difference between the various economic forms of society,* between, for instance, a society based on slave-labour and one based on wage-labour, *lies only in the mode in which this surplus-value is in each case extracted from the actual producer, the labourer* (MEW 23:231; CAP 1:217; my italics).

I don't wish to dwell on this point too long, but the italicized sentence offers us a real key to the understanding of human history, and Marx was fully aware of that fact. In a society based on slave labor, all the products of labor legally belonged to the slave-holder. The slave-holder, however, had to devote a portion of this product to the sustenance of the slaves. Hence this portion was the product of necessary labor rather than of surplus labor. Of course, the important thing in the eyes of the slave holder was the surplus value, and hence surplus labor. And in this case direct, enslaving violence was the way in which surplus value was squeezed out of the direct producer (the slave laborer).

In the medieval system surplus value was again the important thing in the eyes of the lords. It might be extracted from the serfs by forcing them to do surplus labor in the fields of the lord himself or it might be extracted from them by forcing them to give a portion of the harvest from their own plots to the lord. The mode of extracting surplus value was really different in this case from that used in a system employing slave labor. But that is all that was different: the mode or way in which surplus value is extracted. The result was the same: extraction and accumulation of surplus value.

In our present wage system the mode of squeezing out surplus labor consists in the fact that all the means of production are the property of the owners, and that the latter will not allow people to use them unless they are willing to work a certain number of hours a day for the benefit solely of the proprietors. The mode or form is different, but the result is the same.

Obviously in all these three systems the exploiting class must cherish thoughts that tell them that the existing system, which is so nice for them, is a good one. Laws, ideas, and government must be framed in such a way that they dovetail with the way in which workers are constrained to provide surplus labor, which is the basis on which society continually reproduces itself in exactly the same form. The ideas and laws will obviously not say that the system entails undue coercion or exploitation. Although it is not true that all historical causes are ultimately caused by the economic factor, it is true that the mode of production is a cause that accounts for the particular way in which the superstructures are framed. It is a real and effective cause, but not the one and only cause. As elementary logic tells us: *affirmatio unius non est negatio alterius*.

Closely connected with this second part of Marx's central evaluation of capitalism is another basic assertion: since the growth of the capitalist mode of extracting surplus value shows us clearly that differing social formations differ only in their mode of doing this, the revolution against the capitalist mode of extracting surplus value will have to abolish any and all modes of extracting surplus value. Hence this revolution will have to abolish all exploitation, ruling out all the potential ways in which some human beings might plunder other human beings.

This aspect of Marx's thought, which clearly is not only moral but also Christian and eschatological, is something that we shall deal with in Chapter 10. Here I simply wanted to indicate where exactly it fits into his system.

Some people have read amorality in certain expressions that Marx himself called "stoic": in fact they have read amorality *into* them. They should have given more thought to the fact that *Capital* not only ends up unmasking the systematic plunder of surplus value (hidden under the guise of an exchange of equivalents), but also proposes to establish the formula that will enable us to spell out the *degree of exploitation* embodied in each portion of functioning capital. Marx devotes all of Chapter 18 of Book I to discussing various possible formulas or equations. At one point he says: "In all of these formulae . . . the actual degree of exploitation of labour, or the rate of surplus-value, is falsely expressed" (MEW 23:53; CAP 1:531).

In Chapter 14 of Book III the whole first section is devoted to the "increasing intensity of exploitation of labour" (MEW 25:242 f.; CAP 3:232 f.). In Chapter 15 the term *Exploitationsgrad* ("degree of exploitation") appears no less than twenty times. And the problem comes up again in Chapter 23. In *Theories of Surplus Value* Marx repeatedly talks about an increase in the degree of exploitation of the worker, so that one can scarcely count his references (see, for example, MEW 26/3:304, 305, 374, 485, 486, 487).

I don't know who exactly could come up with the idea that a book prescinds from moral judgments when it repeatedly makes statements like the following:

> As a producer of the activity of others, as a pumper-out of surplus-labour and exploiter of labour-power, it surpasses in energy, disregard of bounds, recklessness and efficiency, all earlier systems of production based on directly compulsory labour (MEW 23:328; CAP 1:309–10).

However, the most astounding thing is that some have been able to pin the label "amoral" on a science that appeals to conscience. As we saw earlier, in their *Critique of the Gotha Programme* Marx and Engels maintain that the inability of the leaders of the Social Democrats to understand Marx's analysis is due to their lack of moral conscience (*Gewissen*). I shall say something more about this in Chapter 11, but let me anticipate here with a passage from the *Grundrisse*:

> The bourgeois economists who regard capital as an eternal and *natural* (not historical) form of production then attempt at the same time to legitimize it again by formulating the conditions of its becoming as the conditions of its contemporary realization; i.e., presenting the moments in which the capitalist still appropriates as not-capitalist—because he is still becoming—as the very conditions in which he appropriates *as capitalist*. These attempts at apologetics demonstrate a guilty conscience . . . (GRU:460).

Now if an author accuses those who try to justify capitalism of having a guilty conscience right in the middle of his own economic analysis, then he is not only not prescinding from morality but counting on the existence of moral conscience in both himself and the reader so that his scientific message may be understood. Here moral conscience is an irreplaceable element. That is why, in the passage from the *Grundrisse* cited earlier, Marx wrote: ". . . and for that reason the bourgeois economists are never permitted to understand it clearly" (GRU:553).

To supplement what has been adduced so far in this chapter, I want to present a famous letter that Marx wrote to Engels on 4 November 1864. Here again, those who interpret Marx's thought as being amoral have been completely bamboozled by it. The letter, which recounts some of the background efforts involved in drafting the provisional rules and declaration of principles of the First International (which was just then coming into being), actually supports our proof of the morality of Marx and Engels. Here is the passage that seems to lend support to those who stress the amoral nature of Marx's thought:

> My proposals have all been accepted by the subcommittee. But I was obliged to insert two phrases about "duty" and "right" into the Preamble to the Rules, and also about "truth, morality and justice," but these are placed in such a way that they can do no harm (MEW 31:15; SCME:139).

I shall talk about duty and morality in the next chapter, and the reader will find it hard to believe that anyone ever thought of falsely accusing Marx and Engels of amorality. But the story behind the incident that Marx describes in his letter is really very simple, and it shows that Marx's would-be interpreters did not read his whole letter, that they zeroed in on the above passage, took it out of context as usual, and then based their interpretation on it.

We know the background of the incident from several sources. There is Marx's letter itself. There are the notes of the official editors of Marx's and Engels' complete works (MEW 22:618, ftn. 303). And there is an article by Engels in 1892 on Marx ("Marx, Heinrich Karl") for the *Handwörterbuch* of the Social Sciences published in Jena (MEW 22:37–45).

Through Wolff and Le Lubez, who like Marx were members of the provisional committee for setting up the International, Mazzini sought to "take over and win" (Engels: MEW 22:341) the budding organization for the already existing and powerful European liberal movement. The leader of the latter movement was Mazzini himself. With this aim in mind, Wolff and Le Lubez handed in a preliminary draft of the rules for the International based wholly on the rules of the Italian Workers' Associations, which were part of Mazzini's movement. The terminology used in their draft betrayed this origin clearly, so that the new organization would seem to be a branch of Mazzini's own movement. In addition to that, the rules "aim in fact at something that was utterly impossible, a sort of central government of the *European* working classes (with Mazzini in the background of course)" (MEW 31:14; SCME:138).

According to Engels, the final result of the debate was this:

> The draft of rules and of an inaugural discourse presented in Mazzini's name was rejected. The one drafted by Marx was preferred, and from then on the management of the International remained securely in Marx's hands (MEW 22:341).

Marx, however, gives us more details about the discussion and debate that went on in the provisional committee. Here is what he says:

> The whole Committee met on October 18. As Eccarius had written me that delay would be dangerous, I appeared and was really alarmed when I heard the worthy Le Lubez read out an appallingly wordy, badly written and quite raw preamble, pretending to be a declaration of principles, in which Mazzini could be detected everywhere, the whole coated with the vaguest scraps of French socialism. . . . I . . . was fully determined that if possible not one single line of the stuff should be allowed to stand . . . (MEW 31:14 f.; SCME:138–39).

In the course of the letter Marx relates all the maneuvers he used to alter the draft papers. He proposed that there be an inaugural discourse, and this task was entrusted to him. Then, on the grounds that the same things should not be repeated in the inaugural discourse and the preamble of the rules, he completely reworked the latter also. His reworking was accepted by the subcommittee, except for one change noted in the famous passage cited earlier: "But I was obliged to insert two phrases about 'duty' and 'right' into the Preamble of the Rules, and also about 'truth, morality and justice,' but these are placed in such a way that they can do no harm."

I ask my readers to judge whether commentators have acted in good faith when they cite those words in isolation and then conclude that Marx's thinking is amoral. Instead of standing at the head of the document, as they did in the version of Mazzini's followers, they were placed by Marx in the eighth and ninth paragraphs of the Preamble to the provisional rules (see MEW 16:14 f.; VFI:82 f.). The beginning of the Preamble, reworked by Marx as he saw fit, also talks about rights; but the focus is clearly a class one:

> Considering,That the emancipation of the working classes must be conquered by the working classes themselves, that the struggle for the emancipation of the working classes means not a struggle for class privileges and monopolies, but for equal rights and duties, and the abolition of all class rule . . . (MEW 16:14; VFI:82).

The fourth paragraph talks about the need for "solidarity" and a "fraternal bond of union between the working classes of different countries." And the final paragraph of the whole document (no. 10) sees working men's societies "united in a perpetual bond of fraternal cooperation."

Now if we disregard the eighth and ninth paragraphs of the Preamble, the only ones which Marx felt obliged to rework in a vein that was not his own, the draft still contains three insistent mentions of fraternity and it starts off with a vigorous allusion to rights and duties. The appeal to moral principles is as forceful as it was in the Mazzini-sponsored draft, but this final draft by Marx does not stand under the aegis of Mazzini's European liberal movement. It even stumps for "truth, justice and morality," but it situates this demand in a context which ensures that the International will not be dependent on another organization that evades the class struggle. Thus the International came into being as an achievement of the working class itself, which is what Marx wanted. In what way can this incident be properly interpreted as an indication of Marx's amorality?

But the most noteworthy thing of all is that this document did not stand alone. At the same time Marx alone drafted the famous *Inaugural Address of the International Working Men's Association* and delivered it (MEW 16:5–13; VFI:73–81). In it he came down against "disregard of that bond of brotherhood which ought to exist between the workmen of different countries." The members of the International, he said, have a duty "to vindicate the simple laws of morals and justice, which ought to govern the relations of private individuals, as the rules paramount of the intercourse of nations" (MEW 16:13; VFI:81).

These last words make it clear that Marx's low opinion of the Mazzini-derived expressions has no connection whatsoever with amorality or anything remotely like it.

Now some might imagine that the last words cited above were written or spoken inadvertently. The very fact that they stand as the culminating words at the end of the discourse is enough to rule out such an interpretation. But to confirm that fact, let me remind the reader that Marx alluded to them again six years later. In the *First Address of the General Council on the Franco-Prussian War,* drafted entirely by Marx, we read these words right near the beginning:

> We defined the foreign policy aimed at by the International in these words: "Vindicate the simple laws of morals and justice, which ought to govern the relations of private individuals, as the laws paramount of the intercourse of nations" (MEW 17:3; VFI:172).

Where did people get the idea that Marx attached no importance to morality and justice? On 6 August 1872 Engels drafted, and the whole General Council signed, a message entitled *The General Council to All the Members of the International.* In it we read: "The International demands that all its adherents recognize truth, justice, and morality as the basis of their conduct" (MEW 18:118). To complete the story, two days later Marx and Engels jointly drafted another message of the General Council, this one addressed to the Spanish sections. In it they said: "The International demands that its adherents recognize truth, justice and morality as the basis of conduct" (MEW 18:123). Among the signatures were those of Marx and Engels (MEW 18:124).

If any such statement is to be grounded in the documents of the International, then the messages of 1872 would have to appeal either to the 1864 *Inaugural Discourse* (as Marx did in 1870 by quoting from it) or to the *Provisional Rules* of 1864. The sequence "truth, justice and morality" makes the latter possibility more likely. In fact, it hearkens back to the eighth paragraph of the Preamble (MEW 16:15; VFI:82–83), whose formulation derives from the followers of Mazzini. Thus, even though Marx had been "obliged" to incorporate these words into the rules, he was by no means opposed to their basic content. The anti-moralist interpreters of Marx have rarely been so offbase as they have been in interpreting this whole incident.

There is hardly any force at all to the objection that these are official documents of the International. First of all, the initiative to issue them came from Marx. Secondly, Marx chose the words that go to make up these documents, and those words could have been very different. Thirdly, Marx also signed the documents. Fourthly, another work cited by all Marxists, *The Civil War in France,* is also an official document of the International. Its full title is: *The Civil War in France: Address of the General Council.* Fifthly, as Engels wrote to Laura in a letter dated 24 June 1883, "Marx's life without the International would be like a diamond ring from which one had torn out the precious stone" (MEW 36:43). Sixthly, as Engels wrote in the 1878 *Volks-Kalender,* while Marx was still alive; "To describe Marx's activity in the International would be to write the history of that association itself" (MEW 19:101). Seventhly, Marx always regarded all those messages of the International as his own works (see MEW 34:346; MEW 33:26; MEW 36:458 and 514; MEW 22:188 and 252; MEW 38:45; MEW 18:266). Eighthly, and most decisively, Marx and Engels also appeal to justice in other works that have nothing to do with the International.

IV

In an article for the NYDT (1 February 1862), Marx writes:

> In such circumstances sheer justice demands that we pay attention to the firm attitude of the British working class, all the more so if we contrast it to the hypocritical, boastful, cowardly and stupid attitude of official, accommodating John Bull (MEW 15:440).

Referring to Spain in an article for the NYDT dated 20 October 1854, Marx writes of "the absurd and oppressive fiscal system, *whose injus-*

tice has become proverbial" (MEW 10:453; my italics). In a letter to Engels dated 19 February 1869, Marx writes:

> It seems that our last circular has caused quite a sensation, and that in Switzerland and France a witch-hunt has overtaken the Bakuninists. But *est modus in rebus* ["one can go too far"], and I am going to make sure that *no injustice is done* (MEW 32:448 f.; my italics).

Writing about the war of the French, Spanish, and British against Mexico (declared in the Convention of London, 13 October 1861), Marx had this to say in an article for the NYDT dated 15 February 1862:

> The recently published blue-book on the Mexican intervention contains a very incriminating revelation of modern British diplomacy, with all its sanctimonious hypocrisy, its savage fury against the weak, its servility to the strong, and its *complete disregard for the right of nations* (MEW 15:472; my italics).

In his speech to the German Workers Educational Association on the Irish question, which he delivered on 16 December 1867, Marx talks about the "ignominious violation of the agreement" committed by the British (MEW 16:448). On 2 November 1867 the General Council sent a *Memorial,* written by Marx, to the British Home Secretary, petitioning for the commutation of the death sentences of the five Fenian prisoners condemned for the murder of a policeman. In it Marx wrote: "A mitigation of the verdict, which we request, will be not only *an act of justice* but also an act of political wisdom" (MEW 16:219; my italics).

In *Theories of Surplus Value* Marx writes: "*In all fairness,* however, it must be said, that other economists, such as Ure, Corbet etc., declare over-production to be the usual condition in large-scale industry, so far as the home country is concerned . . ." (MEW 26/2:498; TSV 2:498; my italics).

We could go on like this for pages. In this very chapter we have already cited passages where Marx talks about "justice" or "fairness" with their full meaning. As far as Engels is concerned, we have already cited some of his pertinent remarks on the subject: "This is a very peculiar sort of fairness"; "according to the political economy of the capitalist class, that is the very pink of fairness." Such sentiments could only be expressed in the name of authentic justice. In an article dated 13 October 1872 for the Spanish periodical *La Emancipación,* Engels writes:

To apply these new laws to the congress in session would be to give them retroactive force and *violate every principle of justice* (MEW 18:172; my italics).

Another article of Engels' entitled "Socialism in Germany" was published in the *Almanac* of the French Workers' Party in 1892. In it Engels states:

> As soon as this party attains power, it will not be able to keep it or exercise it without *repairing the injustices* that its predecessors in office have committed against other nations (MEW 22:253; my italics).

In a letter to Marx dated 1 May 1870, Engels asks him if any effort has yet been made to write a worthy obituary for Schapper in the newspaper: "I don't know if Eccarius would be the man to do justice to this superb type of oldtime conspirator" (MEW 37:254).

Having made his will, on 14 November 1894 Engels explains it in a letter to the two surviving daughters of Marx (Laura and Eleanor). He entrusts the children of the late Jenny (Marx's eldest daughter) to them in the following terms:

> Thus you are free of all responsibility before British law, and you can proceed as *your sense of justice* and your love for the children *dictate* (MEW 39:318; my italics).

In a letter to Martignetti dated 2 July 1889, Engels writes: "I hope that the court of appeals will *do justice to you*" (MEW 37:254; my italics).

Engels wrote a series of "Letters from London" for the Italian organ, *La Plebe*. The second in the series (17 November 1872) reports that the British government has issued a regulation governing public meetings that obliges people to inform the police in writing two days before the meeting and to give them the names of the speakers. Engels has this comment:

> This ordinance, carefully kept secret by the British press, abolished with a stroke of the pen *one of the most precious rights* of the working people of London, i.e., *the right to hold meetings* in the parks whenever and however they please. To submit to such an ordinance would have meant *renouncing the right* of the people (MEW 18:189; my italics).

In the 1886 Appendix to the American edition of *The Condition of the Working Class in England,* Engels notes how in the past forty-two years the British bourgeoisie has been giving in to the pressure of the workers' movement and public opinion. Then he remarks:

> The fact is that all these *concessions to justice* and philanthropy were nothing else but means to accelerate the concentration of capital in the hands of the few, for whom the niggardly extra extortion of former years had lost all importance and had become actual nuisances (MEW 21:251; CWC:362).

In short, the list of passages by Engels on right and justice could be extended for pages also. And the reader should note that in the case of both Marx and Engels I have focused exclusively on works written at the height of their maturity.

7

The Moral Conscience of Marx

There are various ways, completely sound and certain, to verify whether a human being acknowledges the existence of a moral imperative. In this chapter I shall explore the main ways in turn, thereby giving some order to my compilation of relevant texts written by Marx. I want to make it clear to my readers that the present chapter is closely linked to the two preceding chapters, because both the profoundly humanist criterion of Marx's work and the content of his economic analysis bear witness to his moral conscience. The material has been divided into three chapters for the sake of ease in reading.

I

One obvious way to see whether an author recognizes morality is to find out if he explicitly mentions it. If he does, then one's research is obviously made easier.

In the Afterword to the 1875 edition of the *Revelations on the Cologne Communist Trial,* originally published in 1852, Marx writes this significant passage:

> At that time Stieber was the name of a lowly police official on a savage hunt for higher pay and office; today Stieber signifies the unlimited rule of the political police in the new holy Prusso-German empire. Thus Stieber has been transformed into a moral person, so to speak; moral in the metaphorical sense that, e.g., parliament is a moral entity (MEW 8:575).

To Marx it is very clear that the adjective "moral" is being used in a purely metaphorical sense when, for example, we talk about contracts between physical persons and moral persons, either in the singular or the plural. The fact is that legislation accords juridical personality to organizations, institutions, associations, and even whole nations; they are then called moral persons. Marx is fully aware of the fact that "moral" in this sense does not mean "moral" in the strict and proper sense. In the latter sense "moral" means something completely different. Marx is aware that morality in the strict and proper sense does exist. Thus he implies a contrast between "moral" in that sense and the "moral person," Stieber, in the metaphorical sense.

In a letter dated 7 October 1876, Marx congratulates Lavrov for having dared to criticize pan-Slavism in his article for the periodical published by Russian exiles. According to Marx, the article is not only "a masterpiece but above all an act of great moral valor" (MEW 34:208). We have already seen that in his article of 17 June 1859 for the NYDT Marx referred to Mazzini's manifesto as "an admirable act of moral valor" (MEW 13:365). In these two cases Marx is obviously using the word "moral" in its strict and proper sense rather than in a metaphorical sense.

In Book I of *Capital* Marx describes the lot of the proletariat as one of "brutalization and moral degradation" (MEW 23:675). He also asserts that in its unbridled hunger for surplus value capital "oversteps not only the moral, but even the merely physical maximum bounds of the working-day" (MEW 23:280; CAP 1:265). In these passages Marx fully realizes that he is using the adjective "moral" in its proper and authentic sense. He is obviously assuming that morality prescribes certain limits to the length of the working day and that the capitalists are thus violating a moral precept.

In an article entitled "British Atrocities in China," which appeared in the NYDT on 10 April 1857, Marx rails against Britain's promotion of opium consumption in China, complaining about the silence of the British press on the matter: "We have heard nothing about the illegal opium trade which, year after year, fills the coffers of the British treasury at the expense of human lives and *morality*" (MEW 12:165; my italics).

Here Marx uses the noun, and hence morality is capitalized in the German text. According to Marx, morality has been harmed through the behavior of the British. A few lines further Marx says:

> We have heard nothing about that or about many other things, first of all because the majority of people outside China are little concerned about the social *and moral* situation of that country, and secondly because politics and astuteness forbid the raising of questions which will result in no financial advantage (MEW 12:165; my italics).

Marx takes complete cognizance of the fact that the moral criterion is clearly distinct from economic interests and all calculations of convenience and advantage. Yet he takes sides with morality, despite all the dictates of political astuteness.

At Marx's initiative the General Council of the International adopted a resolution drafted by Marx on 17 October 1871. The resolution was designed to correct various points in the rules of the French section. The first correction is this:

> (1) From Article 2 strike out the phrase, "bring some verification of one's means of subsistence," and in its place simply put: "To be accepted as a member of the section, the candidate must present *guarantees of morality,* etc." (MEW 17:436; see VFI:290).

This hardly calls for comment. As we saw in Chapter 6, Marx insisted that every member of the International—and we would add here every true revolutionary—must recognize morality as the basis of his conduct. In his article for the NYDT dated 14 July 1853, Marx writes:

> To correctly appreciate the value of strikes and coalitions, we must not let ourselves be deceived by the apparent insignificance of their economic results. Instead we must above all take cognizance of their *moral* and political effects (MEW 9:171; my italics).

As far back as Chapter 1 we examined a letter written twenty-five years later to Liebknecht, in which Marx bears similar witness to the importance of moral considerations (see p. 6). Marx gave his support to the Turkish peasants because they were the more capable and moral people in the Russo-Turkish region of Europe. As is true in this 1853 article, Marx certainly took political factors into account as well, but he gave preeminence to moral ones. We have also seen that in the *Critique of the Gotha Programme* Marx expressed his indignation at the socialist leaders for lowering the moral level of the proletariat (1875). In an article for *Das Volk* dated 30 July 1859, Marx criticizes the policy of Louis Napoleon in these terms:

> In such circumstances it cannot surprise us that the general disposition towards barbarism adopts a certain method, that *immorality is turned into a system,* that illegality wins its legislators and the right of the strongest its legal codes (MEW 13:444; my italics).

Without claiming to be exhaustive, these passages suffice to show that Marx explicitly recognizes the existence of morality, and of an obligatory morality no less.

Insofar as Engels is concerned, we may also adduce a few texts on this point. In December 1889 Gerson Trier, a Danish Socialist, wrote to Engels and expressed his doubts about the advisability of the Social Democrats entering into alliances with other parties, e.g., the progressive or liberal party. Engels replied on 18 December:

> Prescinding from the question of morality—which is not at issue in
> this case and so I leave it aside—for me, as a revolutionary, any
> means is good if it leads to the end, both the most violent means and
> what seems to be the meekest (MEW 37:327).

A good materialist would not interject the qualification that Engels
did. According to traditional morality, as anyone can read in the works
of Thomas Aquinas or any other serious tract of ancient or modern
times, there are situations in which the use of violence is licit. Such is the
case, for example, with an act of self-defense or the overthrowing of a
tyrant. Thus Engels is not adverse to violent means, and he is quite right
on this score. Nor is he opposed to alliances with other political parties,
he goes on to say, "provided that the proletarian class character of the
Party is not jeopardized thereby" (MEW 37:327; SCME:387).

The use of violence is not illicit in and of its very nature, nor are
alliances. That is why Engels says that in this case it is not a question of
morality and so he can leave the latter question aside. But the way he
puts it makes it clear that in other circumstances there could be a moral
question involved in the choice of means. In short, Engels' reply to a
serious question like that of Trier is very cautious: if there is no moral
question involved, any means is good. A good materialist would not
offer any such qualification.

On 23 October 1892 Engels wrote the following to Victor Adler, an
Austrian, about the contemporary customs of the British:

> You have no idea how etiquette dominates everything here, even
> medicine. One infringement of etiquette is more serious than ten
> against the moral law (MEW 38:501).

For Engels, the moral law clearly exists and is obligatory. He
criticizes the British for placing etiquette higher than morality. In a letter
to Bebel dated 24 January 1893, Engels describes the inevitable effects
of the institution known as the stock exchange:

> . . . an excellent medium for the concentration of capitals, the
> disintegration and dissolution of the last remnants of naturally
> formed interconnections in bourgeois society and at the same time
> for the annihilation of *all orthodox moral concepts* and their per-
> version into their opposites . . . (MEW 39:14; SCME:429; my
> italics).

Clearly orthodox, obligatory morality exists for Engels. In his 1886
Appendix to the American edition of *The Condition of the Working
Class in England* Engels talks about the unexpected advances that big
industry has made since 1844. Then he adds:

And in proportion as this increase took place, in the same proportion did manufacturing industry become *apparently moralised* (MEW 21:251; CWC:361; my italics).

Such a diganosis could be pronounced only by someone who believes that a real morality exists alongside any possible morality of mere surface appearances. One must be convinced that real morality exists if one wants to differentiate between real morality and apparent morality. Here we have an irreducible difference between the founders of Marxism and the modern dilettantes of liberation for whom all morality is mere appearance. In Chapter 6 I cited Engels' article of 7 May 1881 where he alluded to the "science of morals" (see pp. 146–47).

Engels' letter of 3 December 1890 to Ferdinand Domela Nieuwenhuis is a veritable moral treatise on a matter of conscience (MEW 37:509 f.) that figures in all the modern tracts: is it licit to get out of military service by buying an exemption or a replacement? Engels, obviously consulted because of the moral authority he enjoyed among the socialists of all countries, concluded that it was licit. But he reached this conclusion by citing moral reasons, not by declaring that moral questions have no importance. The types of argument proffered by Engels are the same types that any serious moralist would use, though of course he, unlike most moralists, frames them in the context of the class struggle. For example, Engels asserts that those who take the place of one who has bought his way out are riffraff (*Lumpen*), not real proletarians.

Whether his arguments are convincing or not, the point here is that their rigorously moral intent and thrust cannot be missed by any reader. In the same connection it is pertinent to cite his remark to Pasquale Martignetti in a letter dated 13 January 1890: "To the extent that I do enjoy the confidence of the workers, it is due to the assumption that in all circumstances I tell them the truth and nothing but the truth" (MEW 37:343). Also relevant is Engels' vehement denunciation of "the violation of their pledged word" in his 1891 Introduction to the reissue of *The Civil War in France* (MEW 22:190 and 192). The same vehemence can be found in his letter to Bebel dated 6 November 1892, where he says: "Among bourgeois politicians one's word is given only to be broken" (MEW 38:509).

How different Engels is from the amoral pseudo-Marxists who regard the fulfillment of one's pledged word as a bourgeois prejudice. These subhuman beings do not seem to know that a human being is worth what his or her word is worth. Also relevant here is Marx's description of Thiers as "a virtuoso at swearing false oaths" (MEW 17:508). The same condemnation of perjury can be found in *Theories of Surplus Value*, where Marx writes: "To swear false oaths is productive for the person who does it for cash" (MEW 26/1:265; TSV 1:293).

In a letter dated 8 March 1895 Engels shows that he is perfectly familiar with the basic difference between a moral obligation and a legal obligation. Richard Fischer was in charge of the publications of the German Social Democratic party and also the quasi-official correspondent with Engels on party matters. Some distinguished members of that Party had just come out accepting unreservedly the new legislation which substantially diminished the government's persecution of socialists. To Fischer Engels writes:

> You would do better to hold the view that the obligation to legality is juridical, not moral . . . and that it ceases completely when the wielders of power break the laws. You people, or at least some of you, have demonstrated weakness in not standing up as you should have to the demand of the enemy: the weakness of acknowledging the obligation to stay within the bounds of the law as a *moral* obligation, as a duty that is obligatory under all circumstances. Instead you should have said: "You hold power, you have the laws. If we transgress them, then you can deal with us in accordance with those laws and we must endure that. But that finishes the matter. We have no other obligation and you have no other right." That is what was done by the Catholics under the May Laws, by the old Lutherans in Meissen, and by that Mennonite soldier who is in all the newspapers; and this point of view is one which you people cannot deny (MEW 39:425).

Engels certainly was a person who was familiar with morality and who recognized the existence of a moral imperative. From the above passage it is clear that he thought that a moral obligation, unlike a juridical one, does not cease to exist when rulers break the laws; that it is a duty that obligates people under any and every circumstance. He even goes on to say that the members of the Social Democratic party cannot deny that viewpoint. The neo-Marxists of our day do not really know the people whom they claim to be following. In his letter of 19 November 1892 to Bebel, the head of the party, Engels says:

> You people are the battle corps of the modern working movement, and if you had promised that in Brussels, you were *morally obliged* to carry it out (MEW 38:518; my italics).

II

There is a surefire way to find out whether a human being recognizes the existence of an obligatory morality or not. One need only ask whether all means are good in his or her eyes.

In a little known book of 143 pages entitled *A Plot Against the*

International, which was written jointly by Marx and Engels in 1873 and published in French before it came out in German, we read the following remark about the international Bakuninist Alliance: "To achieve their aims they do not stop at any means or any dishonesty" (MEW 18:333). In the article on the Mexican intervention which I cited earlier (see p. 162), Marx attacks the vile behavior which prompted the parties involved to use "the most detestable means in undertaking the Mexican intervention" (MEW 15:472). In his lecture on the Irish question (see p. 162 above), Marx condemns "the infamy through which the most ignominious measures were used to *convert* the Irish Catholics *into Protestants* through *'property'* regulations" (MEW 16:448).

In his open letter of 25 August 1871 to the editor-in-chief of *The Sun,* Marx writes: "And Monsieur Thiers is as cowardly in his relations with foreign powers as he is unscrupulous towards his defenseless fellow-citizens" (MEW 17:402). In a letter to Engels dated 9 February 1860, Marx has this to say about Lassalle: "The very same character who uses the most shameful means to get in good with the most shameful people, in the service of the Countess Hatzfeldt!" (MEW 30:31).

In his article of 1 August 1854 (NYDT) on "The British Bourgeoisie," Marx writes:

> For years now the owners have been trying to extend the working day in the factories beyond what is humanly tolerable and, by *unscrupulously* implementing the piece-work system and setting some workers against others, to lower the pay of the skilled worker to the level of the unskilled worker (MEW 10:647; my italics).

In *A Plot Against the International* Marx and Engels describe the tactics of the Bakuninist Alliance as follows: "For them lying, calumny, intimidation, and sneaky blows are equally good" (MEW 18:333). As for Engels himself, he has this to say in a letter to Bebel dated 12 October 1893: "And if the matter is not *completely clear,* there is nothing to do with a character like Reeves; he is completely unscrupulous in his business speculations" (MEW 39:138).

In his article of 8 March 1890 for *Der Sozialdemokrat,* Engels writes: "And we know that Bismarck is one of those people for whom any means is good" (MEW 22:9). Writing of Hyndman in a letter to Bernstein dated 7 December 1885, Engels says: "This man is a pure caricature of Lassalle: totally indifferent to the quality of the means" (MEW 36:404).

In an article on "The Fifteenth Anniversary of the Paris Commune," published in *Le Socialiste* on 27 March 1886, Engels writes: "In Germany Bismarck has exhausted every means, even the most abject ones, to break the worker movement" (MEW 21:258). In an article on "The

172   *The Moral Conscience of Marx*

Death of Marx" for *Der Sozialdemokrat* (17 May 1883), he writes: "From 1867 on, the anarchists sought to take over control of the International by using the most infamous means" (MEW 19:345).

In a letter to Bernstein dated 20 October 1882, Engels writes: "In general all the old Bakuninist tactics, which justify any means—lies, calumniation, secret cliquishness—dominated the preparations for the Congress" (MEW 35:374; SCME:332). Referring to Gottschalk in a letter to Liebknecht on 29 October 1889, Engels writes: "For that he, like a good prophet, was above all scruple and hence capable of any and every sort of base action" (MEW 37:298). And in a letter to Lafargue on 7 December 1885, Engels reiterates his opinion of Hyndman: "But Hyndman is a caricature of Lassalle; to him all means are good" (MEW 36:406).

When Engels was informed that Marx's treatment of Lassalle had caused some bad feelings among the old followers of Lassalle, he felt obliged to give a summary evaluation of Lassalle and his activity to Kautsky in a letter dated 23 February 1891:

> Lassalle has belonged to history for twenty-six years. While under the Anti-Socialist Law historical criticism of him was left in abeyance, the time is at last at hand when it must be expressed and Lassalle's position in relation to Marx be made plain. . . . However highly one may estimate Lassalle's services to the movement, his historical role in it remains an equivocal one. Lassalle the Socialist is dogged at every step by Lassalle the demagogue. Everywhere, Lassalle the conductor of the Hatzfeldt law suit shows through Lassalle the agitator and organiser *the same cynicism in the choice of means,* the same preference for surrounding himself with disreputable and corrupt people who can be used as mere tools and discarded (MEW 38:40; SCME:406; my italics).

On 9 December 1871 Engels wrote the following to Paul Lafargue: "For the rest, the others had worked well and had employed fairly infamous means, as usual" (MEW 33:356). In *The Role of Force in History* (1888), we find this passage written by Engels:

> If Louis Napoleon had learned from his own shady past not to be too scrupulous in his choice of means, Bismarck learned to be even less scrupulous from the history of Prussian policy, especially from the history of the so-called Great Elector (Frederick-William) and of Frederick II (MEW 21:427; RFH:57).

My readers can readily see that Marx and Engels angrily rejected "cynicism in the choice of means" whether it was displayed by institutions or individuals, by socialists, capitalists, or militarists. This total reprobation of unscrupulousness in the use of means was voiced in books, articles, and letters, in both their public and their private statements. Machiavellianism is incompatible with their published thought and with their private everyday thoughts, with their doctrinal pronouncements and their personal views. The new crop of amoral Leninists around today may find support in Thiers, Machiavelli, or Palmerston, but they cannot look to Marx and Engels as their patrons.

III

There are other themes that infallibly indicate whether a human being recognizes the existence of a moral imperative in the strict sense, e.g., egotism, the capacity for self-sacrifice, and the recognition of strict obligation. In this section we shall see what Marx and Engels thought about these matters. Then in Section IV we shall tackle the most direct and important question relating to the matter of morality, the question of conscience.

In Chapter 28 of Book I of *Capital* we read the following passage written by Marx:

> We see that only against its will and under the pressure of the masses did the English Parliament give up the laws against strikes and trades' unions, after it had itself, for 500 years, held, *with shameless egotism*, the position of a permanent trades' union of the capitalists against the labourers (MEW 23:769; CAP 1:740–41; my italics).

In the 103-page pamphlet written jointly by Marx and Engels, *The Great Men of the Exile* (1852), the authors criticize Ruge in these terms: "Sordid egotism appears purified and clean in the shape of a sacrifice allegedly carried out" (MEW 8:276). As we already noted in an earlier chapter (see p. 75), Marx praised Mazzini's manifesto of 1859 and described the current situation in Europe as "a Babel of obfuscation, blind fanaticism, and egotistical falsehood" (MEW 13:365). And in his first draft of *The Civil War in France* (1871), Marx writes:

> What Paris will no longer stand is the existence of *cocottes* ("loose women") and *cocodés* ("fops"). What it is resolved to drive away or transform is this useless, sceptical and *egotistical* [my italics] race which has taken possession of the gigantic town, to use it as its own (MEW 17:563; VFI:268).

In *The Eighteenth Brumaire of Louis Bonaparte* (1852), Marx tells us that some of the members of Parliament, who belonged to the party of order, deserted its camp and went over to Louis Bonaparte out of fear of struggle, fanaticism for compromise, boredom, family regard for relatives holding state salaries, speculation on coming vacancies in ministerial positions (Odilon Barrot), and finally the simple *egotism* which always inclines the ordinary bourgeois citizen to sacrifice the general interest of his class to this or that private motive (MEW 8:172; VSE:209–10; my italics).

In his second draft of *The Civil War in France* (1871), Marx describes Thiers as follows: "In a man like that, the so-called attainments of culture show up merely as the refinement of corruption and of egotism" (MEW 17:577). In an article for the NYDT published 25 June 1853, Marx writes: "England, it is true, in causing a social revolution in Hindustan was actuated only by the vilest interests" (MEW 9:133; VSE:306–07).

Talking about money at one point in the *Grundrisse*, Marx says:

> With that, the independent value of things, except in so far as it consists in their mere being for others, in their relativity, exchangeability, the absolute value of all things and relations, is dissolved. Everything is sacrificed to egotistic pleasure (GRU:839).

In a letter written to Engels from Hannover (24 April 1867), Marx lets us see what he might say when he wants to praise someone:

> Kugelmann bores me at times with his enthusiasm, which runs directly counter to his cold character as a doctor. But he *understands* and is *thoroughly honest,* uncompromising, capable of sacrifice, what is most important, *convinced* (MEW 31:290).

For our purposes here, however, it does not matter whether the last mentioned trait is given first place or not. The important thing is that when Marx wants to appraise a person's worth, he focuses on his honesty and his capacity for sacrifice.

This dovetails with what Marx's wife tells us about Marx himself. On 24 December 1867 she wrote a letter to Kugelmann while Marx himself was confined to bed by an attack of carbuncles. He had finally gotten Book I of *Capital* published. Jenny writes:

> If the workers had any idea of the sacrifice it took to finish this book, which was written solely for their sake and in their interests, they might perhaps show a bit more interest (MEW 31:596).

On 30 April of the same year Marx had written a letter to Siegfried Meyer. The latter had been complaining about not getting a reply to his letters. Marx writes:

Well, why didn't I answer you? Because I was constantly hovering at the edge of the grave. Hence I had to make use of *every* moment when I was able to work to complete my book, to which I have sacrificed health, happiness, and family. I trust that I need not add anything to this explanation (MEW 31:542; SCME:173).

In a letter to W. Bracke dated 18 August 1877, Marx describes Carl Hirsch in this way: "Hirsch is a person worthy of total confidence, with the greatest capacity for sacrifice" (MEW 34:290).

In his article for *Das Volk* dated 20 August 1869 Marx describes the lockout which the builders have forced on the "society" of London bricklayers. Then he adds:

From all parts of the country substantial donations of money are flowing in for the "society," but up to now the workers, without bread, have refused to accept the aid. Honor to the brave ones! Would the bourgeois be capable of such a sacrifice in the interests of *their* class? (MEW 13:488).

In *A Plot Against the International* Marx and Engels write:

The International was already solidly established when Michael Bakunin came up with the idea of playing a role as the emancipator of the proletariat. The International could only offer him the field of activity common to all its members. To be someone in it, he would first have had to win his spurs by constant, *self-sacrificing* work (MEW 18:335; my italics).

This passage by Marx and Engels presents self-sacrifice not only as a part of life but also as a duty in life. Engels once was off base in telling Paul Lafargue that Marx hated the word "sacrifice" (MEW 36:125). The fact is that both he and Marx (see his letter to Engels about Kugelmann above) use it deliberately and frequently.

In an article for *The Secular Chronicle* dated 4 August 1878, Marx criticizes the history of the International presented by George Howell. Among other things he writes:

[Howell] ought to have been more proud to recall his past ties with the workers' association, which won worldwide renown and a place in the history of humanity, not by means of a substantial treasury but by its spiritual force and its *disinterested* energy (MEW 19:147; my italics).

In *The Civil War in France* (1871) Marx includes such unequivocal statements and expressions as the following:

The *self-sacrificing heroism* with which the population of Paris
—men, women and children—fought for eight days after the entrance of the Versaillese, reflects as much the grandeur of their
cause, as the infernal deeds of the soldiery reflect the innate spirit
of that civilization of which they are the mercenary vindicators
(MEW 17:355 f.; VFI:226; my italics).

In all its bloody triumphs over the self-sacrificing champions of a
new and better society, that nefarious civilization, based upon the
enslavement of labour, drowns the moans of its victims in a hue-
and-cry of calumny . . . (MEW 17:357; VFI:228).

The Paris people die enthusiastically for the Commune in numbers
unequalled in any battle known to history (ibid.).

The *cocottes* had refound the scent of their protectors. . . . In their
stead the real women of Paris showed again at the surface—heroic,
noble, and devoted, like the women of antiquity (MEW 17:349;
VFI:219–20).

The working men's Paris, in the act of its heroic self-holocaust,
involved in its flames buildings and monuments (MEW 17:357;
VFI:228).

In a letter to Kugelmann dated 12 April 1871, Marx reminds him of
what he wrote in the final chapter of the *Eighteenth Brumaire* about the
next socialist revolution in France:

The next French Revolution will no longer attempt to transfer the
bureaucratic military apparatus from one hand to another, but to
smash it, and this is the precondition for every real people's
revolution on the Continent. And this is what our heroic Party
comrades in Paris are attempting. . . . History has no comparable
example of similar greatness! (MEW 33:205; SCME:247).

Let us note in passing that the sacrifice of oneself for others is one of
the innumerable contributions of authentic Christianity to the concrete
realization of communism. When the bourgeois criticized the fighters of
the Commune, saying that they were merely a handful of unknowns, the
latter replied "like the twelve apostles." And those who think that the
capacity to sacrifice oneself for others will lose its place and importance
once communism becomes a reality do not know what they are talking
about.
    In a letter to Lassalle dated 28 April 1862, Marx has this to say about
Johann Philipp Becker: "He has been one of the most noble German

revolutionaries since 1830'' (MEW 30:621). Then, contrasting the attitude of the British working class with the baseness of the British middle class, he adds: "By contrast the British working class, which suffers most under the Civil War, has never shown itself more noble or more heroic" (MEW 30:623).

As for Engels, he has this to say to Lavrov in a letter dated 13 June 1893: "I hope you may still be alive on the day when the Russian movement for social revolution, to which you have *fully sacrificed* your entire life, raises its victorious banner on the rubble of Czarism" (MEW 39:84; my italics).

In his major antireformist study, "Trade Unions," published in *The Labour Standard* on 28 May 1881, Engels stresses that the struggle of the working class is not designed simply to modify the existing mode of production. So long as the latter continues to exist,

> the working class remains what it was, and what our Chartist forefathers were not afraid to call it, a class of wage slaves. Is this to be the final result of all this labour, *self-sacrifice,* and suffering? (MEW 19:257; SW:106; my italics).

In his 1890 pamphlet on *The Foreign Policy of Russian Czarism* Engels at one point exalts the Polish Revolution of 1830 and says: "Thus for a second time Poland saved the European revolution through its self-sacrifice" (MEW 22:4).

In a letter to Jules Guesde dated 20 November 1889, Engels reports that:

> In the last four months the workers of east London have not only entered the movement body and soul but also have given their comrades in every other country an example of discipline, *sacrifice,* courage and resistance equalled only by that of the Parisians when they were besieged by the Prussians (MEW 37:315; my italics).

In his open letter to the editorial board of the *People's Friend* in Brno, Engels writes:

> And if the workers of Brno, despite the financial squeeze, have nevertheless managed to keep their newspaper going for ten years without denying their banner in any way, this is another fresh proof of the resistance and *sacrifice* that today can be found only among workers (MEW 2:261; my italics).

On 17 November 1891 *The Daily Chronicle* published the fabrication that in 1871 Marx's late wife had reported to the French authorities the whereabouts of a revolutionary arsenal in order to obtain the release of her son-in-law, Paul Lafargue. Engels wrote to protest this calumny, ending his letter to the editorial board as follows:

> The whole story of the alleged arsenal is nothing but a fairy tale fabricated to smear the memory of a woman whose noble and *self-sacrificing* nature was completely incapable of a vile act (MEW 22:263; my italics).

In a letter to Laura Lafargue dated 13 October 1888, Engels writes of "an heroic woman," Louise Kautsky, and of "a truly heroic letter" that she had written to him (MEW 37:108 and 109). On 25 October he writes about the same matter to Bebel: "Louise had conducted herself with rare heroism in the whole affair" (MEW 37:118). The sad business in question is the fact that Karl Kautsky has separated from his wife. The latter, still in love with him and suffering terribly, nevertheless offers excuses for the man who has abandoned her. On 11 October 1888 Engels replies to Louise:

> You say that Karl's nature is such that it will go to rack and ruin without love and without passion. If that nature manifests itself in the fact that it needs a new love every two years, then he should tell himself that in the present circumstances such a nature ought to be repressed, or else it will involve himself and others in endlessly tragic conflicts. That, dear Louise, is what I feel obliged to say to you (MEW 37:107).

So here we have Engels recommending the mortification of nature and even feeling obliged to make that recommendation. His moral criterion is the only truly valid one: something that causes suffering to one's neighbor should be repressed.

The above texts are enough to document the feelings of Marx and Engels about egotism and self-sacrifice. In fact the very same texts also bear witness to the fact that there is something known as moral obligation, but here we might do well to add others which mention that notion explicitly.

In an article for the NYDT dated 23 September 1858, Marx set out to denounce the complicity of Mehmed Bey (alias Colonel Bangya) with the Russian government and various ministers of other Western regimes. Marx begins by way of prologue with the following words:

> I feel that I would be violating my obligation if I did not object to the cowardly maneuvers which seek to stifle any further investigation and draw a veil of silence over the entire matter (MEW 12:557).

In *A Plot Against the International* (1873) Marx and Engels write:

Thus the resolutions enacted by the Hague Congress against the Alliance were purely *acts of obligation;* the Congress could not allow the International, this great creation of the proletariat, to get caught in the trap laid by the exploiting class (MEW 18:440 f.; my italics).

In a letter to Engels dated 20 February 1866, Marx writes: "I am proud of the Germans. It is *our obligation* to emancipate this 'profound' people" (MEW 31:183; my italics). In a letter to the editor-in-chief of the *Times* (29 January 1852), Marx writes:

Sir, the annihilation of the last remnants of an independent press on the continent means that the English press is bound in honor to report any and every act of illegality and oppression anywhere in Europe (MEW 8:219).

Remember Marx's 1875 letter to Bracke, which he sent along with the *Critique of the Gotha Programme*. In the letter he tells Bracke: *"It is my duty* not to approve, even by diplomatic silence, a programme which in my opinion is thoroughly reprehensible and demoralizing for the party" (MEW 19:13; VFI:340; my italics). And he concludes the *Critique* with the words: *"Dixi et salvavi animam meam"* (MEW 19:32; VFI: 359). No author, ancient or modern, could affirm the existence of an absolute moral obligation in clearer or more convincing terms.

In a letter to Kautsky dated 27 August 1881, Engels writes the following:

J. Simon is a public health official, a doctor in private practice, for all practical purposes the director of British medical policy. He is the same person that Marx cites so often and so approvingly in *Capital,* perhaps one of the last of the oldtime functionaries who remained true to his vocation and preserved his delicacy of conscience between the years 1840 and 1860. At every turn he came up against the interests of the bourgeoisie as the first and major obstacle to his *fulfillment of his obligation* and found himself forced to fight them (MEW 35:223; my italics).

The biography of W. Wolff (alias "Lupus") was composed by Engels in 1876, but Marx worked closely with him and contributed to it also. It was published as a series that same year in *Die Neue Welt*. In the introductory article we read:

But it took long years of cooperation and friendly conversation in the struggle, in triumph and defeat, in good times and bad, to test and ascertain the full measure of his indomitable strength of character, his absolute reliability which left no room for doubt, and his unwavering *sense of duty* which was equally strict towards his enemies, his friends, and himself (MEW 19:55; my italics).

The highest praise that the founders of Marxism can envision for someone is the fact that the person in question has a strict and unwavering sense of duty. This makes short shrift of the image of Marx and Engels concocted by the reactionaries who seek to discredit them and by the materialists who try to appeal to the authority of Marx and Engels to excuse their own absurd evasion of moral obligations. Their image of Marx and Engels is nothing else but calumny, devoid of the slightest basis in the work or personality of those two men.

Marx himself was a gentleman of the old school. Is it an insignificant detail, for example, that he used a monocle all his adult life? He completely scorned popularity, felt an overwhelming sense of implacable moral responsibility, and the depth of that feeling made him a communist. The notion that he wanted to "liberate" human beings from moral obligation is the sheerest nonsense propagated in recent times.

I have already quoted the letter of Engels to Fischer on 8 March 1895 (see p. 170). The matter at issue was the weak attitude of the Social Democrats, who were willing to accept what was only a legal obligation as a moral obligation. The situation was complicated by the fact that at the time Fischer was also publishing Engels' new Introduction to *The Class Struggles in France*. Some of the leaders of the Social Democrats found some of Engels' comments to be too forceful. Right after the passage cited earlier, Engels discusses their proposed corrections and accepts most of them. He is even willing to have his remarks on Bismarck toned down to some extent. But there is a limit:

> Why you people find it hazardous to allude to Bismarck's conduct in 1886, when he violated the Constitution, is totally incomprehensible to me. It is an incomparable argumentum ad hominem. But, very well, I will give in to your request.
>
> That far! I *absolutely* cannot go any farther. I have done as much as I could to preclude difficulties for you in the debate. But you would have done much better to sustain the viewpoint that the obligation to legality is juridical, not moral . . . (MEW 39:425).

Here we have Engels consciously obeying an absolute moral norm: "I *absolutely* cannot go any farther." Engels cannot agree to a doctrinal error on a matter of ethics, i.e., confusing a legal obligation with a moral one. Political opportunism, then and now, behaves quite differently.

The opportunists are willing to say anything that sounds good at the moment, even if they have no intention of carrying out their word. When the time comes to act, they will do what suits them even if it contradicts everything they had promised before.

Engels absolutely could not accept that outlook. Today people frequently overlook the fact that condemnation of opportunism necessarily implies some absolute moral criterion. Otherwise there would be no difference between opportunism and political effectiveness. (Recall what Engels wrote to Gerson Trier about alliances: all means are good, so long as the question of morality is not involved (see p. 168). When some neo-Marxists maintain that we need politics, not morality, they are really espousing the bourgeois criterion of opportunism. Recall Engels' letter cited earlier (p. 170): "And if you had promised that in Brussels, you were *morally obliged* to carry it out."

According to the founders of Marxism, it is characteristic of the revolutionary not only to proclaim rights as the bourgeois *Declaration of the Rights of Man* does, but also to acknowledge certain obligations. Correcting the Erfurt Programme in 1891, Engels puts it this way:

> Instead of "in the name of the equal right of all" I propose: "in the name of equal rights and *equal obligations* of all." For us, *equal obligations* are an especially essential complement to the bourgeois-democratic *equal rights;* they divest the latter of their specifically bourgeois sense (MEW 22:232).

Paradoxical as it may seem to the fashionable new currents around today, the founders of Marxism viewed the denial of obligations as a step backward into what should be the past.

IV

There is a fourth theme that enables one to verify infallibly whether an author recognizes the existence of an absolute moral imperative. It is the notion of "conscience." In this case I need hardly remind the reader that I am going to present only passages from the writings of Marx and Engels that mention the term *Gewissen* ("moral conscience"), not passages where they use the term *Bewusstsein* ("consciousness" in general).

At this point the reader might be a bit puzzled by my insistence on citing more passages from Marx and Engels. Their testimony on the existence and importance of morality already seems so explicit and frequent that it looks like I am trying to batter down a door that is already open. I must admit that there are indeed many Marxists who do recognize the existence of an unmistakable moral conscience. (Why do they call themselves materialists? We must ask.) But those Marxists who deny the existence of moral conscience are much more logically consistent, and this section is directed at their thinking. So that there will be no doubt in the reader's mind, I will begin by citing two passages from Althusser. His merit lies in the fact that he spells out the logical consequences of a materialism which many profess without realizing the implications. Althusser writes:

> Of course everyone, unless one lives one of these ideologies as the truth (e.g., if one "believes" in God, justice, duty, etc.), admits that as a "conception of the world" the ideology—speaking of it from a critical perspective and examining it as an ethnologist examines the myths of a "primitive society"—is in large part imaginary: i.e., that it "does not correspond to reality".[1]

> They recognize the existing state of affairs (*das Bestehende*). They acknowledge that "things are the way they are, not otherwise"; that it is necessary to obey God, conscience, the parish priest, De Gaulle, the engineer; that it is necessary "to love one's neighbor as oneself"; and so forth.[2]

In the first passage Althusser mocks duty, in the second passage he makes fun of conscience. Of course he is free to profess what he chooses, but there is an objective way to find out whether Marx professed the same thing or not.

Let us begin by recalling the *Critique of the Gotha Programme*, where Marx attributed a lack of conscience to those who had betrayed his economic message:

> The mere fact that the representatives of our party were capable of making such a monstrous attack on an insight which has gained wide acceptance among the mass of the party is surely sufficient proof of the criminal levity and complete lack of conscience with which they set to work on the formulation of the compromise program (MEW 19:26; VFI:352).

In Chapter 26 of Book III of *Capital* we read the following:

> Instead of enlightening us on this point, Norman offers us the sage opinion that the demand for money-capital is not identical with the demand for money as such; and this sagacity alone, because he, Overstone, and the other Currency prophets, constantly have *pricks of conscience* since they are striving to make capital out of means of circulation as such through the artificial intervention of legislation, and to raise the interest rate (MEW 25:434; CAP 3:419; my italics).

Back in the preceding chapter I cited a similar passage from the *Grundrisse* (see p. 157) which ends: "These attempts at apologetics demonstrate a guilty conscience" (GRU:460).

In section 14 of Chapter 4 of *Theories of Surplus Value*, Marx writes:

> If the labourer's overproduction is *production for others*, the production of the normal capitalist, of the industrial capitalist as he ought to be, is *production for the sake of production*. It is true that the more his wealth grows, the more he falls behind this ideal, and becomes extravagant, even if only to show off his wealth. But he is always enjoying wealth *with a guilty conscience* [my italics], with frugality and thrift at the back of his mind. In spite of all his prodigality he remains, like the miser, essentially avaricious (MEW 26/1:254; TSV 1:282).

In Chapter 20 of the same book Marx first has this to say about James Stuart Mill:

> Thus no solution of the matter is possible here, only a sophistic explaining away of the difficulty, that is, only *scholasticism*. Mill begins this process. In the case of an *unscrupulous blockhead* like McCulloch, this manner assumes a swaggering shamelessness (MEW 26/3:83; TSV 3:87).

In the same book he categorizes the doctrine of McCulloch as "conscienceless eclecticism," both in a subheading and in the body of his text (see MEW 26/3:168 and 171; cf. TSV 3:168 and 171).

After mentioning the indescribable atrocities of the primitive accumulation of capital in Chapter 1 of Book I of *Capital*, Marx writes:

> With the development of capitalist production during the manufacturing period, the public opinion of Europe had lost the last remnant of shame and conscience (MEW 23:787; CAP 1:759).

In Chapter 4 of *Theories of Surplus Value* Marx notes that once the bourgeoisie has won the battle to take over its share of control of the state, it then pays the intellectual and spiritual workers to enter its service. At that point

> the bourgeoisie tries to justify "economically," from its own standpoint, what at an earlier stage it had criticised and fought against. Its spokesmen and *conscience-salvers* in this line are the Garniers, etc. (MEW 26/1:274; TSV 1:301; my italics).

If Marx could have looked ahead to the second half of the twentieth century, he would have added the names of various neo-Marxist theoreticians to the list of Garnier and others. For the best way to salve consciences is to deny that moral conscience corresponds to reality and to laugh at those who believe in conscience.

In Chapter 1 of Marx's *Contribution to the Critique of Political Economy,* which provides a classic analysis of the commodity, we find this sentence:

> On the other hand, exchange-value as we have considered it till now has merely existed as our abstraction, or, if one prefers, as the abstraction of the individual commodity-owner, who keeps the commodity as use-value in the warehouse, and has it on his conscience as exchange-value (MEW 13:30 f.; CCPE:44).

In Chapter 17 of *Theories of Surplus Value* we read this long protasis:

> Altogether, the phrase *over-abundance of capital* instead of *over-production of commodities* in so far as it is not merely a prevaricating expression, or conscienceless thoughtlessness, which admits the existence and necessity of a particular phenomenon when it is called A but denies it as soon as it is called B, in fact therefore showing scruples and doubts only about the *name* of the phenomenon and not the phenomenon itself; or insofar . . . (MEW 26/2:499; cf. TSV 2:499).

There is hardly need to point out that when Marx rebukes such traits as "conscienceless thoughtlessness," he is rebuking people who have no conscience (*Gewissen*) and separating himself irretrievably from them. The mockery of neo-Marxists against those who "believe" in moral conscience strikes first and foremost against Marx himself; and the ultimate outrage is to equate Marx's system with a denial or rejection of conscience. It is a falsification without the least semblance of plausibility, plain old cynicism in the style of Adolf Hitler, and an outrageous offense against public opinion.

In a letter to Engels dated 9 February 1860, Marx writes:

> Vögele, who was asked to come yesterday, did *not* come. Of course Blind [and] Hollinger kept him away with money, but that money is down the drain. I know the man has a conscience, and I am going to buck up his resolve (MEW 30:33).

In another letter to Engels dated 11 January 1868, Marx writes about the failings of Feuerbach:

The gentlemen in Germany (except reactionary theologians) think that Hegel's dialectics is a "dead dog." On this point Feuerbach has many things weighing on his conscience (MEW 32:18).

To the same intimate friend Marx talks about his own conscience in an important letter dated 7 May 1867:

> Without you I would never have been able to finish the work. And I assure you that it has always weighed heavily on my conscience that you have squandered your time in business and allowed your egregious energy to be frittered away for my sake in particular; and that in addition you have also had to share all my petty miseries (MEW 31:296 f.).

For his part, Engels directs the following question to Marx in a letter dated 3 September 1873:

> Are you willing to communicate what I have said above to Le Moussu, if you are of the opinion that I can in good conscience proceed thus with regard to Lafargue? (MEW 33:91).

The last two letters are an even more irrefutable argument than the preceding ones, if that is possible. Writing to each other, Marx and Engels talk about their respective consciences as realities which undoubtedly exist and which serve as an obligatory norm for their behavior. On 5 November 1892 Engels, deeply immersed in preparing Book III of *Capital* for publication, writes as follows to his friend Sorge:

> There still remains a pile of work, but now I have progressed far enough to glimpse the end. No one will be more pleased than I; this piece of work has weighed like an incubus on my conscience (MEW 38:507).

When Martignetti asked him for a letter of recommendation for Buenos Aires, Engels replied in a letter dated 13 January 1890. After first reminding him that the confidence which the workers placed in him was due to the fact that they believed he always told the truth, Engels says:

> To foresee any contingencies, I am enclosing to you a card on which I say on your behalf all that I can say in good conscience (MEW 37:343).

In a letter to Marx dated 8 July 1866, Engels writes:

As far as the Russians are concerned, Monsieur Bismarck is the man who can threaten them with a new Polish insurrection; and they know that the man is sufficiently lacking in conscience for such a thing (MEW 31:236).

I have already quoted Engels' letter to Kautsky (see p. 179) in which he talks about Dr. J. Simon, "perhaps one of the last of the oldtime functionaries who remained true to his vocation and preserved his delicacy of conscience" (MEW 35:223). On 26 April 1853 Marx begins a letter to Engels as follows:

Dear Frederic:
I am afraid the planned trip will come to nothing. Bamberger cannot discount the note for me and Friedlander, who had halfway promised, definitely does not want to. I have written to Strohn about it, but I regard this as a mere formality which I have carried out to discharge my conscience and for my wife's sake, without hoping in any result (MEW 28:235).

In a letter dated 13 August 1887, Engels invites Bebel to spend a few days resting with him in England when he gets out of prison. Then he goes on to say:

But you must do me the favor of accepting my proposal in its entirety, especially this part: at my expense, since I could not be at peace with my conscience if I were to impose any sacrifice, however small, upon you (MEW 36:694).

On 22 February 1885 Engels writes as follows to Hermann Schlüter:

The last section of Book II of *Capital* goes off tomorrow. The day after that it is Book III— So long as I have this on my conscience, I cannot think seriously about anything else (MEW 36:285).

In his second draft of *The Civil War in France* Marx offers this clear and concise description of Thiers. It would serve as a fine characterization of some theoreticians today who claim to be interpreters of Marx:

. . . with national and class prejudices instead of ideas, and with petulance instead of a conscience (MEW 17:576).

In the article on Bangya cited earlier (see p. 178), Marx also writes the following:

The Poles did not rest content with communicating to Türr and other Hungarians the content of these missives, which later were published by the *Tribune*. They gave still another unequivocal proof of their delicacy of conscience . . . (MEW 12:558).

In an article for the *Neue Oder-Zeitung* dated 28 June 1855, Marx writes:

In both cases we find a conspiracy between the Church and the capitalist monopolies, and in both religious penal laws aimed at the lower classes to set at rest the conscience of the privileged classes (MEW 11:323; VSE:289).

Writing about Louis Napoleon for the NYDT (8 March 1853), Marx says

that this adventurer without conscience, over whom no parliament or press exercises control, would try like the dickens to fall upon England like a pirate after squandering his own public treasury by extravagance and waste (MEW 8:532).

And since we are talking about Louis Napoleon, let us recall another comment by Marx on this person: "Everything that debases the conscience of the nation consolidates the power of Napoleon" (MEW 12:511). In another article for the NYDT (31 March 1858), Marx calls him

a gambler without conscience, a rash adventurer who would bet the bodies of kings as readily as those of others in any game that promised him profit (MEW 13:286).

Referring to the pretender to the throne of Prussia in an article dated 27 December 1858 (NYDT), Marx says:

Whereas he and his followers imagine they can deceive the country, they only bear witness to their own lack of conscience (MEW 12:661).

By way of contrast, here is Marx's opinion of the great antislavery agitator, Wendell Phillips, which was published in *Die Presse* on 30 August 1862:

For thirty years, and at the risk of his own life, he has incessantly raised the battle cry of the emancipation of the slaves, without consideration for either the mockery of the press or the furious cries of paid ruffians and the conciliatory representations of prejudiced friends. He has been recognized, even by his enemies, as one of the greatest orators of the North, as a character of iron who unites violent energy with *the purest intention* (MEW 15:530; my italics).

This passage makes it clear that Marx knows very well what he is saying when he talks about conscience in the other passages cited above. He is discerning enough to pinpoint the man of integrity who obeys his conscience despite threats, jibes, and alluring appeals to the easy way out.

On 7 or 8 May 1869 the General Council of the International published a flyer written by Marx, "The Belgian Massacres: To the Workmen of Europe and the United States." In it Marx noted:

> The Belgian ministers are certainly excellent patriots of the stamp exemplified by the Irish minister. Even as he has been the conscienceless instrument of the planters of western India, so they are the conscienceless instruments of the Belgian capitalists (MEW 16:352).

This message was translated into German by Eccarius, and his text was published in the *Demokratisches Wochenblatt* on 22 May and in the *Vorbote* in June. Eccarius, who lived in London and worked closely with Marx, used the German word *gewissenlose* ("without moral conscience") here, not the word *unbewusst* ("unconscious," "unknowing"). The import of the passage is clearly the same as the ones we have cited above.

At this point I would like to point out that many Marxists, particularly those who use the Romance languages (French, Spanish, Italian, and Portuguese), play dirty when they proffer their theories of ideology. They translate Marx's term *böses Gewissen* ("bad conscience" or "guilty conscience") as *mala conciencia,* and then imply that Marx's term is *schlechtes Bewusstsein* ("bad consciousness"). Thus they completely disregard the moral connotation in Marx's term, implying that he is talking about nothing more than a mistaken mental reflex. English-language writers may do the same thing by erroneously translating *Gewissen* as "consciousness" instead of "conscience."

The fact is that Marx himself consistently characterized ideological lines of reasoning in one and the same way. He suggested that they were meant to soothe consciences, to allay any hints or suspicions of *moral* blindness or hypocrisy. When his translators and interpreters reduce his term "conscience" to mere "consciousness," they proceed to construct epistemologies that have absolutely no connection with that of Marx himself. This nonsensical brand of interpretation cannot be attributed to unfamiliarity with the German language because the surrounding context eliminates any potential ambiguity. All one has to do in this case is read what is in Marx's text. Instead the nonsensical interpretations must be attributed to an unfamiliarity with, or disregard for, Marx's work. If one starts off with a materialist presupposition, as these interpreters do, then obviously it makes no sense to talk about moral conscience. But as I have pointed out before, in his *Theses on Feuerbach* Marx rejected *all* prior versions of materialism. And that of course includes the most obvious and well-known version of materialism, i.e., the one that consists in denying the existence of spirit. Prescinding from the work of Marx, some of his would-be interpreters fabricate a philosophic system of their own. While it may be more or less consistent, it has about as much relationship to Marx as it does to Dante Alighieri. I wonder why they impute their ideas to the former rather than to the latter.

In his article for the *Neue Oder-Zeitung* (22 March 1855), which criticized the day of fasting promulgated by the London government, Marx writes:

> Official England orders the people to humble themselves before the Lord; to fast and do penance for the opprobrium that the bad administration of the previous government brought down upon their heads, for the millions of pounds sterling that were uselessly extorted from them, and for the thousands of lives that were carried off from them without a twinge of *conscience* (MEW 11:133; my italics).

On 25 February 1859 Marx published an article on British industry in the NYDT. At one point he writes:

> In other words, Mr. Horner tells us that in the present state of society, in the opinion of economists and the classes for which they speak, a principle can be put forward as "sound" even though it not only *contradicts all the dictates of human conscience* but also creeps in like a cancer to corrupt the life of a whole generation (MEW 13:203; my italics).

One could not assert more clearly that moral conscience prescribes dictates and norms. In this case Marx was talking about the principle of laissez-faire competition and the growth of constant capital. So the issue in question is a strictly economic one, yet Marx objects to the principle on the grounds of the dictates of conscience. In an article for the NYDT dated 25 February 1860, Marx discusses the budget of the Gladstone government:

> That Mr. Gladstone maintains a war tax on such vital necessities as tea and sugar instead of seriously taxing territoral property is an act of cowardice that must be attributed more to the aristocratic composition of Parliament than to the mental narrowness of Mr. Gladstone. If he had dared to lay a hand on the income of the owning class, this cabinet, whose view of life is quite insecure, would have felt obliged to walk out immediately. An old refrain says that the belly has no ears; but it is just as true that *the income of the owning classes has no conscience* (MEW 15:24; my italics).

Notice that Marx adds to the "materialist" maxim another one that is typically spiritual, and that he thinks the latter is more explanatory. In this case he suggests that economic decisions depend on the absence or presence of real moral conscience in people. The point is put even more strongly in Marx's letter to Engels about Vögele (see p. 184). Marx thinks that Vögele still has a conscience, and so he will be able to overcome the economic "determinations" imposed by Blind and Hollinger. And there is one other point worth noting in the above passage on the British budget: while the materialist maxim is a traditional one, the spiritually oriented one is deliberately coined by Marx as his own.

In his article for the NYDT dated 15 March 1853, Marx reports:

> On the continent hangings, firing-squad executions, and deportations are the order of the day. But the executioners, too, are beings who can be trapped and hung; and their deeds are indelibly imprinted on the conscience of the entire civilized world (MEW 8:540).

As for Engels' remarks on conscience, I shall confine myself to a relatively brief sampling of texts. For here again the listing could include hundreds of texts, as is the case with Marx. In his 1890 treatment of "The Foreign Policy of Russian Czarism," Engels reports the existence of a secret society recruited from foreign adventurers. This gang has managed to retain control over the important government posts in Russia right up to the moment that Engels is discussing. Engels' description of the people involved is: "This gang—as talented as it is without conscience . . ." (MEW 22:15; RME:26).

At one point in his article for *Der Volksstaat* dated 6 October 1874, Engels remarks:

> The union could be maintained of course only if we gave in immediately to the wishes of the Bakuninists and handed over the

International, bound hand and foot, to their secret conspiracy. *We were not so devoid of conscience as to do that.* We threw down the gauntlet; the Hague Congress made its decision, expelled the Bakunists, and voted to publish the official proceedings which justified this expulsion (MEW 18:537; my italics).

Even in articles dealing with military history Engels rightfully injects conscience into the picture. His article for the NYDT on "The Attack on Sebastopol" was published on 14 October 1854. He describes the siege of Silistria by the Russians, when thirty thousand French and twenty thousand British soldiers abandoned their Turkish ally to an attack from a far superior number of Russians even though they (the French and British) were bivouacked within a few days' marching distance. Here is Engels' comment on their conduct:

> There is no instance in the history of war of an army within easy reach, thus cowardly leaving its allies to shift for themselves. No expedition to the Crimea, and no victory will ever clear away that stain from the honour of the French and English commanders. Where would the British have been at Waterloo if old Blücher, after his defeat at Ligny two days before, had *thus conscientiously* acted in the manner of Raglan and Saint-Arnaud (MEW 10:508 f.; TEQ:476; my italics).

The allusions of Marx and Engels are frequent and abundant. They crop up at key points in their economic works, in private affairs, and in their explanations of historical and political events. How is it possible that a certain brand of materialism has sought to justify and certify its own absurd theses by appealing to their names? In particular, how could it appeal to Marx and Engels to justify its mockery of moral conscience? The answer is simple: it is due to a complete lack of conscience on the part of the materialists involved. (I do not insult them, for they themselves deny the existence of conscience.)

V

Since Marx so clearly and unequivocally recognizes the existence of an absolute moral imperative and an inescapable moral conscience, it does not really matter much whether he explicitly affirms the existence of God in this connection or not. In fact we shall see that he does affirm the existence of God explicitly. But for someone who realizes that the God of the Bible is revealed solely and exclusively as a moral imperative of justice, the important point has already been resolved in this and the preceding chapters.

Here in this section I simply want to add some statements of Marx and

Engels about moral matters that do not fit neatly into any one of the four previous sections. Here I am talking about their use of qualifying words that are undeniably ethical in import even though Marx and Engels may not explicitly bring out the fact that it is a question of morality, or the liceity of certain means, or a matter of duty and sacrifice, or a question of egotism or conscience.

For example, in Chapter 26 of Book III of *Capital* Marx remarks on "the *dishonesty* of our banking lord, and his narrow-minded banker's point of view . . ." (MEW 25:439; CAP 3:424; my italics). In a letter to Talandier (10 November 1878), Marx says: "After that, there is no need to add another word more about the *integrity* of your client and bondsman" (MEW 34:354). In a letter to Kugelmann (17 February 1870), he writes about Jacoby: "Old Jacoby himself is very praiseworthy. What other oldtime radical in Europe has had the *integrity* and the courage to take his stand so directly on the side of the proletarian movement? (MEW 32:651; my italics). Writing to Engels about Ernest Jones (24 November 1857), Marx says:

> I consider him *honest* [my italics], and as in England it is impossible for a *public character* to become impossible because of the follies, etc., he commits, it is only a question of his extricating himself as quickly as possible from his own snare (MEW 29:218; SCME: 92).

Referring to Juch, Marx writes this to Engels on 31 January 1860: "Now and then I must give encouragement to this man, who otherwise is *completely honest* in his own fashion" (MEW 30:18). In another letter to Engels dated 27 August 1860, Marx writes: "Weydemeyer is now at last discovering that he is too honest for American journalism" (MEW 30:85).

As for Engels, in a letter to the editor-in-chief of *La Roma del Popolo* dated 21 December 1871, he writes:

> Dear Editor-in-Chief: Relying on your *integrity,* I request that you publish the attached statement. Since we are at war, let us engage in it *honorably* (MEW 17:472).

In his obituary for Robert Shaw published in *L'Internationale* on 16 January 1870, Marx writes:

> He was one of the most active members of the Council, a man of pure heart, manly character, passionate temperament, a truly revolutionary spirit, and far above vile ambition and personal interests (MEW 16:392).

In a letter dated 5 March 1895, Engels writes that "in France the Socialists are the only honest Party" (MEW 39:421). In his article for *Der Volksstaat* dated 5 July 1871, he writes: "And the *Examiner,* the only newspaper that acted *with real decency,* came down decidedly on the side of the International in a detailed article" (MEW 17:381; my italics).

In a letter to Kautsky dated 4 September 1892, Engels has this to say about George Bernard Shaw: "The paradoxical man of letters Shaw— very talented and witty as a writer but absolutely useless as an economist and politician, although honest and not a careerist . . ." (MEW 38:446; SCME:422).

In the CCPE Marx has this to say about Petty and Boisguillebert by way of contrast:

> But whereas Petty was just a frivolous, grasping, unprincipled adventurer, Boisguillebert, although he was one of the intendants of Louis XIV, stood up for the interests of the oppressed classes with both great intellectual force and courage (MEW 13:40 n; CCPE:55, ftn. 2).

In *The Great Men of the Exile* (1852) Marx and Engels describe Arnold Ruge in the following terms:

> Furthermore, a character richly endowed with all sorts of vices, coarse habits and meannesses, with the perfidy and stupidity, the cunning narrowness and dullness, the servility and arrogance, the rusticity and falseness of the emancipated serf, the peasant (MEW 8:276).

In the first draft of *The Civil War in France* Marx offers a typically moral characterization of Thiers: "pompous, skeptical, an epicurean" (MEW 17:512). Equally moral is the statement of Engels in his article for *Der Sozialdemokrat* (17 May 1883): "a premeditated liar" (MEW 19:345).

In his article for the NYDT entitled "Kossuth and Louis-Napoleon" (24 September 1859), Marx establishes an important criterion of moral uprightness in politics. This criterion is clearly incompatible with any and all amoralism, which thinks only of efficacy and is inclined to play any role to achieve its aims. Marx writes:

> It is no longer tolerable that one and the same people take in payment from the murderer of the French republic with one hand while waving the banner of liberty with the other; that they perform two roles, that of martyrs and that of courtesans; that after having

been converted into tools of the cruel usurper, they still pose as representatives of an oppressed nation (MEW 13:500).

In *The Class Struggles in France* (1850) Marx denounces "the same prostitution, the same blatant swindling, the same mania for self-enrichment" (MEW 7:14; VSE:39). In an article for the NYDT (22 April 1857), he indicts "the cruel greed of the manufacturing gentlemen" (MEW 12:185). In Chapter 24 of Book I of *Capital* he condemns the fact that "at the historical dawn of capitalist production—and every capitalist upstart has personally to go through this historical stage—avarice and desire to get rich are the ruling passions" (MEW 23:620; CAP 1:593). And earlier in the same book he denounces the *auri sacra fames* of the business capitalist (MEW 23:168, ftn. 9). In an article on the situation in Spain for the NYDT (30 September 1854), Marx denounces the "adulation, intriguing, and office-seeking" (MEW 10:495).

Engels denounces the same sort of thing in the Russian bureaucracy in his article for *Der Volksstaat* dated 21 April 1875: "The administration completely *corrupt* from start to finish, the officials living more off theft, bribery and extortion than off their pay" (MEW 18:567; my italics).

Again speaking of the Spanish government, Marx has this to say in the NYDT (20 October 1854): "the mountain of debts that an age-old series of *corrupt* governments has accumulated" (MEW 10:453; my italics).

On the French government Engels writes the following in his 1891 Introduction to *The Civil War in France:*

> In compensation for this his [i. e., Louis Bonaparte's] rule encouraged speculation and industrial activity, in a word, the rise and enrichment of the whole bourgeoisie to an extent unknown. To an even greater extent, it is true, *corruption* and mass robbery developed, clustering round the imperial court, and drawing their heavy percentages from this enrichment (MEW 22:191; SW:300–01; my italics).

In his letter of 27 October 1894 to the editorial board of the *Social Critic,* Engels writes:

> Perhaps our testimony will not be completely in vain in the face of the odious and shameful calumnies of an official and *corrupt* press (MEW 22:478; my italics).

I shall not stop to dwell on the rigorously moral import that Marx and Engels give to the word "calumny." Counting their letters, articles, and books, we can say that this word (or its corresponding adjective) is mentioned no less than two hundred times. It would take a whole monograph to study their use of it. And the same applies to their use of such words as "robbery," "swindle," "cruelty," "infamy," "abjectness," and "canaille." They are abundantly used in *Capital* in particular.

Here it would be better to allude to their use of the word "crime," whose moral connotations strike one immediately. In particular, there is Marx's prophetic conclusion to Chapter 25 of Book I of *Capital*, which ends with an intentionally tragic and ominous strain from Horace:

> *Acerba fata romanos agunt*
> *Scelusque fraternae necis* (MEW 23:740; CAP 1:712).

The crime of fratricide has never been so substantiated with documentation as it is in this chapter by Marx on the process of capitalist accumulation. Marx's article on "Tortures in India," which was published in the NYDT on 17 September 1857, concludes with these words:

> And if the English could do these things in cold blood, is it surprising that aroused Hindus, in the rancorous heat of rebellion and struggle, have become guilty of the crimes and cruelties that were committed against themselves? (MEW 12:273).

The whole article is replete with similar statements. Marx's denunciation of the Prussians in another text cuts even deeper. It is in the second address of the General Council on the Franco-Prussian War (9 September 1870):

> History will measure its retribution, not by the extent of the square miles conquered from France, but by *the intensity of the crime* [my italics] of reviving, in the second half of the nineteenth century, *the policy of conquest!* (MEW 17:274; VFI:182).

In an article for the NYDT entitled "Population, Crime and Pauperism" (16 September 1859), Marx writes:

> Something must be rotten in the core of a social system which increases its wealth without diminishing its poverty, and in which *crimes* grow even faster than the population figures (MEW 13:492; my italics).

Of all the clearly moral categories we have documented here in Section V, the most important may well be that of honesty (or integrity). The brand of materialism that is much in evidence today, and that claims to be "Marxist" and "revolutionary," maintains that the moral qualities of human beings are of no importance. Such a thesis is about as revolutionary as a call to return to brute animality. According to Marx and Engels, integrity and honorableness are absolutely indispensable in an authentic revolutionary, because the future world we hope to construct will be a world of integrity and authentic morality.

Notes

1. "Ideología y aparatos ideológicos del estado," in *La Filosofía como arma de la revolucíon,* 17th Spanish edition, Mexico City: Siglo XXI, 1976, p. 124.
2. Ibid., p. 137 f.

8

The Gospel Roots
of Marx's Thought

Jesus Christ asks his listeners: "Is not life more than food? Is not the body more valuable than clothes?" (Matt. 6:25). Then, after alluding to the birds in the sky, he asks: "Are not you more important than they?" (Matt. 6:26). In another context he voiced his subversive statement: "The sabbath was made for man, not man for the sabbath" (Mark 2:27). In making these remarks Christ was formulating the very same value judgment that constitutes the essence of Marx's humanism as we saw it in Chapter 5. It was in the name of this humanism and its attendant value judgments that Marx's whole economic message revolted against capitalism. Why? Because in the capitalistic system "the process of production has the mastery over man, instead of being controlled by him" (MEW 23:95; CAP 1:81). Because "the workers themselves appear as that which they are in capitalist production—mere means of production, not an end in themselves and not the aim of production" (MEW 26/2:549; TSV 2:548). Hegel had earlier pointed out that the conviction that a human being is an end in itself is not a "natural" one. It has not always existed and not every civilization has arrived at it on its own. Thus Kant was wrong in believing that such a conviction is "natural" to reason. Instead it has an historical origin. It was from Jesus Christ that the West learned that a human being is an end in itself, and the rest of the world learned it from the West.

In Chapter 5 I called particular attention to this statement by Marx: "As in religion man is governed by the products of his own brain, so in capitalistic production he is governed by the products of his own hand" (MEW 23:649; CAP 1:621). The term *Machwerk* ("artificial work") is a technical term in the German Bible. And as I have already noted, it is used there to refer to the false gods that are the products of human hands. So Marx's thesis is that the domination of human beings by the works of their own hands is even more true in the capitalistic mode of production than in religion.

197

I

Both Marxists (e.g., Balibar) and anti-Marxists (e.g., Delekat and Künzli) have called attention to the central importance of the category "fetish" in Marx's writings. It shows up specifically in those scientific and technical sections of his economic works to which Marx himself attributed greater originality. The term "fetish" is a technical one derived from ethnology, the sociology of religion, and the history of religions. However, Marx uses the words: "Moloch," "Baal," and "Mammon" just as often, if not more often. These three words are taken from the Bible. Moloch (probably identical to Milcom) was the god of the Ammonites (see Sam. 12:30; 2 Kings 23:13; Jer. 49:1–3; Zeph. 1:5). Baal, the god of the Canaanites, is mentioned frequently (see Judg. 6:25–32; 1 Kings 16:31 f.; Hos. 2:15; 11:2). The third term "Mammon" (originally Aramaic *mamonas*) is the most important of the three, but it only appears in the Gospels: three times in Luke's Gospel (Luke 16:9,11,13) and once in Matthew's Gospel (Matt. 6:24). Each time it appears on the lips of Jesus himself. The point here is that the German translation of the Gospels retained the word "Mammon," whereas it has been translated as "money" or "wealth" in Spanish, French, and English versions of the Bible. The saying, "You cannot serve God and Mammon" (Matt. 6:24 and Luke 16:13), is one of those whose historical authenticity on the lips of Jesus is not denied by any modern researcher. And "Mammon" is not the name of some god or idol; it means "money," or "capital" to be specific.[1]

Both the Old and the New Testaments repeatedly prohibit idolatry, the worship of false gods. For example, the anathematized golden calf (Exod. 32), to which Marx also alludes, was not worshipped as gold; it was worshipped as an idol, as an image and representation of a false god. It is in this connection that the unsettling originality of Jesus Christ appears. The rest of the Bible talks about idols and false gods. It refers to them as "demons" (e.g., Deut. 32:17; Ps. 105:37; 95:5; Bar. 4:7; 1 Cor. 10:20.21) or "things of nought" (e.g., Lev. 19:4; 1 Chron. 16:26; Hab. 2:18; Jer. 14:22; 16:19). Jesus, however, denounces money as the real object of idolatry. He is the first human being in history to denounce money as the real object that is the true rival of the one and only God.

The Christian churches have not fully realized the unprecedented originality in this saying of Jesus. The premeditated saying, "You cannot serve God and money," evokes in its hearers the Old Testament contrast between serving Yahweh and serving other gods (e.g., Deut. 6:13; 7:16; 10:20). For the first time, however, that other god is something real and recurring. For the first time covetousness and the lust for gain are denounced as the real idolatry. They are not to be found solely in a few rare human beings who indulge in the whimsicality of worshipping false gods that are not real. They are to be found in all human beings who place their confidence in money, and hence in any economic system that depends on money. St. Paul understood the point when he referred to "that lust which is idolatry" (Col. 3:5; Eph. 5:5). Here we have another phrase that strikes the exegetes as unique and surprising; its precedent is to be found in the surprising and aggressive saying of Jesus that we have just noted.

Of course the spontaneous reaction of the "average" Christian is this: how can we stop trusting in money so long as we live in a world in which everything depends on it? Jesus Christ was no fool, and he anticipated this reaction. The point is that we must choose between two possible types of Christianity: an authentic Christianity and a pseudo-Christianity. In trying to carry out the message of Jesus Christ, those who choose authentic Christianity will also accept its political and socioeconomic consequences. Others will accept a pseudo-Christianity which maintains that this dictum makes no sense and cannot be carried out "in the present circumstances" (which have lasted for two thousand years). Or else this pseudo-Christianity tries to foster a sense of guilt in us so that justification will depend on God's gratuitous gift rather than on our own works. But if we are to carry out the teaching of Jesus Christ in all its originality, then the fact remains that we must get rid of any mode of production in which money is of necessity the supreme god. We have already noted that Marx mocked the superficiality of people like Proudhon, who hoped to get rid of money while still retaining the commodity mode of production. For the absolute dominion of money over everything is inevitable in that particular mode of production.

It can hardly be a coincidence that the exact same skeptical reaction occurs in the face of all similar remarks by Jesus. Another saying of his, which no modern investigator would deny as authentic and historical, is: "It is easier for a camel to pass through the needle's eye than for a rich man to enter the kingdom of God" (Mark 10:25; see Matt. 19:24). It has already been proven that the kingdom is to be realized on earth. In fact the prayer composed by Jesus says: "Your kingdom come" (Matt. 6:10). It does not say: "Bring us to the kingdom." Thus in the future social organization that we call the kingdom of God only those who are poor will participate; those who are rich now cannot participate. Another certainly authentic saying of Jesus is: "Blest are you poor; the reign of God is yours" (Luke 6:20). It is complemented by another saying: "Woe to you rich, for your consolation is now" (Luke 6:24).

I shall not stop here to show that Jesus is not condemning the physical fact of being rich in this saying. What he is condemning is the fact that some are rich while others are poor, that existing society is divided into classes. All this means that the kingdom will be communist. No subtlety of reasoning or hemming and hawing can evade that conclusion.

Of course, the communist effort of the primitive Christian community (Acts 2:44 and 4:32) did fail. However, that fact does not strip the primitive communism of the early church of its normative character vis-à-vis the essence of Christianity. Instead we must ask ourselves why it failed and eradicate the causes for that failure. According to Marx, it failed because the primitive Christians neglected the political struggle. In the midst of a world based upon commodity production and private property, an isolated community cannot avoid the penetrating influence of money and anti-communist factors. Centuries later Christians would betray the cause by asserting that the elimination of private property is not an obligation but a way to higher perfection. Today that felonious "interpretation" is still being taught; while it claims to adore Jesus Christ as God, it actually stabs him in the back. That is the only way to keep the gospel message from revolutionizing the world.

Delekat is correct in pointing out that Christian discussion of Marxism is theological and that it does not end with debating the theme of historical materialism.[2] He and most other commentators sidestep the fact that the discussion really centers on the question as to whether we are or are not disposed to accept the message of Jesus Christ. It should not be imagined that Marx, with all his hatred for capitalism, disregards or conceals the fact that worship of the god money has existed from antiquity. On the contrary, he states that capital made capitalism, not vice versa.

First, then, I shall try to show that the conception of money as a false god cannot be excised from Marx's work. After that I shall bring his earlier works into the picture to point up the Christian roots of this conception in Marx's mind.

In considering his mature writings first, I shall focus on the message of his economic treatises, then his letters, and finally a series of important articles dealing with political and economic affairs.

II

Insofar as Marx's mature economic works are concerned, we cannot excise the notion of money as a false god from them as some materialists already propose to do. There are two reasons why we cannot: first, because in it is rooted the humanism which lies behind Marx's economic analysis and which condemns the subordination of human beings to things; second, because the central problem of the birth of capitalism— around which Marx's whole economic effort turns, according to Rosdolsky—is solved by focusing on the god money as the cause and then spelling out its impact.

Reading *Capital* and the *Grundrisse,* a materialist would scarcely imagine that Marx is dealing with the history of the god Mammon, that his work is a commentary on Jesus Christ's denunciation of the worship of money.

Materialists have difficulty in trying to understand Marx's explanation of the birth of capitalism. Psychologically speaking, their difficulty does not begin when Marx talks about the false god as an actor, protagonist, and subject. It begins a bit earlier when Marx notes that money "suddenly presents itself as an independent substance, endowed with a motion of its own, passing through a life-process of its own" (MEW 23:169; CAP 1:154). Materialists had thought that the mode of production was the cause of everything. What matters to Marx, however, is how the different causes exert their impact on the mode of production (see Chapter 4). In this case we are dealing with a cause that creates a whole mode of production suited to itself. If materialists cannot appreciate the fact that the cause of the historical birth of capitalism is the god money, Mammon, it is because they cannot see money as a substance with a motion of its own.

Let us begin, then, by ruling out the usual explanation given for the rise of capitalism. So long as we do not get beyond that evasion, we will not be able to give any real attention to the positive explanation Marx offers for the historical rise of capitalism. In *Theories of Surplus Value* we read:

> Originally, *trade* is the pre-condition for the transformation of guild, rural domestic and feudal agricultural production into capitalist production. It develops the product into a commodity, partly by creating a market for it, partly by giving rise to new commodity equivalents and partly by supplying production with new materials and thereby initiating new kinds of production which are based on trade from the very beginning because they depend both on production for the market and on elements of production derived from the world market.
>
> As soon as manufacture gains strength (and this applies to an even greater extent to large-scale industry), it in turn creates the market, conquers it, opens up, partly by force, markets which it conquers, however, by means of its *commodities.* From now on, trade is merely a servant of industrial production. . . (MEW 26/ 3:461 f.; TSV 3:470).

In the *Grundrisse* we find a statement that directly contradicts those who think that the origin of capitalism lies in some mode of production: "Production based on capital originally came out of circulation" (GRU:542). In Book II of *Capital* we find the same thought expressed in different words: "The capital-relation during the process of production arises only because it is inherent in the act of circulation, in the different fundamental economic conditions in which buyer and seller confront each other, in their class relation" (MEW 24:37; CAP 2:30). Book III is equally clear on this point: "Usurer's capital employs the method of exploitation characteristic of capital, yet without the latter's mode of production" (MEW 25:611; CAP 3:597).

Those who only read Book I of *Capital* will find Marx saying that the origin of capitalism lies in violence. Marx never retracts that view. The problem is that his materialist readers assume that the capitalist mode of production is the cause of this violence, a view Marx explicitly contradicts in Book III:

> It is again forgotten that . . . this complete expropriation of the labourer from his conditions of labour is not a result which the capitalist mode of production seeks to achieve, but rather the established condition for its point of departure (MEW 25:609; CAP 3:595).

Furthermore, in the *Grundrisse* and Book I of *Capital* we find Marx repeatedly maintaining that the separation between producers and means of production was the indispensable precondition for the rise of capitalism. Hence it is not the mode of production that is the cause of the violence attending this separation. Here we can add a passage from Engels' pamphlet of 1882 entitled *Age of the Franks:*

> There is an inexorable law in all societies based on the production of commodities and commodity interchange. It is that in them the distribution of property becomes increasingly unequal, the contrast between wealth and poverty becomes increasingly greater, and property becomes increasingly concentrated in the hands of a few. This law certainly reaches its full development in modern capitalist production, but it is not at all correct to say that it occurs there for the first time (MEW 19:476).

In history the class division between possessors and dispossessed is caused outside the sphere of production; but that division has an impact on the sphere of production, settles there, and is crystallized, and then continues to persist there because that is where it is reproduced.

Now let us follow Marx in the *positive* exposition of the dialectics of money. At some point money becomes god, and at some point this god creates the mode of production called capitalism.

First, commodity production (i.e., noncommunist production) necessarily causes one commodity to detach itself and become the medium or measure of concrete value. With equal necessity this concrete measure of value then turns into the means of payment and is called money. Next, for objective reasons that Marx enumerates, gold and silver gain an exclusive monopoly in this area and become the means of payment or money. To fill in the gap here, I shall briefly enumerate the six reasons given by Marx in his *Contribution to the Critique of Political Economy* of 1859 (MEW 13:129 f.; CCPE:153–57):

1. The uniform quality of these metals enables them to objectify merely quantitative differences. In them all differences and relationships are reduced to the single one of quantity.
2. They can be divided into as small a number of parts as you wish, and then these parts can be put together again into wholes.
3. Their great density or specific weight allows them to contain a great deal of exchange value (= labor time) in a small volume. So they are easily transportable.
4. Their relative indestructibility and incorruptibility makes gold and silver the natural material for hoarding.
5. We can prescind from gold and silver as means of life and objects of consumption. Thus they can enter the process of circulation without undermining the process of production.
6. It is possible to transform gold and silver from money pieces into bullion, and from bullion into luxury articles and articles of adornment, and vice-versa. Gold and silver are not tied to one particular form of use once and for all.

Now we may continue. Once money exists in the form of gold and silver, it inevitably tends to turn into capital. Before we consider this point, however, we must dwell a bit on what Marx calls the third attribute of money in itself. Its first attribute is to be a measure of value. Its second is to be a means of payment and of circulation. Its third attribute, which already contains its quality as capital in latent form (GRU:216), is its ability to have exchange value and live an independent existence outside circulation. However, this independence does not mean the elimination of every relationship with circulation; instead it signifies a *negative* relationship with circulation. For if every relationship were eliminated, then gold and silver would merely be natural objects; they would not be money and they would not possess exchange value.

Looked at in terms of this third attribute, then, the relationship of money to the economy is a power relationship. Standing outside production and circulation, money nevertheless dominates both. It is the epitome of wealth, the autonomous existence of value, and the concrete materialization of human labor. So true is this that it is no longer money that represents commodities but commodities that represent money. Insofar as a commodity has a price, it is merely a representative of gold; if it cannot be exchanged for money, then it suffers devaluation and depreciation: "From having been a servant of commerce, says Boisguillebert, money became its despot" (GRU:199).

> Thus, wealth (exchange value as totality as well as abstraction) exists, individualized as such, to the exclusion of all other commodities, as a singular, tangible object, in gold and silver. Money is therefore the god among commodities (GRU:221).

> In the period of the rising absolute monarchy with its transformation of all taxes into money taxes, money indeed appears as the moloch to whom real wealth is sacrificed. Thus it appears also in every monetary panic (GRU:199).

The problem is not that money is the god of commodities. The problem is that money becomes the god of this world and the god of human beings living under the commodity mode of production. That was already the case back in the time of Jesus Christ, and Marx's analysis is the best commentary on Jesus' remark about Mammon. Let us first see how Marx explains the transformation of money into a god ruling human beings:

> Since it is an individuated, tangible object, money may be randomly searched for, found, stolen, discovered; and thus general wealth may be tangibly brought into the possession of a particular individual (GRU:221).

> Money is therefore not only *an* object, but is *the* object of greed [*Bereicherungssucht*]. It is essentially *auri sacra fames*. Greed as such, as a particular form of the drive—i.e., as distinct from the craving for a particular kind of wealth such as clothes, weapons, jewels, women, wine etc.,—is possible only when general wealth, wealth as such, has become individualized in a particular thing: i.e., as soon as money is posited in its third quality. Money is therefore not only the object but also the fountainhead of greed. The mania for possessions is possible without money; but greed itself is the product of a definite social environment, not *natural* as opposed to *historical*. Hence the wailing of the ancients about money as the source of all evil (GRU:222).

> When the aim of labour is not a particular product standing in a particular relation to the particular needs of the individual, but

money, wealth in its general form, then, firstly, the individual's industriousness knows no bounds (GRU:224).

If its quality as general wealth is given, then there is no difference within it, other than the quantitative. It represents a greater or lesser amount of general wealth according to whether its given unit is possessed in a greater or lesser quantity. If it is general wealth, then one is the richer the more of it one possesses, and the only important process, for the individual as well as the nation, is to pile it up [*Anhäufen*] (GRU:229).

If gold and silver represent general wealth, then, as specific quantities, they represent it only to a degree which is definite, but which is capable of indefinite expansion (GRU:230).

The formation of hoards therefore has no intrinsic limits, no bounds in itself, but is an unending process, each particular result of which provides an impulse for a new beginning (MEW 13:110; CCPE:132).

This unlimitedness, this "bad infinity," is what makes a god out of money. Marx offers a genetic analysis of the phenomenon that Christ was the first to formulate in such striking terms. Long before it engenders capitalism, money is already a god:

One sees how the piling-up of gold and silver gained its true stimulus with the conception of it as the material representative and general form of wealth. The *cult of money* [my italics] has its asceticism, its self-denial, its self-sacrifice—economy and frugality, contempt for mundane, temporal and fleeting pleasures; the chase after the *eternal* treasure. Hence the connection between English Puritanism, or also Dutch Protestantism, and money-making (GRU:232).

The *Contribution* of 1859 says the same thing more succinctly: "Our hoarder is a martyr to exchange-value, a holy ascetic seated at the top of a metal column" (MEW 13:111; CCPE:134). Book I of *Capital* is more explicit:

In order that gold may be held as money, and made to form a hoard, it must be prevented from circulating, or from transforming itself into a means of enjoyment. The hoarder, therefore, makes a sacrifice of the lusts of the flesh to his *gold fetish* [my italics] (MEW 23:147; CAP 1:133).

Temples with the ancients served as the dwellings of the gods of commodities (MEW 23:146, ftn. 90; CAP 1:132, ftn. 1).

But hoarding is not the only way of worshipping the god money. There is also commerce and usury, and they date back to antiquity. Here is what the *Contribution* of 1859 has to say:

> Whereas the commodity-owner as the guardian of a hoard was a rather comical figure, he now becomes terrifying, because he regards, not himself, but his neighbour as the embodiment of a definite sum of money, and turns his neighbour and not himself into a martyr to exchange-value. The former believer becomes a creditor, and turns from religion to jurisprudence (MEW 13:117; CCPE:140).

I have dwelt on this third quality of money, prior to its becoming capital, because it is in this aspect that Marx sees money becoming a god: first the god of commodities, and then a god ruling over human beings themselves. And it is precisely in this aspect—as a gold fetish exacting asceticism and the sacrifice of human beings—that money becomes capital and gives rise to capitalism: "The period which precedes the development of modern industrial society opens with general greed for money on the part of individuals as well as of states" (GRU:225). In the *Contribution* of 1859 Marx cites a whole paragraph of Boisguillebert with evident satisfaction:

> These metals (gold and silver) have been turned into idols, and disregarding the goal and purpose they were intended to fulfil in commerce—i.e., to serve as tokens in exchange and reciprocal transfer—they were allowed to abandon this service almost entirely in order to be transformed into *divinities* to whom more goods, important needs and even human beings were sacrificed and continue to be sacrificed, than were ever sacrificed to the false divinities even in blind antiquity . . . (MEW 13:103, ftn.; CCPE:125, ftn. 3).

It seems quite obvious to me that *it is from this attack on the worship of Mammon that Marx derives his humanist criterion which we examined in Chapter 5. And on the basis of that criterion he condemned the fact that human beings should be sacrificed as such and turned into means in the service of objectified, reified wealth.* For the fact is that Marx's hostile critique of Mammon and its worship antedates his humanist criterion and its implementation.

Let us get back to the origin of capitalism. It is in its role as god, as

Mammon, as a false deity, that money gives rise to capitalism. Book I of
Capital says so:

> Today industrial supremacy implies commercial supremacy. In the
> period of manufacture properly so called, it is, on the other hand,
> the commercial supremacy that gives industrial predominance.
> Hence the preponderant role that the colonial system plays at that
> time. It was "the strange God" who perched himself on the altar
> cheek by jowl with the old Gods of Europe, and one fine day with a
> shove and a kick chucked them all of a heap. It proclaimed
> surplus-value making as the sole end and aim of humanity (MEW
> 83:782; CAP 1:754).

The expression "strange God" is a deliberate allusion to the way the
Bible refers to all deities besides the one true God. One can find numerous examples of this in the Bible (e.g., Gen. 35:2; Exod. 20:3; Josh.
24:23; Jer. 11:10; 16:11; 5:19; Deut. 32:12). In what was originally the
sixth chapter of Book I of *Capital,* and which has been published only
recently,[3] we find this passage:

> In material production, in the real process of social life (for that is
> what the process of production is), we find exactly *the same*
> relationship that *religion* presents in the realm of ideology: the
> conversion of subject into object and vice-versa. Viewed *histori-
> cally,* this conversion appears as the necessary moment of transi-
> tion for achieving by violence, and at the expense of the majority,
> the creation of wealth as such—that is to say, the inexorable
> development of the productive power of social labor, which is the
> only thing that can constitute the material basis of a free human
> society.

Thus capitalism is born. The conversion or switching of subject into
object, of end into means and vice-versa, is something that Marx first
perceived in the realm of false religion. He then applied it to economics.
Again in Book I of *Capital* we read:

> The money capital formed by means of usury and commerce was
> prevented from turning into industrial capital, in the country by the
> feudal constitution, in the towns by the guild organization. These
> fetters vanished with the dissolution of feudal society, with the
> expropriation and partial eviction of the country population. The
> new manufactures were established at sea-ports, or at inland
> points beyond the control of the old municipalities and their guilds
> (MEW 23:778; CAP 1:751).

In itself money already possessed all the dynamism needed for its conversion into capital and the creation of capitalist social relations. That is how capitalism arose. Book III of *Capital* says the same thing in different words:

> Usurer's capital employs the method of exploitation characteristic of capital yet without the latter's mode of production. . . . Usury, in contradistinction to consuming wealth, is historically important, inasmuch as it is in itself a process generating capital. Usurer's capital and merchant's wealth promote the formation of moneyed wealth independent of landed property (MEW 25:611; CAP 3:597–98).

> It is futile to speak of the stimulus given by Australian gold or a newly discovered market. If it were not in the nature of capital to be never completely occupied—i.e., always partially *fixated*, devalued, unproductive—then no stimuli could drive it to greater production (GRU:623).

> The quantitative delimitation of exchange-value conflicts with its qualitative universality, and the hoarder regards the limitation as a restriction . . . (MEW 13:109; CCPE: 131–32).

> Money in its final, completed character now appears in all directions as a contradiction, a contradiction which dissolves itself, drives towards its own dissolution. As the *general form of wealth*, the whole world of real riches stands opposite it. It is their pure abstraction—hence, fixated as such, a mere conceit. Where wealth as such seems to appear in an entirely material, tangible form, its existence is only in my head; it is a pure fantasy. . . . Further, [the notion that] to accumulate it is to increase it, [since] its own quantity is the measure of its value, turns out again to be false. If the other riches do not [also] accumulate, then it loses its value in the measure in which it is accumulated. What appears as its increase is in fact its decrease (GRU:233–34).

Thus money must rush into circulation once again so as not to be devalued, so as to retain its value. However, it does not move into circulation to be consumed, for then it would disappear; instead it moves into circulation in order to produce value. In the case of capital it is all the same whether it is embodied in money or in commodities. But it cannot maintain its value if it does not produce, which is to say, if it does not increase. In an early draft of the *Grundrisse,* to be found in the German edition, we find these words:

Its very entrance into circulation must be a phase of its remaining in itself, and its remaining in itself must be its entrance into circulation (German *Grundrisse*: 931).

Hence, for value which clings to itself as value, increasing itself and preserving itself coincide. It is conserved only by continually moving beyond its quantitative limit, which latter aspect contradicts its intrinsic universality. Thus self-enrichment is an end in itself (German *Grundrisse*: 936).

So money rushes into circulation once again. Unfortunately the exchanges that constitute circulation consist in interchanging equivalents. Capital, however, must find some way to exchange itself for some commodity that produces more value than the commodity itself has. As we saw in Chapter 6, that privileged commodity is labor power. Of course the latter must be put to work, otherwise it will not produce any increase in value. Capital moves into production insofar as it is grounded on an exchange with the commodity known as labor power; and the ultimate basis of this process is the relationship between capital and labor. The fact is that the only form of labor that can complement capital as such is wage labor, i.e., the worker who possesses nothing except his labor power. If that particular commodity did not exist in the market, then capital would have to invent it. Indeed it was the dictates of the god capital that brought about the violent separation of direct producers from the land.

Once the mode of production proper to capital is established, it must reproduce this type of laborer, just as it must reproduce itself in increasing measure. Capitalism consists in this relationship between money that seeks to convert itself into more money and the laborer that lacks the means of production. In the dimensions of the whole economy, one cannot exist without the other. The relationship itself must be reproduced, hence so must the terms of the relationship:

Capital posits the permanence of value (to a certain degree) by incarnating itself in fleeting commodities and taking on their form, but at the same time changing them just as constantly; alternates between its eternal form in money and its passing form in commodities. Permanence is posited as the only thing it can be, a passing passage—process—life. But capital obtains this ability only by constantly sucking in living labour as its soul, vampire-like (GRU:646).

Book I of *Capital* says the same thing in different words:

Capital is dead labour that, vampire-like, only lives by sucking living labour, and lives the more, the more labour it sucks (MEW 23:247; CAP 1:233).

In truth, however, value is here the *subject* in a process in which, while constantly assuming the form in turn of money and commodities it at the same time changes in magnitude, differentiates itself by throwing off surplus-value from itself; the original value, in other words, expands spontaneously. For the movement in the course of which it adds surplus-value, is its own movement; its expansion, therefore, is automatic expansion. Because it is value, it has acquired the occult quality of being able to add value to itself. It brings forth living offspring, or, at the least, lays golden eggs (MEW 23:169; cf. CAP 1:153–54; my italics).

All social powers of production are productive powers of capital, and it appears as itself their *subject* (GRU:585; my italics).

Constant capital, the means of production, considered from the standpoint of the creation of surplus-value, only exists to absorb labour, and with every drop of labour a proportional quantity of surplus-labour. . . . The prolongation of the working-day beyond the limits of the natural day, into the night, only acts as a palliative. It quenches only in a slight degree the vampire thirst for the living blood of labour (MEW 23:271; CAP 1:256).

By turning his money into commodities that serve as the material elements of a new product and as factors in the labour-process, by incorporating living labour with their dead substance, the capitalist at the same time converts value—i.e., past, materialized, and dead labour—into capital, into value big with value, a live monster that is fruitful and multiplies (MEW 23:209; CAP 1:195).

III

All these vivid descriptions of money—as active subject, vampire, and so forth—should not be allowed to lead us astray. We must remember that right from the early part of Book I of *Capital* Marx insists that we are dealing here with a *theological* question. The key section, of course, is the one on the "Fetishism of Commodities and the Secret Thereof" (MEW 23:85 f.; CAP 1:71–83). Marx himself says: "A commodity appears, at first sight, a very trivial thing, and easily understood. Its analysis shows that it is, in reality, a very queer thing, abounding in metaphysical subtleties and theological niceties" (MEW 23:85; CAP 1:71). The allusion is clear and unmistakable. The study of a false god has to be a theological study. Marx repeatedly uses the term "fetish" as a noun or adjective in this section, and he also uses such terms as "enigmatical," "perceptible and imperceptible," "mysterious," and "magical." He alludes to "the whole mystery of commodities, all the magic and necromancy that surrounds the products of labour as long as they take the form of commodities" (MEW 23:90; CAP 1:78). The riddle presented by the money fetish is merely the riddle presented by the commodity fetish, "only it now strikes us in its most glaring form" (MEW 23:108; CAP 1:93).

Lest someone think that Marx does not know the real name of this fetish, the main character of his analysis, a remark in a later chapter should be noted here: "Even in the middle of the eighteenth century, the Rev. Mr. Tucker, a notable economist of his time, excused himself for meddling with the things of Mammon" (MEW 23:645, ftn. 75; CAP 1:617, ftn. 2). And *On the Jewish Question* of 1843 cites another author speaking in similar terms:

> Captain Hamilton informs us that the pious and politically free inhabitant of New England is a kind of Laocoön who does not make even the slightest effort to free himself from the snakes that are choking him. *Mammon* is his idol and he prays to him not only with his lips but with all the power of his body and his soul (MEW 1:373; VEW:237).

We cannot excise this denunciation of money as a false god from Marx's economic analysis because it is an intrinsic part of his thought from Chapter I of *Capital* to his study of interest-bearing capital in Book III of *Capital* and the three volumes of *Theories of Surplus Value*.

> In interest-bearing capital the movement of capital is contracted. . . . Capital is now a thing, but as a thing it is capital. Money now has passion in its veins (MEW 25:406; CAP 3:393).

> As interest-bearing capital, and particularly in its direct form of interest-bearing money-capital . . . capital assumes its pure fetish form . . . (MEW 25:406; CAP 3:393).

> In interest-bearing capital, therefore, this automatic fetish, self-expanding value, money generating money, are brought out in their pure state; and in this form it no longer bears the birthmarks of its origin (MEW 25:405; CAP 3:392).

> It is the capacity of money, or of a commodity, to expand its own value independently of reproduction—which is a mystification of capital in its most flagrant form (MEW 25:405; CAP 3:392).

After a lengthy quote from Luther against interest on loans and several follow-up citations, Marx concludes:

> In its capacity as interest-bearing capital, capital claims the owner-ship of all wealth which can ever be produced, and everything it has received so far is but an installment for its all-engrossing appetite. By its innate laws, all surplus-labour which the human race can ever perform belongs to it, Moloch (MEW 25:410; CAP 3:397).

> The concept of capital as a fetish reaches its height in interest-bearing capital . . . (MEW 25:412; CAP 3:399).

From these statements we can see the roots of Marx's revolt against the subordination of human beings to a thing. Here is the source of his humanism, which we studied in Chapter 5. Indeed Marx himself points up the relationship in his *Theories of Surplus Value:*

> If in capitalist production—hence in political economy, its theoret-ical expression—past labour were met with only as a pedestal etc. created by labour itself, then such a controversial issue would not have arisen. It only exists because in the real life of capitalist production, as well as in its theory, *materialised labour* appears as a contradiction to itself, to *living labour*. In exactly the same way in religious reasoning, the product of thought not only claims but exercises domination over thought itself (MEW 26/3:271 f.; TSV 3:276).

> The complete *reification, inversion* and *derangement* of capital as interest-bearing capital—in which, however, the inner nature of capitalist production, [its] derangement, merely appears in its most palpable form—is capital which yields "compound interest." It appears as a Moloch demanding the whole world as a sacrifice belonging to it of right (MEW 26/3:448; cf. TSV 3:456).

> It is in *interest-bearing capital*—in the division of profit into inter-est and [industrial] profit—that capital finds its most objectified form, its pure fetish form (MEW 26/3:489; TSV 3:498).

> Thus the nature of surplus-value, the essence of capital and the character of capitalist production are not only completely obliter-ated in these two forms of surplus-value, they are turned into their opposites. But even insofar as the character and form of capital are complete [it is] nonsensical [if] presented without any intermediate

links and expressed as the subjectification of objects, the reification of subjects, as the reversal of cause and effect, the religious *quid pro quo*, the pure form of capital expressed in the formula M—M. The ossification of relations, their presentation as the relation of men to things having a definite social character is here likewise brought out in quite a different manner from that of the simple mystification of commodities and the more complicated mystification of money. The transubstantiation, the fetishism, is complete (MEW 26/3:484 f.; TSV 3:494).

In these passages we glimpse clearly the derivation of the humanism in *Capital,* its denunciation of the reversal in the relationship between persons and things. It clearly derives from Marx's denunciation of the worship of money as a god.

Here I would simply like to add a few phrases from *Theories of Surplus Value* which mirror those in Book III of *Capital* on interest-bearing capital:

The form of revenue and the sources of revenue are the *most fetishistic* expression of the relations of capitalist production (MEW 26/3:445; TSV 3:453).

However, of all these forms, the most complete fetish is interest-bearing capital (ibid.).

Interest-bearing capital is the perfect fetish (MEW 26/3:446; TSV 3:454).

Interest-bearing capital is the consummate *automatic fetish* (MEW 26/3:447; TSV 3:455).

Let no one imagine that Marx is presuming to develop this thesis, a thesis that runs through his whole major economic work, without seeing any connection between it and the New Testament. At the most critical stage in his whole dialectical reasoning process, at the point where one of the commodities stands apart and becomes money, that is to say, at the point when money is born in history, Marx cites two whole verses from the Apocalypse (17:13 and 13:17). He cites them in Latin, to be sure, and he makes it clear that they are from the Apocalypse. Here is the passage in Book I of *Capital:*

The social action therefore of all other commodities sets apart the particular commodity in which they all represent their values. Thereby the bodily form of this commodity becomes the form of the socially recognized universal equivalent. To be the universal equivalent becomes, by this social process, the specific function of the commodity thus excluded by the rest. Thus it becomes— money. "Illi unum consilium habent et virtutem et potestatem suam bestiae tradunt. Et ne quis possit emere aut vendere, nisi qui habet characterem aut nomen bestiae, aut numerum nominis ejus" (Apocalypse) (MEW 23:101; CAP 1:86).

Marx had stored that quote away for himself for at least ten years, if not longer. We find it in the published form of the *Grundrisse* (GRU:237) and in an early draft for the *Grundrisse* (German edition, p. 895); in this work he even notes that the citation is taken from the Vulgate Bible. The "beast" of this citation is the same monster or vampire or fetish or Moloch that Marx continues to refer to throughout his work. At the very point where the god money begins its trajectory we find a citation from the New Testament, and the citation holds in its literalistic sense.

Thus, on the basis of Marx's economic work and its content, the very least we could say in all truth is that Marx was certainly used by the gospel message as an unconscious tool for its scientific elaboration and for the propagation of Christ's teaching about the god Mammon. However, this biblical citation proves that Marx was not unaware of this connection with the message of the New Testament and that he did not disavow it. Indeed he could not be unaware of it. For as we shall see further on when we examine *On the Jewish Question,* Marx there rebukes the Christian world with an *ad hominem* argument as few had done before.

It should be obvious that neither Jesus Christ nor Marx was trying to construct a mythology. They were not trying to suggest that money is a superhuman entity really existing on its own. Rather, they were denouncing the construction of such a mythology and were trying to undermine it. Christ's message, for which Marx provides the detailed commentary, obviously implies that the worship of Mammon is a free act of human beings; otherwise Christ would not have exhorted them to stop it. Idolatry is a two-way relationship in this case. Money is a god only insofar as human beings treat it as such; but insofar as they do, it really *is* a god.

Marx shows his agreement with this point of view when he points out that in itself the accumulation of capital is not enough to give rise to capitalism in history automatically. The latter requires a certain type of human being, a certain kind of civilization, and a particular set of "historical circumstances." In his well-known letter of November 1877 to the editor of the *Otechestvennie Zapisky* on Book I of *Capital,* Marx rejects the notion that one can turn his "historical sketch of the genesis of capitalism in Western Europe" into "an historico-philosophic theory of the general path imposed by fate upon every people, whatever the historic circumstances in which it finds itself'' (MEW 19:111; MESC:354). As proof of the silliness of such a proposal, Marx points to the case of ancient Rome. In that society there arose an enormous accumulation of capital and the complete separation of the plebeians from the means of production:

> And so one fine morning there were to be found on the one hand free men, stripped of everything except their labour power, and on the other, in order to exploit this labour, those who held all the acquired wealth in possession. What happened? The Roman proletarians became, not wage labourers but a mob of do-nothings more abject than the former "poor whites" in the southern section of the United States; and alongside of them there developed a mode of production which was not capitalist but dependent on slavery. Thus events strikingly analogous but taking place in different historical surroundings led to totally different results (MEW 19:111 f.; MESC:354–55).

The same point is made in *Theories of Surplus Value* and the *Grundrisse*. In the former work he notes that in our day

> this great majority of producers necessarily remains more or less excluded from the consumption of wealth—insofar as wealth goes beyond the bounds of the necessary means of subsistence.
> This was indeed also the case, and to an even higher degree, in the ancient mode of production which depended on slavery. *But the ancients never thought* of transforming the surplus product into capital. Or at least only to a very limited extent. (The fact that the hoarding of treasure in the narrow sense was widespread among them shows how much surplus product lay completely idle.) (MEW 26/2:528 f.; TSV 2:528; my italics).

In the *Grundrisse* he says:

> The *mere presence of monetary wealth*, and even the achievement of a kind of supremacy on its part, is in no way sufficient for this *dissolution into capital* to happen. Or else ancient Rome, Byzantium etc. would have ended their history with free labour and capital, or rather begun a new history (GRU: 506).

Commenting on the end of the Middle Ages in a letter to Annenkov dated 28 December 1846, Marx notes:

Under the protection of this regime of corporations and regulations capital was accumulated, overseas trade was developed, colonies were founded. But the fruits of this would themselves have been *forfeited* if men had *tried to retain the forms* under whose shelter these fruits had ripened (MEW 4:549; MESC:8; my italics).

So we see that when Marx attributes the rise of capitalism to the god money, he is not talking about some automatic god that exists on its own even though human beings do not serve it as a god. Idolatry is a two-way relationship. I could have cited the last four passages in Chapter 3, for they clearly show Marx's belief that human beings freely decide the course of history. However, the most dialectical aspect of the whole dialectics lies in the reciprocal causality existing between the false god and its worshipper. Indeed that is part of the very definition of a false god. While the worshipper, humanity, never ceases to be the real active subject of history (see Chapter 2), idolatry consists in the fact that humanity creates a counter-subject (an idol) that ends up dominating humanity itself. Here is what Marx says in *Theories of Surplus Value*, as we noted earlier: "*Materialised labour* appears as a contradiction to itself, to *living labour*. In exactly the same way in religious reasoning, the product of thought not only claims but exercises domination over thought itself" (MEW 26/3:271 f.; TSV 3:276).

Those who reject the category of fetish for materialist reasons cannot rest content with disregarding all the economic works of Marx. That they must do, of course, since it is central to the *Grundrisse,* the *Contribution* of 1859, and *Capital.* But it is equally central to the mature Marx and his thought when he is founding the First International. Even then his thought cannot be reconciled with any such pseudo-Marxian materialism. Right in the heart of his *Inaugural Address* of 1864 we find this passage:

Through their most notorious organs of science, such as Dr. Ure, Professor Senior, and other sages of that stamp, the middle class had predicted, and to their heart's content proved, that any legal restriction of the hours of labour must sound the death knell of British industry, which vampire-like, could but live by sucking blood, and children's blood, too. In olden times, child murder was a mysterious rite of the religion of Moloch, but it was practised on some very solemn occasions only, once a year perhaps, and then Moloch had no exclusive bias for the children of the poor (MEW 16:11; VFI:79).

Such materialists would also have to disregard Marx when he talks or writes to his intimate friends and tells them what he really thinks. In a letter of 19 October 1877 to F. A. Sorge he says: "Though I gladly grant translation rights *in any part* of Europe where copyright exists with England, nevertheless I do not do so in this land of Mammon known as England'' (MEW 34:302). In like manner they must also disregard Marx the revolutionary columnist writing for the *New York Daily Tribune* and other periodicals. In an article on ''The Situation of the British Factory Industry'' dated 15 March 1859 (NYDT), Marx inserts this pregnant paragraph without any apparent reason:

> At the same time I take advantage of the occasion to express my admiration for those British factory inspectors who, in the face of all-powerful class interests, have assumed the task of protecting the oppressed masses. In these days *when Mammon is worshipped* one can hardly find any parallel for their moral courage, their unflagging energy, and their spiritual superiority (MEW 13:203; my italics).

In his article of 20 September 1858 (NYDT) we read:

> Whereas the emperor of China prohibited the importation of the poison by foreigners and its consumption by the native population, the East India Company quickly made the growing of opium in India and its smuggling into China an essential and indispensable part of its financial system. While the semi-barbarian was upholding the principle of morality, the civilized party countered with *the principle of Mammon* (MEW 12:552; my italics).

In his article of 8 March 1853 (NYDT) Marx says:

> The Milan uprising is significant as a symptom of the revolutionary crisis that is drawing near everywhere on the European continent. We see an admirable act of heroism in the action of a handful of proletarians. Armed only with knives, they dare to attack the fortress of a garrison and an army of forty-thousand men composed of the best troops in Europe. Meanwhile *the children of Mammon* were singing, dancing, and merry-making amid the blood and tears of their humiliated, martyred nation (MEW 8:527; my italics).

Similar comments can be found in other articles for the same publication. In an article dated 21 April 1853 Marx notes: ''The sentimental bourgeoisie has everywhere sacrificed the revolution to its god called property'' (MEW 9:38). In an article dated 31 March 1859, on the occasion of Louis Napoleon's visit to Queen Victoria, Marx writes:

> The British stock-exchange toasted the French stock-exchange. The apostles of stock speculation congratulated each other and

shook hands. The prevailing conviction was that finally the golden calf had been enthroned as the omnipotent god, and that its Aaron was the new French autocrat (MEW 13:284 f.).

Writing for the same publication (NYDT) on 11 January 1859, Marx noted: "No sooner had the French stocks started to drop than people rushed headlong to the *temple of Baal* to divest themselves at any price of the state bonds and stocks of Crédit Mobilier and railroad companies" (MEW 13:169; my italics). In his article for the *Neue Oder-Zeitung* (22 March 1855) Marx writes:

> We know that the despots of Tyre and Carthage placated the wrath of their deities, not by sacrificing themselves, but by buying children of the poor to throw them into the flaming arms of Moloch. England bids the people to . . ." (MEW 11:132 f.).

In an article dated 4 October 1853 (NYDT) Marx spells out one of the major principles of his philosophy of civilization and history. We shall return to this matter in the next chapter, so I would ask the reader to take serious note of the next two citations for their programmatic value. The article of 4 October says:

> One thing must be evident at least, that it is the stockjobbers, and the peace-mongering bourgeoisie, represented in the Government by the oligarchy, who surrender Europe to Russia, and that in order to resist the encroachments of the Czar, we must, above all, overthrow the inglorious Empire of those mean, cringing, and infamous *adorers of the golden calf* (MEW 9:325; TEQ:132; my italics).

On 8 August 1853, Marx laid down the same revolutionary principle in slightly different words:

> When a great social revolution shall have mastered the results of the bourgeois epoch, the market of the world and the modern powers of production, and subjected them to the common control of the most advanced peoples, then only will human progress cease to resemble that hideous pagan idol, who would not drink the nectar but from the skulls of the slain (MEW 9:226; VSE:325).

IV

My point should be clear. Honest materialists must reject the entire work of the mature Marx. We need go no further than the last two quotes to see that. His revolutionary sincerity is thorough and it is also profoundly creative. Indeed he identifies himself completely with western civilization, seeing it menaced from without by Russian barbarism and from within by the treachery of those who worship money as a god. No honest reader could interpret his denunciation of money and its rule as a god as a superficial attitude or a mere literary artifice. Marx's opposition to Mammon is so much a part of his personality and his thought that capitalists find themselves forced to indulge in barefaced "psychological" interpretations to discredit him, as they do with every revolutionary. They see in him a maladjusted personality riddled with unresolved conflicts. They "sense" some complex proper to those who never succeed in life (whatever that means). They "discover" the syndrome of the Jew who has been persecuted for centuries, and who therefore comes to hate everything in himself that looks like a vestige of his Jewish nature.[4]

This amateur brand of psychoanalysis takes no notice of the fact that it would have to say exactly the same thing about Jesus Christ and his personality, and for exactly the same reasons. (By the way, we first persecute the Jews and then accuse them of suffering from a persecution complex.) All such maneuvers betray a complete lack of insight and an inability to understand human beings. They are pure escapism. They refuse to face up to Christ's denunciation of idolatry or to the objective reasons that Marx offered by way of scientific support.

Here I do not intend to trace Marx's denunciation back year by year from his mature works to his earliest works. It is his mature works that are of prime interest to us here, and we have already considered them in detail. However, I would like to go back to his first statement on the subject in 1842 and then link it up with *On the Jewish Question* of 1843 and the *Economic and Philosophic Manuscripts* of 1844. The Stalinists, by the way, are more avid in their rejection of the 1844 Manuscripts of Marx than they are in their rejection of Hegel.

The first statement, then, is his article of 14 July 1842 for the *Rheinische Zeitung*. It is a strong plea to the bourgeoisie, addressed to them directly. Here is the relevant passage:

Don't most of your processes and civil laws deal with property? But you have been told that your treasures are not of this world. And if you reply that one must give to Caesar what is Caesar's and to God what is God's, then at least *let the Caesar of this world include not only the Mammon of gold* but also free reason to the same extent. And the "activity of free reason" is what we call philosophizing (MEW 1:101; my italics).

For the so-called Christian bourgeoisie, then, Mammon is the Caesar of this world, according to Marx. In another article for the same periodical (3 November 1842) Marx attacked the new law of the Rhineland Diet that prohibited the peasants from gathering timber for firewood and from trapping rabbits as game. His series on the new law governing forest thefts ended with the article we are now considering. It concludes:

> The savages of Cuba regarded gold as *the fetish of the Spaniards.* They celebrated a feast in its honor, sang around it, and then threw it into the sea. If the savages of Cuba had attended a session of the Rhineland Diet, would they not have come to view *wood* as the *fetish* of the *Rhinelanders?* But at the next session they would have learned that fetishism is linked up with the cult of animals, and the savages of Cuba would have thrown the *hares* into the sea in order to save *human beings* (MEW 1:147).

Comparing these two articles of 1842, we see that the July article is a bit diffuse and vague. It advocates the use of free reasoning and wants philosophizing to hold a place equal to that of Mammon in the bourgeois world. The November article, by contrast, is more focused and pointed. It argues for human beings, for the poor specifically, and it applies the label "fetish" to anything for the sake of which human beings are sacrificed. However, the very vagueness and generality of the allusion to money as a god in the July article clearly shows that Marx was taking the idea over ready-made from the Christian tradition without yet realizing its deeper import and its sharp point. In that article Marx is simply reiterating the Christian idea without getting to the bottom of it.

The correct focus came to him while he was writing *On the Jewish Question* between August and December 1843. Despite its sometimes forced style, it is a work of major importance. Here we already find Marx's thesis that political and juridical reforms and revolutions are useless so long as there is no alteration of the economy. But there is a further point which is of the utmost importance in our present context: when Marx takes a stand against the economic factor for the first time, seeing that as the decisive thing, he views the economic realm in terms of the god money. There is no talk about the mode of production as yet; instead he talks about bourgeois society. Yet Marx will never be forced to retract what he says in *On the Jewish Question* because it turns out that money as god, as capital, creates the mode of production that is perfectly suited to itself. Furthermore, this 1843 work also focuses attention on the most characteristic feature of this mode of production, i.e., private property (MEW 1:354; VEW:219). In short, it is already a communist work.

There is irrefutable testimony that both Marx and Engels were communists already in 1843. In an article for the Owenite periodical, *The New Moral World,* written in that year, Engels makes that clear:

Communism is so *necessary* a consequence of Neo-Hegelian philosophy that no opposition can stop it (MEW 1:494).

The Germans are a philosophical nation. They cannot and will not renounce Communism insofar as it is based on sound philosophical principles, particularly if it flows as an inevitable consequence from *their own* philosophy (MEW 1:495).

Engels names some of the neo-Hegelians who have arrived at the communist consequences of Kant's and Hegel's philosophy: Hess, Herwegh, and Marx. And he expressly states that Feuerbach did not dare to go that far (MEW 1:494).

Let me sum up the substance of Marx's position in his 1843 article by quoting from *On the Jewish Question:*

What is the secular cult of the Jew? *Haggling.* What is his secular God? *Money.*

Well then! Emancipation from *haggling* and from *money,* i.e., from practical, real Judaism, would be the same as the self-emancipation of our age (MEW 1:372; VEW:236).

The Jew has emancipated himself in a Jewish way not only by acquiring financial power but also because through him and apart from him *money* has become a world power and the practical Jewish spirit has become the practical spirit of the Christian peoples. The Jews have emancipated themselves insofar as the Christians have become Jews (MEW 1:373; VEW:237).

The god of *practical need and self-interest* is *money.* Money is the jealous god of Israel before whom no other god may stand. Money debases all the gods of mankind and turns them into commodities. Money is the universal and self-constituted *value* of all things. It has therefore deprived the entire world—both the world of man and of nature—of its specific value. Money is the estranged essence of man's work and existence; this alien essence dominates him and he worships it.

The god of the Jews has been secularized and become the god of the world. Exchange is the true god of the Jew. His god is nothing more than illusory exchange (MEW 1:374 f.; VEW:239).

It is of the utmost significance that in this connection Marx quotes the first practical revolutionary of the capitalist age, Thomas Münzer, the Protestant pastor who rejected private property as incompatible with Christianity and what he read in the Bible. Marx writes:

In this sense Thomas Münzer declares it intolerable that "all creatures have been made into property, the fish in the water, the birds in the air, the plants on the earth—all living things must also become free" (MEW 1:375; VEW:239).

Marx ends this article with the following words: "The *social* emancipation of the Jew is *the emancipation of society from Judaism*" (MEW 1:377; VEW:241).

It is so obvious that here Marx sees himself as a Christian that he has been accused of anti-Semitism on the basis of this article. Insofar as certain details of history are concerned, the accusation might well be merited. But as a general accusation it is one of the most superficial and escapist tacks in history. It is true, for example, that Marx assumed that the Jews were involved in money-lending activity to a degree that later statistics have not verified. We now know that only about 2 percent of them were engaged in such activity. It is also true that Marx does not allude to the historical fact that for centuries in Europe the Jews were excluded from almost every profession except commerce and trade, which obviously involves exchange. That fact is of real importance.

But the point of Marx's argument goes much deeper. First, Marx says that society as a whole has turned Jewish. He is not attacking the Jews but capitalist society as a whole. Second, the Judaism in question here consists in the worship of the god Mammon, and Marx says so explicitly. Third, Marx uses the popular image of the Jew—without verifying how true and objective it is—to confront those who hold that image and tell them: you are precisely that! Fourth, and most important, the objection to Marx's argument on the grounds of its anti-Semitism is merely a way of closing one's ears to the real message of this work and all Marx's later economic writings, i.e., that the capitalist system is essentially the institutionalization of the idolatrous worship of Mammon. This is the point I want to stress here. In this article Marx focused on the economic realm as the decisive factor for the first time; and he equated that realm with the god Mammon.

Insofar as the *Economic and Philosophic Manuscripts* of 1844 are concerned, I only want to make two brief observations. Citing Shakespeare's *Timon of Athens* in the section on "money," Marx arrives at two conclusions that are very much in line with the New Testament:

Shakespeare brings out two properties of money in particular: (1) It is the visible divinity, the transformation of all human and natural qualities into their opposites, the universal confusion and inversion of things; it brings together impossibilities. (2) It is the universal whore, the universal pimp of men and peoples (MEW/EB 1:565; VEW:377).

In the section on "Rent of Land" Marx arrives at this conclusion:

In this way the medieval saying *nulle terre sans seigneur* gives way to the modern saying *l'argent n'a pas de maître* [money knows no master], which is the expression of the complete domination of dead matter over men (MEW/EB 1:507; VEW:319).

Here again we have the notion of money as a god underlying this work as it will all the future economic works of Marx. Here, too, we already find the notion of inversion (*Verkehrung*) and the domination of matter over human beings. But the latter notion flows from the first, as we have already seen it do in *Capital* and the *Grundrisse*. To reiterate Marx's remark in *On the Jewish Question:* "Money is the estranged essence of man's work and existence; this alien essence dominates him and he worships it" (MEW 1:375; VEW:239).

By way of exception, then, I have gone back to some of the early works of Marx in this chapter. I have done so for two reasons. First, I wanted to corroborate the deliberately and strictly Christian origin of the notion of money as a god in the mind of Marx, though it is evident from the very logic of *Capital* and his reference to the Apocalypse in that later work. Second, I wanted to show that the repudiation of Marx's early works by neo-Marxists will not help them get around their difficulties. The things they reject in Marx's early works do not add one iota to the most basic and central theses of his mature economic works. The latter may add something to the former, but not vice versa. If one wishes to reject some of Marx's earliest works—not including *The Holy Family* and *The German Ideology*—then one must also reject the most central, underlying theses of *Capital* itself.

Notes

1. See Friedrich Hauck, *Theologisches Wörterbuch zum NT,* 4:392. Eng. trans., Kittel's *Theological Dictionary of the New Testament,* Grand Rapids, Mich.: Eerdmans, 1967. Also see Julius Schniewind, *Das Evangelium nach Matthäus,* 11th ed. (Das Neue Testament Deutsch), Göttingen: Vandenhoeck, 1964, p. 92; K. H. Rengstorf, *Das Evangelium nach Lukas,* 12th ed. (Das Neue Testament Deutsch), Gottingen: Vandenhoeck, 1967, p. 190.

2. See F. Delekat, *Marxismusstudien,* Tübingen: Mohr, 1954, 1:55.

3. Spanish edition translated by P. Scaron, Buenos Aires: Signos, 1971, p. 19.

4. See the monumental work (869 pages) of Arnold Künzli, *Karl Marx:Eine Psychographie,* Vienna: Europa Verlag, 1966. Though hatred of Marx is the guiding thread of this work, the author shows a mastery of the complete works of Marx that no Marxist author seems to possess.

9

Marx's Thought as a Conscious Continuation of Early Christianity

Marx's attack on religion has frequently been interpreted as an attack on Christianity. But Christianity is not a religion, as I have tried to demonstrate in my previous works.[1] In them I have offered detailed arguments to prove that the God of the Bible is incompatible with religion, and that Jesus Christ not only stressed this unmistakable trait of Yahweh but also expressly attacked the cultic worship and the temple that were allegedly dedicated to the true God. Strictly speaking, one can say that the interpretation of Christianity as a religion has been the most radical falsification ever perpetrated in history.[2]

I

Marx does attack Christianity insofar as it has been converted into religion, but he does not say very much. I am not insinuating that in making a distinction between true and false Christianity Marx uses the same words that I have just used. But obviously some such distinction is assumed by Marx when he makes such statements as the following. In an article for the NYDT dated 21 August 1852, Marx reproaches the British Whigs for being "fosterers of family-nepotism, grand masters of corruption, *hypocrites of religion, Tartuffes of politics*" (MEW 8:340 f.; VSE:261; my italics).

Here Marx is obviously assuming that in the matter of religion one can be a hypocrite or not. Whatever the conceptual distinction implied in the above quote may be, we find Marx coming down on the side of Christianity in a letter to Antonieta Philips dated 17 July 1861:

My gracious little sorceress, I hope that you will not prove to be too severe but instead that you, like a good Christian, will soon send me one of your little letters, without taking revenge on my silence that has lasted far too long (MEW 30:611).

In this passage, obviously in a rather light-hearted vein, Marx asks Antonieta Philips not to hold a grudge against him for his overly long silence. Instead of being severe with him, she should act like a "good Christian." A good Christian presumably would be forgiving and generous enough to send him a quick little letter.

Here is another letter to a friend in which the same phrase occurs. Writing to Kugelmann on 26 March 1870, Marx says:

Today I am writing you only a few lines because a Frenchman dropped in just as I had gotten set to renew my correspondence with you after a long break. Now it is afternoon, I am not yet rid of the fellow, and the post office closes at 5:30.

But tomorrow is Sunday, and so a good Christian like me is permitted to interrupt work and fill you in more fully, particularly on the Russian case which has unfolded beautifully (MEW 32: 663).

Here again Marx brings up the phrase, "a good Christian," this time applying it to himself. Here again he is speaking in a rather light-hearted vein. Is it just a matter of tongue-in-cheek banter? I don't think so. I would suggest that Marx felt an affinity to authentic Christianity: to the radical personality and message of Jesus Christ and the career of the early Church in particular.

Perhaps the best and most surprising testimony to this affinity comes from his daughter, Eleanor, in her book entitled *Erinnerugen an Marx:*

How well I remember the time when I had religious doubts at the age of five or six. (We had been listening to spectacular music in a Catholic Church.) Of course I confided these doubts to the Moor [Marx's family nickname]. How the Moor explained everything to me in his calm way, so clearly and lucidly that from that point until today I have never been overtaken by even the slightest doubt!

And how he narrated to me the story of the carpenter's son who was put to death by the rich, in a way I don't think it has ever been narrated before or since! I often heard him say: despite everything, we can forgive Christianity many things because of the fact that it has taught us to love little ones.[3]

There isn't the slightest objective reason to doubt the veracity of this testimony. If Marx taught his own daughter to admire the carpenter's son, and of course in the context of the class struggle ("who was put to death by the rich") and with full recognition of the fact that institutional Christianity has committed atrocities ("we can forgive Christianity many things"), the intrinsic nature of the testimony itself in this case vouches for its very high likelihood.

As I noted in the previous chapter, the standpoint of *On the Jewish Question* is that of a Christian denouncing the fact that the Christian world has turned Jewish. In fact Marx was baptized in Trier in 1824. (His father had become a Christian in 1817, a year before Marx's birth.) His high-school paper of 1835 on a passage from St. John's Gospel (MEW/EB 1:598–601) demonstrates that Marx was not only baptized but did in fact hold the Christian faith. But much more than any merely *de facto* Christianity is involved here.

The report of the General Council of the International to the 1869 Basle Congress was drawn up by Marx alone at the end of August. It was subsequently published as a pamphlet in English (London), German (Basle), and French (Brussels). Later it appeared in article form in French, German, Italian, and Russian (see MEW 16:655 f., n. 262). In this report Marx recounts the reaction of the factory owners of Basle and Baden to the economic revolt of their workers, a revolt that was supported by members of the International. Among other things, the factory owners tried to expel the International from their midst because it allegedly fostered the spirit of rebellion. And Marx goes on to say:

> To London they expressly sent a messenger on the fantastic errand of ascertaining the dimensions of the International general "treasury-box." Orthodox Christians as they are, if they had lived at the time of nascent Christianity, they would, above all, have spied into St. Paul's banking accounts at Rome (MEW 16:372; VFI:101).

Could one imagine anything more indicative and significant than this comparison between the International and early Christianity in its nascent stage, a comparison that bears the indelible imprint of Marx's genius? Neither in the preceding nor the following pages of the report is Christianity mentioned at all. Nor is there any mention of some hypocritically pious organization of the owners. Suddenly, out of the blue, we are hit with the passage I have just cited. From it one can infer not only that a distinction must be made in Christianity between a conservative orthodox current and a revolutionary one but also that Marx's communist movement is to be compared to the latter current.

On 25 September 1871 a dinner was held to celebrate the seventh anniversary of the International. Marx delivered a speech for the occasion, which was reported in the New York *World* on 15 October 1871. At one point in his speech Marx said:

> The persecutions of the governments against the International were like the persecutions of ancient Rome against the primitive Christians. They, too, had been few in numbers at first, but the patricians of Rome had instinctively felt that if the Christians succeeded the Roman empire would be lost. The persecutions of Rome had not saved the empire, and the persecutions of the present day against the International would not save the existing state of things (MEW 17:432; VFI:271).

In both of the preceding citations Marx clearly identifies his movement with early Christianity. As we shall see, it is Engels who will explain the doctrinal rationale for this identification or continuity. But before we consider what he has to say, let us note the same parallel being reiterated by Marx in a letter dated 22 February 1881. Ferdinand Domela Nieuwenhuis had urged upon him the need to anticipate the organizational and structural measures that would have to be adopted by the revolutionaries at the moment when the socialist revolution triumphed. Marx replies that this is not an urgent question, that concrete circumstances themselves will decide the proper *modus operandi*. However, note the reasoning he offers to convince Nieuwenhuis that he should not worry about that question now:

> The doctrinaire and inevitably fantastic anticipation of the programme of action for a revolution of the future only diverts one from the struggle of the present. The dream that the end of the world was near inspired the early Christians in their struggle with the Roman Empire and gave them confidence in victory. Scientific insight into the inevitable disintegration of the dominant order of society, a disintegration which is going on continually before our eyes, and the ever-growing fury into which the masses are lashed by the old ghostly movements, and the enormous positive development of the means of production taking place simultaneously— all this is a sufficient guarantee that as soon as a real proletarian revolution breaks out the conditions of its immediately next *modus operandi* (though it will certainly not be idyllic) will be in existence (MEW 35:161; SCME:318).

Here we can readily see Marx's desire that the communist movement imitate primitive Christianity in its confidence in victory and in its unconcern about how precisely they are to act in their moment of victory. At this point it should be remarked that the same objection is still being hurled at communists today, i.e., that they have no precise plans about what they are going to do. But Marx asks us to look to the revolutionary Christian experience for support on this issue and to rise above that objection. And if there were no continuity between the two movements, the Christian precedent would not constitute an authority to which Marx could look for support.

In writing the first draft of *The Civil War in France* (April 1871), Marx alludes to the Central Committee elected by the workers during the reign of the Paris Commune:

> These twenty delegates, chosen by the majority of the battalions of the National Guard, composed the Central Committee, which on 18 March initiated the greatest revolution of this century and still holds its post in the present glorious struggle of Paris. Never were elections more sifted, never delegates fuller representing the masses from which they had sprung. To the objection of the outsiders that they were unknown—in point of fact, that they only were known to the working classes, but no old stagers, no men illustrious by the infamies of their past, by their chase after pelf and place—they proudly answered, "So were the twelve apostles," and they answered by their deeds (MEW 17:538; VFI246).

It would be silly to try to sidestep the force of this description by saying that Marx here is simply narrating facts. Anyone familiar with literary analysis knows that the very manner of narrating itself tells the whole story. When Marx adds the word "proudly," he is certainly identifying with their reply. And of course there is the additional fact that Marx chose to highlight this particular piece of information, selecting it from among all the events and details that were at his disposal. We have already seen (p. 226) how spontaneously Marx evoked the figure of St. Paul in his 1869 report to the Basle Congress.

I am not at all trying to deny that there are differences between the early Christian movement and the communist movement of Marx. My point is that according to Marx himself these very differences are grounded on an even more basic identity between the two. Consider this decisive passage from the speech which Marx delivered in Amsterdam on 8 September 1872, right after the close of the Hague Congress of the International (the only Congress which Marx personally attended, by the way):

> The workers will have to seize political power one day in order to construct the new organization of labour; they will have to overthrow the old politics which bolster up the old institutions, unless

they want to share the fate of the early Christians, who lost their chance of the *kingdom of heaven on earth* because they rejected and neglected such action (MEW 18:160; cf. VFI:324; my italics).

Thus the identity between the two movements lies in their efforts to build the heavenly kingdom on earth; and the difference lies in the fact that the new Christians—the communists—must not neglect the political struggle because it is an indispensable tool for turning this communist kingdom into a reality.

This 1872 statement is definitive. In 1847 Marx had spoken against "the social principles of Christianity" because they inculcate submissiveness. When speaking in such terms, however, Marx was referring either to the Christian social movement of Bishop Ketteler (MEW 4:200) or in general to the age-old religious falsification that I mentioned at the start of this chapter. This reference is clear in a letter dated 17 November 1862 (MEW 30:301), where Marx writes that the British workers display "the Christian nature of slaves" because they fail to rebel. Marx's letter of 16 June 1862 (MEW 30:627), in which he expresses his preference for Julian the Apostate, should be interpreted in the same vein. In any case, whatever the differences may be between the early Christian movement and that of Marx, his 1872 speech makes it quite clear that there is a conscious and basic identity between authentic Christianity and Marx's movement in their efforts to establish the heavenly kingdom on earth.

I should point out that Marx's speech in Amsterdam was published in the Dutch, Belgian, French, and German press. There are variant readings, but not in the passage I have cited above. The official Russian editors of the MEW have been able to reconstruct the exact text, relying especially on the French and Belgian newspapers whose versions dovetail word for word (see MEW 18:730, n. 182).

Before moving on to Engels, who did more historical studies than Marx, I want to introduce an article that was drawn up by Engels but that is really *Marx's article*. Entitled "What Is To Be Done With European Turkey?" it was published in the NYDT on 21 April 1853. The danger under consideration in this article is, as usual, the barbarous influence of Russia in the strict sense of the word. By contrast, "the western serfs in the interior of the region are the exclusive bearers of civilization" (MEW 9:34). The issue is then posed in the following terms:

The Christians in Bulgaria, Thrace, Macedonia, and Bosnia see in Serbia the center around which they all must gather in the upcoming struggles for national independence. In brief, it must be said that the more Serbia and Serbian nationality has been consolidated, the more the influence of Russia on the Turkish serfs has been pushed back. The reason is that Serbia, in order to maintain her own position as a Christian state, has had to borrow from Western Europe her institutions, her schools, her science, and the organization of her industry (MEW 9:34).

The article then goes on to propose solid support for Serbia from the West. The important point for us here, however, is what is said in the last paragraph of the article by way of summing up the problem of the Turkish Empire:

> Here, then, is the simple and *definitive* solution of the problem. Both history and the events of our own day point equally to the necessity of erecting a free and independent *Christian* state on the ruins of the Muslim Empire (MEW 9:35; my italics).

Few of our present-day Marxists have envisioned any such *definitive* solution. And "state" does not necessarily mean government; it can mean country, nation, a way of organizing society. In this passage it is obviously meant in this last sense.

I want to stress the fact that these early articles were not sent to New York by Engels from Manchester; they were sent by Marx from London after he had read them and signed them as his own. The same is true of the nineteen articles in the series entitled *Revolution and Counter-Revolution in Germany*, which were published in the NYDT between October 1851 and October 1852. Engels wrote them up in English, but on 30 August 1853 Marx writes the following to the editor of *The Morning Advertiser:*

> In my reports on "Revolution and Counter-Revolution in Germany" for the *New York Daily Tribune*, I was the first German author, as far as I know, to express due admiration to Bakunin for his participation in our movement, and particularly in the Dresden uprising (MEW 9:295 f.).

One can hardly imagine a more complete assumption of authorship and responsibility for the articles written by Engels. It is not merely a matter of loyalty to a friend. It is an assumption of complete personal responsibility for what is said in these articles and the very fact that it is said. Marx counts the articles as his own, and wants everyone to so regard them. When he had to correct or retract something written in them, Marx did so as if the error had been his. For example, he writes this in connection with the articles on the Russo-Turkish question:

> When I reported the news that the Prussian government ordered certain artillery officers, who were vacationing abroad, to return

immediately to service, I erroneously indicated that those officials were occupied with training the Russian army in combat exercises. What I really meant to say was they were occupied in training the Turkish artillery corps (MEW 9:117; NYDT, 22 June 1853).

Insofar as the article on the definitive solution for the problem of European Turkey is concerned (see p. 230), there was never the slightest indication that Marx wanted to correct or retract what was written there.

II

There is no need for me to expatiate on the thesis that the definitive solution for European Turkey is a free and independent Christian state. Instead let us move on to Engels' testimony on the continuity between Christianity and Marx's communist movement. In his biblical study "On the History of Early Christianity" (1894), Engels writes:

> If, therefore, Prof. Anton Menger wonders in his *Right to the Full Product of Labor* why, with the enormous concentration of land-ownership under the Roman emperors and the boundless sufferings of the working class of the time, which was composed almost exclusively of slaves, "socialism did not follow the overthrow of the Roman Empire in the West," it is because he cannot see that this "socialism" did in fact, as far as it was possible at the time, exist and even become dominant—in Christianity (MEW 22:449; OR:316–17).

The parallelism which we saw Marx affirm so vigorously is unmistakably based on the fact that early Christianity *was socialism,* and from that socialism is consciously derived the socialism of the Commune and that of the International founded by Marx. Here is another passage from the same article:

> The parallel between the two historical phenomena forces itself upon our attention as early as the Middle Ages in the first risings of the oppressed peasants and particularly of the town plebeians. . . . This appeared most splendidly in the organization of the Bohemian Taborites under Jan Zizka, of glorious memory; but this trait pervades the whole of the Middle Ages until it gradually fades away with the workingmen Communists after 1830. The French revolutionary Communists, as also in particular Weitling and his supporters referred to early Christianity long before Renan's words: "If I wanted to give you an idea of the early Christian

communities I would tell you to look at a local section of the International Working Men's Association"... (MEW 22:450; OR:317–18).

One could not ask Engels to be more explicit. He is fully aware of the continuity between early Christianity and the modern communism for which he and Marx are fighting, and he documents it. In *The Peasant War in Germany* (1850), he notes that "the Revolutionary opposition to feudalism was alive throughout all the Middle Ages" (MEW 7:344; TGR:35). Among the precursors of Thomas Münzer were Joachim of Calabria and the medieval mystics, who were "the main subject of his studies" (MEW 7:351; TGR:44). But they included many others: the Englishmen John Wycliffe and his Lollards (MEW 7:345; TGR:36), Ball, and Tyler; the Czech preacher Jan Hus and the Taborites; the French and Italian Albigensians of the twelfth and thirteenth centuries (MEW 7:345; TGR:36); Peter Wald of Lyons in the twelfth century and his followers (MEW 7:344; TGR:35), who still survive today; and in general the various medieval Christian sects which, despite countless devastating persecutions on the part of the official Church, appeared uninterruptedly on the scene from the earliest centuries right up to the sixteenth century.

The point that must be stressed here is that Engels knows what lies at the root of this uninterrupted process that constitutes the history of authentic Christianity. In his 1892 Introduction to the English edition of *Socialism: Utopian and Scientific*, Engels recounts the many recourses to religious indoctrination used by the British bourgeoisie in the nineteenth century to keep the proletariat docile. Then he goes on to say:

> Finally, he accepted the dangerous aid of the Salvation Army, which revives the propaganda of early Christianity, appeals to the poor as the elect, fights capitalism in a religious way, and thus fosters an element of *early Christian class antagonism,* which one day may become troublesome to the well-to-do people which now find the ready money for it (MEW 22:306 f.; SUS:34–35; my italics).

Thus, according to Engels, the very same class struggle which today is the principle weapon of the communist movement is an element of primitive Christianity. And the reason why Christianity included it among its constitutive elements is that the Christian message "appeals to the poor as the elect." Though Engels does not expressly mention it here, this is undoubtedly based on the words of Jesus Christ: "Blest are you poor" (Luke 6:20); and "Woe to you rich" (Luke 6:24).

It is also worth stressing the fact that Engels is aware of the continuity despite the fact that he, prejudiced by the prevailing dogmatic interpretation, thinks that the liberation proclaimed by early Christianity is that of the "life beyond" (see the same article, MEW 22:449 f.; OR:316; also his letter to Kautsky dated 28 July 1894, MEW 39:276). The fact is, as I have tried to show in my earlier books, that the resurrection of the body does not at all mean that the kingdom of God is realized in another world.[4] On this point Marx was better informed than Engels, for in his Amsterdam speech he talks about the early Christians losing their chance of the *kingdom of heaven on earth* (see pp. 228–29).

Yet *despite* a seeming difference, which Engels took for real but which in fact is not, he still repeatedly affirmed the continuation between early Chrstianity and modern socialism. For example, in the article we have been considering, Engels mentions the seeming difference and then writes:

> Both are persecuted and baited, their adherents are despised and made the objects of exclusive laws, the former as enemies of the human race, the latter as enemies of the state, enemies of religion, the family, social order. And, in spite of all persecution, nay, even spurred on by it, they forge victoriously, irresistibly ahead. Three hundred years after its appearance Christianity was the recognized state religion in the Roman World Empire, and in barely sixty years socialism has won itself a position which makes its victory absolutely certain (MEW 22:449; OR:316).

In a letter to Kautsky dated 8 November 1884, Engels describes the socialist movement as follows:

> . . . a force whose existence and spread is just as incomprehensible and mysterious to the rulers and old ruling classes as was the surge of the Christian wave for the authorities of *Romanitas* that it submerged, but a force which stands erect with the same sureness and invincibility as did Christianity back then (MEW 36:230).

The parallelism verges on almost complete identification. Not surprisingly, then, we find Engels writing as follows in his article for *The Labour Standard* dated 6 August 1881 (thus while Marx was still alive):

> The teachings of Marx, which all the reactionary parties, both feudal and democratic, have wasted such monstrous efforts on repressing, have now been preached from the housetops in all civilized nations and languages (MEW 19:292).

There is not the slightest trace of malice in Engels' statement. He is perfectly aware of the continuity between Marx's message and that of early Christianity. The phrase "preached from the housetops" is taken literally from Matthew 10:27 and Luke 12:3. They are the words of Jesus Christ describing what is to happen with his own teaching. And as far back as Chapter 5 in this volume (see p. 110), I noted how literally and faithfully Engels applied the gospel phrase "wolves in sheep's clothing" to those who urged union and harmony in order to dissuade the exploited class from fighting for their liberation.

In a letter dated 12 September 1892, Engels offers encouragement to the young communist Conrad Schmidt who is confronted with friction and the loss of old friendships because of his turn to communism. Engels tells him that he, too, had to face similar situations, but in his case it was with members of his own family. This is how he concludes:

> As far as the harrassment and bitterness is concerned, it is in fact impossible to see things through without this happening: "I have not come to bring peace but the sword." In these days I am sending you the *Condition of the Working Class*. With every best wish. Yours. Frederick Engels (MEW 38:459).

Engels even puts the phrase of Jesus Christ (Matt. 10:34) in quotation marks. If it had been of his own choosing, he would probably have written "war" instead of "the sword." Any leftist knows that the quoted phrase is used in its genuine, original sense. Whatever the Jacobins and the Lopez-Trujillos of this world may think, Engels consciously saw his work as a continuation of the authentic message of Christ and explored the continuity between communism and Christ's message in depth. It is one of the most impressive and well-documented facts available to any reader.

In the above passages from Engels' writings there are certain points that deserve more detailed consideration. For example, he tells us that Weitling and his supporters in particular "referred to early Christianity" long before Renan did (see pp. 231–32). The reader might well wonder who Weitling was and how Engels knows enough to say what he says about him. Wilhelm Weitling (1808–71) was "the founder of German communism," as Engels explicitly acknowledges in his English article of 1843 (MEW 1:490). Marx and Engels *entered* the organization founded by Weitling. In a letter to Stefanoni dated 7 February 1872, Engels writes: "I belonged to that organization. It was founded, not by Marx, not in the year 1850, and not in Cologne. It was already in existence more than ten years earlier" (MEW 17:485). The significant point here is that Weitling based his communism entirely on the gospel, as can be seen from his 1845 book entitled *The Gospel of a Poor Sinner*.

Thomas Münzer (1490–1525) organized and directed the first anti-capitalist revolution near the start of the capitalist age. But let Engels tell us about him. Here is what he says in *The Peasant War in Germany:*

There is more than one communist sect of modern times which, on the eve of the February Revolution [1848], did not possess a theoretical equipment richer than that of Muenzer of the Sixteenth Century. His programme, less a compilation of the demands of the then existing plebeians than a genius's anticipation of the conditions for the emancipation of the proletarian element that had just begun to develop among the plebeians, demanded the immediate establishment of the kingdom of God, of the prophesied millennium on earth. This was to be accomplished by the return of the church to its origins and the abolition of all institutions that were in conflict with what Muenzer conceived as original Christianity, which, in fact, was the idea of a very modern church. By the kingdom of God, Muenzer understood nothing less than a state of society without class differences, without private property, and without superimposed state powers opposed to the members of society (MEW 7:353 f.; cf. TGR:47).

In other words, what Münzer took to be the kingdom of God (and what the Bible in fact regards as the kingdom of God) is precisely communism: nothing more or less than what we today understand by communism. Incidentally we might note that Marx too regarded the Peasants' War as "the most radical episode in German history" (MEW 1:386; VEW:252). What about the "genius's anticipation," of which Engels speaks in the above text? His meaning is clear when we recall what Marx pointed out: that the ends and goals of prior forms of socialism "are the last ends proclaimed by the Paris revolution and by the International; only the means are different . . ." (MEW 17:557; VFI:262).

Thus we get a clearer picture of what Marx means by humanity when he writes in the CCPE: "Mankind thus inevitably sets itself only such tasks as it is able to solve" (MEW 13:9; CCPE:21). By humanity here he means the whole human species, the whole aggregate of human beings. And when he goes on to say that the problem or the task itself "arises only when the material conditions for its solution are already present or at least in the course of formation" (ibid.), we must understand "course of formation" in a sufficiently broad-based way. For capitalism has been in the process of formation ever since the production of commodities existed (see Chapter 8), and the latter existed even back in Christ's time.

In his 1875 Preface to the reissue of *The Peasant War in Germany*, Engels writes:

German theoretical Socialism will never forget that it rests on the shoulders of Saint Simon, Fourier and Owen, the three who, in spite of their fantastic notions and Utopianism, belonged to the most significant heads of all time and whose genius anticipated numerous things the correctness of which can now be proved in a scientific way . . . (MEW 7:541; TGR:17).

The appeal of these three socialists to the gospel is so well known that it does not call for further comment. Engels acknowledges that their "genius anticipated" numerous things as well. But let me continue by citing some further remarks of Engels on Thomas Münzer:

> Already among these precursors of the movement we notice an asceticism which is to be found in all medieval uprisings that were tinged with religion, and also in modern times at the beginning of every proletarian movement (MEW 7:359; TGR:53).

> The most outspoken revolutionaries among the peasants were mostly his [Muenzer's] disciples, defending his ideas (MEW 78:379; TGR:77–78).

> Muenzer's revolutionary party was everywhere in the minority but it formed the backbone of the peasant camps (MEW 7:381; TGR:79).

> Not only the movement of his time, but the whole century, was not ripe for the realisation of the ideas for which he himself had only begun to grope (MEW 7:401; TGR:105).

> Nevertheless he was bound to his preachings of Christian equality and evangelical community of possessions. He was at least compelled to make an attempt at its realisation (MEW 7:402; cf. TGR:105).

> Luther had given the plebeian movement a powerful weapon—a translation of the Bible. Through the Bible, he contrasted feudal Christianity of his time with the simple Christianity of the first century. In opposition to decaying feudal society, he held up the picture of another society which knew nothing of the ramified and feudal hierarchy. The peasants had made extensive use of the weapon against the forces, the nobility, and the clergy (MEW 7: 350 f.; cf. TGR:43).

Engels then proceeds to tell how Luther, frightened by the revolution *provoked by the reading of the Bible,* betrayed that revolution and turned his weapons against Münzer.

I have already mentioned the bevy of medieval precursors that Engels mentioned in connection with Münzer. All those precursors based their views on early Christianity, so we must follow Engels and go back to early Christianity. But first I would simply like to cite an observation on the sixteenth century that Engels makes in his 1892 Introduction to the English edition of *Socialism: Utopian and Scientific:*

> Calvin's church constitution was thoroughly democratic and republican; and where the kingdom of God was republicanized, could the kingdoms of this world remain subject to monarchs, bishops, and lords? While German Lutheranism became a willing tool in the hands of princes, Calvinism founded a republic in Holland, and active republican parties in England, and, above all, Scotland (MEW 22:300; SUS:26).

As far as early Christianity is concerned, it should be noted that Engels was no dilettante on the subject. He had angrily expressed his opposition to certain superficial opinions that can be readily heard today in certain Marxist circles. He published three conscientious studies of the subject: "Bruno Bauer and Early Christianity" (1882: MEW 19:297–305; OR:194–204); "The Book of Revelation" (1883: MEW 21:9–15; OR:205–12); and "On the History of Early Christianity" (1894: MEW 22:447–73; OR:316–47). He devoted himself with deep interest and seriousness to the new science; its elaboration was recognized to be due to the Germans, for it applied the historicocritical method to the study of the Bible: "German criticism of the Bible, so far the only *scientific* basis of our knowledge of the history of early Christianity . . ." (MEW 22:455; OR:323). And since he is writing from England, he points out the following:

> A *Science* almost unknown in this country, except to a few liberalizing theologians who contrive to keep it as secret as they can, is the historical and linguistic criticism of the Bible, the inquiry into the age, origin, and historical value of the various writings comprising the Old and New Testament (MEW 21:9; OR:205).

Engels was quite adept at Greek and Hebrew, as can be seen by anyone who reads these investigations. For the problem of the date of the composition of the Apocalypse (or Book of Revelation) Engels proposes a solution based on the Hebrew term for *Neron Kaisar* and its numerical value (MEW 21:14 and MEW 22:468 f.; OR:210–12 and OR:341–42). The letters of the alphabet signify numbers. We also find Hebrew citations in Engels' letters (e.g., in 1889; MEW:37, 188, and 216). In a letter dated 29 May 1891 to Marx's son-in-law, Paul Lafargue, where he disputes a certain biblical study published by the latter, he appeals to the *patah furtive* of the name Eloah (MEW 38:109); it is a matter that really falls within the competence of linguistic students and lexicographers. But even as far back as 1841 we find that Engels' writings reveal a knowledge of Hebrew (see MEW/EB 11:478).

It should be noted that Engels was opposed to the unfounded radicalism of Bauer, which was repeatedly refuted at a later date and which sought to attribute the origin of Christianity to Philo and Neo-platonic thought. The question at issue was how much of a historically genuine nucleus could sound scientific methods attribute to the founder of Christianity. Engels took his stand between some kind of maxi-malism, which he attributes to the Tübingen School, and the minimalism of Bauer: "The factual truth lies between these two limits" (MEW 22:456; OR:325).

Besides the despair and the oppression prevailing in the decaying Roman Empire, one of the causes of the success of early Christianity stressed by Engels is the monotheism of the Old Testament, which was taken over by Christianity (MEW 19:304 and MEW 22:466–70; see OR:203 and 339–44). This gave Christianity a dimension of universality that other religions did not possess. Other factors mentioned by Engels are the resultant elimination of purificatory and discriminatory cere-monies and the consciousness of sin. To the obvious objection that Judaism, too, was monotheistic, Engels had this reply:

> Judaism, too, with its new universal god, had made a start on the way to becoming a universal religion; but the children of Israel always remained an aristocracy among the believers and the cir-cumcised . . . (MEW 19:304; OR:203).

As far as equally monotheistic Islam is concerned: "Islam itself, on the other hand, by preserving its specifically Oriental ritual, limited the area of its propagation . . ." (ibid.).

Engels believed that he had found the oldest Christian work in the Book of the Apocalypse:

> Here we have neither the dogma nor the ethics of later Christianity but instead a feeling that one is struggling against the whole world and that the struggle will be a victorious one; an eagerness for the struggle and a certainty of victory which are totally lacking in Christians of today and which are to be found in our time only at the other pole of society, among the socialists (MEW 22:460; OR:330).

To conclude, let me cite the last thing that Engels published in his lifetime. We find it in the concluding section of his famous 1895 Intro-duction to the reissue of *The Class Struggles in France* (written by

Marx). He was in the midst of writing this Introduction when he wrote to Paul Lafargue, telling him that Marx's 1850 work could not be published without a new introduction. Why? Because we must explain "why we were then justified in counting on an immediate and definitive victory of the proletariat, why that did not happen, and how the course of events has helped us to view things differently than we did then" (MEW 39:412). In the course of the Introduction Engels writes:

> History has proved us, and all who thought like us, wrong (MEW 22:515; SW:285).

> But we, too, have been shown to have been wrong by history, which has revealed our point of view of that time to have been an illusion (MEW 22:513; SW:283).

And the chief point is the one that stressed the necessity of violent means for the revolution. In his 1895 Introduction Engels writes:

> The irony of world history turns everything upside down. We, the "revolutionaries," the "rebels"—we are thriving far better on legal methods than on illegal methods and revolt (MEW 22:525; SW:296).

Most noteworthy, however, is the fact that Engels corroborates everything I have been saying here in the final page of his Introduction, which is devoted entirely to the victory of Christianity in the early part of the fourth century. Engels begins as follows:

> It is now, almost to the year, sixteen hundred years since a dangerous party of revolt made a great commotion in the Roman Empire. It undermined religion and all the foundations of the State; it flatly denied that Caesar's will was the supreme law; it was without a fatherland, international; it spread over all countries of the Empire from Gaul to Asia, and beyond the frontiers of the Empire (MEW 22:526; SW:297).

Engels then proceeds to recount all the persecutions, chicanery, and illegal acts perpetrated by the Roman authorities against Christianity. He ends up telling how seventeen years after this last persecution, the subversive movement (Christianity) succeeded in putting Constantine on the throne as emperor and soon getting itself proclaimed as the state religion. Thus ends the last written work published by Engels.

The thesis that violent means are not indispensable seems debatable to me, but we have already seen that Marx said as much about some of the more democratic countries in his speech in Amsterdam (see VFI:324). The interesting thing about Engels' last page above is his clear intent to identify the socialist hope with that of early Christianity. The goodness of the cause is so clear and certain that one can be sure that it will impose its stamp on the whole world by virtue of its own merit. In the book for which Engels wrote this Introduction Marx had employed a biblical comparison that earlier had been very dear to early Christians:

> The present generation is like the Jews, whom Moses led through the wilderness. They not only have a new world to conquer; they must perish in order to make room for the men who are equal to a new world (MEW 7:79; VSE:112).

The idea of somehow comparing early Christianity with the same Hebrew generation of the desert years can be found in the writings of the New Testament (e.g., Acts 13:18; Heb. 3:17; John 6:49; and Heb. 3:8,10). In a series of articles for *Der Volksstaat* in 1872 and 1873 on "The Housing Question," Engels alluded to the same comparison in talking about the plight of the workers. Granting that the workers' situation under capitalism was bad, he went on to ask:

> But are we then to look back nostalgically to the (equally bitter) fleshpots of Egypt, to small rural industry which engendered nothing but slavish souls, or to the "savages"? Quite the contrary (MEW 18:220).

The allusion to Exodus 13:3 is perfect. This base nostalgia for the fleshpots of Egypt typified the desert generation; for that very reason, according to Marx, it had to perish. On the other hand Engels identifies all of human history and civilization with the grandiose happening of the Exodus. And that brings us to the next topic to be discussed in the chapter.

III

I think that the above treatment has abundantly proved that Marx and Engels saw their communism as a conscious continuation of authentic Christianity. I could end the chapter right here. The occidentalism and even nationalism of the two men is of much less importance, and the reader uninterested in this topic could skip the following pages and move on to Chapter 10. The unfortunate thing is that commentators have not seen, or have not chosen to see, the essential connection between this topic and the Christianity of Marx and Engels.

To some commentators who criticize both the nationalism and the

Europeanism of Marx and Engels, the Christianity that lies at its base is even more unacceptable. So they isolate the topic and thus render it even more open to criticism. The only correct and fair way to approach it, however, is to present it as a derivative topic, an appendix to the Christianity of Marx and Engels that we have just been discussing, even though the material is as ample as that of the previous sections.

The fact that Marx postulated the existence of a primitive communism at the dawn of prehistory has prompted many readers to assume that his struggle to achieve communism was a struggle to return to nature; that the human race was supposed to return to some supposedly idyllic natural state that prevailed before civilization corrupted it. I myself held this mistaken view in *Being and the Messiah* (Chapter 3). To have espoused this Romanticism, however, Marx would have had to fail to understand Hegel's arguments, which really annihilate all such naturalism.

The primitive communism postulated by Marx is entirely negative: there is no private property in it because there is no property of any sort. If property is to exist, there must exist values that have not been consumed; but since there was no surplus labor at that point, the existing products contained only use values that were consumed. The productivity of hunting, fishing, and food gathering was the minimum required to prevent the tribe from dying off out of starvation. The fields, the woods, and the river were common only in the sense that they belonged to nobody. This communism is a theorem, not an ideal or a desirable state to which humanity could or should return.

Already in the *Communist Manifesto* Marx and Engels point out that bourgeois capitalism

> has created enormous cities, has greatly increased the urban population as compared with the rural, and has thus rescued a considerable part of the population from *the idiocy of rural life* (MEW 4:466; VRV:71; my italics).

This pitilessly negative judgment about the "natural" life of the peasant was never altered one iota throughout the writings of Marx and Engels. In Chapter 17 of *Theories of Surplus Value* Marx writes:

> The proportion of persons engaged in agriculture cannot therefore be directly determined by the number of individuals immediately employed in agriculture. In countries with a capitalist mode of production, many people participate *indirectly* [Marx's italics] in agricultural production, who in less developed countries are directly included in it. The difference therefore appears to be greater than it is. *For the civilization of the country as a whole, however,*

242 Conscious Continuation of Early Christianity

this difference is very important, even in so far as it only means that a large section of the workers involved in agriculture do not participate in it directly; they are thus saved from *the idiocy of country life* and belong to the industrial population (MEW 26/2:475 f.; cf. TSV 2:475; my italics).

Thus even though a certain type of labor may be associated with agriculture, because it transforms or processes agricultural products, the significant thing in Marx's eyes is the fact that those who do this work do not live in the country. This is of decisive importance for a nation's level of civilization. For so long as people are directly immersed in rural labors, they have not been snatched away from the idiocy of rural life. Thus any appeal to naturalism or the rural soil is wholly incompatible with Marx's thought. This implacably pejorative evaluation of the "natural" is of decisive importance in Marx's thought, and it has not been duly appreciated.

In "The Housing Question" (1872–73), Engels tells us that it is a matter of "rescuing the peasant population from the isolation and stupidization in which it has vegetated almost without change for millennia" (MEW 18:280). In their refutation of Daumer (1850), Marx and Engels write: "Mr. Daumer flees from the tragedy of history, which comes too close for comfort to so-called nature—that is, to the stupid peasant idyll" (MEW 7:201 f.). And in *The Great Men of the Exile* (1852), Marx and Engels offer this evaluation of another German refugee. What matters here is the comparison made:

> Furthermore, a character richly endowed with all sorts of vices, coarse habits and meannesses, with the perfidy and stupidity, the cunning narrowness and dullness, the servility and arrogance, the rusticity and falseness of the emancipated serf, *the peasant* (MEW 8:276; my italics).

One of Marx's classic theses—that it is necessary to pass through capitalism in order to arrive at socialism—has been totally misunderstood and hence rejected precisely because people have not taken seriously his mercilessly negative judgment of any and all so-called naturalism. But if one disregards this negative judgment, one cannot understand Marx's whole system at all. Marx is on the side of civilization. If ethnologists and anthropologists had confronted him with the objection that primitive tribes possess a civilization of sorts, he would have doubled over with laughter. So here we would do well to see exactly what Marx and Engels mean by the word "civilization."

In his article for the NYDT dated 5 June 1857, Engels writes about "Asiatic ignorance" (MEW 12:212). In his article for the NYDT dated

12 August 1853, Marx asserts that *"the intrinsic barbarism of Russia* is documented in the stereotyped uniformity of this policy" (MEW 9:235; my italics). And in a joint article of February 1850, Marx and Engels write:

> Californian gold is pouring in torrents over America and the Asiatic coast of the Pacific and is drawing the reluctant barbarian peoples into world trade, into the civilized world (MEW 7:220 f.; VRV:275).

Here they apply the label "barbarian" (in the original sense of the word) to all the peoples who border the Pacific Ocean except those in North America. The clear implication is that Marx and Engels are hoping that the growth of capitalism will force the barbarian peoples to enter civilization. Russia and all of Asia are in the same situation. As far as China is concerned, the aforementioned article has this to say:

> Chinese socialism may, of course, bear the same relation to European socialism as Chinese to Hegelian philosophy. But it is still amusing to note that the oldest and most unshakeable empire on earth has, within eight years, been brought to the brink of a social revolution by the cotton bales of the English bourgeoisie; in any event, such a revolution cannot help but have the most important consequences for the civilized world (MEW 7:222; VRV:277).

In his article for the NYDT dated 14 June 1853, Marx has this to say about China:

> Before the British arms the authority of the Manchu dynasty fell to pieces; the superstitious faith in the eternity of the Celestial Empire broke down; *the barbarous and hermetic isolation from the civilized world* was infringed; and an opening was made for that intercourse which has since proceeded so rapidly under the golden attractions of California and Australia (MEW 9:96; VSE:326; my italics).

Marx then proceeds to comment as follows on the effects of the opium trade on China:

> It is almost needless to observe that, in the same measure in which opium has obtained the sovereignty over the Chinese, the emperor and his staff of pedantic mandarins have become dispossessed of their own sovereignty. It would seem as though history had first to

make this whole people drunk before it could arouse them out of *their hereditary stupidity* (MEW 9:96; VSE:327; my italics).

Once again it is clear that the absence of civilization, the "state of nature," in the eyes of Marx and Engels, means that human beings are submerged in stupidity and idiocy. This thesis, which is expressed without reservations or provisos, is completely central to the thought of Marx and Engels. They fully realize that some of the barbarian peoples are less uncivilized than others. For example, the people of China and India are less barbarous than the Mongols, the Arabs, the Tartars, and the Turks. But that is only comparatively speaking, and such semicivilization is not what Marx and Engels mean by civilization. They prefer to call such cultures "semi-barbarian."

Thus in his article for the NYDT dated 20 September 1858, Marx wrote: "Whereas the semi-barbarian defended the principle of morality, the civilized [party] countered with the principle of Mammon" (MEW 12:552). In *Socialism: Utopian and Scientific* (1880) Engels discusses the crisis in "production and exchange among all civilized peoples and their more or less barbarian appendages" (MEW 19:218; SUS:86). Alluding to the American aborigines in *The Origins of the Family, Private Property and the State* (1884), Engels calls for "closer investigation among the peoples still at the upper stage of savagery in the northwest, and particularly in South America" (MEW 21:54; OF:44).

In a letter to Engels dated 14 June 1853, Marx has this to say about India:

> These idyllic republics, where only the *boundaries of their village* are jealously guarded against the neighbouring village, still exist in a fairly well-preserved form in the North-Western parts of India, which were only recently acquired by the English. I do not think that one can envisage a more solid foundation for Asiatic despotism and stagnation. And however much the English may have Hibernicised the country, the breaking up of those stereotyped primitive forms was the *sine qua non* for Europeanization (MEW 28:268; SCME:80).

By "civilization" Marx and Engels mean western civilization. All the rest represent natural idiocy in their eyes. If people are scandalized by this central evaluation in Marx's system, it seems to me it is because they have not understood the rationale behind it. But before I explain that rationale and get off on that point, I want to stress once again Marx's rejection of primitive communism as an ideal to be returned to.

In his 1857 Introduction Marx is talking about the increasing versatility of the modern worker, his ability to handle all sorts of different work.

This versatility, of course, will reach its acme when the ultimate stage of communism is reached. Here is what Marx has to say about the difference in this versatility as examplified in the United States on the one hand and Russia on the other:

> One could say that this indifference towards particular kinds of labour, which is a historic product in the United States, appears e.g. among all the Russians as a spontaneous inclination. But there is a devil of a difference between barbarians who are fit by nature to be used for anything, and civilized people who apply themselves to everything. And then in practice the Russian indifference to the specific character of labour corresponds to being embedded by tradition within a very specific kind of labour, from which only external influences can jar them loose (MEW 13:635 f.; GRU:105).

Thus the disposition in question is very different, according to Marx, if it is a natural result of barbarianism than if it is a product of civilization and is impregnated with all the cultural and human weight of the latter. Thus there is a big difference in the benefits to be derived from some sort of primitive communism on the one hand and a communism produced by civilization on the other. In a letter to Kautsky dated 16 February 1884, Engels spelled out this point quite clearly. Indeed the pertinence of this letter as a criticism of certain modern-day brands of socialism is so obvious that it hardly calls for comment. The parentheses in the text are those of Engels himself:

> It would be a good thing if somebody took the trouble to explain state socialism, which is now so prevalent, by the example of *Java* where its practice is in full bloom. All the material for that can be found in *Java, or How to Manage a Colony*, by J. W. B. Money, Barrister at Law, London 1861, 2 vols. Here it will be seen how on the basis of the old community communism the Dutch organised production under state control and secured for the people what they considered a quite comfortable existence. The result: the people are kept *at the stage of primitive stupidity* and 70 million marks (by now presumably more) are annually collected by the Dutch national treasury. This case is highly interesting and the practical conclusions can easily be drawn. Incidentally this demonstrates that today primitive communism (so long as it has not been stirred up by some element of modern communism) furnishes the finest and broadest basis of exploitation and despotism there, as well as in India and Russia, and that in the conditions of modern society it turns out to be a crying anachronism (which has either to be removed or is almost going backwards) as much as were the

independent mark communities of the original cantons (MEW 36:109; cf. SCME:347; my italics).

To repeat: no comment is necessary. In the eyes of Marx and Engels civilization is more important than the bare fact of communism or the mere absence of private property. The surviving remnants of primitive communism must be eliminated, for they are part of the stage of natural stupidity that can be suppressed only by civilization. One cannot comprehend Marx and Engels if one does not grasp that absolutely central thesis. Even the capacity to perform different kinds of labor, which is physically identical, is totally different depending on whether it is exercised by a civilized or an uncivilized human being.

In a letter to Annenkov dated 28 December 1846, Marx writes: "If North America were wiped off the map of the world, the result would be anarchy, the total decay of trade and of modern civilization" (MEW 4:554; SCME:36). In *Anti-Dühring* (1878) Engels argues that a revolution must take place if modern civilization is to survive: "If the whole of modern society is not to perish, a revolution of the mode of production and distribution must take place, a revolution which will put an end to all class divisions" (MEW 20:146 f.; AD:174). The task can be evaded only "on pain of sinking to the level of the Chinese coolie" (ibid.). In a letter to Bebel (9–10 November 1891) Engels writes: "The mass of day-laborers east of the Elbe are still too much the medieval serf (as also the English) for our direct propaganda to have much effect on them before they get some education on progress" (MEW 38:212).

The biggest irony in this whole story is the fact that in the eyes of Marx and Engels all socialists who want communism without western civilization are reactionaries. Here is what Engels has to say about a socialist author in his series of articles on "The Housing Question" (1872–73):

> In this jeremiad we have Proudhonism with all its reactionary trappings. To create the modern class of the proletariat it was absolutely necessary to cut the umbilical cord which still bound the worker of yesterday to the land and the soil. The hand-weaver, who had his little cottage, garden, and plot of land besides his loom, was a tranquil man in the midst of all his poverty and political oppression. . . . He took off his hat to the rich, the clergy, and the government functionaries; and inside he was a serf in every way. It is precisely modern big industry that transformed the worker attached to the soil into a proletarian stripped of all property, divested of all the traditional chains, and free and clear as a bird. It is precisely that economic revolution that created the unique conditions under which the exploitation of the laboring classes in its ultimate form—i.e., capitalist production—can be overthrown.

And now along comes this tearful Proudhonist deploring the dislodgement of the worker from house and hearth as a great step backward, when that is clearly the first and foremost condition for his spiritual emancipation (MEW 18:219).

Marx and Engels are grateful to capitalism for having served as the material instrument whereby human beings, uprooted from the idiocy of natural circumstances, could achieve spiritual emancipation for the first time in history. According to them, capitalism has been the great vehicle of western civilization, though a wholly involuntary one. In his article for the NYDT dated 25 June 1853, Marx writes:

England, it is true, in causing a social revolution in Hindustan was actuated only by the vilest interests, and was stupid in her manner of enforcing them. But that is not the question. The question is, can mankind fulfil its destiny without a fundamental revolution in the social state of Asia? If not, whatever may have been the crimes of England, she was the unconscious tool of history in bringing about that revolution (MEW 9:133; VSE:306–7).

Let us disregard for the moment the moral objection that is wont to be raised here. This exceptionally forceful passage of the mature Marx justifies us in citing another passage from the *Economic and Philosophic Manuscripts of 1844*. It is far less radical, but it refers explicitly to the matter of communism:

The crude communism is merely the culmination of this envy and desire to level down on the basis of a *preconceived* minimum. It has a *definite, limited* measure. How little this abolition of private property is a true appropriation is shown by the abstract negation of the entire world of culture and civilization, and the return to the *unnatural* simplicity of the *poor*, unrefined man who has no needs and who has not even reached the stage of private property, let alone gone beyond it (MEW/EB 1:534 f.; VEW:346).

I might add here that in the famous three drafts of Marx's reply to Vera Zasulitch (written in February and March 1881), Marx insists that the primitive agrarian communism of Russia does not have the least chance of surviving unless it adopts the institutions of western civilization; and also that the Russians are very lucky in living as contemporaries of the modern progress going on in the West (MEW 19:388f.,390, 392, 398, 404, 405; see RME 218–28). Engels recapitulated this line of thought in the 1894 Afterword to his articles on "Russian Social Problems." In his Afterword, entitled "Russia and the Social Revolution

Reconsidered,'' Engels maintains that "the initiative for such a possible transformation of the Russian village community can only originate, not in the community itself, but solely among the industrial proletariat of the West" (MEW 22:426 f.; RME:232–33).

Similarly, in his letter to Nikolai Frantsevich Danielson (17 October 1893), Engels remarks:

> I would go further and say, that no more in Russia than anywhere else would it have been possible to develop a higher social form out of primitive agrarian communism unless that higher form was *already in existence* in another country, so as to serve as a model. . . . It could not be developed directly out of the agrarian commune, unless in imitation of an example already in existence somewhere else (MEW 39:149 f.; SCME:438–39).

In the 1894 Afterword cited just above, Engels adds two significant passages:

> In fact agrarian communism, a derivative of gentile society, has never developed anywhere out of its own forces anything but its own destruction (MEW 22:427; RME:233).

> On the other hand, it is not only possible but certain that, after the victory of the proletariat and the transfer of the means of production to common ownership among Western European peoples, the countries which have just entered the stage of capitalist production and have still preserved institutions of gentile society or remains of them will derive from the remnants of common ownership and the corresponding folkways a powerful means of appreciably shortening their process of development to a socialist society and of escaping most of the sufferings and struggles through which we in Western Europe have had to labor. But in this process the example and the active support of the formerly capitalistic West is an unavoidable prerequisite. . . . And this goes for all countries in a pre-capitalistic stage of development, not merely for Russia (MEW 22:428 f.; RME:234–35).

The use of the adjective "gentile" in these two passages is terribly significant. It refers to nations or institutions that are not Christian. In the first part of this chapter we saw that western communism, in the view of Marx and Engels, is a continuation of authentic Christianity. Now we are told that the pagan world cannot arrive at communism without the example and help of the Christian West. This dovetails with the thesis we saw earlier (see p. 230), i.e., that the simple and definitive solution for eastern Europe is "a free and independent Christian state on the ruins of the Muslim Empire" (MEW 9:35). And here "state" means the way society is organized.

However, the two 1894 passages of Engels have a worldwide dimension. One version of orthodox Marxism asserts the economically determined necessity of passing through capitalism in order to reach communism. In reality Marx and Engels maintained that the necessity involved was a civilizing one; economic development was to be used as a mere tool in order to break down the hermetic isolation of the other areas of the world.

As early as an article dated 10 September 1848, Marx and Engels bring up the demands of civilization. Commenting on Denmark, which is acting as an obstacle to the advance of civilization in some way, Marx and Engels plump for:

> . . . the right of civilization against barbarianism, of progress against stability. And even if the treaties were in Denmark's favor—which is very doubtful—this right counts more than any treaty because it is the right of historical development (MEW 5:395; *Neue Rheinische Zeitung*).

Let no one think that Marx and Engels ever backed down on their insistence over this point. After alluding to "the intrinsic barbarism of Russia" in an article for the NYDT dated 12 August 1853 (MEW 9:235; TEQ:80), Marx stresses the same thesis with reference to the Turkish question:

> Constantinople is the eternal city—the Rome of the East. Under the ancient Greek Emperors, Western civilization amalgamated there so far with Eastern barbarism, and with the Turks, Eastern barbarism amalgamated so far with Western civilization, as to make this center of a theocratical Empire the effectual bar against European progress (MEW 9:236; TEQ:81).

> It is cheering to see the American intervention in Europe beginning just with the Eastern Question. . . . America is the youngest and most vigorous representative of the West (MEW 9:236; TEQ:81).

> Constantinople is the golden bridge thrown between the West and the East, and Western civilization cannot, like the sun, go around the world without passing that bridge; and it cannot pass it without a struggle with Russia. The Sultan holds Constantinople only in trust for the Revolution, and the present nominal dignitaries of Western Europe, themselves finding the last stronghold of their

"order" on the shores of the Neva, can do nothing but keep the question in suspense until Russia has to meet her real antagonist, the Revolution (ibid.).

Here we have the important second half of Marx's thesis: the true bearer of western civilization is the socialist revolution. It is the same basic point that Engels makes in *Anti-Dühring:* communism is needed if western civilization is not to perish. The contemporary rulers of the West and the "order" they represent are so stupid that they see Russian barbarism as their bulwark and rock of Gibraltar. The real enemy of barbarianism, however, is the communist revolution. Recall what Marx himself stated in his article for the NYDT dated 8 August 1853:

> England has to fulfil a double mission in India: one destructive, the other regenerating—the annihilation of old Asiatic society, and the laying of the material foundations of Western society in Asia (MEW 9:221; VSE:320).

Capitalism is merely a material instrument. The real carrier of western civilization is communism. Eleven years after the above article, in his *Inaugural Address of the International Working Men's Association* (1864), Marx concludes on this note:

> The shameless approval, mock sympathy, or idiotic indifference, with which the upper classes of Europe have witnessed the mountain fortress of the Caucasus falling a prey to, and heroic Poland being assassinated by Russia; the immense and unresisted encroachments of that *barbarous* power, whose head is at St. Petersburg, and whose hands are in every cabinet in Europe, have taught the working classes the duty to master themselves the mysteries of international politics; to watch the diplomatic acts of their respective governments; to counteract them, if necessary, by all means in their power; when unable to prevent, to combine in simultaneous denunciations, and to vindicate *the simple laws of morals and justice,* which ought to govern the relations of private individuals, as the rules paramount of the intercourse of nations (MEW 16:13; VFI:81; my italics).

Here Marx anticipates any question we have as to what constitutes civilization. It is morals and justice. But the important point for us here is that he clearly implies the aim and purport of the communist movement. It is to fight against barbarianism, to snatch the banner of western civilization away from the ruling classes, who not only are incapable of bearing it but also are traitors to it because they are acting as accomplices of the barbarian powers.

In a letter to Palladino dated 23 November 1871, Engels writes that "the Council of the International will always remain faithful to the banner entrusted to its keeping for the past seven years by *the workers of the civilized world*" (MEW 33:337; my italics). In a letter dated 12 September 1882, he tells Kautsky: "A reorganised Europe and North America will have such colossal power and provide such an example that the semi-civilized countries will automatically follow in their wake; they will be pushed in that direction even by economic needs alone" (MEW 35:358; SCME:331). And in the *History of the Communist League* (1885), Engels remarks on "the intuition that any revolution must be European if it is to triumph" (MEW 21:210). However, Marx himself had already formulated the most explicit statement of this position in his article for the NYDT dated 5 August 1853:

> The revolutionary party can only congratulate itself on this state of things. The humiliation of the reactionary Western Governments, and their manifest *impotency to guard the interests of European civilization against Russian encroachment,* cannot fail to work out a wholesome indignation in the people who have suffered themselves, since 1849, to be subjected to the rule of counter-revolution (MEW 9:215 f.; TEQ:75; my italics).

In an article for the NYDT ten days earlier (25 July 1853), Marx had reported:

> While the English Queen is, at this moment, feasting Russian Princesses; while an enlightened English aristocracy and bourgeoisie lie prostrate before the barbarian Aristocrat, the English proletariat alone protests against the impotency and degradation of the ruling classes (MEW 9:199; TEW:62).

Now as far as the intrinsic reason for this bourgeois impotency and degradation is concerned, Marx tells us about it in an article for the NYDT dated 4 October 1853, which we have already cited in Chapter 8 (see p. 218). In it he also tells us why communism is the authentic carrier of a western civilization that is truly Christian. Here is what he writes:

> One thing must be evident at least, that it is the stockjobbers, and the peace-mongering bourgeoisie, represented in the Government by the oligarchy, who surrender Europe to Russia, and that in order to resist the encroachments of the Czar, we must, above all,

overthrow the inglorious Empire of those mean, cringing, and infamous adorers of the golden calf (MEW 9:325; TEQ:132).

The same idea is to be found in the passage from his article of 8 August 1853, to which I called the reader's attention above (see p. 250). Thus it is not correct, as Habermas says, that for Marx industrial and technological development is the be-all and the end-all, or even the main thing. It is merely a means, a material tool, however indispensable as such it may be. Engels' view is the same. Here is what he writes in his series of articles on "The Housing Question" (1872–73):

> It is through this industrial revolution that the productivity of human labor has reached the point where, for the first time in the existence of humanity, through the ongoing division of labor among all, it is possible not only to produce enough for the abundant consumption of all the members of society and for an ample reserve-fund but also to provide each and every individual with the leisure required, not only to preserve what deserves to be preserved of the culture transmitted to us by history—science, art, urbanity, etc.—but also to transform it from a monopoly of the ruling classes to a common good of society as a whole and perfect it even more. *And this is the decisive point* (MEW 18:220 f.; my italics).

IV

Now we are in a position to probe the why and wherefor of the intransigent occidentalism of Marx and Engels. Its underlying motivation is misunderstood both by the anti-Marxists who try to ridicule Marx's Europeanism and by the "magnanimous" Marxists who feel that their Marxism is mature and solid enough to admit the "understandable" errors and flaws of the founders.

The first point that should be noted, and it is often overlooked even though it is decisive, is that Marx and Engels do not limit the charge of idiocy and hereditary stupidity to non-European peasants. They bring the same charge against European and German peasants as well. They are against "the idiocy of peasant life" wherever it is found. One is being very superficial if one thinks that Marx and Engels suffer from some ill-founded predilection for Europe and Germany. There is a universal disposition towards barbarianism, according to Marx, and it can be found just as easily among Europeans as among Asians or Polynesians. In an article for *Das Volk* dated 30 July 1859, in which Marx writes about the military armaments and the financial chicanery of Louis Napoleon, he remarks:

In such circumstances it cannot surprise us that *the universal disposition towards barbarism* adopts a certain method, that immorality is turned into a system, that illegality wins its legislators and the right of the strongest its legal codes. Hence, if there is such frequent recourse to "Napoleonic ideas," it is because these absurd fantasies of the prisoner of Ham have become the Pentateuch of the modern religion and the Revelation of the bellicose and stockjobbing imperial swindle (MEW 13:444; my italics).

Barbarism is the conduct of ruffians and swindlers, the assertion of the right of the strongest. Civilization is what stands opposed to this barbarism. In his address at Cambridge Hall on 22 January 1867 Marx said:

As far as the liberation of the peasant serfs in Russia is concerned, it has liberated the supreme government authority from the obstacles which the nobility were capable of placing in the way of its centralizing activity. It created a broad field for the recruiting of its army, dissolved the collective property of the Russian farmers, divided them, and made fast their faith in their dear father, the Czar. *It has not freed them from Asiatic barbarism, since civilization is forged through the centuries.* Every effort to *raise the moral level* of the peasants is regarded as a crime and punished. I recall to you only the official persecutions of the abstinence associations that were trying to rescue the Muscovite from what Feuerbach calls the material substance of his religion, i.e., liquor. Whatever may be hoped for from the liberation of the peasants in the future, right now it is clear that in any case it has bolstered the forces at the Czar's disposal (MEW 16:203 f.; my italics).

The moral import of what Marx understands by "civilization" is clear-cut. If it is Christianity that has been the promoter of civilization in that sense and has struck deeper roots in Europe, it is not Marx's fault. Aside from that, Marx finds that the capitalist economy, for all its intrinsic evilness, has been the effective instrument in battering down the walls that block the entry of western civilization into the rest of the world. As he wrote to Engels in his letter of 14 June 1853: "The breaking up of those stereotyped primitive forms was the *sine qua non* for Europeanization" (MEW 28:268; SCME:80).

In Section II of Chapter 7 we saw that Marx was not a person who felt that the end justifies the means. Thus we cannot give credence to the moralistic objection that is often raised on this ground, an objection often voiced by superficial people who are incapable of ever learning anything new. It is frequently taken for granted by many people that Hegel and Marx could not possibly be intending to teach us something totally new that would uproot our existing categories from their very foundation. Cherishing this prejudice, they do not even make any effort to *understand* the message of these men.

Marx incessantly condemns the unpardonable atrocities of capitalism and the immoral actions of Britain. He does so in the most forceful terms, and there is no need to repeat those condemnantions here. But the big question remains: how are we to save humanity from the endlessly repetitive round of vegetal and animal idiocy, from the natural eternal return of all things to which humanity has been chained for millennia? Marx stressed, with all the force that human speech possesses, that human beings cannot become truly human until they manage to break away from that cycle.

People often forget the very plain and simple fact that we do come from the animals. It seems unbelievable that a century after Darwin this fact must be called to people's attention every time some problem takes on depth and seriousness. As Hegel put it: the natural is the nonhuman; in becoming human, a human being ceases to be natural. This supernaturalism is rigorously Christian. But its opponents must first grasp the scope of the problem because, as Marx points out, the very import of human history and humanity's existence is at stake here.

To "impose civilization on humanity" would certainly seem to be paternalistic and imperialistic. It sounds thus if expressed in those terms. But here we are not at one of those name-calling meetings where people cannot pose authentic questions and broach real problems. Without civilization human beings cannot reach the point where they are capable of making decisions for themselves, yet such decision making is the only way to keep them from being manipulated by all the varied forms of paternalism and imperialism. It is not certainly correct that a human being is free in and by himself or herself. As such, a human being is as enslaved and devoid of freedom as the animals and plants are. Though by nature a human being possesses a human body, it is civilization that makes a human being truly human. As Marx put it in an early work (*Critique of Hegel's Philosophy of Right: Introduction*): "But how does the history of our freedom differ from that of the wild boar, if it is only to be found in the forests?" (MEW 1:380; VEW:246). Philosophies obtuse enough to confuse "being free" with "being at large" will never comprehend that it is the moral imperative that makes a human being free.

In the article on Denmark cited earlier (see p. 249), Marx and Engels uphold "the right of civilization against barbarianism, of progress against stability . . . the right of historical development" (MEW 5:395). To place such comments in their proper context, we can recall the thesis which Marx offered in his article on India for the NYDT dated 8 August 1853: "Indian society has no history at all . . ." (MEW 9:220; VSE:320). And also his thesis in the 1857 Introduction: "Mere hunting and fishing peoples lie outside the point where real development begins" (GRU: 107).

Naturalism and barbarism signify vegetal stagnation in a repetitive cycle, the absence of history, and total dependence with respect to matter. Vegetative existence means subordination to the annual cycle of vegetation, which in turn depends on the cyclic return of the orbiting stars and planets in their immutable course where nothing new can occur. And though they are alive, animals and plants represent repetitive stagnation by very definition.

Such is the realm of nature. To say that the human being is a cultural and civilizing entity rather than a natural entity is to say that the human being is a historical entity. The human being is not human until it begins to have a history. Annual festivals and religions themselves were originally agricultural in nature, reinforcing humanity's role as a cog in this monstrously repetitive machinery. Nature consists in this endlessly repeated and loathsome cycle, this stupefying tautology. This is why Marx alludes to the "hereditary stupidity" and the "idiocy" of peasant life. There can be no real intelligence or understanding in these conditions, and hence there can be no freedom either. For human beings are free only insofar as they are familiar with something more than the confining routine of the natural horizon. As Marx wrote for the NYDT on 25 June 1853:

> We must not forget . . . this undignified, stagnatory, and vegetative life . . . this passive sort of existence. . . (MEW 9:32; VEW:306).

> We must not forget that these idyllic village communities, inoffensive though they may appear, had always been the solid foundation of Oriental despotism, that they restrained the human mind within the smallest possible compass, making it the unresisting tool of superstition, enslaving it beneath traditional rules, depriving it of all grandeur and historical energies (ibid.).

Far from being open to any accusation of amorality, Marx's transcendental option for civilization seeks to give humans, for the first time, the very possibility of morality. It is concerned to provide the conditions that make moral living possible. Marx argues from the very reality that makes objections possible, a reality of which his objectors are not aware.

V

Finally, let us focus on something even more specific than the occidentalism of Marx and Engels. Let us consider their Germanism. Here again it would be completely unreasonable to accuse them of chauvinist sympathies without examining their motives and reasons. In an article for the NYDT dated 24 April 1852, which was written by Engels and signed by Marx, we read the following:

> If all of the territory east of the Elbe and the Saar was once inhabited by interrelated Slavic tribes, this fact only demonstrates the historical tendency and the physical and intellectual ability of the German nation to subdue its ancient Oriental neighbors, to absorb and assimilate them; this absorptive tendency of the Germans has been, and continues to be, one of the most powerful means of expanding western civilization in Eastern Europe (MEW 8:81).

Thus in the eyes of Marx and Engels, Germany is a means of propagating western civilization; and to them western civilization *is* civilization *tout court*. And in this task Germany has been a noticeably effective means. There is no trace of chauvinism in their view. For in other places they maintain that England, or the United States, or the French Revolution has been the great means of propagating civilization.

In early 1887 Adolf Sorge, a long-time confidant of Marx and Engels residing in the United States, wrote a letter to Engels. In it he remarked on how minimal had been the effect of the *Communist Manifesto* on American workers over a period of almost forty years as compared with its immediate and revolutionary impact on German workers like himself in 1848. Engels replied to him in a letter dated 4 May 1887:

> Moreover, forty years ago you people were Germans, with the theoretical sense of the Germans, and that is why the *Manifesto* had an impact; on the other hand among the other peoples it had absolutely no impact though it was translated into French, English, Flemish, Danish, etc. (MEW 36:648).

In a letter to Bernstein dated 9 August 1882, Engels writes:

> In all questions of international politics the French and Italian publications of the Party should be used with extreme caution. In

this area, too, we Germans are obliged to display, through our criticism, the theoretical superiority which in fact we possess (MEW 35:349 f.).

Some commentators, scandalized by such remarks from Engels, have tried to suggest that Marx thought differently on this matter and that his Germanism waned as he grew older. It is not true. At the time of the Franco-Prussian War, Marx wrote the following to Engels in a letter dated 20 July 1870:

If the Prussians win, the centralization of state power will be useful for the centralization of the German working class. German preponderance would shift the center of gravity of the working-class movement in Western Europe from France to Germany; and one need only compare the movement in both countries from 1866 to today to see that the German working class is superior to the French one both in theory and in organization. Their victory over the French on the world stage would simultaneously be the victory of *our* theory over that of Proudhon, etc. (MEW 33:5).

The theoretical superiority of the German people is an indubitable fact for Marx just as it is for Engels. The reader should note that the passages cited above discuss the German proletariat in terms of the world revolution that must take place in accordance with Marx's theory. Insofar as this dimension of scientific socialism is concerned, Marx and Engels regard the German proletariat as superior to other proletariats and other peoples.

Thus there is no question of racism here. Marx and Engels acknowledge that all peoples are capable of developing themselves and reaching full civilization and communism. The question is who is leading the way in this process of development. It would be pure a priori hypothesizing to maintain that all peoples are equally advanced in this respect. I don't see any prejudice in the fact that someone maintains that one person or party is more advanced than others, particularly when that assertion can be verified. Indeed nationalist prejudice lies much more in denying the possibility that some other people may be more civilized than my own. That really is chauvinism, and jt often underlies discussions of this topic. If one does maintain the latter thesis, then one is forced to profess moral relativism; for it is as if no objective criterion existed which could be used to settle the question. And such a position is clearly incompatible with the thought of Marx and Engels.

Now we must take the bull by the horns and face the fact that Marx and Engels attribute the very existence of scientific socialism to the theoretical superiority of the German people. In a review of Marx's recently published Book I of *Capital,* which was published in the *Demokratisches Wochenblatt* on 21 March 1868, Engels writes:

> As long as capitalists and workers have existed, no book has appeared which is of such importance for the workers as *Das Kapital.* The relation between capital and labour, the hinge on which our entire present system of society turns, is here treated scientifically for the first time and with a thoroughness and acuteness of which only a German is capable. Valuable as are the writings of Robert Owen, Saint-Simon and Fourier—valuable as they will be in the future—it has been reserved for a German first to climb to the heights from which the whole field of modern social relations can be clearly seen in full view just as the lower mountain scenery is observed by someone standing on the topmost point (MEW 16:235; SW:177–78).

In his Preface to the first German edition of *Socialism: Utopian and Scientific* (1882), Engels writes:

> Such readers will also be surprised to encounter the Kant-Laplace cosmogony, modern natural science and Darwin, classical German philosophy and Hegel in a sketch of the history of the development of socialism. But scientific socialism is indeed an essentially German product and could arise only in that nation whose classical philosophy had kept alive the tradition of conscious dialectics in Germany (MEW 19:187; SUS:7).

When present-day Stalinism and neo-Stalinism deny that the socialism of Marx and Engels is derived directly and consciously from Hegel, they are simply ignoring the explicit statements of Marx and Engels on this very point. On an engraving Heinrich Scheu made for him Engels wrote the following dedication (4 January 1891):

> We German socialists are proud of the fact that we are descendants not only of Saint-Simon, Fourier and Owen, but also of Kant, Fichte and Hegel. The German working-class movement is the inheritor of German classical philosophy (MEW 38: opposite page 16).

The very last sentence is the concluding one of Engels' work entitled *Ludwig Feuerbach and the End of Classical German Philosophy* (MEW

21:307; LF:60). The first sentence of the dedication appears earlier in the 1882 Preface to *Socialism: Utopian and Scientific* (MEW 19:188; SUS:7–8). Particularly noteworthy is the deliberate omission of Feuerbach's name in the philosophical lineage of socialism whenever Engels recounts that lineage. This dovetails with what Marx wrote to Engels in a letter dated 24 April 1857: on rereading some of his early work he found the cult of Feuerbach in them "very humorous" (MEW 31:290). If today we find Alfred Schmidt trying to reestablish a connection between Marxism and Feuerbach, it is because he is not really familiar with the works of Marx and Engels. But let me get back to the point at issue.

Serious attention should be paid to the fact that it was Marx himself who pointed out to Engels the strictly German origin of his work. He did so in a letter written *prior* (20 February 1866) to all the testimony later given by Engels. As he was finishing up Book I of *Capital*, Marx wrote the following to Engels:

> You realize, dear friend, that in a work such as mine many deficiencies in detail must exist. But the *composition*, the linking-up, is a triumph of German science, a triumph which an individual German must recognize as due to no merit of *his own* but as belonging to the *nation* (MEW 31:183).

The letter ends with these words: "I feel proud of the Germans. It is our obligation to emancipate this 'profound' people."

The German science whose triumph is to be seen in scientific socialism is obviously what Kant, Fichte, and Hegel understood to be science. Those three figures talked a great deal about the scientific nature of their philosophy and analyzed what went to make it "scientific." And apart from biblical exegesis and its auxiliary disciplines, there had as yet been no other specifically German science. So in listing those names and attributing the working-class movement to the merit of the German nation as such, Engels is being perfectly faithful to the opinion of Marx himself. Here I would like to add one more lengthy piece of testimony from Engels. It is found in his Addendum to the Preface to the second edition of *The Peasant War in Germany* (1870):

> The German workers have two important advantages compared with the rest of Europe. First, they belong to the most theoretical people of Europe; they have retained that sense of theory which the so-called "educated" people of Germany have totally lost. Without German philosophy, particularly that of Hegel, German scientific Socialism (the only scientific Socialism extant) would

never have come into existence. Without a sense for theory, scientific Socialism would have never become blood and tissue of the workers. What an enormous advantage this is, may be seen on the one hand from the indifference of the English labour movement towards all theory, which is one of the reasons why it moves so slowly in spite of the splendid organisation of the individual unions; on the other hand, from the mischief and confusion created by Proudhonism in its original form among the Frenchmen and Belgians, and in its caricature form, as presented by Bakunin, among the Spaniards and Italians (MEW 18:516; TGR:16–17).

The second advantage, which I am not going to discuss here, is the fact that the German working-class movement came after the experiences of the French and English working-class movements and hence could learn lessons from them. The issue of concern to us here, however, is the reason for the theoretical superiority of the Germans which, according to Marx and Engels, produced Marx's system and the German working-class movement. The reason or cause is not racial. As we have already seen, they disparaged the "idiocy of peasant life" in Germany as much as anywhere else. This fact is confirmed in a passage of Marx's *Critique of Hegel's Philosophy of Right: Introduction,* where he sarcastically rebuts the famous historical school of law:

> On the other hand, good-natured enthusiasts, German chauvinists by temperament and free-thinking liberals by reflection, seek the history of our freedom beyond our history, in the primieval Teutonic forests. But how does the history of our freedom differ from that of the wild boar, if it is only to be found in the forests? And besides, everyone knows that what is shouted into a forest is echoed back again. So peace to the primeval Teutonic forests! (MEW 1:380; VEW:246).

It is a classic passage. The "natural" explains nothing. It is the "historical" that is the key. If the Germans are superior, we must look to history for the explanation; and history begins after the Teutonic forests, after the racial element. The implication is clear: western civilization is the cause of German superiority, not a result of the latter.

We have explicit testimony from Engels on the cause of German theoretical superiorty in the notes entitled *Varia über Deutschland.* In them he drew up the outline for a history of Germany that he never got to publish, though he did manage to write a few sections in full. From a letter to Liebknecht dated 27 January 1874 (MEW 33:615), we know that he planned to use the material to write a pamphlet at least. He divides this history into three periods: from 1500 to 1789, from 1789 to 1815, and from 1815 to 1873.

In the first period Engels mentions Böhme, Kepler, Leibniz, and Bach (stressing the latter), and ends up with the names of Lessing, Kant, Goethe, Schiller, Wieland, Herder, Händel, Gluck, and Mozart. The second period is that of "the splendour of literature and philosophy and the culmination of music in Beethoven" (MEW 18:593). In various sections dealing with the third period, Engels maintains that "German Protestantism is the only modern form of Christianity worthy of criticism" (MEW 18:595). He writes about historical, philological, and philosophical criticism, stresses the fact that Germany furnished it, and maintains that it would have been impossible without German Protestantism (which is the plain truth, be it noted in passing). But the passage in which we are interested here has to do with the first period. In it Engels notes:

> The specifically theologico-theoretical character of the German revolution in the sixteenth century. Predominant interest in the things that are not of this world. Abstraction from wretched reality—the basis of the later theoretical superiority of the Germans from Leibnitz to Hegel (MEW 18:590).

One could not ask for greater explicitness on the theological cause of German theoretical superiority, to which latter factor both Marx and Engels attributed the rise of the scientific socialism elaborated by Marx. This hardly takes us by surprise because Marx has already told us that it is a matter of realizing "the kingdom of heaven on earth" (which is the goal of authentic Christianity); and because both he and Engels have already told us that the definitive solution is a Christian state.

Notes

1. See J.P. Miranda, *Marx and the Bible: A Critique of the Philosophy of Oppression,* Eng. trans., Maryknoll, N.Y.: Orbis Books, 1974; *Being and the Messiah: The Message of St. John,* Eng. trans., Maryknoll, N.Y.: Orbis Books, 1977.

2. *Translator's note:* For the sake of readers who may be unfamiliar with Miranda's thought, I should like to present a passage from his last book that summarizes his negative view of religion and the tragic reabsorption of Christianity into a religious framework:

Perhaps the greatest disaster of history was the reabsorption of Christianity by the framework of religion. It is difficult to imagine a greater falsification of Christianity; and the masters of this world could not have invented a more effective stratagem for preventing the revolution of oppressed humanity. Religion does not alter the prevailing order; it has always had an accepted place in society; the successive gods, no matter what their names, are of absolutely no importance. Christianity fell into this pattern because of the understandable weakness of the persecuted as well as the subtle, invincible strength of the oppressors.

The anthropological, apologetic thesis that all people are innately religious is in a certain sense true, but it has no relation to Christianity. Or rather, it is related insofar as religiosity can reabsorb and annihilate Christianity. It is as if we were told that all people are innately alienated. So what?

Far from challenging consumeristic society, religion constitutes an integral part of it. We need only glance at the work of the urban planners: parks, schools, bus stations, theatres, churches, stores, parking lots, packing houses, sports arenas. A society that wants to preserve itself has to attend to the various needs of the people—religious needs, recreational needs, nutritional needs, etc. For many centuries religious authorities have taken advantage of this fact. But the message of the Bible has no place in such a program, it does not fit; it does not satisfy these needs nor was it meant to. Yahweh does not come to occupy a place reserved for him in the cosmos by the social structure. He comes to revolutionize this cosmos and this entire social structure from their very foundations.

Therefore Yahweh rejects cultus, because it would be a way of domesticating him, of reducing him to religion. See Matt. 5:23; 1 Cor. 11:20–22; Matt. 7:21–23; Amos 5:21–25; Isa. 1:10–20; Hos. 5:1.2.6; 8:13; Mic. 6:6–8; Jer. 6:18–21; 7:4–7, 11–15, 21–22; Isa. 43:23–24; 58:2; 6–10; etc. In these passages Yahweh does not demand interpersonal justice ''in addition to'' cultus, nor does he ask that cultus be reformed, nor does he require—as the theology of the status quo has unrepentantly interpreted the above passages—that cultus be continued but with better internal dispositions on the part of the worshippers. The message of these passages can be summarized in this way: *I do not want cultus but rather interpersonal justice.* Anything we do to find some other meaning in this message is pure tergiversation. . . .

Religion lubricates the cycles of the eternal return in history. Rebellion against religion is mandatory for anyone convinced that justice must be achieved, because persons with moral conscience cannot resign themselves to the eternal return of all things. But the eternal return is an iron circle, unbreakable as long as we fail to perceive the Absolute in the outcry of suffering humanity. Mechanistic materialism and bourgeois nihilism are perfectly interchangeable. Their common denominator—which renders them both ultimately without significance—is the insipid triviality to which they reduce the world when they deny the transcendence of the ''other.'' Nothing but an intervening Absolute can cause the banal circumvolutions of history to stop. Without it, everything will continue to consist of deducible combinations and permutations of either material particles or eternal spiritual essences, but in either case the result is the same: Without this Absolute there can be no *ultimum* which is the achievement of justice in the world (*Being and the Messiah*, pp. 40–42).

3. Cited by Irving Fetscher in his *Marxistische Portrats*, Stuttgart: Frommann, 1975, p. 27. The title of Eleanor Marx's book is *Erinnerungen an Marx*.
4. See my books cited in note 1.

10

The God of Historical Eschatology

Although this chapter stands on its own arguments, I would like to stress the fact that it is not meant to be read in isolation from the nine preceding chapters. Affirmation of the existence of God means nothing if it is hedged in by merely utilitarian motives, unappealable determinism, antihumanist skepticism, the denial of morality, and the denial of Christianity, if we are dealing with an author reared in a Christian world. The opposite holds true just as well: in order to be able to maintain its denial of God, and precisely for that purpose, materialism has had to deny humanity, morality, liberty, and spiritual motivating forces. But if the unexpected day arrives when it is obliged to acknowledge the reality of these things, then I do not see how it can logically or purposefully continue to deny the existence of God.

In other words I am saying that from what we have seen in the preceding chapters, the existence of God seems to me to be logically inescapable. By the same token, in the absence of the themes and commitments brought out in the previous chapters, the affirmation of God's existence would be totally devoid of intelligible meaning.

This is the massive logic of the question. Of course, it should not surprise us to find inconsistencies or hesitancies in the thought of individual authors. For authors usually have not been able to fully explicitate or deduce all the logical consequences of their own thought. In particular, when their message is vigorous, new, and revolutionary, the authors have not managed in their own lives to explore this message all the way to the end, to detect and resolve all their personal convictions that are incompatible with it and that have their origin *elsewhere*.

I

Now aside from the absolutely fundamental theses in the thought of Marx and Engels that we have examined in the preceding chapters, we also find another conviction in their thought that may well be even more important. It is the conviction that history has an end and a goal, and that this end is good. The full realization of communism is the end or conclusion of history envisioned in this case, which takes place within history.

Marx's denunciation of the worship of the god of money, which we examined in Chapter 8, clearly and undeniably has its origin in a teaching of Jesus Christ. Many Christians dare not take that teaching seriously because it is purposely designed to revolutionize every aspect of life and society, since it is aimed directly against the mode of production itself. Marx's use of the word "mammon" shows that he himself was aware of the source and origin of this denunciation that is the central axis of his own economic analysis.

But there is another teaching of Jesus Christ that is even more central and equally pervasive in its revolutionary impact on everything. It is his proclamation of the final end and outcome of history. The Greek term for it is *eschaton;* the Latin term is *ultimum*. Now it is true that one branch of later theology gave an ultraworldly cast to eschatology. It is also true that those around today who thrive on the opiate of the people understand the term in that unearthly sense. Yet the fact remains that in the Bible this end of history is viewed as something within history itself, something occurring not in another world but in this very world where the historical process has unfolded.

The origin of this eschatological awareness is also certain and unmistakable. It is the very definition that Jesus Christ gave to the meaning and content of his good news, his evangelical message: "This is the time of fulfillment. The reign of God is at hand! Reform your lives and believe in the gospel!" (Mark 1:15). Some individuals—the postponers—interpret this statement to mean that the *eschaton* is approaching, that it is not as far away as it was yesterday. But that is hardly news. Such escapist interpretations would turn Jesus into a common fool who puts enormous enthusiam and passion into announcing a trite commonplace as big news.

Many Christians as well as official Christian churches have refused to accept this message, and continue to do so today, even though the term "Messiah" can have no specific meaning without it. We find, all the same, that the most striking feature of Marx's thought is its full eschatological awareness. What is more, no one who lacks that awareness can be a revolutionary. For the only other alternative that one can profess in its place is the eternal return of all things. One must assume that one injustice will succeed another, that one form of oppression will succeed another, and that we cannot possibly realize justice in the world in any definitive way.

But contrary to what is the case with respect to other doctrines or teachings about history, we find that eschatological awareness has something very characteristic about it, i.e., in strict logical consistency we cannot believe that a good end exists for history unless we believe that God is directing history. The *eschaton* is the definitive triumph of good over evil. Scientifically speaking, however, we cannot demonstrate that good ultimately has to triumph over evil unless we include in our demonstration the proof of God's existence (the scientifically demonstrative procedure followed by Hegel).

The fact that some thinkers or currents of thought have affirmed the *eschaton* and denied the existence of God simply proves what I said above, i.e., that no author manages to draw all the ultimate conclusions of his or her own thought.

Perhaps we really needed a half century of ravaging, brain-crushing, logical positivism to bring out this logical implication clearly: that we cannot scientifically affirm that history has an *eschaton* unless we, in one of our premises, affirm the existence of a God who guides history. The atheistic Marxists of today, who have gone through the devastating school that goes by the name of formalism, prefer to deny the *eschaton*, or to say that they have no idea what a final end of history might be. On this point it seems to me that they are being perfectly logical.

The fact is, to be sure, that there is nothing incomprehensible about the term *eschaton* or its meaning. It does not refer to any universal conflagration or to a disastrous end of the world. Nor does it mean that human beings will turn into pillars of salt and cease to be human. It means that injustice and exploitation will disappear once and for all. And if that notion does not have a crystal-clear meaning, then no notion does.

When this point is explained to atheistic Marxists, they prefer to go back to the first approach. They disown the *eschaton* and deny that Marx affirmed it. Quite apart from the question as to whether Marx and Engels were consistent enough to face up to the logical implications of affirming that there is an end for history, we will have made some progress if we show, with explicit texts, that both men repeatedly and emphatically maintained the reality of the *eschaton*. In this way we will at least have firmly established that particular fact in investigations of Marx's thought.

II

First, however, we would do well to go over other texts of Engels and Marx that are not directly eschatological in import but that provide a vision of history that serves as a suitable framework for the directly eschatological passages we will consider in the next section of this chapter.

Consider, for example, the following monumental thesis in Engels' letter of 18 June 1892 to Nikolai Frantsevich Danielson:

> In fact, there is nothing in history that ultimately does not serve the cause of human progress in one way or another, but frequently in a terribly roundabout way. And that may well be the case with the current economic revolution in your own country (MEW 38:363).

It would be hard for a Christian to find a better formulation for his or her conviction that God does guide the whole pageant of human history, and ultimately directs it toward a good end. The important point here, in any case, is the fact that Engels' thesis is not empirical in any way.

Again, in a letter of Engels to Friedrich Adolph Sorge dated 8 June 1889, we read the following:

> It has cost me tremendous effort to make even Bebel understand what it is all really about, although the Possibilists know it very well and proclaim it every day. And with all these mistakes I had little hope that things would work out well, that immanent reason, which is gradually evolving to consciousness of itself in human history, would win out as early as this (MEW 37:231; cf. SCME:383).

That is pure Hegel. Only superficial minds could have accused him of pantheism, and they did so because they did not realize that in Hegel's mind the assertion that God resides in another world is atheism in its most obstinate form. For the "atheist" is a person "without God," and the transcendental notion of God just mentioned really leaves the world "without God," and hence "atheistic." Engels himself does not seem to advert to the fact that Hegel's reason immanent in history is God, the true God who was fleshed out in Jesus Christ. That is why I will not try to offer this text as proof of the theism of Engels. But the fact is that the "hope" to which Engels alludes in the above passage is identical to the hope that Marx alluded to when he was writing about the Maryland campaign of the American Civil War (*Die Presse,* 12 October 1862):

And yet the breakthrough into Maryland took place under the most favorable possible circumstances: an ignominious series of unexpected defeats for the North; the Union army demoralized; Stonewall Jackson, the hero of the day; Lincoln and his government, the butt of children's jokes; the Democratic Party further strengthened in the North and taking for granted the presidency of Jefferson Davis; France and England lying in wait to openly proclaim the legitimacy of the slave states that they now recognize within! *"E pur si muove."* Despite everything, reason triumphs in world history.

Even more important than the campaign in Maryland is Lincoln's Proclamation. . . . In the history of the United States and humanity, Lincoln will occupy the place right next to Washington! (MEW 15:552 f.).

In this same context let me cite the letter of Engels to Vera Ivanovna Zasulich (23 April 1885):

People who boasted that they *made* a revolution have always seen the day after that they had no idea what they were doing, that the revolution *made* did not in the least resemble the one they intended to make. That is what Hegel calls the irony of history, an irony which few historical personalities escape (MEW 36:307; SCME: 362).

On his rough draft of this letter Engels crossed out the next phrase: "Perhaps the same thing will happen to us."

In a letter to Nikolai Frantsevitch Danielson (13 November 1885), Engels talks about the vulgar economists who seem to be incapable of understanding Book I of *Capital*. To them it will always remain a closed book. Then Engels goes on to say: "It is a fine example of what Hegel calls *die Ironie der Weltgeschichte* ("the irony of world history") (MEW 36:384; SCME:366).

In his 1895 Introduction to the *Class Struggles in France* Engels brings out the same point incisively, as we have seen: "The irony of universal history upsets everything. We, the 'revolutionaries,' the 'rebels'—we are thriving far better on legal methods than on illegal methods and revolt" (MEW 22:525; cf. SW:296). In another letter (4 January 1888) to Ion Nadejde, he almost sounds like St. Paul: "Come what may, I am sure that in the end everything will work out to the advantage of the Socialist movement" (MEW 37:6). And in an article for *Der Sozialdemkrat* on 15 January of the same year, Engels addresses the following words directly to the bourgeoisie: "At the end of the tragedy you will be in ruins, and the triumph of the proletariat will have been achieved or will be clearly inevitable" (MEW 21:351).

Another monumental thesis, one just as nonempirical, is formulated by Engels in a letter to Ferdinand Domela Nieuwenhuis dated 11 January 1887: "Only a European war can hinder us and momentarily cause us to fall back a good distance; but even that, *like any other event,* must ultimately work to our advantage" (MEW 36:593; my italics). It is the same eschatological certainty that St. Paul expressed in these words: "We know that God makes all things work together for the good of those who have been called according to his decree" (Rom. 8:28).

In his treatise-letter dated 11 March 1895 to Werner Sombart, an economist, Engels offers the following comment on Marx's *Capital:*

> According to Marx's views all history up to now, as far as the great events are concerned, has come about unconsciously—that is, the events and their further consequences have not been intended. The ordinary actors in history have either wanted to achieve something different, or else what they achieved has led to quite different unforeseeable consequences (MEW 22:525; SCME:455).

All this Marx learned from Hegel. The cunning or subtlety of reason squeezes out of the historical process the results it was seeking in spite of, and even contrary to, the ends that we human beings were consciously pursuing. There may be many steps backward and roundabout maneuvers, but "reason triumphs, despite everything, in the history of the world."

Such expressions evidently mean an intelligent principle that is superior to human beings and that is guiding history to ends and by means which limited human reason cannot succeed in dominating by thought or perverting by willful action. For to assume that this principle is an abstraction rather than a being that really exists is to commit a logical mistake of the first order; indeed, the appeal to this principle is an appeal to a factor whose operation and effectiveness explain why history takes one particular course rather than another, and arrives at one particular result rather than another. Logically speaking, then, we are dealing here with a real being, not an abstraction. We are equally obliged by logic to say that this being possesses a personal character and is not just a brute thing. For the name given to this principle is "reason." If it is reason, then it understands; and if it understands, it is personal.

But what exactly is Engels talking about in the above-cited letter to Sombart when he implies that the cunning of reason is Marx's historical conception in *Capital?* Well, the fact is that it would be hard to find any corpus of writings that are so decidedly based on this certitude as Marx's economic analyses. The "irony of history" *par excellence* is the fact that the capitalist mode of production, historically speaking, constitutes the major means whereby humanity will manage to fashion the definitive form of society; and it constitutes this means despite its unspeakable atrocities and its systematic forms of exploitation, and even despite the unprecedented devastation of the truly human that is part and parcel of it.

We could cite practically all of *Capital* and the *Grundrisse* in this connection. In every chapter of those works we can find laconic passages by Marx which deliberately point in this direction and which are far more eloquent than any formal discourse on the cunning of reason. Let me cite a couple of examples here.

In Chapter 5, Section II, of Book III of *Capital* ("Savings in Labour Conditions at the Expense of the Labourers"), we find this passage, the first sentence of which was cited earlier:

> Capitalist production . . . more than any other mode of production . . . squanders human lives, or living labour, and not only blood and flesh, but also nerve and brain. Indeed, it is only by dint of the most extravagant waste of individual development that the development of the human race is at all safeguarded and maintained in the epoch of history immediately preceding the conscious reorganization of society (MEW 25:99; CAP III:88).

The certainty-in-spite-of-everything evident in the second sentence ("Indeed, it is only by dint . . .") seems to me to be deliberately strident. Here we see the irony of history, the cunning of reason, in all its nakedness. The rash Hegel never went so far in his remarks. In Chapter 15 of the same Book III we read:

> The means—unconditional development of the productive forces of society—comes continually into conflict with the limited purpose, the self-expansion of the existing capital. The capitalist mode of production is, for this reason, a *historical means* of developing the material forces of production and creating an appropriate world-market and is, at the same time, a continual conflict between this, *its historical task,* and its own corresponding relations of social production (MEW 25:260; CAP III:250; my italics).

The whole capitalist system, the whole historical epoch of capitalism, is a means, an instrument. To it is assigned a mission that it must carry out in history. But it is not a means in the hands of human beings because we are told specifically that everything happens *in spite of* the goals that human beings set for themselves. So we are faced with a good question: a means in whose hands? Who is the subject that assigns capitalism its historical mission?

As we shall see, Marx does not leave us without an explicit, conclusive response to that question. But the laconic cast of such passages as the above has provided the occasion for some Marxists to believe that "reason" with its cunning could be a mere abstraction, that it need not be a real, existing entity. But a nonexistent entity cannot be the subject in whose hands capitalism functions as a mere instrument. An abstraction cannot fill the role of an active agent that assigns a historical mission to the bourgeois mode of production. For we would then be dealing with a mythical being which we know did not exist. How can anyone think that Marx consciously explains the course of history by appealing to a mythical entity?

And if abstract "reason" does not fill the bill, still less does "progress" or "history" itself (except in metaphorical phrases that only postpone a real explanation for later on). The crux of Marx's whole conception of history is that the protagonists, both individuals and the capitalist system in its entirety, do not know what they are doing. His conception affirms a higher principle that does know where history is going. "Progress" is not an entity that knows, nor is it a knowing subject, nor does it exist as a real being. And if history is the sum total of the actors in history, that means that history itself does not know where it is going. If, on the other hand, there is some entity called "history" existing above and beyond all those actors, then it is nothing but a myth. And in this case it is inferior to the myth called "reason" because reason, even if it does not exist any more than history does as an entity, is at least conceived as endowed with reasoning power. But that disregards the fact that Marx views human beings as the ones who make history, not vice versa.

If we do not wish to present nonexistent abstractions as historical factors, then this "reason" must be "Reason" in Hegel's sense, i.e., God.

Writing about the capitalist in Chapter 24 of Book I of *Capital,* Marx presents the following passage that we have already considered in another context:

> Fanatically bent on making value expand itself, he ruthlessly forces the human race to produce for production's sake; he thus forces the development of the productive powers of society, and creates those material conditions which alone can form the real basis of a higher form of society, a society in which the full and free development of every individual forms the ruling principle (MEW 23:618; CAP I:592).

Here again we have the irony of history in all its nakedness. Behind Marx's reticence is a desire that the reader grasp the contrast here. On the one hand the capitalist is a totally blind fanatic who wants only to produce for the sake of producing. The cunning of reason, on the other hand, ensures that he unwittingly creates the indispensable bases for a higher, definitive society that is truly humane. Or as Marx put it in an article for the NYDT dated 8 August 1853: "The bourgeois period of history must create the material basis of a new world" (MEW 9:226).

We have every right to ask at this point: why *must* it do this? Obviously the answer is that an *eschaton* of justice and human fulfillment is a certainty in Marx's mind.

Here is another passage from the *Grundrisse:*

> The theft of alien labour time, on which the present wealth is based, appears a miserable foundation in face of this new one created by large-scale industry itself. As soon as labour in the direct form has ceased to be the great well-spring of wealth labour-time ceases and must cease to be its measure (GRU:705).

In this passage Marx spells out the strident contrast. Up to now economic systems have desired and sought to extract surplus value from alien labor. That is their miserable foundation, and it looks all the worse in comparison with the new foundation that they have thus created without even wishing to. The new foundation is obviously not their work in any conscious, deliberate sense. The thing that they seek to do consciously is something pretty miserable. But what they have created in fact is the basis for a superior and definitive form of society:

> The growing incompatibility between the productive development of society and its hitherto existing relations of production expresses itself in bitter contradictions, crises, spasms. The violent destruction of capital not by relations external to it, but rather as a condition of its self-preservation, is the most striking form in which advice is given it to be gone and to give room to a higher state of social production (GRU:749–50).

But who gives this advice, since the destruction of capital is only the immanent form in which the advice is expressed? Here Marx obviously presupposes a reason that directs history, a conscious, higher principle that says when one social formation must withdraw and cede its place to another.

III

Having considered the above passages, which provide us with a context centered around the philosophy of history, let us now tackle the directly eschatological passages of Marx and Engels. For it is the final turn of events that best demonstrates that "reason triumphs, despite everything, in the history of the world."

Back in Chapter 6, I already stressed the point that there is something of extraordinary dimensions in the fact that capitalism produces the material means to eliminate not only its own form of human exploitation but also all the forms of exploitation that have existed in history. This thesis of Marx is 100 percent eschatological, envisioning a final goal where all forms of exploitation and injustice will have disappeared. And no minimalist disquisition will manage to extirpate that thesis from Marx's work because his most persistent economic analyses are orientated around it from the very start. So let us now document the wholly eschatological awareness of Marx.

In a letter of 11 September 1858 to Elsner (published by Stanislav Schwann in the *International Review of Social History,* 1959, p. 86), Marx writes the following:

If the *Neue Oder-Zeitung* had to disappear, we must find consolation in the knowledge that everything we are doing, undertaking, and putting into practice now is merely provisional and simply "better than nothing."

We must try to find out why the editors of the MEW did not include this letter in their compilation of the complete works of Marx and Engels. Künzli's comment on it is quite apt: "This is certainly one of the most important passages from Marx's pen. It proves him to be an extreme eschatologist. . . ."[1] So it does. Of all the more avowedly eschatological authors, none could have written a more typically eschatological remark. What Albert Schweitzer describes as the New Testament mind or attitude vis-à-vis the imminent end of the world does not differ one iota from the view expressed in this sentence of Marx.

But it should not be thought that this is an isolated sentence that escaped Marx's lips involuntarily (though it might be even more significant if that were the case). Marx was very familiar with Hegel's refutation of the "bad infinity" of Kant whose categorical imperative is always being reiterated one more time but never manages to be fully realized. In the *Eighteenth Brumaire of Louis Bonaparte* Marx alluded to the French promonarchists of 1850 who keep postponing the restoration of the monarchy "in infinitum" (MEW 8:140). To make mock of them in the *Class Struggles in France,* he sets up a comparison between them and their views on the one hand and Kant and his bad infinity on the other:

> The royalists made of *the monarchy* what Kant makes of the republic—the only rational form of state: a postulate of practical reason, which can never be realized but whose achievement must always be the goal striven for and adhered to in one's beliefs (MEW 7:76; VSE:108).

It is not usually appreciated that this is a point where the dilemma does not allow for any middle term or harmony, even as there can be no concord or compromise between Ptolemy's geocentric conception of the solar system and Copernicus's heliocentric view. Within the "bad infinity" of Kant are included the philosophy of indefinite progress, the Whiteheadian conception of process, and all antieschatological and antimessianic attitudes—though they may not have heard the term.

Hegel has been criticized for affirming the final end of history. Now there are certainly things open to criticism in Hegel's thought, but those who reproach him on this point do not seem to have the remotest inkling that what is at stake here is the most important message of Jesus Christ. Indeed it is so important that it is the very definition of the evangel, the "good news." Clearly conservatives cannot accept this message because the *eschaton* signifies the total revolution.

In this particular opposition between two options, where there is no middle ground and no third choice, Marx is on the side of the gospel even more clearly and specifically than Hegel was. Kant and the bourgeoisie are in favor of eternal deferral and postponement (and, of course, respectful obeisance). They decide that history is to be perpetual process and progress, provided of course that it never arrives at the definitive realization of justice. In reality they opt for the eternal return of all things, though of course they whitewash the facade. And this is precisely the same reaction of so-called Christians to the message of Jesus Christ. They are willing to accept and profess all the doctrines and dogmas foisted on them, so long as it is understood that they relate to some infinitely postponable future.

In their *Circular Letter* of 1879 addressed to the leaders of the German Socialist party, Marx and Engels describe and then reject the conciliatory and renegade plan of the Swiss:

> The programme is not to be *given up* but only *postponed*—for an indefinite period. One accepts it, though not really for oneself and one's own lifetime but posthumously, as an heirloom to be handed down to one's children and grandchildren. In the meantime one

devotes one's "whole strength and energy" to all sorts of trifles and the patching up of the capitalist order of society so as to produce at least the appearance of something happening without at the same time scaring the bourgeoisie (MEW 19:162; SCME: 304).

The antieschatological attitude criticized and rejected in this passage is exactly the same as that of those present-day Marxists who not only deny the *eschaton* out of ignorance of Marx's works but also allege that he never maintained it. But as I have already indicated, one cannot be a revolutionary if one denies the *eschaton*. One must then necessarily fall back into the eternal return of injustices and patchwork remedies, oppression and compromise, exploitation and compensatory measures— the "old shit," as Marx put it. Neo-Marxists give it the laughable appellation of "non-antagonistic contradictions."

Making fun of the bourgeois classes, Engels makes an apt remark in his letter to Laura Lafargue dated 2 October 1886:

> Even if they come round to our views they will say: of course communism is the ultimate solution, but it is far off, maybe 100 years before it can be realized—in other words: we do not mean to work for its realisation neither in our, nor in our children's lifetime (MEW 36:540; SCME:372).

In the *First Address of the General Council on the Franco-Prussian War* (1870), which was drafted by Marx for the First International and then published worldwide, we read:

> . . . in contrast to old society, with its economical miseries and its political delirium, a new society is springing up, whose international rule will be *Peace,* because its national ruler will be everywhere the same—*Labour!* The pioneer of that new society is the International Working Men's Association (MEW 17:7; VFI:176).

After reading Marx's mockery of any indefinite postponement, we already know what Marx has in mind when he talks about a new society based on peace and labor in contrast to preceding societies. He is not talking about a goal to which one merely pays lip service and which one simply makes sure to "keep in mind." He is talking about a definitive *eschaton*.

The above passage was reiterated and reaffirmed in Marx's *Report to the Hague Congress* (1872: MEW 18:130 f.; VFI:316). Equally eschatological is the famous statement in the 1859 *Contribution to the*

Critique of Political Economy about the social formation known as capitalist production:

> The prehistory of human society accordingly closes with this social formation (MEW 13:9; CCPE:22).

There is an equally significant passage in the *Civil War in France* (1871) because it sets up an explicit contrast between something that is repeated or reactivated time and again and something that will be *definitive in the end:*

> After Whit Sunday 1871, there can be neither peace nor truce possible between the working men of France and the appropriators of their produce . . . the battle must break out again and again in ever-growing dimensions, and there can be no doubt as to who will be the victor *in the end*—the appropriating few or the immense working majority. And the French working class is only the advanced guard of the modern proletariat (MEW 17:361; VFI:232; my italics).

Now there could be no real contrast with the old society, such as is mentioned in the earlier passage on the Franco-Prussian War above, if the new society were not final and definitive in the fullest sense of the word. The older societies are characterized by ever recurring promises of a future that is never attainable, by the eternal postponement espoused by Kant and the bourgeoisie. As Marx sees it, the new society grounded on peace and labor is the final and definitive victory of the workers. It is eschatological. The words used in the *Grundrisse* to describe it say it all:

> *The last form of servitude* assumed by human activity, that of wage labour on one side, capital on the other, is thereby cast off like a skin . . . (GRU:749; my italics).

Engels is equally explicit in his 1883 Preface to the *Communist Manifesto,* when he sums up Marx's thought thus:

> . . . to liberate the whole of society *once and for all* from exploitation, oppression, and class struggles (MEW 21:3; my italics).

Now if the above remarks are not talking about the *eschaton,* then there never has been and never will be any author who talks about the *eschaton* because there simply are no words at all to express or embody that outlook! Neither in the Bible nor elsewhere among avowedly eschatological authors do we find more explicit and undeniably eschatological statements. In the last analysis, the Marxists who deny the eschatologism of Marx and Engels must simply deny that eschatologism exists at all!

In his Preface to the 1888 English edition of the *Communist Manifesto*, Engels sums up the thought of Marx as follows:

> . . . nowadays, a stage has been reached where the exploited and oppressed class—the proletariat—cannot attain its emancipation from the sway of the exploiting and ruling class—the bourgeoisie—without, at the same time, *and once and for all,* emancipating society at large from all exploitation, oppression, class distinctions and class struggles (MEW 21:367; VRV:65; my italics).

To say it again: one cannot find a more eschatological statement than one of this sort. Consider this closing statement in Engels' *Socialism: Utopian and Scientific* (1880):

> Men, at last masters of their own mode of social organization, consequently become at the same time masters of nature, masters of themselves—free (MEW 19:228; SUS:100).

Such passages are very similar to Old Testament passages that talk about the *eschaton*. And even more forceful is this passage by Marx in the *Grundrisse:*

> These barriers to production based on capital are even more strongly inherent in the earlier modes of production, in so far as they rest on exchange. But they do not form a law of production pure and simple; as soon as exchange value no longer forms a barrier to material production, as soon as its barrier is rather posited by the total development of the individual, *the whole story with its spasms and convulsions is left behind* (GRU:623; my italics).

Comment is hardly necessary. The same tenor of thought can be found in dozens of biblical passages (e.g., Rev. 12:2). In any case we have already seen the unsurpassable expression of Christian eschatological thought in Marx's speech about the Hague Congress of the International that he delivered in Amsterdam:

> The workers will have to seize political power one day in order to construct the new organization of labour; they will have to overthrow the old politics which bolster up the old institutions, unless they want to share the fate of the early Christians, *who lost their*

chance of the kingdom of heaven on earth because they rejected and neglected such action (MEW 18:160; cf. VFI:324; my
italics).

On page 387 of the German *Grundrisse* Marx uses the phrase, *"das
absolute Herausarbeiten,"* to talk about "the absolute working-out"
(GRU:488) of humanity's creative potentialities. The idea clearly implies and assumes the eschaton. Beyond it there can be nothing further.
Indeed it would be difficult to find a more conclusive way to describe the
final goal of history as some definitive reality that is not to be confused
with any intermediary stage. And I must also remind the reader that
there are many other remarks in *Capital* and the *Grundrisse* which,
while seemingly less explicit insofar as they do not stress the chronological aspect, embody content regarding the absolutely radical change in
the relations between human beings and nature and human beings with
each other that dovetails with the vision of Old Testament prophecy
about the nature of the historical *eschaton*. Let me cite some examples:

> With that, production based on exchange value breaks down, and
> the direct, material production is stripped of the form of penury
> and contradiction (GRU:705–6).

> Modern industry, indeed, compels society, under penalty of death,
> to replace the detail-worker of today . . . by the fully developed
> individual, fit for a variety of labours, ready to face any change of
> production, and to whom the different social functions he per-
> forms, are but so many modes of giving free scope to his own
> natural and acquired powers (MEW 23:512; CAP I:488).

> Modern industry . . . imposes the necessity of recognizing, as a
> fundamental law of production, variation of work, consequently
> fitness of the labourer for varied work, consequently the greatest
> possible development of his varied aptitudes (MEW 23:512; CAP
> I:487–88).

> . . . the germ of the education of the future, an education that will,
> in the case of every child over a given age, combine productive
> labour with instruction and gymnastics, not only as one of the
> methods of adding to the efficiency of production, but as the only
> method of producing fully developed human beings (MEW 23:508;
> CAP I:484).

> The free development of individualities, and hence not the reduc-
> tion of necessary labour time so as to posit surplus labour, but
> rather the general reduction of the necessary labour of society to a

minimum, which then corresponds to the artistic, scientific, etc. development of the individuals in the time set free, and with the means created, for all of them (GRU:706).

Free time—which is both idle time and time for higher activity—has naturally transformed its possessor into a different subject . . . (GRU:712).

This process is then both discipline, as regards the human being in the process of becoming; and, at the same time, practice [*Ausübung*], experimental science, materially creative and objectifying science, as regards the human being who has become, in whose head exists the accumulated knowledge of society (GRU:712).

And without dwelling on the matter, I shall simply cite the description of this state given by Marx in the *Critique of the Gotha Programme* (1875):

In a more advanced phase of communist society, when the enslaving subjugation of individuals to the division of labour, and thereby the antithesis between intellectual and physical labour, have disappeared . . . (MEW 19:21; VFI:347).

The word translated as "intellectual" in English is the German word whose basic root is *Geist* ("spirit"), and the contrast may just as well be between "spiritual" and "bodily" labors.

Marx's thought is rigorously eschatological in the most technical sense of the word. And this is true quite apart from the question as to whether he did or did not go so far as to spell out the theological premise which today's strict logic proves is necessary if one wishes to assert the reality of the *eschaton*.

IV

Having said that much, I could consider this chapter to be finished because I am not going to deny the atheism of Marx and Engels. In the writings of Engels we find affirmations of atheism from his university days to the end of his life. In Marx's case, on the other hand, we must round out the picture in a much more nuanced way. This is true, quite apart from the questions raised by the famous packet of letters to his daughters that has disappeared.

We find atheism in his writings as far back as his doctoral thesis (*On the Difference between the Democritean and Epicurean Philosophy of Nature*). The same holds true for his early writings, though his profession of atheism is not always as explicit as it is in his letter to Hardmann dated 14 October 1840 (when he was twenty-two). What is noteworthy is the fact that from 1850 on, atheism, or at least the explicit profession of it, disappears from his writings—with one exception. He avowedly professes atheism in an interview with R. Landor, a reporter for the *New York World*. This interview, published on 18 July 1871, does not appear in the forty-three volumes of the MEW. Its publication in English came to my attention after the Mexican edition of my book had appeared. Here is the relevant passage:

> *Reporter:* And as to religion?
> *Dr. Marx:* On that point I cannot speak in the name of the society [i.e., the International]. I myself am an atheist. It is startling, no doubt, to hear such an avowal in England, but there is some comfort in the thought that it need not be made in a whisper in either Germany or France (VFI:399).

There are no two ways about it. Chronologically speaking, we must say that the last explicit remark of Marx on this theological theme that we have so far is a declaration of atheism. I have already indicated that this view is inconsistent with an eschatological outlook, and there is no need to insist on that point here. However, every interpretation of Marx's thought is obliged to strive for objectivity. I think that obligation obliges me to present other texts that also belong to Marx's mature years and that, at the very least, point in a direction different from atheism.

The chief text is the simply perfect address that Marx gave in London on 14 April 1856, on the occasion of the fourth anniversary of the *People's Paper*. In a footnote the official editors of the MEW try to minimize it, insinuating that Marx's affirmation of the existence of God was an act of diplomacy or prudent politeness for the sake of his audience of believers, or else that it was plainly a slip of the tongue which escaped from Marx in the perfervid heat of the moment. Before we consider such points, let us read the main passage and evaluate it ourselves. And since the phraseology is strictly and deliberately Hegelian, we first need to consider the texts already cited in this chapter; for they provide the right philosophical context and backdrop. Marx said:

> All our invention and progress seem to result in endowing material forces with intellectual life, and in stultifying human life into a material force. This antagonism between modern industry and science on the one hand, modern misery and dissolution on the other hand; this antagonism between the productive powers and the social relations of our epoch is a fact, palpable, overwhelming, and not to be controverted. Some parties may wail over it; others

may wish to get rid of modern arts in order to get rid of modern conflicts. Or they may imagine that so signal a progress in industry wants to be completed by as signal a regress in politics. *On our part, we do not mistake the shape of the shrewd Spirit that continually manifests himself in all these contradictions.* We know that to work well the new-fangled forces of society, they only want to be mastered by new-fangled men—and such are the working men (MEW 12:4; VSE:300; my italics).

Here it is no longer a question of talking about "reason," or the "irony of history," or the "cunning of reason"—phrases that could be interpreted as abstractions. Marx refers concretely to the "shrewd Spirit" (and "Spirit" is *Geist* in German), who is guiding the course of history and who manifests itself in the clashes and contradictions that I have indicated in the previous pages of this chapter. The sentence in the passage which I italicized above is perfectly consistent with Marx's whole system and, above all, with his conception of history. Indeed Engels himself has already told us that the historical conception in *Capital* implies the cunning of reason. In particular, the above sentence is very much consistent with the certainty, evident in all Marx's economic analyses, that there is a truly human *eschaton* as the Bible maintains ("the kingdom of heaven on earth": MEW 18:160). Here the reader need only compare it with the expressions I have brought together in Chapter 4 and Chapter 5 of this book.

The above italicized sentence would fit in perfectly with numerous pages of *Capital* or the *Grundrisse,* with Marx's articles on British colonization, and with his articles on the American Civil War. We are obliged to acknowledge and register the fact that in this 1856 text, at least, Marx managed to achieve consistency with his systematic thought as a whole. In this superbly brilliant page of economic analysis he drew the important logical conclusion that his affirmations of atheism illogically denied.

It should also be noted that in the interview with Landor Marx explicitly indicates that he himself, as an atheist, cannot speak in the name of the international communist movement. It is a strictly personal conviction. The same contrast and separation should be made with respect to the economic, philosophic, and historical system that Marx constructed for the world communist movement. In other words, the atheism that the individual named Karl Marx professes in the private forum has nothing to do with the system of revolutionary thought known as scientific socialism. The materialistic interpretations that have been made of the latter system—and indeed without studying Marx's texts—are expressly rejected by Marx and Engels over and over again, as we saw in the preceding chapters.

Now if there was any solid foundation for the efforts of the MEW editors to minimize Marx's 1856 statement, Marx himself would have stopped his friend Ernest Jones from publishing the text as it stands five days later in the *People's Paper* (no. 207, 19 April 1856). Jones always did what Marx asked of him. He had been a friend of Marx long before he founded that newspaper. And if it were true that Marx later regretted having uttered the theological statement in question, at the very least he could have sent a clarifying note to Jones, the editor-in-chief, to be printed in the paper as a way of toning down or relativizing what he said in his speech. Marx had recourse to this very tactic quite a few times in the course of his life.

Insofar as the text in question is concerned, the certain fact is that Marx actually did utter the phrase transcribed above and did allow it to be published. The 1856 speech is one of the most authentic, indisputable, and creditable documents in Marx's whole corpus. It is certainly on a footing of equality with the 1871 interview with Landor, to say the least. And the two items cannot be reconciled for the reason that I stated earlier in this chapter, i.e., it is impossible to ask an author to be totally consistent insofar as the ultimate implications and ramifications of his thought are concerned.

Bakunin, an atheist, had indeed caught the scent of something in the wind when he unleashed "vehement attacks against the International as a denier of atheism" (MEW 33:402; letter of Engels to Liebknecht dated 15 February 1872). On the other side of the coin, one of the main reasons why Marx's International rejected the Bakuninist Alliance was the fact that the Alliance insisted upon "*atheism as a dogma* dictated to the members" (Letter of Marx to Friedrich Bolte dated 23 November 1871: MEW 33:329; SCME:254).

Finally, and merely to complete the picture, I should like to cite Marx's article of genius on the freedom of the press. It was first published in 1842, but Marx himself tried to get it published again in 1851 and I believe that he succeeded. In my opinion, it contains an explicit assertion of the existence of God, but I will not insist on that point. I will leave that up to the reader to decide. In this passage Marx is criticizing those who defend the institution of censorship and prohibit freedom of the press:

> It is impurity of heart and imagination feeding on frivolous images of the omnipotence of evil and the impotence of good. It is the imagination taking pride in sin, the impure heart shrouding its worldly pride in mystical images. It says: "It is despair of one's own salvation that tries to stifle the voice of conscience by the denial of God." It is despair of one's own salvation that turns personal frailties into frailties of humanity in order to exonerate its own conscience from them. It is despair over the salvation of humanity that prevents the latter from following innate, natural

laws and preaches irresponsibility as a necessity. *It is hypocrisy simulating a God without believing in his reality, in the omnipotence of good.* It is egotism caring more about its own private salvation than the salvation of all" (MEW 1:65; my italics).

This "lead article" on freedom of the press was published in the *Rheinische Zeitung* in six installments (5, 8, 10, 12, 15, and 19 May 1842) while Marx was the editor-in-chief. In his classic biography of Marx, Franz Mehring had this to say about his work on this subject:

> And for the freedom of the press his rapier play has never been equalled in brilliance and trenchancy. Without envy Ruge admitted: "It would be impossible to say anything more deep or more thorough in favour of the freedom of the press. . . ."[2]

Those who claim that Marx disavowed these pages do him very little service. His comments constitute one of the most lucid and enduring works in the journalistic literature of the world. It is not just that the claim is completely gratuitous but also that Marx himself refuted it long ago. The editors of the MEW have no recourse but to acknowledge that in 1851 Marx tried to get these articles republished, long after the *Rheinische Zeitung* had ceased to exist (MEW 1:595, footnote 1, *ad finem*). This intention is verified by Marx's letter to Hermann Becker, a Cologne publicist, dated 28 February 1851 ("I hope that you have received the *Rheinische Zeitung*": MEW 27:546), and also by his letter to Engels dated 22 January of the same year: "I still have no news, either from Schabelitz, who expressed a desire to handle the continuation of our "review," or from Becker, who wanted to take charge of publishing my articles" (MEW 27:165).

The editors of the MEW (27:649, footnote 170) inform us that at the end of April 1851 the first installment of the *Complete Articles of Karl Marx* appeared in Cologne. Besides containing Marx's "Comments on the Latest Prussian Censorship Instruction" (published in Ruge's *Anekdota*, February 1843, in Switzerland), the first fascicle contained a part of the famous "lead article" mentioned above. But the MEW editors do not indicate how much of the article was printed in that fascicle. And the German authorities blocked further publication of the projected series.

It is very much worth noting that in 1851 Marx is not trying to republish *The Holy Family, The German Ideology, On the Jewish Question, A Contribution to the Critique of Hegel's Philosophy of Right,* his doctoral thesis, or even his *Economic and Philosophical Manuscripts of 1844*. Of all his earlier works it is his articles on the freedom of the press that he is concerned about republishing; and in them we find the passage that I cited above.

Moreover, he is not thinking at all about publishing his *Complete*

Works. At the age of thirty-three only a nut would entertain such an outlandish idea. That possibility is ruled out in this specific case because the next year Marx made fun of Ruge in *The Great Men of the Exile* because Ruge was trying to publish his own complete works (MEW 8:275,278,280).

Notes

1. Arnold Künzli, *Karl Marx: Eine Psychographia* (Vienna: Europa Verlag, 1966), p. 813. The passage from Marx's letter to Elsner is taken from Künzli also.
2. Franz Mehring, *Karl Marx: The Story of His Life*, Eng. trans. (London: Allen and Unwin, 1936), p. 39.

11
Appendix on Marx's Epistemology

Marx was far more concerned about knowing reality than about knowing the methodology of knowing reality. In this respect, too, he was a disciple of Hegel rather than of Kant. He would never have shared the tendency of that brand of neo-Marxism which prefers to discuss knowledge rather than to practice it. That is why the present chapter must be considered merely an appendix to this work.

However, in addition to certain epistemological contributions implicit in his exercise of congnition, Marx also contributed certain explicit elements that are valuable. The full utilization of these elements for constructing a complete epistemology would require an entire monograph of its own. This is not the place for such a task, and so I shall set myself a more limited objective. First we shall examine Marx's anticipatory rejection of certain epistemologies which now label themselves "Marxist." Then we shall examine his important contribution to the current debate about the theory of science.

I

Proceeding in orderly fashion, we must first note the passages that reject the primitive notion that science does not exist at all, that only ideologies exist. Adopting this gnoseological nihilism, some assume the right to use science and philosophy as mere means in the political struggle. They are not at all scrupulous about logical coherence, much less about the quest for truth. As far back as Chapter 2 (see pages 45–50) I presented citations from Marx's writings that expressly reject such a Neanderthal point of view, and I would refer the reader back to them. By the way, I myself would raise a question here and direct it to all those who hold such a view. What about the thesis that science does not exist, that only ideologies exist? Is it a scientific or an ideological thesis? If it is

285

an ideological thesis, then it is false and science does exist. If it is scientific, then it itself is science and science does exist.

More widespread and recurrent is the pseudo-Marxist thesis that any and every scientific pronouncement is dependent on the social class of the one who pronounces it. The more I examine this thesis, the more I feel that it denies rationality, all rationality, as well as all hope of reaching the truth. But my opinion is not what matters here. Let us see what Marx maintained at a meeting of the General Council of the International held on 17 August 1869:

> Disciplines which permit class or partisan interpretation ought not to be introduced in elementary schools or the higher schools. Only such disciplines as the natural sciences, grammar, etc. can be taught in the schools. For example, the rules of grammar do not differ whether they are expounded by a religious tory or a freethinker. Disciplines which allow for differing conclusions should not be taught in school lessons. They can be the concern of adults under the direction of teachers such as Mrs. Law, who gives religion classes (MEW 16:564).

This is the version reported in the official minutes of the meeting. A more succinct report of Marx's words can be found in the issue of the *Bee-Hive* dated 21 August 1869:

> Insofar as political economy, religion, and other disciplines are concerned, they should not be introduced in the elementary schools or the upper schools. This sort of education is for adults, and it should be imparted in the form of lessons by teachers such as Mrs. Law (ibid., ftn.).

The first point to note is that Marx brings out clearly here that not all knowledge is affected by production relationships; that not all knowledge is an echo of the social class to which those who formulate or possess it belong. Now in his letters on linguistics, even Stalin admitted that this science does not depend on whether its practitioners are bourgeois or socialist. The narrow, sectarian outlook of certain Marxists today is that Stalin's view was a sign of weakness and inconsistency. But while such narrow sectarianism may be very consistent with materialism, it is explicitly and roundly rejected by Marx in the passage cited above—and not just with respect to linguistics.

In reality Stalin was not familiar with Marx's view of the question, as he was not familiar with most of Marx's writings. On this point, however, he agreed with Marx. We can hardly call it a matter of chance because the evidence itself shows that some types of knowledge are indeed independent of ideology and production relationships. Marx cites as examples the natural sciences and grammar. He then adds an "etc." ("other disciplines" in the *Bee-Hive*), which is hardly to be ignored. Only an irrational, sectarian point of view would maintain that a grammatical rule—e.g., if the subject is plural, the verb must be plural too—depends on the political affiliation of the one who pronounces it. Of course, such sectarianism may maintain whatever it likes. The point here is that it cannot appeal to Karl Marx.

Second, it is worth noting that in the above passage Marx is not even opposed to the teaching of religion, provided that it is addressed to adults.

Third, it is obvious that Marx would be opposed to the brainwashing that is today institutionalized in some of the socialist countries which call themselves "Marxist." Marx would not allow the teaching of Marxism in either the lower schools or universities. (Marx is scientific in his approach. Marxism is not by a long shot, as we saw in Chapter 4.) He would be even more appalled by the narrow sectarianism that can be found today among certain university faculties, those in Mexico, for example.

II

Our second step is to consider the positive side of the issue, to see what Marx means by scientific knowledge. We can begin our approach to that task by seeing which disciplines he calls "scientific," noting his total disagreement with modern-day empiricism and positivism in this regard. As we have already seen in Chapter 9, Engels consciously referred to biblical exegesis as a "science" (MEW 21:9; MEW 22:455). Indeed the first of his own three exegetical studies, the one dealing with the views of Bauer, was published a year before Marx's death; and the second, on the Apocalypse, was published the year that Marx died.

In their joint article for the NYDT dated 10 July 1854, Marx and Engels write about the "science of war" or "military science" (*Kriegswissenschaft:* MEW 10:294). They do so again in their joint article for the *Neue Oder-Zeitung* dated 8 January 1855 (MEW 10:597). On his own, Marx writes in the name of "scientific military criticism" in his article for the same publication dated 26 June 1855 (MEW 11:315) and in his review dated 18 March 1865 (in *Hermann*) of a pamphlet of Engels (MEW 16:84). Engels does the same in his solo articles for the NYDT dated 14 October 1854 (MEW 10:508 and 513–14) and 17 February of the same year (MEW 11:16).

As for the "science" in question, let no one think that Marx or Engels is talking in these articles about physics, biology, geology, or mathematics. They are talking about tactical and strategic considerations:

supplies, the terrain, distances, the psychology of the contending parties, the moral trustworthiness of the generals, the possibility of new alliances and different coalitions, the relatively civilized or barbarian status of the two sides, the political leanings of their governments, the variability of public opinion, the constructive capabilities of the engineers, the military traditions and training programs of the various nations, the time available for preparation, the authority of Clausewitz, the precedents set by the great geniuses of warfare, and so forth. Thus they are talking about a conglomeration of various kinds of knowledge that no positivist definition would call "science."

In his article for the *Neue Oder-Zeitung* dated 24 April 1855, Engels refers to philology as a science. In his 1891 Preface to *The Origins of the Family, Private Property and the State,* he refers to the investigation of prehistory as a science (MEW 21:481), as he also does in a letter to Laura dated 13 June 1891 (MEW 38:117). In an article for *The Labour Standard* (7 May 1881), he mentions the "science of morals" (MEW 19:247; SW:98). In *On the History of the Communist League* (1885) he writes about "the science of history." The particular context in the latter case is not to be overlooked. In writing about Marx's great discovery of the basic factor called the mode of production, Engels says that this discovery revolutionized the science of history (MEW 21:212); but in no way does he state or imply that historical study began to be a science only with Marx's discovery. The presupposition is that history already existed as a science. There is no doubt that this was also the opinion of Marx himself, as we can readily infer from his footnote about Darwin and Vico in Book I of *Capital* (MEW 23:392 f., ftn. 89; CAP 1:372, ftn. 3).

The point is clear enough. If morals, exegesis, and history are sciences in the full sense of the word according to Marx and Engels, then their view is clearly incompatible with any and every brand of positivism and empiricism. This is not the time or the place to determine which view is right. The important point is that we can offer objective documentation to show the incompatibility of one view with the other.

Insofar as philosophy is concerned, a certain snobbish view in vogue today, which should be called Comtism by right, has come out with the statement that Marx buried philosophy and that henceforth the natural sciences are to occupy the place once usurped by philosophy. I shall not entertain the reader here with some of Marx's letters from London that refute any such negative view of philosophy. In them Marx requests a portrait of Hegel, acknowledges receipt of it, and informs the sender that the portrait has been given a prominent place in his study. A more interesting detail, perhaps, is the fact that Marx asked Kugelmann for two pieces of tapestry from Leibnitz's home when it was slated for demolition by the municipality of Hannover. Kugelmann got them for Marx, and in a letter to Engels dated 10 May 1870 Marx writes: "I have both things hanging in my work room. You know my admiration for Leibnitz'' (MEW 32:504).

These details are not without significance. If Marx was still studying and admiring Hegel and Leibnitz after he had written Book I of *Capital*, then he obviously did not think that he had buried philosophy. The intent to bury philosophy, which some would attribute to Marx today, is something that never crossed his mind at all.

There is a decisive passage written by Marx about Proudhon's philosophy that has not been given due attention. It is in his letter to Johann Baptist Schweitzer dated 24 January 1865. The letter, actually a small treatise, was subsequently published by *Der Sozialdemokrat* with Marx's approval. Here is the passage:

> At the same time he attempted to present the *system* of economic categories dialectically. In place of *Kant's* insoluble *"antinomies,"* the *Hegelian "contradiction"* was to be introduced as the means of development.
>
> For an estimate of his book, which is in two fat volumes, I must refer you to the refutation I wrote. There I have shown, among other things, how little he has penetrated into the secret of scientific dialectics . . . (MEW 16:27 f.; SCME:144).

Now one can cite a whole series of counterbalancing texts to argue whether Marx did or did not stand Hegel on his feet, whether he was or was not indignant about Dühring and company treating Hegel as "a dead dog" (MEW 32:18), and whether he really was proud to be a disciple of "that great man" (MEW 23:27). But this passage in his letter to Schweitzer goes right to the heart of the key question and saves us a lot of trouble. For in this letter Marx makes clear that *Hegel's dialectics is scientific*. Proudhon tried to use the Hegelian contradiction in his treatment of economics, but Marx asserts that he failed to penetrate into the secret of Hegel's scientific dialectics.

As far as I am concerned, the dependence of Marx's economic analysis on Hegel is as clear as day. This fact has been demonstrated by Rosdolsky, Reichelt, and Landgrebe.[1] But to appreciate this fact, one must obviously have understood the message in Marx's economic analysis; and the materialism of the anti-Hegelians prevents them from doing this. By contrast, Marx's letter to Schweitzer breaks the Gordian knot and states that Hegel's dialectics is scientific. Hence it survives, and Marx neither buried it nor thought of burying it. Furthermore, in the latter part of Chapter 9 we saw that Marx and Engels explicitly affirmed their dependence on German scientific thought, which is none other than the thought of Fichte and Hegel.

Another passage dealing with philosophy might well be cited here. It is far less important than the one cited above, but it adds another anti-empiricist standpoint that Marx will deepen later, as we shall see. It is taken from a series of articles against Karl Heinzen, which were published in the *Deutsche-Brüsseler Zeitung* (October-November, 1847):

> It is characteristic of the *muddle-headedness* of "sound common sense" that it drinks deep of the "full life" and does not allow its *natural* dispositions to be corrupted by philosophy and other studies; that when it manages to see the *difference* it does not see the *unity*, and when it sees the *unity* it does not see the *difference* (MEW 4:339).

The sarcastic point is obviously that philosophy is needed to escape from the muddleheadedness of good old common sense. The latter, in Marx's view, is akin to the state of nature that we considered in Chapter 9. There is at least the implication that philosophy continues to be necessary and needed. People today may maintain that philosophy has reached its end and that it has now been replaced by physics, biology, and mathematics; but they cannot appeal to Karl Marx's support for that position.

III

Now let us take a third step and register Marx's explicit rejection of positivism. In a letter to his daughter Jenny dated 10 June 1869, thus *after* the publication of Book I of *Capital,* Marx writes:

> Dakyns is also a declared enemy of the Comtists or Positivists. He agrees with me that there is nothing positive about them, except their arrogance (MEW 32:614).

The same year he writes to Engels (20 March):

> With a few incidental notes of mine I have mailed to Beesley, for him to read, the pamphlet of Vermorel that I also sent you (with Castille). He sent it to me with the attached little letter, as silly as it is masterfully arrogant. It seems to me that the Positive Philosophy is identical with ignorance about everything positive (MEW 32:284).

In a letter to Engels dated 19 March 1870, Marx reports to him on the last meeting of the General Council of the International:

> On receiving an announcement of affiliation from the "positivist proletarians," the General Council reminded them courteously

that it could not permit their incorporation until it had examined their program. They subsequently sent a program—genuine orthodox Comtism—which was discussed last Tuesday. The meeting was chaired by Mottershead, an old Chartist who is very intelligent (though anti-Irish) and who is a personal enemy of Comtism, with which he is familiar. After a long debate: Since they are workers, they are permitted to enter as a simple branch. However, they cannot enter as a "positivist branch," since the principles of Comtism directly contradict those of our Statutes (MEW 32:463).

Notice that Marx knows who is familiar with Comtism and who is not, and that he distinguishes between authentic positivism and other less orthodox versions. No pseudo-Marxist positivists of today can say that Marx rejected positivism without really knowing it well. Notice also that these remarks come from Marx at the height of his maturity. To Beesley, who is mentioned in the letter to Engels cited above, Marx wrote directly on 12 June 1871:

> Permit me to observe in passing that as a Party man I take up an entirely hostile attitude towards Comtism, while as a scholar I have a very poor opinion of it. I regard you, however, as the only Comtist both in England and in France who deals with historical turning points (crises) not as a sectarian but as an historian in the best sense of the word (MEW 33:228; SCME:250).

In the first draft of *The Civil War in France* there is a subsection entitled "Workmen and Comte." It begins as follows:

> If the workmen have outgrown the time of socialist sectarianism, it ought not be forgotten that they have never been in the leading strings of Comtism. This sect has never afforded the International but a *branch* of about half a dozen men, whose programme was rejected by the General Council (MEW 17:555; VFI:260).

Marx could not have declared war more openly against positivism, both on the political and the scholarly level. And note that the principal feature of positivism is a specific definition of science. This decided hostility should not suprise readers at this point, for the previous chapters of this book have made it clear what constitutes Marx's own science. Nor can present-day positivists who call themselves "Marxists" allege that Marx's ill will here is directed against only the political line of the positivists. For Marx expressly distinguishes between the politics and the science of Comtism and berates both. He himself makes clear that he is talking about "genuine orthodox Comtism"; and he also alludes to the "principles of Comtism."

This might well be the moment to express astonishment that any positivists would dare to call themselves "Marxists." But nothing can really surprise us any more. Throughout this book we have encountered absolutely basic theses which hold exactly the opposite of what Marx held and which yet are barefaced enough to claim Marx as their source.

IV

Let us take a fourth step and see what Marx thinks of empiricism. We have already noted that Marx, as a good philosopher, regards the demands of truth as something that go further than the ingenuousness of the natural scientist and of common sense insofar as they stick to "the facts" of direct observation or controlled experimentation. Here we are dealing with a matter of the utmost importance in every sense. It is regrettable, then, that even the minds of some Marxists are clogged with the hard-nosed presupposition that the only scientific knowledge is that which sticks to the surface appearance of things. This prevents them from learning from Marx something that they did not already know and that supposedly no one in his or her right mind would contradict.

What is to be understood as "the facts" always depends on a theory that is not noticed as something existing. Without subjecting it to discussion, people presuppose a particular tradition on which both thought and observation depend, as well as the experimental procedures that are a combination of thinking and observation. People simply suppose, or presuppose, that "the facts" do not depend gnoseologically on theories which describe what are facts and the interrelationships between them. Thus people presuppose that experiment puts theories to the test in facts which do not depend on theories. But in defining the conditions of verification one is determining ahead of time what goes to make up the empirical validity of the activities that constitute the substantiation of facts. Thus the *quaestio facti* depends on the *quaestio juris*. There are no raw facts. Right from the start our sense organs and our focusing of attention always imply an interpretation of the facts. In a letter to Kugelmann dated 11 July 1868, Marx says this:

> And then the vulgar economist thinks he has made a great discovery when, in face of the disclosure of intrinsic interconnection, he proudly states that on the surface things look different. In fact, he boasts that he sticks to appearances, and takes it for the ultimate. Why, then, have any science at all? (MEW 32:553; SCME:197).

When the publishing of Book I of *Capital* was in its final stage, Marx wrote to Engels, telling him what the content of Book III would be (27 June 1867):

There it will be seen how the philistine's and vulgar economist's *way of looking at things* arises, namely, because it is only the immediate *phenomenal form* of these relations that is reflected in their brains and not their *inner connection*. Incidentally, if the latter were the case, what need would there be of *science?* (MEW 31:313; SCME:179).

In other words, the vulgar and the bourgeois economists stick to the empirical; they are empiricists. For them, appearance constitutes "the facts." If the senses perceived the intrinsic and essential connection between things, there would be no need for science. Empirical cognition sticks to appearance as if it were the ultimate there is to know.

After these explicit, fighting words from Marx, empiricists may certainly deny that the work of Marx is scientific; but they certainly cannot maintain that Marx's science is an empiricist one. In *Value, Price and Profit* (1865), Marx had already expressly denied that *empeiria* gives us knowledge of reality as it is:

> To explain, therefore, the *general nature of profits,* you must start from the theorem that, on an average, commodities are *sold at their real values,* and that *profits are derived from selling them at their values,* that is, in proportion to the quantity of labour realised in them. If you cannot explain profit upon this supposition, you cannot explain it at all. This seems paradox and contrary to everyday observation. It is also paradox that the earth moves round the sun, and that water consists of two highly inflammable gases. Scientific truth is always paradox, if judged by everyday experience, which catches only the delusive appearance of things (MEW 16:129; VPP:36–37 in WLCVPP).

The real choice is between the Hegelian concept of science on the one hand and the empiricist "modern" concept of science on the other. Marx could not be more explicit in insisting on the antiempiricist thrust of his own science. In Chapter 11 of Book I of *Capital,* Marx formulates the law governing the mass of surplus value. Then he adds: "This law clearly contradicts all experience based on appearance." A few lines later he says:

> Vulgar economy which, indeed, "has really learnt nothing," here as everywhere sticks to appearances in opposition to the law which regulates and explains them. In opposition to Spinoza, it believes that "ignorance is a sufficient reason" (MEW 23:325; CAP 1: 307).

The *Grundrisse* moves along the same line, attempting to distinguish the real from the apparent that is offered to *empeiria*. The passage I am going to cite here provides us with a truly decisive example, and it has no parallel insofar as its importance to Marx's whole analysis is concerned:

> Circulation, therefore, which appears as that which is immediately present on the surface of bourgeois society, exists only in so far as it is constantly mediated. Looked at in itself, it is the mediation of presupposed extremes. But it does not posit these extremes. Thus, it has to be mediated not only in each of its moments, but as a whole of mediation, as a total process itself. Its immediate being is therefore pure semblance. *It is the phenomenon of a process taking place behind it* (GRU:255).

In his CCPE (1859) Marx insists on the same radical and irreducible antiempiricism:

> Although encompassed by this bourgeois horizon, Ricardo analyses bourgeois economy, *whose deeper layers differ essentially from its surface appearances,* with such theoretical acumen that Lord Brougham could say of him: "Mr. Ricardo seemed as if he had dropped from another planet" (MEW 13:46; CCPE: 60–61; my italics).

In a letter to Sorge (19 October 1877) Marx maintains: "The workers themselves, when, like Mr. Most and Co., they give up work and become *professional literary men,* always cause 'theoretical' mischief . . ." (MEW 34:303; SCME:290). In an earlier letter to Kugelmann (28 December 1863) Marx had said that "the *scientific* efforts to revolutionize a science can never be really popular" (MEW 30:640). On 18 July 1877 he offers the same explanation for refusing an invitation to collaborate on a popular periodical:

> The first condition for any and all criticism, which is a disregard for all extraneous considerations, becomes impossible in that company. Furthermore one must constantly be trying to make things readily comprehensible, to expound things to ignorant people (MEW 34:48).

And we have already seen in this chapter what he thought about the muddleheadedness of common sense when it refuses to be enlightened by philosophy.

The point is not just that the principle and absolutely central concepts of Marx's science are not empirical. It is also that Marx himself openly and earnestly stresses that they are not empirical and that sticking to the empirical impedes the possibility of science. It is a matter of intellection, not of empiricism. Thus in Chapter 24 of Book I of *Capital* Marx notes: "We can neither see nor smell in this sum of money a trace of surplus-value" (MEW 23:605; CAP 1:579). In Chapter 1 of the same volume he writes: "So far no chemist has ever discovered exchange-value in a pearl or a diamond" (MEW 23:98; CAP 1:83). On the first page of the massive section in the *Grundrisse* dealing with "Capital," we read:

> Gold and silver, in and of themselves, are not money. Nature does not produce money, any more than it produces a rate of exchange or a banker. . . . To be money is not a natural attribute of gold and silver, and is therefore quite unknown to the physicist, chemist etc. as such (GRU:239).

When one adverts to the fact that exchange value is the central piston of Marx's whole analysis, one can gauge the depth and extent of the antiempiricism in the quote from Chapter 1 of *Capital* cited above (MEW 23:98). It shows how off-base are the efforts of those who want to reduce Marx's science to empiricism or positivism. Such efforts really are a complete falsification and annihilation of Marx's science. It is not without reason that these same people have felt obliged to deny the existence of subjects. Marx's whole efforts, on the other hand, were aimed at dissolving *things* that are apparently tangible and empirical in order to make people realize that the reality in question consists of relations between *persons*. The contentual scope of this rigorously scientific effort on Marx's part was spelled out in the preceding chapters; here I want to bring out its epistemological dimension.

In Chapter 4 of *Theories of Surplus Value*, Marx expressly states: "The mystification here arises from the fact that a social relation appears in the form of a thing" (MEW 26/1:142; TSV 1:172), when in truth the exchange value of a commodity "has nothing to do with its corporeal reality" (ibid., p. 141). If this seems antiscientific to empiricists, it is because they have illusions about the nature of the so-called natural sciences and infect the practitioners of those sciences with their illusions. But the most paradoxical thing is the fact that anyone would attribute any such empiricist character to the science of Marx, when he himself applied the term "scientific" to the nonempirical. In Chapter 10 of Book II of *Capital,* Marx quotes passages from Adam Smith and comments at length on them. Here are two comments relevant to our present discussion, followed by a third from Chapter 11:

> What strikes one here above all is the crudely empirical conception of profit derived from the outlook of the ordinary capitalist, which

wholy contradicts the better esoteric understanding of Adam Smith (MEW 24:199; CAP 2:198).

But the physiocratic conception too lurks in Smith's analysis, although it contradicts the esoteric—really scientific—part of his own exposition (MEW 24:214; CAP 2:212).

In Ricardo the uncritical adoption of the Smithian confusion is more disturbing not only than in the later apologists, in whom the confusion of ideas is rather something not disturbing, but than in Adam Smith, because Ricardo, in contrast to the latter, is more consistent and incisive in his analysis of value and surplus-value, and indeed upholds the esoteric Adam Smith against the exoteric Adam Smith (MEW 24:221; CAP 2:219).

If we compare the identical aspects and thoughts in these three passages from Book II of *Capital,* then we see clearly that for Marx being scientific by very definition means understanding value, the very same value which, according to the quote from *Theories of Surplus Value* above, has "nothing to do with the corporeal reality" of commodities. That is why the understanding of value is esoteric: because it cannot be reduced to empiricist knowledge. In Book III of *Capital* Marx insists on the following point:

Surplus-value and rate of surplus-value are, relatively, the invisible and unknown essence that wants investigating, while rate of profit and therefore the appearance of surplus-value in the form of profit are revealed on the surface of the phenomenon (MEW 25:53; CAP 3:43).

V

Empiricism is thingism. It cannot possibly grasp value because value is not a thing but a relationship between persons. But this raises a big question and brings us to the fifth step we must take: what accounts for the fact that the bourgeois and their apologetes do not understand value, and hence do not understand surplus value either? Why do they opt for empiricism, sticking to empirical data that certainly do not include value and surplus value? On Marx's answer to this question depends the great contribution he can possibly make to resolve the complicated epistemological problematics of our own day.

Capital is a minute and thorough dissection of the bourgeois ideology and its mechanism. It dismantles that ideology completely, but only insofar as one tackles the issue at the deeper level where Marx tackles it and does not just go around shouting "ideology!" right and left. The peculiar relationship between persons which Marx makes evident, and which empiricism endeavors to overlook, is morally intolerable and rouses indignation. It is also a production relationship, and hence it cannot be altered unless the corresponding mode of production is eliminated.

In Chapter 19 of Book I of *Capital* Marx writes: "It is naturally still more convenient to understand by value nothing at all" (MEW 23:560, ftn. 26; CAP 1:537, ftn. 2). He is referring to Say, who uses this dodge to avoid examining what underlies such common expressions as the "value of labor" or the "price of labor." If one is bold enough to face up to the problem, the first thing that is seen in this case is that any such expression is an absurdity: "And 'price of labour' is just as irrational as a yellow logarithm" (MEW 25:826; CAP 3:818). Obviously this argument of Marx is not empirical, no matter from what angle we view it. Note this point made by Marx:

> That which comes directly face to face with the possessor of money on the market is in fact not labour, but the labourer. What the latter sells is his labour-power. As soon as his labour actually begins, it has already ceased to belong to him; it can therefore no longer be sold by him. Labour is the substance, and the immanent measure of value, but *has itself no value* (MEW 23:559; CAP 1:537).

What is sold in the transaction between the capitalist and the laborer is labor power, not labor. And labor power is indeed sold at its value (i.e., exchange value), which is equal to the quantity of commodities required to reproduce it (food, clothing, etc.). Once the notion of value is taken seriously, it becomes obvious that labor power produces much more than it itself is worth in exchange value; for the laborer obviously works more hours than he must to produce his own sustenance. Bourgeois ideology sticks with empiricism and avoids thinking about value for this reason. For once it started to think about it, it would be obvious that there is such a thing as surplus labor and that the capitalist system consists in snatching surplus value away from the worker; and it does so not in spite of the fact, but precisely by virtue of the fact, that it pays labor power at its real value. Thus the vulgar empiricist expression "price of labor" is the ideal mechanism used to conceal the true nature of the wage system as a system:

> But here the vulgar economist is all the more satisfied, because he has gained the profound insight of the bourgeois, namely, that he pays money for labour, and since precisely the contradiction be-

tween the formula and the conception of value relieves him from all obligation to understand the latter (MEW 25:826; CAP 3:818).

In fact these bourgeois economists instinctively saw, and rightly so, that it is very dangerous to stir too deeply the burning question of the origin of surplus-value (MEW 23:539; CAP 1:516).

But one and the same commodity, money etc., can represent capital or revenue etc. Thus it is clear even to the economists that money is not something tangible. . . . It is then evident that it is *a relation, and can only be a relation of production* (GRU:514).

In the second draft of his letter to Vera Zasulich (1881), Marx writes: "Finally the capitalist mode of production has shown to everyone its purely transitory character, *except to those who are blinded by virtue of their own interests*" (MEW 19:397; my italics). If one wants to appreciate the epistemological contribution of Marx, the first thing one must realize is that the danger of ideology crops up, in Marx's eyes, only when we have people "who are blinded by virtue of their own interests." Marx never thought that any and every sort of knowledge was "determined" by the social class to which a person belongs (see the citations on page 286 of this chapter). Once this materialist dogmatism has been rejected, Marx's dissection of the mechanism of ideology reveals that there is an element of morality or immorality in cognition. Contemporary epistemology cannot continue to evade this element, however much empiricist naiveté may protest. In the Afterword to the second German edition of Book I of *Capital* (1873), Marx recounts what happened in the history of economic theory after the decline of the genuine Ricardian school:

It was thenceforth no longer a question whether this theorem or that was true, but whether it was useful to capital or harmful, expedient or inexpedient, politically dangerous or not. In place of disinterested inquirers, there were hired prize-fighters; in place of genuine scientific research, the bad conscience and the evil intent of apologetic (MEW 23:21; CAP 1:15).

So two things should be clear. First, according to Marx there can be authentic, objective, impartial, truth-seeking science. Second, according to Marx there is a moral cause for the lack of a real scientific attitude. As I indicated in Section IV of Chapter 7, *böses Gewissen* means "bad conscience" and has moral connotations. Thus Marx is not denouncing a mere misunderstanding or a simple cognitive error. He is saying that its cause is a moral perversion of conscience.

This fact is made clear in many of Marx's writings. Referring to the post-Ricardian school of economics in *Theories of Surplus Value,* Marx alludes to "conscienceless thoughtlessness" (MEW 26/2:499; cf. TSV 2:499). In the *Grundrisse* he comments: "These attempts at apologetics demonstrate a guilty conscience" (GRU:460). In Book III of *Capital* he writes: "Norman offers us the sage opinion that the demand for money-capital is not identical with the demand for money as such; and this sagacity alone, because he, Overstone, and the other Currency prophets constantly have pricks of conscience . . ." (MEW 25:434; CAP 3:419). In his article for the NYDT dated 28 June 1855, Marx writes that the ideological efforts to sell the Sunday Trading Bill in England and encourage church-going are designed "to set at rest the conscience of the privileged classes" (MEW 11:323; VSE:289). In his article dated 25 February 1860 (NYDT) he assures his readers that the revenues of those living off rent and interest "have no conscience" (MEW 15:24).

Why is this? What about the capitalist? In *Theories of Surplus Value* Marx tells us that the capitalist "is always enjoying wealth with a guilty conscience" (MEW 26/1:254; TSV 1:282). In his CCPE he tells us that the capitalist is one who "keeps the commodity as use-value in the warehouse, and has it on his conscience as exchange-value" (MEW 13:30 f.; CCPE:44). In Book III of *Capital* Marx writes:

> So far as the individual capitalist is concerned, it is evident that he is only interested in the relation of the surplus-value, or the excess value at which he sells his commodities, to the total capital advanced for the production of the commodities, while the specific relationship and inner connection of this surplus with the various components of capital fail to interest him. And it is, moreover, rather in his interests to draw the veil over this specific relationship and this intrinsic connection (MEW 25:53; CAP 3:43).

Even earlier, in the *Grundrisse,* Marx had noted that "this creation is identical with the appropriation of alien labour *without exchange,* and for that reason the bourgeois economists are never permitted to understand it clearly" (GRU:553). That is why Marx praises Ricardo for "the scientific impartiality and love of truth characteristic of him" (MEW 23:461, ftn. 213; CAP 1:438, ftn. 1). That is why he condemns the attempts of vulgar economy to idealize capitalism, for this need has replaced "all need for love of truth and inclination for scientific investigation" (MEW 25:853; CAP 3:844, ftn.).

VI

Now let me take a sixth step and show that Marx, besides dealing directly with the question of value, also dissects the empiricist ideologies of the vulgar economists throughout the pages of *Capital.* The assumption that the capitalist system is the ''natural'' state of affairs is of course attacked time and again, and I shall not consider that particular point here. Instead I shall consider three mechanisms associated with empiricism that are particularly noticeable and striking: supply and demand, the three sources of value, and the makeup of capital as fixed and circulating capital.

In Book III of *Capital* Marx enumerates certain phenomena that are reflected to some extent in competition (supply and demand). In the course of his treatment he makes the following points:

> All these phenomena *seem* to contradict the determination of value by labour-time as much as the nature of surplus-value consisting of unpaid surplus-labour. *Thus everything appears reversed in competition* (MEW 25:219; CAP 3:209).

> What competition does *not* show, however, is the determination of value, which dominates the movement of production; and the values that lie beneath the prices of production and that determine them in the last instance (MEW 25:219; CAP 3:208).

> Supply and demand determine the market-price; and so does the market-price, and the market-value in the further analysis, determine supply and demand (MEW 25:200; CAP 3:191).

> In other words, the ratio of supply to demand does not explain the market-value, but conversely, the latter rather explains fluctuations of supply and demand (MEW 25:202; CAP 3:192).

> Even the ordinary economist . . . must admit that, whatever the market-value, supply and demand must coincide in order for it to be established (MEW 25:202; CAP 3:192).

> If supply and demand balance one another, they cease to explain anything, do not affect market-values, and therefore leave us so much more in the dark about the reasons why the market-value is expressed in just this sum of money and no other (MEW 25:199; CAP 3:189).

In Book I of *Capital* Marx had written:

> Classical political economy . . . soon recognized that the change in the relations of demand and supply explained in regard to the price of labour, as of all other commodities, nothing except its changes, i.e., the oscillations of the market-price above or below a

certain mean. If demand and supply balance, the oscillation of prices ceases, all other conditions remaining the same. But then demand and supply also cease to explain anything. The price of labour, at the moment when demand and supply are in equilibrium, is its natural price, determined independently of the relation of supply and demand. And how this price is determined, is just the question (MEW 23:560; CAP 1:537–38).

Thus the economists do not explain what accounts for the price, or how this thing we call price arises. They simply deal with what accounts for fluctuations in price, and it is there that supply and demand enter the picture. But why do they not ask questions about the very existence of price in the first place? Because that would force them to confront the problem of value, and here lies the key. The flood of tautologies about supply and demand concentrate on the empirical surface appearance of the facts in question, on the fluctuations in price. Thus they constitute an ideology which tends automatically and unbidden to operate in an anti-scientific direction, to obscure the nonempirical reality known as value. So the big question, which has to do with the origin of value (see Chapter 6), is evaded. By contrast, Marx's concept of science includes the honesty required to face up to the whole problem of justice.

A naive approach is to divide up the value of a product into one part known as rent, one part known as profit, and a third part known as wages. This approach makes it look as if the original sources of value, independent of human labor, are the earth and nature on the one hand and machines and raw materials on the other. Here is what Marx has to say in Chapter 48 of Book III of *Capital:*

> The conversion of surplus-value into profit, as we have seen, is determined as much by the process of circulation as by the process of production. Surplus-value, in the form of profit, is no longer related back to that portion of capital invested in labour from which it arises, but to the total capital. The rate of profit is regulated by laws of its own, which permit or even require, it to change while the rate of surplus-value remains unaltered. All this obscures more and more the true nature of surplus-value and thus the actual mechanism of capital. Still more is this achieved through the transformation of profit into average profit and of values into prices of production, into the regulating averages of marketprices. . . . The average profit of a particular capital differs from the surplus-value which this capital has extracted from the labourers employed by it. . . . Normal average profits themselves seem immanent in capital and independent of exploitation . . . (MEW 25:836 f.; CAP 3:828–29).

Thus, if wage-labour coincides with labour generally, then so do wages with the produce of labour, and the value portion representing wages with the value created by labour generally. But in this way the other portions of value, profit and rent also appear independent with respect to wages, and must arise from sources of their own, which are specifically different and independent of labour; they must arise from the participating elements of production, to the share of whose owners they fall; i.e., profit arises from the means of production, the material elements of capital, and rent arises from the land, or Nature, as represented by the landlord . . . (MEW 25:834; CAP 3:826).

Vulgar economy actually does no more than interpret, systematize and defend in doctrinaire fashion the conceptions of the agents of bourgeois production who are entrapped in bourgeois production relations (MEW 25:825; CAP 3:817).

Apart from the ideology over supply and demand and the ideology proclaiming the above three sources of value, I think we would do well to consider the ideology that upholds the composition of capital into fixed and circulating capital. This empiricist division prevents people from grasping the real underlying division at work, i.e., that between constant capital and variable capital. In Book II of *Capital* Marx writes:

By this means the distinction between variable and constant capital, which decides everything, is blotted out, hence the whole secret of the production of surplus-value and of capitalist production, the circumstances which transform certain values and the things in which they present themselves into capital, are obliterated. All constituent parts of capital are then distinguished merely by their mode of circulation (and, of course, circulation of commodities concerns itself solely with already existing given values); and the capital laid out in wages shares a peculiar mode of circulation with the part of capital laid out in raw materials, semi-finished products, auxiliary materials, as opposed to the part of capital laid out in instruments of labour.

It is therefore understandable why bourgeois political economy instinctively clung to Adam Smith's confusion of the categories "constant and variable capital" with the categories "fixed and circulating," and repeated it parrotlike, without criticism, from generation to generation for a century (MEW 24:221; CAP 2:218–19).

The three examples of mystifying ideology cited above share certain traits in common with the bourgeois refusal to confront the reality of value. They stick to the empirical. They tranquilize the consciences of capitalists by preventing them from seeing their systematic exploitation. And their mystifying mechanisms can be overcome only by an act of moral honesty that deliberately chooses to know the truth.

VII

Now let me take the seventh step. I shall try to impress upon my readers the fact that Marx's earnest efforts to point up the moral substance of science is undoubtedly bound up with his systematic work of dereification. Empiricism sticks to things. Marx dissolves things into relations between persons because conscience is not troubled by any moral obligation whatsoever when it confronts things.

As we have just seen in the last section, Marx maintains that vulgar economic theory transfers to the level of systematic thinking the same outlook and the same type of surface-bound knowledge that prevails in the practical world, where human persons are exploited and crushed as if they were things. Thus it is not too surprising that positivism and empiricism should posit the absence of moral valuations as the criterion of real "scientific" thinking, or reduce everything to things. For the manipulation of things does not involve any appeal to a moral imperative. That is why positivism and empiricism are really nothing more than ideology. What they do in fact is provide a "scientific" tranquillization of conscience.

Here would be a proper place to repeat all the dereifying passages of Marx that were cited in Chapter 2 and Chapter 5. Instead, however, I will simply refer my readers to those chapters and add a few more passages by way of reminder:

These *objective* dependency relations also appear, in antithesis to those of *personal* dependence (the objective dependency relation is nothing more than social relations which have become independent and now enter into opposition to the seemingly independent individuals; i.e., the reciprocal relations of production separated from and autonomous of individuals) in such a way that individuals are now ruled by *abstractions*, whereas earlier they depended on one another (GRU:164).

Human labour-power is by nature no more capital than are the means of production. They acquire this specific social character only under definite, historically developed conditions, just as only under such conditions the character of money is stamped upon precious metals, or that of money-capital upon money (MEW 24:43; CAP 2:35).

> Like all economists worth naming . . . Ricardo emphasises that labour as *human activity,* even more, as socially determined *human activity,* is the sole source of value. . . . All these economists understand more or less clearly, but Ricardo more clearly than the others, that the exchange-value of *things* is a mere expression, a specific social form, of the productive activity of men, something entirely different from things and their use as things, whether in industrial or in non-industrial consumption. For them, value is, in fact, simply an objectively expressed relation of the productive activity of men, of the different types of labour to one another (MEW 26/3:181; TSV 3:181).

Marx is absolutely implacable in carrying through this personalizing demolition of all *things.* It does not matter if the land and beasts of burden produce more value than they consume. Marx is not impressed at all with this argument put forth by McCulloch, which is discussed just after the above passage in *Theories of Surplus Value.* The important thing is that neither the land nor beasts of burden are persons, that the only important and decisive reality is to be found in relations between persons. This is the sharp cleavage we noted in Chapter 5, when we considered Marx's criticism of Adam Smith (see pages 113–14). Indeed Marx's whole analysis and system becomes vulnerable at this point if one does not adopt his dereifying epistemological focus. The moral dimension of scholarly science does not surface at all if Marx fails in his effort to bring us face to face with the appeal and the summons of human beings, of persons, precisely as such.

That is why positivism and empiricism, which really are concerned about things and hence empirical appearances, must seek to suppress the notion of value. And that comes down to suppressing Marx. At bottom these two schools of thought are pragmatism, not science. Science demands responsibility, and responsibility exists only vis-à-vis persons.

VIII

My eighth step will be to engage in some comment and discussion. When positivism asserts that none of the words I have just used above mean anything because their content is not reducible to sensations, it is clearly revealing its ideological interest in immunizing itself against anything and everything not reducible to what it knows already and in sheltering itself from any and all criticism of its own irrationality. For it is certainly irrational to limit ourselves to the realm of the knowable that we share with other nonhuman animals. Behind the same set of sense data that we can register, irrational cognition does not perceive a person *as such* whereas rational knowledge does. Far from demanding rationality as prerequisite, as they claim, positivism and empiricism demand irrationality. It is rational to recognize the irreducible nature of the summons of one interiority to another. It is not rational to deny it on the pretext that it does not consist of sense data that can be verified through predetermined procedures. The empiricist appearance of objectivity has serious repercussions on the knowing subject; it animalizes and reifies him or her.

Since the verifiability spoken of by positivism and empiricism consists ultimately in the procedures and operations that scientists indicate, the criterion they give us comes down to this: "scientific" is what scientists tell us is scientific. Any demand for greater scientificity coming from outside the fraternity is rejected on principle. But if people systematically reject greater demands with respect to what is scientific, then their self-complacent hermeticism and their self-fed vicious circle is merely an illusion of scientificity. It completely lacks the universality and the unconditional openness to criticism that originally characterized science. It is scientism, not science. By virtue of the initial, dogmatic definitions that constitute it, it is incapable of self-criticism; and it has invented those preliminary definitions for the sole purpose of shielding itself from the outside world once and for all.

I noted above that the positivist scientists are mistaken about the nature of their sciences. They forget that their "simple observations" are preformed by society. An unconditionally scientific outlook would demand the right to criticize those observations as well as the society that had preformed them. Obviously such criticism could not be made on the basis of other "simple observations" because the uncriticalness of the latter would affect the whole process and render it useless. In any case the whole matter of verifiability would require dialogue and discussion, hardly reducible to *empeiria,* in order to arrive at some common definition of the method of verification and to determine the conditions that must be met before one could say that a theory had been proved. All the natural sciences and even mathematics practice this extraempirical, dialogic discussion and presuppose it. This is evident from the very existence of metalanguages, without which people cannot reach agreement in trying to determine the very conditions of scientificity. But dialogic discussion implies an interpersonal relationship marked by honesty and integrity, and it is necessarily based on morality. So the value judgments that had gone out the door have had to come back in through the window. And Marx is a thousand times more correct when he makes scientificity depend on conscience and integrity.

Scientists must always dialogue with each other to decide whether a particular descriptive formulation of the facts is or is not sufficiently motivated by experience. Then they will compare this descriptive formulation (called a basic proposition) with the theory, or better, with the formulations that describe what should happen according to their theory. But whether the basic proposition is or is not adequately grounded on the experience of observations or experiments is something that the members of the fraternity must *decide* by consensus. And this decision cannot be forged by *empeiria* because it is the very thing that must decide exactly what is empirical and what is not. The consensus may be grounded on *ad hominem* arguments: if we accepted A last year, then with the same plausibility we must accept B today. It may be grounded on the authority of a prominent member or group in the fraternity. Or it may be grounded on some other type of reasoning process. But in any event the latter are not empirical, because the reasons used will decide whether a descriptive statement is empirical or not.

If people ingenuously go on believing that it is things and the immediate data provided by things that ultimately decide which theories are true and which are not, then the consensus-generating process is removed from collective reflection and systematic rationality. It is much more scientific to start out with the realization that this interpersonal discussion exists, and to make it a part of the object of study and of rational reflection. The formidable lucidity of Marx lies in his discovery that relations between persons are the truly basic factor behind and underneath the surface appearance of relations between things and with things. The communitarian process leading to consensus can evade the arbitrariness or naiveté of extrascientific motives only if we, in all frankness, realize that dialogic discussion does exist, that it is moral in character, and that it is thus a matter of conscience. I am thinking, in particular, of those who think that the social sciences can attain real maturity by some other route. Such people, it seems to me, do not realize what is really at stake in the social sciences. And economics is not to be exempted here, though it imagines itself to have reached maturity precisely at the point when it has turned into nothing more than an ideology for the tranquillization of consciences.

If we decree by definition that morality lies outside science, then we decree irrationality for the whole complex of consensus—items already existing and for all those that are to follow—the latter being the decisive ones, when all is said and done. Adorno is quite right when he says that positivism has suffered from a secret anti-intellectualism ever since

Hume dogmatically degraded ideas to mere copies of impressions. For positivism, thinking must be reduced to imitating and copying; anything beyond that comes from the devil. At bottom it is materialism, and as far back as Hobbes such materialism identified ideas with images. This anti-intellectualism is characterized by an absence of reflection and, as Adorno points out, by a certain resentment against the spiritual attitudes that are geared toward reflection. In the latter there are no copies, and materialism fears superiority in others. Marx calls it "thoughtlessness without conscience" (*gewissenlose Gedankenlosigkeit*).

The lack or absence of value judgments is equivalent to a separation between norms and facts. Essentially it presupposes that history, equated with nature, cannot have a meaning. The *eschaton* of Marx, which is the same as that of the gospel, is what gives meaning to history. Of course, positivism must deny any *eschaton* and operate in and with the eternal return of all things. Since there are no subjects for it, there can be no end either. Insofar as ends are concerned, they become a matter of arbitrariness completely. If on the other hand history itself does have an end, then facts and events themselves are good or bad depending on whether they lead toward that end or not. Values are then imbedded in facts and events themselves; and no science that prides itself on being objective can prescind from axiological judgments because goodness or evilness are an essential constituent of the facts to be studied.

Merely technical solutions, which please positivism so much because they are devoid of valuation and only say, "If you want B, you must do A," cannot solve the real problems that do actually pertain to action. Such solutions are scarcely practical at all. So long as we have no genuine criterion for deciding about the end envisioned, it will not help us at all to say "If you want such and such an end, you must employ such and such means." The conditional considerations are of no help when there are no apodictic ones. If positivism were right, then science would leave us in the lurch. The real decision would remain submerged in irrationality and isolated from any control by demonstrative scientific lucidity. In fact positivism is more than a little responsible for the fact that our human capacities for reflection refrain from taking up moral questions and leave decisions about ends in the hands of the barbarism that stalks the field today. Indeed the barbarism that stalks the world today is one of the most unbridled, homicidal, and life-destroying barbarisms that has ever roamed the field of human history.

In the last analysis, positivism is astonishingly superficial and has not at all adverted to what language really is. It thinks that things are what names say they are, quite apart from whether names exist or not. The use of names conditions all our science since the meaning of sense objects themselves, to which empiricism appeals, depends on what has been "already said" about them. When two people debate or discuss, they already take for granted the application of certain names to certain things; indeed they assume that certain things *are* what these names signify. The speaker presupposes a primeval act of speaking. In the very act of talking he assumes this primeval act as his own, assumes responsibility for this denomination which is really nominating because it makes something to be something. The very act of speaking implies fidelity to those hoary denominations. It also believes in the honest intention of the interlocutor to be faithful to what has been "already said," to take things for what language says they are even though nothing empirical guarantees that they are. It is a communitarian effort to denominate things and to take them for what the words say they are. And this communitarian project has an equally communitarian end in view. It is a project that arose out of the nature of human beings, an end that must be in accord with what they are: persons engaging in dialogue and living in relationship with each other. Responsibility lies at the core of the astonishing phenomenon called speech, and hence at the core of the interpersonal discourse called science.

But here we must note what Levinas points out. The things to which speech refers are not first "given" or thematicized, to receive a meaning later. They are given by the meaning they possess. Human beings would not have bothered to name them if it were not for the meaning that they possess. What is certain is that all talk and all science move directly between denominations, not directly between objects. It is not the objects themselves that are going to decide the discussion or the debate; that will be decided by the naming that "we" have given to the objects. If the object in question is "that thing" or "such and such a thing," then such and such consequences must be acknowledged. It is not that knowing exists first and then we add on the speaking later. Speaking is the first activity of knowing, its essential and ineradicable symbolism.

Now the conceptual and symbolic character of knowing is not a deficiency or limitation of human thought, which thereby proves its inability to open up intuitively "to things themselves." What do people think knowing is? This opening up is, in and of itself, imaginative and symbolical, creating meaning and realizing ends. Expectation is not posterior to experiences. It is a prior condition for the very existence of experiences. The names that knowing gives are not descriptive. (What does "descriptive" mean here anyway?) They are figurative and metaphorical from the very start. Objects would not interest cognition one bit, if they did not have any meaning; but they do, thanks to words.

What does intelligibility signify? It is a focus or framework that we give to the life we share with each other. Indeed, what does reality, what does "signifying" mean? No one can reduce these words to neutral empirical data. The interpersonal realm is the origin of all signification, of all meaning, We say something to *someone*. We want it to signify something, to have meaning for that person. We make signs between subjects to call attention to each other. We would not understand each other if we did not refer each other to the experiences of interiority that we share.

For example, it is much easier to say when there is consensus or agreement (we know it automatically when there is) than to describe the external reality with which the consensus is concerned. Even the work of formulating a basic proposition is geared toward consensus as something whose existence or nonexistence is easier to discern; and thus inner consensus between us gives meaning to the external data. The interpersonal is what is comprehensible first and most readily, so much so that in the practice of science it is the presence of consensus that decides between various possible descriptive propositions.

And reciprocal understanding of the interpersonal experiences of life, such as that of agreement or consensus, implies honesty and integrity between the parties involved, between each in relation to all. What does "understanding" mean if not understanding each other? If it does not consist in "understanding each other," how can we talk about "understanding a thing"? Understanding cannot be merely an individual process. Understanding is always a type of consensus. I have come to understand a thing when I have the same understanding of it that some one else may have of it. The word "understanding" has meaning always in terms of some interpersonal meaning.

When Marx appeals to the activity of production, he is arguing *ad hominem:* all human beings have had to "reach an understanding" about that activity at least; if they had not, they would not be alive. The reference is not to objects themselves, but to the interpersonal relations that have had to arise in connection with material production. If there is no understanding between persons, then speech is impossible. And science as well.

Notes

1. Roman Rosdolsky, *Zur Entstehungsgeschichte des Marxschen "Kapital,"* 4th ed., Frankfurt: Europäische Verlagsanstalt, 1974; Eng. trans., *The Making of Marx's Capital*, New York: Urizen, 1977. Helmut Reichelt, *Zur logischen Struktur des Kapitalbegriffs*, 4th ed,, Frankfurt: Europäische Verlagsanstalt, 1973. Ludwig Landgrebe, "Hegel and Marx," in *Marxismusstudien*, Tübingen: Mohr, 1954, 1:19–53.

Epilogue

This book has attempted to offer a positive exposition of Marx's thought, at least of those aspects that seem to be the most important. Indeed it is so positively oriented that it might seem to be little more than a mere anthology of Marxian themes. But in many instances I have found it necessary to contrast Marx's thesis with directly opposed theses—theses that involve differing interpretations of the term "materialism." That is not really surprising. After all, in his *Theses on Feuerbach* Marx expressly noted that he disagreed with all the versions of materialism that had existed up to then. The mechanistic version of materialism is only one such interpretation. To claim, as some do, that Marx rejected only mechanistic materialism is to turn him upside down and distort his thought beyond recognition.

Marx's materialism is the materialism that I have spelled out in Section VI of Chapter 4 (see pages 99–105). Underlining the incomparable importance of the mode of production, Marx stands Hegel back on his feet and demonstrates the falsity of any mystifying "reconciliation" restricted to ideas or to juridical and political entities. Any and every attempt at improvement or change must be fleshed out in a new mode of production that is communist; otherwise it will not be new at all.

Now that all the other interpretations of materialism have been carefully compared with the thought of Marx and rejected, perhaps the moment for revolutionary unification has arrived for the western worker, who does indeed exist and who is not materialistic (see Chapter 1). Marx regarded that worker as the only possible protagonist of the revolution, and that thesis continues to remain valid so long as we do not mistake the one to whom it is addressed.

Index

Adler, Victor, 168
Adorno, T., 306
Aeschines, 120
Afghans, 78
agriculture, 94, 103, 241-42, 248
Albigensians, 232
Alighieri, Dante, 189
Althusser, Louis, 29, 32-34, 39-46, 51n.12, 182
Annenkov, Marx's letter to, 215, 246
anti-intellectualism, 306
antireformism, 105, 124, 143, 177
anti-Semitism, see Judaism
Anti-Socialist Law, 172
Aquinas, see Thomas Aquinas
Arabs, 73, 244
Aragonese, 73
Aristotle, 65, 70, 87
Austerlitz, 80
Austro-Prussian conflict, 85
Avenarius, 46

Bach, Johann Sebastian, 261
Bachofen, 88
Bakunin, Michael, 175, 230, 260, 282
Bakuninist Alliance, 90, 162, 171, 172, 175, 190, 282
Balibar, Etienne, 198
Ball, John, 232
Bamberger, 186
Bañez, Domingo, 93
del Barco, Oscar, 51n.12
Barrot, Odilon, 174
barter, 138-39
Bauer, Bruno, 237, 238, 287
Bebel, 67, 267
  Engels' letter to, 82, 83, 134, 168, 169, 171, 178, 186, 246
  letter of, to Engels, 82
Becker, Hermann, Marx's letter to, 283
Becker, Johann Philipp, 120, 176
Beesley, 290, 291
Beethoven, Ludwig van, 261
Belgium, 188
Bentham, Jeremy, 5, 30

Bernadotte, Jean Baptiste Jules, 78, 87
Bernstein, Eduard, 67
  Engels' letter to, 71, 171, 172, 256
Berthollet, Claude Louis, 98
Bey, Mehmed (Colonel Bangya), 178, 186
Bismarck, Otto von, 82, 83, 90, 171, 172, 180, 186
Blanquism, 88-89
Blind, 184, 190
Bloch, Joseph, Engels' letter to, 72, 77, 80
Blücher, Gebhard Leberecht von, 191
Blum, Robert, 88
Böhme, Jakob, 261
Boisguillebert, Pierre le Pesant, sieur de, 193, 204, 206
Bolte, Friedrich, Marx's letter to, 282
Bonaparte, Napoleon, 73-74, 77-78, 87
Bonaparte, Napoleon III (Louis)
  and Bismarck, 83
  corruption of, 2, 3, 5, 17, 85, 167, 172, 173-74, 187, 194, 252-53
  expansionist designs of, 83
  intervention of, in Italy, 74
  visit of, to Queen Victoria, 217
Borkheim, Sigismund, 84
Bourbons, 73
Bracke, W., 67
  Marx's letter to, 175, 179
Brentano, Lujo, 49
Brindley, 92
British Parliament, 78, 111-12, 134n.1
Brno, workers of, 177
Brougham, Lord, 294
Bury, J.B., 31, 50n.4

Cadiz assembly, 77
Calvin, John, 237
Canton, see China
Carbonari, 3
Cardanus, 93
Carey, Henry Charles, 39, 56
Carmaux, miners of, 134
Carthage, 218
Cartwright, Edmund, 98
Castille, 290

311

Catherine II, 88
Ceres, 73
Chartists, 177, 291
Cherbuliez, 21
Chevalier, M. Michel, 142
China, 47, 91, 118, 166, 217, 244
    Canton, 107
    Manchu dynasty of, 243
    and socialism, 243
Church
    Catholic, 225
    Fathers of, 124
    primitive, 199, 224-41
Civil War (U.S.), 61, 80, 86, 89, 267-68, 281
civilization, 64, 242-59
Cobden, Richard, 122
Coeur-de-Lion, Richard, 81
Commune, *see* Paris Commune
Comtism, 288, 290, 291
Constantine, 239
Constantinople, 249-50
Constitution of 1812, 76-77
Copernicus, Nicholas, 274
Copleston, F., 30, 50n.1
Corbet, 162
corruption, 193-96
Cortes of Cadiz, 76-77
Crimean War, 73, 79, 191
Cuba, 220
Czarism, 177, 195, 251, 253

Dakyns, 290
Danielson, Nikolai Frantsevich, 248, 267, 268
Darwin, Charles, 38, 55, 108, 254, 258, 288;
    see also Social Darwinism
Daumer, George Frederick, 146, 242
Davis, Jefferson, 80, 268
Davy, Humphrey, 98, 99
Delekat, 198, 200, 223n.2
Denmark, 249, 254
Dionysius, 73
Dresden uprising, 230
Dühring, Eugen Karl, 57, 289

Eccarius, 159, 163, 188
education, 31, 278, 286-88
egotism, 173-78
Ehrenfreund, Isadore, Engels' letter to, 63
Elsner, Marx's letter to, 273, 284n.1
Emancipation Proclamation, 80, 86, 268
empiricism, 287, 292-309
Engels, Charlotte, Engels' letter to, 48
Engels, Emile, 48
Enlightenment, *see* French Enlightenment
etiquette vs. morality, 168
exchange value
    capitalist production and, 40, 126, 141, 152, 206, 297, 299

conflict of, 208
definition of, 138
in the sales process, 27
of wages, 14

Factory Act, 55
Faust, 87
February revolution, 235
feminism, 146
Ferguson, A., 115
fetishism, *see* idolatry
Fetscher, I., 51n.10, 263n.3
feudal system, 91, 101, 231, 232, 236
    and capitalism, 207, 215
    and labor, 139
Feuerbach, Ludwig, 30, 79, 120, 185, 221, 253, 259
Fichte, Johann Gottlieb, 258, 259, 289
Fischer, Engels' letter to, 170, 180
Fourier, Charles, 88, 235, 258
Francis II, 73
Franco-Prussian War, 2, 160, 195, 257, 276
fratricide, 195
Frederick II, 88, 172
Frederick, William, 172
freedom, *see* liberty
Freiligrath, Marx's letter to, 3, 102
French Constitution of 1791, 76
French Enlightenment, 30-31
French revolution, 63, 75, 89, 256
French Workers' Party, 163
Friedlander, 186
Friedrich, Wilhelm IV, 66

Galiani, Ferdinando, 4, 113
Garibaldi, Giuseppe, 79, 87-88
Garnier, 183-84
German Protestantism, 261
German scientific Socialism, 88, 99, 258, 259-60
German Social Democrats, 10, 67
German Workers Educational Association, 162
"Germanism" of Marx and Engels, 256
Gilbart, 143, 146
Gladstone, William, 49, 190
Gluck, Christoph Willibald von, 261
Goethe, Johann Wolfgang von, 261
Gotha Programme, 113, 139, 149, 157, 167, 279
Gottschalk, 172
Grimm, Jakob, 88
Guesde, Jules, 177

Habermas, Jürgen, 28n.2, 252
Haeckel, Ernst Heinrich, 46
Hamilton, 211
Händel, Georg Friedrich, 261
Hapsburgs, 73

Hardmann, Marx's letter to, 280
Hatzfeldt, 171, 172
Hauck, Friedrich, 223n.1
Hegel, Georg Wilhelm Friedrich, 221, 261, 269, 280, 285, 288, 289
  and capitalism, 270
  concept of science of, 293
  and the development of socialism, 258, 259
  dialectics of, considered dead, 185, 289
  on human beings as ends, 197
  on Kant, 273
  on material conditioning, 70
  and naturalism, 241, 254
  on reason and history, 89, 271, 274
  rejection of, by the Stalinists, 219
  on subjects and the existence of God, 33, 266, 267, 274
Heine, Heinrich, 5
Heinzen, Karl, 290
Helvetius, 31, 50n.3
Herder, Johann Gottfried von, 261
Herwegh, Georg, 221
Hess, Moses, 221
Hinduism, 122-23, 195
Hindustan, social revolution in, 174, 247
Hirsch, Carl, 175
Hitler, Adolf, 184
Hobbes, Thomas, 1, 46, 307
Hochberg, 67
Hodgskin, 4
Hollinger, 184, 190
Holy Alliance, 83, 84
Horace, 195
Horner, 189
Howell, George, 175
Hume, David, 307
Hus, Jan, 232
Hyndman, Henry Mayers, 171, 172
  Marx's letter to, 86

idolatry, 123-24, 198-200, 205-23
India, 54, 122, 188, 244, 245, 250, 255
Inkermann, battle of, 73
International, Congress of the
  attempts to take over, by anarchists, 89, 172
  1865 (First), 5, 151, 158-61, 216, 275
  1868 (at Brussels), 111
  1869 (at Basle), 226, 228
  1872 (at the Hague), 86, 179, 191, 277
  goals of, 235
  history of, 175, 231
  support for, 193
International, General Council of the
  1865, 151, 158-61
  1868, 111
  1869, 151, 188, 226, 228, 286
  1871, 167, 251

International Working Men's Association, 111, 232, 275
Irish problems, 119-21, 162, 171, 188, 291
Isabella of Spain, 90
Islam, 238
Italian Workers' Associations, 158

Jackson, Stonewall, 80, 268
Jacobinism, 76, 234
Jacoby, 192
Jews, *see* Judaism
Joachim of Calabria, 323
John Bull, 161
Jones, Ernest, 192, 282
Jones, Richard, 129
Juch, 192
Judaism, 221, 238
  and anti-Semitism, 220, 222
Julian the Apostate, 229
Julius Caesar, 93

Kant, Immanuel, 197, 221, 258, 259, 261, 273, 274, 276, 285, 289
Kautsky, Karl, 75, 178
  Engels' letter to, 49, 63, 172, 178, 179, 186, 193, 233, 245, 251
Kautsky, Louise, Engels' letter to, 178
Kepler, Johannes, 261
Ketteler, Bishop Wilhelm Emmanuel von, 229
Kittel, Gerhard, 223n.1
Kugelmann, 174, 175
  Marx's letter to, 77, 81, 120, 133, 176, 192, 225, 288, 292, 294
Künzli, 198, 223n.4, 273, 284, n.1

Lafargue, Laura, 83
  Engels' letter to, 108, 120, 134, 161, 178, 275, 288
Lafargue, Paul, 71, 185
  Engels' letter to, 48, 108, 120, 172, 175, 178, 237, 239
Landgrebe, Ludwig, 289, 309n.1
Landor, R., 280, 282
Lang, Engels' letter to, 108
Lanz, Johannes, 46
Laplace, Pierre Simon, Marquis de, 32, 53, 258
Lassalle, Ferdinand, 24-25, 26, 50, 56, 67, 154, 171-72
  Marx's letter to, 176
Latin America, 45
Lauderdale, 92
Lavrov, Peter, 89
  Engels' letter to, 177
  Marx's letter to, 166
Leibniz, Gottfried Wilhelm, Baron von, 261, 288, 289
leisure, 138, 279

Le Lubez, 158
Le Moussu, 185
Lenin, V.I., 45, 46, 50n.9, 54, 68n.1
Leninists, 173
Lessing, Gotthold Ephraim, 261
Levinas, Emmanuel, 308
Lewis, 32, 45
liberalism, 63, 160
liberty, psychological vs. political, 58-68
Liebig, Justus, 98, 99
Liebknecht, Wilhelm
    Engels' letter to, 172, 261, 282
    Marx's letter to, 6, 67, 167
Lincoln, Abraham, 80, 86, 268
List, Friedrich, 47
Lombardy, War in, 74
Longuet, Jenny Marx, 88, 119, 163, 174, 290
Lopatin, G.A., 71
López Trujillo, Alfonso, 234
Louis XIV, 193
Louis XV, 89
Luther, Martin, 107, 212, 236-37

Mach, 46, 50n.9
Machiavelli, Niccolò, 173
Maine, Sir Henry, 54
Malthus, Thomas, 46-47, 55-56, 98-99, 129
Mamelukes, 74
Mandeville, 50
Marcuse, Herbert, 28n.2
marriage, 119
Martignetti, Pasquale, Engels' letter to, 163, 169, 185
Marx, Eleanor, 49, 163, 225, 263n.3
Marx, Jenny, *see* Longuet, Jenny Marx
Marx, Laura, 163
Marxism-Leninism, 45
May Laws, 170
Mazzini, Giuseppe, 75, 87, 158-61, 166, 173
McClellan, David, 135n.2
McCulloch, John Ramsay, 4, 183, 304
mechanics, science of, 91-95
Mehring, Franz, 81, 283, 284n.2
Menger, Anton, 231
mental illness, 121
Mexico, 162, 171
Meyer, Siegfried, Marx's letter to, 3, 174
Middle Ages, *see* feudalism
Milan uprising, 217
military service, 169
Mill, John Stuart, 183
Mirabeau, 55
Miranda, José Porfirio, 69, 210, 261nn.1 and 2
Moleschott, 120
Money, J.W.B., 245
Mongols, 244

monotheism, 238
Morgan, 88
Most, 294
Mottershead, 291
Mozart, Wolfgang, 261
Münzer, Thomas, 221-22, 232, 235-36
Muslims
    empire of, 230, 238, 249
    Sunni vs. Shiite sects of, 78

Nadejde, Ion, Engels' letter to, 268
Napoleon, *see* Bonaparte
nationalism, 240-41
necessary labor, 137-38, 278
neo-Hegelianism, 221
neo-Marxists, 153, 170, 181, 184, 223, 275
neo-platonism, 238
neo-Stalinism, 258
Nieuwenhuis, Ferdinand Domela, Engels letter to, 169, 227, 269
Norman, 182, 299

opium trade and consumption, 166, 217 243
Orsini, Felice, 3
Oschanina, M.N., 71
Overstone, 182, 299
Owen, Robert, 88, 109, 117, 235, 258

Palladino, 251
Palmerston, Henry John Temple, 173
Pannekock, A., 50n.9
pan-Slavism, 166
Paris Commune, 54, 81, 107, 118, 176, 228 231, 235
Parliament, *see* British Parliament
Paul, Saint, 199, 226, 228, 268
pauperization, 6-11, 20-21, 22-23, 28
Peasants' War, 235
Peelites, 78-79
Persians, 78
Peter the Great, 88
Petty, William, 87, 193
Philip Augustus, 81
Philips, Antonieta, 224-25
Phillips, Wendell, 187
Philo, 238
philosophes, 30
Pianori, 3
Plato, 65
plebeian movement, 236
Plekhanov, Georg, 88
Poles, 83, 84, 187, 250
Polish revolution, 177
Polish uprising, 83, 186
Polyphemus, 73
population, 55
positivism, 35, 287, 290, 291, 306-7; *see also* Comtism

³otter, 114
³rotestantism, *see* German Protestantism
³roudhon, P.J., 58, 68, 144, 146-47, 151, 199, 246, 257, 260, 289
'psychologizing,'' 219
³tolemy, 274

Quesnay, François, 87

racism and prejudice, 257-58
Ramsay, 21
Rancière, Jacques, 30, 50n.2
Reeves, 171
Reichelt, 289, 309n.1
Renan, Ernest, 231, 234
Rengstorf, K.H., 223n.1
Rhineland Diet, 190
Ricardo, David
    and Adam Smith, 296
    decline of theory of, 298
    on labor and production, 4, 15, 39, 46-47, 49, 127, 137, 294, 304
    law of, on land and rent, 98
    moral implications of, 142
    on rate of profit, 56
    on wages, 113
Roman Empire, 73, 238, 239
Rosdolsky, 7, 28n.3, 200, 289, 309n.1
Rossi, 96
Rousseau, Jean Jacques, 30
Ruge, Arnold, 173, 193, 283, 284
Russian revolution, 83, 88, 106
Russo-Turkish region of Europe, 167
Russo-Turkish War, 6, 84, 109, 230

sacrifice, 173-78, 205-6
Saint-Simon, Claude Henri de Rouvroy, comte de, 88, 235, 258
Salvation Army, 232
Saxon army corps, 107, 118
Scaron, P., 223n.3
Schabelitz, 283
Schapper, 163
Scheu, Heinrich, 258
Schiller, Friedrich von, 261
Schlüter, Hermann, Engels' letter to, 186
Schmidt, Alfred, 9, 28n.1, 259
Schmidt, Conrad, 49
    Engels' letter to, 71, 75, 234
Schniewind, 223n.1
scholasticism, 38
Schramm, 67
Schwann, Stanislav, 273
Schweitzer, Albert, 273
Schweitzer, Johann Baptist, Marx's letter to, 289
scientific Socialism, *see* German scientific Socialism
Sebastopol, battle of, 85, 191

Senior, Nassau, 216
Serbia, 229-30
Serrano y Domínguez, Francisco, 90
Shakespeare, William, 222
Shaw, George Bernard, 193
Shaw, Robert, 192
Sicily
    campaign in, 79
    massacre in, 73
Siegel, August, 63
Silistria, siege of, 191
Simon, J., 179, 186
slavery, 17-19, 27-28, 35, 61, 80, 187
Smith, Adam
    on human freedom, 60, 64
    Marx's criticism of, 95, 113-14, 133, 302, 304
    Marx's praise of, 87
    on mechanical industry, 92, 93
    vis-à-vis Ricardo, 296
social Darwinism, 108-9, 111, 114; *see also* Darwin
Social Democratic Party, 48, 109, 157, 167, 170, 180
    Erfurt Program of the, 108, 181
Sombart, Werner, 7, 28n.3
    Engels' letter to, 269
Sorge, Friedrich Adolph
    Engels' letter to, 185, 267
    letter of, to Engels, 256, 267
    Marx's letter to, 67, 146, 216, 294
Spanish revolution, 76-77
Spencer, Herbert, 108
Spinoza, Baruch, 293
Stalin, Josef, 29, 46, 51n.10, 286
Stalinism, 45, 219, 258
Stefanoni, 234
Stieber, 165
Stiebling, 48
stock exchange, 168, 217-18
Strauss, David Friedrich, 88
Strohn, 186
Strousberg, 67
Sunday Trading Bill, 299
surplus labor, 40, 137-40, 155-57, 210, 212, 278
surplus value
    in capitalist production, 40, 54-55, 126, 210, 212, 299, 301
    and labor power, 11-12, 300
    limited by labor, 15, 38-39
    in medieval times, 103
    origin and existence of, 137-56, 296
    produced by capital, 12

Taborites, 231, 232
Talandier, Marx's letter to, 192
Tartars, 244
Ten Hours Bill, 52, 53

Ten Hours Law, 122
Terence, 114, 135n.2
Thiers, Adolphe, 171, 173, 174, 193
Thomas Aquinas, 65, 168
von Thünen, J.H., 125
trade unions, 5, 10
Trier, Gerson, 168, 181
Tübingen School, 238
Tucker, 50, 211
Turgot, Anne Robert Jacques, 87, 91
Turks, 6, 84, 230, 231, 244, 249
Türr, 187
Tyler, Wat, 232
Tyre, 218

Ulrich, 90
United States' labor, 245
Ure, 92, 162, 216
use value, 138, 141
usury, 207-8, 212
utilitarianism, 1, 2-3, 5
    and the principle of nature, 5
    and the principle of utility, 5

value
    measure of, 139
    theory of, 138
de Vaucanson, Jacques, 93

Vermorel, 290
Vico, Giovanni Battista, 38, 55, 288
Victoria, Queen, 217
violence, 103-4, 168, 202
Vögele, 184, 190
Voltaire, François Marie Arouet de, 30

Wagner, A., 44-45, 142-43, 145, 150
Wald, Peter, 232
Washington, George, 80
Waterloo, 80, 191
Watt, James, 98
Weitling, Wilhelm, 88, 231, 234
Weydemeyer, 192
Whitehead, Alfred North, 274
Wieland, Christoph Martin, 261
Wilhelm I, 83
Wischnewetsky, Florence Kelley, Engels
    letter to, 134
Wolf, W., 158, 179
women's rights, *see* feminism
Wycliffe, John, 232

Zasulich, Vera, 88
    Marx's letter to, 54, 88, 247, 268, 298
Zeuss, Johann Caspar, 88
Zizka, Jan, 231
Zurich Commission, 67